HOW
THE SCOTS
INVENTED
CANADA

Ken McGoogan

HOW
THE SCOTS
INVENTED
CANADA

A PHYLLIS BRUCE BOOK

HARPERCOLLINS PUBLISHERS LTD

A Phyllis Bruce Book, published by HarperCollins Publishers Ltd

First published in a hardcover edition by HarperCollins Publishers Ltd: 2010
This trade paperback edition: 2011

HarperCollins Publishers Ltd
2 Bloor Street East, 20th Floor
Toronto, Ontario, Canada
M4W 1A8

www.harpercollins.ca

Library and Archives Canada Cataloguing in Publication
McGoogan, Kenneth, 1947–
How the Scots invented Canada / Ken McGoogan.
"A Phyllis Bruce Book."

ISBN 978-1-55468-234-8

1. Scots—Canada—History. 2. Scottish Canadians—History.
3. Canada—Civilization—Scottish influences. I. Title.
FC106.S3M34 2011   971'.0049163   C2011-903739-4

*Frontispiece: This evocative 1888 photograph, James Croil and Party,
is the work of Scottish-born William Notman, the foremost
Canadian photographer of the nineteenth century.*

Printed and bound in Canada

DWF 9 8 7 6 5 4 3 2 1

THIS BOOK IS DEDICATED TO

Sheena, Carlin, Sylwia, Keriann, Travis
&
James Jerzy McGoogan

CONTENTS

Introduction

Early this century, Arthur Herman published his foundational *How the Scots Invented the Modern World*. Given the scope of that work, whose subtitle embraces "our world and everything in it," Herman can hardly be faulted for devoting relatively few pages to Canada. Yet, except for the homeland, this is the country where Scots and their descendants have accomplished the most. In taking up where *Modern World* left off, and proceeding differently, I hope to round out the Canadian story.

In his book, the scholarly Herman presents a systematic argument, marshalling evidence to demonstrate that the Scots of the eighteenth and nineteenth centuries proved extraordinary, both intellectually and practically. He gives the Scots their due in global history. This book, *How the Scots Invented Canada*, is deliberately less academic. Biographical in approach, it is meant to be accessible to the general reader. Still, my research in Canada and Scotland turned up recurring themes and currents and not a few surprises. In tracking the Scottish contribution across three centuries, I tell the story of Canada, showing how, down through history, a handful of Scots and Scottish Canadians invented one of the world's most pluralistic countries.

Never have the Scots, even broadly defined, exceeded 16 percent of the Canadian population. Yet no matter how you approach the history of Canada—through exploration, politics, business, education, or literature—you find them playing a leading role. Of Canada's twenty-two prime ministers, for example, thirteen are of Scottish heritage. The challenge has not been to find remarkable Scots but to choose from among too many of them. This pre-eminence has inspired academic studies and popular treatments, all of which concentrate on first-generation immigrants and terminate soon after the First World War. *How the Scots Invented Canada* reaches back to include seminal figures who never set foot in this country, and moves forward to track Scottish influence through second, third, and succeeding generations. Gathering up

A sorrowful young man of the Clan MacAlister prepares to emigrate to Canada during the Highland Clearances.

Ulster Scots along the way, the book culminates near the close of the twentieth century with the emergence of what, more than a decade ago, Richard Gywn called the world's first postmodern nation.

As a Canadian whose various ancestors arrived between six and fourteen generations ago, I have a hybrid heritage: Scottish, yes, but also French, German, Irish, and, further back, Danish Viking. Such ethnic complexity is characteristically Canadian, and this is largely because those who arrived early from Auld Scotia brought integrationist attitudes. Those Scots had been born of ancient meldings (Picts, Gaels, Britons, Angles, Danes). They had been shaped by the early alliances with the French, the precocious development of widespread literacy, and the celebrated Scottish Enlightenment. As a result, the Scots were the first major settler group to introduce the political and cultural pluralism that would later become the hallmark of Canadian identity.

In eighteenth-century Montreal, heart of the fur trade, alliances involving the Scots, the French, and the Native peoples evolved out of Old World sympathies forged during the Scottish struggles for independence. In Book One of *How the Scots Invented Canada,* we see how fur-trade allegiances gave rise to figures like Cuthbert Grant, whose father was a Scottish trader and whose mother was of Cree and French heritage. Born in Canada half a century before Louis Riel and educated in Scotland, the multicultural, multilingual, and multiracial Grant made the Métis aware of themselves as a nation.

Also in Book One, which introduces various Scots charting coastlines, creating settlements, and establishing geographical boundaries, we encounter Major John Norton, who demonstrates that Scottish-Canadian pluralism extended beyond the fur trade. Born in Scotland, the son of a pure-blood Cherokee, Norton became a Canadian hero during the War of 1812 when he led hundreds of warriors from the Six Nations of the Iroquois. He also inspired John Richardson's *Wacousta,* generally regarded as the first Canadian novel.

Book Two tracks Scottish Canadians who unified the far-flung British colonies of North America. Sir John A. Macdonald launches Confederation in 1867, Nellie McClung and Agnes Macphail insist on the inclusion of women as equal partners, and sundry other Scots, from George Brown to Lady Aberdeen, create a multifaceted infrastructure encompassing railways, newspapers, and nomadic nurses. Here too, we begin to see that despite our pluralism—our languages, our regions, our ethnic diversities—as Canadians, we inhabit a coherent, continuous political entity thanks to the Scots.

In Book Three, thinkers Harold Adams Innis and Donald Creighton lay bare the country's mercantile foundations. By elaborating the so-called Laurentian thesis, they show how a numerically insignificant population of Scottish fur traders in Quebec drove the economic expansion that opened up the west. And here we find Scots exploring the uniquely Canadian tension between identity and pluralism. Hugh MacLennan, best known for his novel *Two Solitudes,* proposes that being Scottish means living with internal contradictions.

In the 1970s, MacLennan judged Canada's chances of survival to be excellent, despite the country's proximity to a superpower ten times its size. For this he gave one main reason: "We obstinately refuse to become a melting pot." Canada, he argued, remains "a light shining in the darkness of an almost universal tendency" to homogenize and reduce humankind to sameness.

This idea would find a political champion in yet another product of the old Scottish–French alliance. In 1971, Prime Minister Pierre Elliott Trudeau set up a royal commission to examine "the whole question of cultural and ethnic pluralism in this country and the status of our various cultures and languages." Nine years later, during a fiercely divisive referendum battle, he responded to a Quebec nationalist taunt about his mixed, half-Scottish heritage: "Yes, Elliott was my mother's name," he said. "It was the name borne by the Elliotts who came to Canada more than two hundred years ago. . . . My name is a Quebec name, but my name is a Canadian name also, and that's the story of my name."

In 1982, Pierre Elliott Trudeau gave Canada a constitution that recognized individual rights and multiculturalism. And with that, a hybrid Scottish Canadian finished the political job begun in 1867 by a

Scottish immigrant, Sir John A. Macdonald. Did Canada finally stand invented? Or did this ending represent just another beginning?

Anyone who goes hunting can find books arguing that the French, the English, the Italians, the Blacks, the Irish, the Chinese, and the Aboriginal peoples have shaped or created Canada. Certainly, all of these groups contributed, and a national history of the country would include these people and more, as new immigrants keep coming. In making a case for the Scots, I acknowledge other claimants, other perspectives. Yet the title of this book, *How the Scots Invented Canada,* declares my bias, and I have refused to let fairness take the fun out of the tale.

Book One

THE PIONEERS

Prologue

CANADIANS IN SCOTLAND

A visitor driving into the Scottish town of Mauchline cannot fail to notice a singular, towering monument that looks out over the landscape. This is the Robert Burns National Memorial, a three-storey edifice built in 1896 to honour Scotland's most celebrated poet. Constructed of red sandstone and soaring sixty-seven feet (20 m) into the air, the memorial features diverse window treatments, unexpected balconies, and a curious turret that, taken all together, render it unforgettable: clearly one of a kind. For me and for my wife, Sheena Fraser McGoogan, this memorial provided one of the greatest moments of our eight-week ramble in Scotland.

Canada is home today to almost five million people of Scottish descent. We wanted to know more about where they came from. Why did so many Scots emigrate in the first place? And how was it that, once in Canada, they had proven so influential? Robbie Burns was an extreme case. He never set foot in Canada. Yet every January, throughout the country, tens of thousands of Canadians gather to celebrate his birthday.

On arriving at Glasgow Airport, we had made a beeline for Burns country, a one-hour drive to the south. Within two days, we visited the farmhouse in Alloway where Burns was born. We stood on the Brig O'Doon, the bridge over the River Doon where his fictional Tam O'Shanter narrowly escaped the pursuit of furious witches. And we marvelled at a mural glorifying his life from birth to death.

Before long, we travelled southeast to Dumfries and sat in the pub chair where, in his later years, Burns himself had often sat reading newspapers. We visited the upstairs bedroom where he sometimes slept. And down the street, in the humble home where he lived for three years, we visited his study and the bedroom in which he died.

In driving from Alloway to Dumfries, from one end of Burns country to the other, we followed the scenic route, winding along the coastal highway to Kirkcudbright (pronounced Kir-coo-bree), a town of great significance to Scottish Canadian history. From this harbour in 1622, the first boatload of would-be Scottish settlers sailed for North America. They failed to establish an enduring colony. But before harsh conditions drove them home to Auld Scotia, or Old Scotland, they did name the place where they landed: Nova Scotia.

More than a century later, in 1771, Kirkcudbright became the birthplace of Thomas Douglas, fifth Earl of Selkirk. He was the great early champion of Scottish emigration to British North America. His native town is probably the loveliest in the Scottish Lowlands. Here you find stone-built Georgian houses, a harbour crowded with colourful boats, and, on the outskirts, the ruins of an abbey and a castle.

Near the centre of town, behind a stone wall that encircles the parish churchyard, we found a plaque erected by Manitobans in 1978. Dedicated to the memory of "one of Kirckudbright's greatest sons," it rightly credits Selkirk with creating Scottish colonies in three provinces: Prince Edward Island, Ontario, and Manitoba.

From that plaque, well instructed by locals, we drove to the south end of town, swung off the two-lane highway and followed a tree-lined road to a bay that opens onto the Irish Sea. In the 1700s, the Selkirk estate, more accessible by boat than by horse and carriage, could be found at the tip of this peninsula, called St. Mary's Isle. The grand mansion was lost to fire decades ago, and today there is not much to see: many trees, a few grazing horses.

Yet later, after we had explored Dumfries, I found myself juxtaposing Robbie Burns and Lord Selkirk, the beloved poet and the visionary colonizer. Both made a mark on Canada. But the one was a ploughman born in a croft, the other a nobleman who inherited an estate. What could these two figures possibly have in common? The question brought only one answer: the Scottish Enlightenment.

Born just twelve years apart, Burns and Selkirk were both products of that magical period in the late 1700s when Scots surfaced as world leaders in science, literature, philosophy, engineering, and economics. Scholars talk about the Highland Clearances that extended into the next century, when thousands of tenant farmers were driven from their ancestral lands by rapacious landlords. Certainly the Clearances played a role in shaping Canada. But by the time Sheena and I drove north out of the Lowlands, I was leaning to a different hypothesis: that the Scots who came to Canada made a difference because most of them had been influenced by the Scottish Enlightenment.

Nowhere did the Enlightenment blaze more brightly than in the regal city of Edinburgh. Out striding along the Royal Mile in the heart of town, so recently arrived that the skirling bagpipes and blaring tourist-shop signs made me consider spending money on a kilt, I retreated into St. Giles Cathedral. This magnificent edifice, Scotland's answer to

Westminster Abbey, is filled with statues and other memorials. While strolling around among the portraits, marble busts, and stained-glass windows, suddenly I came face to face with a life-size statue of John Knox. And I found myself thinking that this "graven image" must have made that earliest dour Presbyterian spin in his grave.

On the east coast of Scotland, at St. Andrews, Sheena and I had visited the ruins of the cathedral where, in the mid-1500s, Knox emerged as a fierce prophet. We had also explored the ruins of the castle from which he was taken to France to serve as a galley slave. In the castle museum, we had listened, bemused, while a talking effigy of Knox railed against "idolatry" and "hawkers of papistry"—a hokey exhibition that, even so, evokes the spirit of the man.

In the mid-1500s, John Knox emerged from St. Andrew's Cathedral (shown here in ruins) as a fiery prophet. Galvanized by a stint as a French prisoner and galley slave, Knox led the Protestant Reformation in Scotland.

For many years, John Knox sermonized at St. Giles. The irony was that, while preaching fire and brimstone, and railing against the excesses of Roman Catholicism, he made changes that brought on the Scottish Enlightenment. Knox decreed that everyone had to read the Bible, and figured out ways to make that happen. By 1750, 75 percent of Scots could read—a level of literacy unprecedented in Europe. Widespread literacy gave rise to broader education and so to the Enlightenment.

Increased literacy also fostered more liberal attitudes. When individuals are encouraged to study a complex holy book, and then to dispute its meanings with their religious leaders, they begin to think that all people are created equal. This egalitarianism, transported to the wilds of British North America, made Scottish immigrants, as a group, more able than many others to forge alliances with the Native peoples, who proved invaluable allies.

Scotland's rugged environment also played a role in preparing Scots for early Canada. Our sojourn in Orkney, that wind-swept island-world in the northern reaches, reminded me that Scotland is a northern country with a challenging climate—two qualities it shares with Canada. This prepared seventeenth- and eighteenth-century Orcadians, especially, for life in Rupert's Land, which encompassed much of western Canada at that time. Soon after the Hudson's Bay Company was created in 1670, it began hiring Orcadians to cross the Atlantic Ocean and work in the fur trade.

Tough, resourceful men who knew their way around boats, these Orcadians proved wonderfully adaptive. The London-based HBC filled its ranks with them. In 1794, one observer wrote that the Orcadians were "more sober and tractable than the Irish, and they engage for lower wages than either the English or Irish." Young Orcadians joined the company in droves, trading hardship and poverty for secure employment. In 1799, of the 530 men employed in Canada by the HBC, 416 came from Orkney—almost 80 percent.

Some Orcadians, after working several decades for the HBC, returned home and resettled. But many married Native women and remained in Canada, especially in Manitoba, which is home today to thousands of people with Orcadian surnames like Sinclair, Flett, Spence, Sutherland, and Isbister.

In Orkney, Sheena and I stayed in the house in Kirkwall where in the 1860s explorer John Rae lived for two years after returning to his native Orkney with his Canadian wife. Rae was the son of a factor, or land agent, who had moved to Stromness from a town south of Glasgow. The young man trained as a surgeon in Edinburgh before he joined the HBC, eventually becoming the greatest rough-country traveller of the age.

From what was once Rae's living room, we could sit gazing out at various headlands and islands beyond which flowed Hoy Sound—the gateway to Canada. In that living room, rummaging among books, I realized that, among Scottish emigrants, the Orcadians were the exception. From the outset, they came to Canada in relatively large numbers. Yet even counting these exemplary workers, the early-to-mid-1700s brought only a trickle of settlers to Canada. Through most of the eighteenth century, the majority of Scottish emigrants went to the warmer, more established American colonies.

During the Highland Clearances, landlords evicted tens of thousands of clansmen from crofts like this one.

This trend began to change in 1776 with the American Revolution. Afterwards, Highlanders who had fought with the British against the American rebels merged with other United Empire Loyalists, many of them Scottish in origin, who had been driven north. Together, these groups increased the Canadian population by 40,000 people.

Meanwhile, here in Scotland, the Highland Clearances had begun. Landlords were evicting tens of thousands of crofters from their ancestral plots to create more profitable sheep farms. During a wave of emigration that started in 1792, the "Year of the Sheep," hundreds of crofters were forced onto emigrant ships that sailed most often for Nova Scotia. During the half-century leading up to 1812, when the British–American war launched another wave of immigration, roughly 15,000 Highlanders moved to Canada.

Yet the greatest waves came still later, and included both Highlanders and Lowlanders. During the last thirty years of the nineteenth century, 80,000 Scots came to Canada. The next three decades, between 1901 and 1931, brought the greatest numbers of all. As Scotland endured a series of economic downturns, people cast about for a chance to build a better life, and estimates of Scottish immigrants to Canada range from 370,000 to 440,000. In addition, Canada has received 500,000 immigrants from Northern Ireland, and if U.S. ratios are any indication, almost 300,000 of those are Scottish in origin: Ulster Scots.

Despite these various waves, at Canada's first census in 1871, out of a total population of 3.7 million people, only 16 percent claimed Scottish roots—a lower percentage than those citing English, French, or Irish ancestry. What's more, that percentage has remained almost constant. In 2006, out of a far more diverse population of 32 million, 15 percent (4.7 million) claimed Scottish heritage. And so we come to the question that drives this book: given that the Scots have remained few in number, how did they manage to invent Canada?

Diverse as they were, those Scots who moved to this country did share distinctive commonalities: a maritime tradition, for example. This came home to me during a one-week visit to Northern Ireland, which is also called Ulster. While staying at a B&B near the town of Ballycastle, we drove along the coast to Torr Head. After parking the car, we climbed a steep hill to a ruined shelter and gazed across the North Channel. Sure enough, we could see Scotland: not just the Mull of Kintyre, a dozen miles (20 km) away, but a scattering of Scottish islands to the west of that peninsula.

The previous evening, we had hiked along an arduous cliffside path to the ruins of a castle overlooking these waters. We had wondered why anyone would build a castle here, in a location so difficult to reach. Then we had realized that this once-grand edifice, almost inaccessible by land, had belonged to a thriving water-world. From here, throngs of people had come and gone by boat.

Now, standing in the wind at Torr Head, I grasped that for centuries, parts of Scotland and Northern Ireland had composed a single entity: a Gaelic-speaking world of seafarers. Around AD 500, the Irish, whom the Romans called "Scotti," had climbed into their rough boats, crossed this sea and, in present-day Argyll, established a kingdom called Dalriada.

Eleven centuries later, in the early 1600s, some of their descendants were among those who recrossed this channel. In *The Invention of Scotland,* Hugh Trevor-Roper wrote that "western Scotland was an extension of Ulster long before Ulster became an extension of western Scotland." This back-and-forth movement of peoples by water continued into the 1800s, when Scots and Ulster Scots were also emigrating to the colonies of British North America.

By the time we settled into Inverness, that most Scottish of cities, my head was bursting with ideas. I saw now that explorer John Rae was not unique. He belonged to a subset of Scots who went to Canada and made remarkable contributions. They were well-educated, energetic, hard-working products of the Scottish Enlightenment, and they had grown up into an economy that could not accommodate all of them.

One morning, from our Inverness B&B, we decided to drive north to visit the ancestral turf of the foremost of these outstanding Scottish Canadians: John A. Macdonald. We had already visited the old churchyard in Avoch, where a walled memorial celebrates Alexander Mackenzie, the first explorer to travel overland from the Atlantic to the Pacific Ocean. We had poked around in Dingwall, the boyhood home of two cousins who loom large in the fur-trade history of Canada: Thomas and George Simpson.

We had also explored three locations related to the Scottish creation of the Canadian Pacific Railway. We had driven to Forres, the birthplace of Donald Smith, who eventually drove the symbolic last spike in the railway; and Dufftown, in the heart of nearby whisky country, where a clock tower honours George Stephen, chief financier of that railway; and finally to Aviemore, where, at the great bluff called Craigellachie, the clan Grant would gather during times of trouble and the woods would ring out with a battle cry later echoed by the men who built the CPR: "Stand fast, Craigellachie!"

Now, bent on tracking the history of Canada's first prime minister, a Scot of course, we drove north out of Inverness for an hour before swinging west off the highway. The country is rugged enough that anyone who grew up here would be well prepared for Canada. For ten minutes we followed a secondary road, and then, at a hamlet called Pittentrail, we turned north. After passing through the still smaller Rogart, we spotted a hand-printed sign and veered onto a rutted, one-lane road that wound away into the trees.

As we rattled and bounced along, I found myself reflecting that those Scots who played such key roles in Canada would have made a contribution wherever they had gone. Ambitious, industrious, and resourceful, these children and grandchildren of the Scottish Enlightenment were products of a superior education system. They lacked only opportunity. The secret of Scottish success in Canada, so disproportionate, could be summarized in three words: Scotland sent leaders.

Certainly, the country dispatched poor, uneducated people, some of them victims of the Highland Clearances and other grim circumstances. But with them, Scotland also sent many of its best and brightest: well-educated, hard-working young men—and women—who crossed the ocean to make their fortune.

In Glasgow, the birthplace of John A. Macdonald has been razed. But near Rogart, after following that dirt track under a train trestle and around a sharp bend, we came over a rise and there it stood: a cairn marked by a bench and a Canadian flag. We had reached the ancestral site of Canada's first prime minister. We got out of the car to investigate. The cairn is built of stones from the family's original croft. It bears a plaque inscribed to Macdonald, and identifies him as the father of Confederation: "His monument is a nation," it tells us. "This cairn is but a footnote to his greatness."

At this spot, Macdonald's grandfather—also named John—fell victim to the Highland Clearances of the late 1700s. He moved his family to Dornoch, a dozen miles (20 km) south, and in that bustling town became "the merchant Macdonald." His son, Hugh Macdonald, grew up, married well, and moved south to Glasgow, where he tried without success to break into the textile business. Ambitious, energetic, and not quite trapped by fate and circumstance, Hugh Macdonald and his wife pulled up stakes in 1820 and crossed the Atlantic to start a new life in Kingston, Upper Canada. They brought four children—one of them five-year-old John Alexander.

From Rogart to Dornoch to Canada: starting from a Highland croft, these Macdonalds had made their move in three generations. For many other Scots, the transition proved more traumatic. And as I sat on that memorial bench outside Rogart, I realized that even this ancestral cairn would not allow me to capture in a single image who they were and where they came from, these Scots who invented Canada. Theirs was a narrative with countless storylines.

Finally, what of Mauchline? The Robert Burns National Memorial provided special excitement for Sheena and me because her grandfather, an architect born in Lochgilphead, Argyll, designed it. The red sandstone monument grows wider as it gets higher, and features several odd angles and circular substructures. Experts describe it as exemplifying the "Scottish baronial style" of the late nineteenth century. According to a 2004 article in the *Scotsman*, the monument is "regarded worldwide as a shrine central to the poet's life and times."

The memorial is remarkably evocative of the wild and original spirit of Robbie Burns. It is also sufficiently intricate that the editor of the online journal *Scotland One* suggested that stonemasons who worked on it must have wondered "what was going through the mind of Willie Fraser the Glasgow architect who designed it."

That we will never know. Probably he was thinking of Robbie Burns, as he should have been. We do know that on July 23, 1896, when he was twenty-eight years of age, William Fraser visited Mauchline to attend a celebration mark-

The Robert Burns National Memorial in Mauchline, Ayrshire, known to Burns-lovers around the world, is a superb example of the Scottish baronial style of architecture.

ing the hundredth anniversary of the death of Burns. Having won the commission in an architectural competition, he had designed not only the memorial but also a dozen nearby cottages, and he had travelled south from Glasgow to witness the laying of the foundation stone.

Five days before, *Black and White* magazine had described the cottages as "intended for the benefit of old couples, ploughmen or cottars [peasant farmers] in ill-health, or persons not quite destitute, to whom, when misfortune comes, such a haven, with an endowment, will be a veritable godsend."

When Sheena and I visited the memorial, a light rain was falling, yet a cottager named George Mitchell was tending his garden. On learning of our connection with the monument, he showed us around the beautifully kept grounds and dwellings, which together function as a convivial seniors' centre. He told us that the monument is open to the public on only two or three days a year. Then visitors can climb a circular staircase to the roof, gaze out through a telescope and, if the weather is clear, see all the way to distant Ben Lomond, a mountain in the Highlands.

At some point, William Fraser would have savoured that view. Two years after watching masons lay the first stone, he married his sweetheart, Maud Marion Timpson, and moved to Dunoon, a train-and-ferry ride west of Glasgow. There he designed an imposing red-brick school and a landmark hotel before creating the Dunoon Pavilion, which, according to a local newspaper, gave the town a focal point in the "free classic renaissance" style. The pavilion included shops, reception rooms, and an octagonal concert hall that could accommodate 3,500 people.

In 1907, with commissions drying up locally during one of those economic downtowns, William Fraser received an invitation to join C.M. Miller and Company, a thriving firm of architects based in Canada. With his wife, son, and daughter, the designer of the Burns National Memorial packed up and moved to Toronto. Soon enough, by fathering a second son, Frederick, the architect set in motion that sequence of events which would see him become the grandfather of my wife, the great-grandfather of our adult son and daughter, and an ancestor of future generations.

1

Early Explorers

Apart from Vikings who briefly settled in Newfoundland around AD 1000, and the Basque and British fishermen who visited the Grand Banks some time afterwards, the first European to reach North America may well have been a Scottish nobleman named Henry Sinclair (or St. Clair). In 1398, almost a century before Christopher Columbus and John Cabot sailed from Europe, and more than two centuries before Samuel de Champlain did the same, Sinclair apparently spent a winter exploring Nova Scotia.

In *Prince Henry Sinclair: His Expedition to the New World in 1398,* author Frederick J. Pohl makes a strong case that, having become the Earl of Orkney, this Edinburgh native crossed the Atlantic on a voyage of discovery. Drawing on a collection of letters published in 1558 (the *Zeno Narrative*), and also on his own extensive research in Nova Scotia and New England, Pohl recreates the expedition in impressive detail. As well, he presents evidence that Sinclair served as the original model for Glooscap, the hero of Algonquian (Mi'kmaq) mythology.

Unfortunately, the Sinclair saga has been caught up with fanciful tales of the Knights Templar and the Holy Grail. So while many historians regard this expedition as an established fact, including some from Canada's First Nations, other scholars dismiss the whole saga as a hoax. And still other authors, including this one, would prefer to await further evidence—DNA findings, for example, that link contemporary Mi'kmaqs with the Sinclair family of Scotland.

On this much everyone can agree: after Sinclair, more than three centuries elapsed before Scots began arriving in numbers to explore and settle those territories that would one day form part of Canada. Those early explorers were backed by commercial interests. In the 1600s, hats made from beaver pelts became fashionable in Europe just as beavers on that continent were dying out from over-hunting. In 1670, the king of England, Charles II, responded by granting the fur-trading Hudson's Bay Company (HBC) control over all land draining into Hudson Bay. This vast New World territory, which had been inhabited for centuries by Aboriginal peoples, he rather grandly named Rupert's Land in honour of his cousin Prince Rupert, the company's first governor.

By this time, the French had developed a profitable fur trade along the more readily accessible St. Lawrence River. In 1682, to challenge the HBC interlopers, they established the Compagnie du Nord and began pushing west. That initiative failed. But during the 1700s, Montreal-based merchants created small partnerships and began competing successfully by hiring voyageurs and conducting a canoe-and-river-based trade with western Native peoples.

But now came the turning point that led to exploration—and so to the proliferation, even though much uncharted territory had already been named locally by Native peoples, of Scottish place names that today dot the map of Canada. After the conquest of New France in 1759, Scottish merchants gained control of the thriving, Montreal-based fur trade. By the 1780s, they had created the North West Company, which used a far-flung system of canoe brigades to trade 20,000 beaver pelts a year. By the late 1780s, the expansion-minded Nor' Westers were seeking a river that would give them access to the Pacific Coast—a move that would bring them into direct competition with the Hudson's Bay Company. To find that river, the Nor' Westers turned to a strong-minded Highlander.

Alexander Mackenzie: First to the Pacific

Alexander Mackenzie was born in 1764 near Stornoway, a port village on the Isle of Lewis. His father was a tacksman, a middleman who rented lands from their owner, collected rents on smaller holdings from crofters or tenant farmers, and lived on the difference.

By the 1770s, when Mackenzie was growing up, landlords throughout the Scottish Highlands had discovered that they could make far more money by devoting their properties to sheep rather than to farmers. They raised rents to drive tenants off the land. This practice would escalate and eventually become infamous as the Highland Clearances.

Some middlemen, rightly anticipating the worst, began emigrating to North America of their own accord—mainly to present-day Massachusetts, New York, New Jersey, Pennsylvania, Delaware, North and South Carolina, and Virginia.

Several members of Mackenzie's extended family emigrated to these American colonies. In 1774, after his mother died of natural causes and his older brother drowned in a shipwreck, his father left Lewis to join a relative in New York. Accompanied by two maiden aunts, the ten-year-old Mackenzie soon followed, sailing to New York on the *Peace and Plenty* with a hundred other emigrants.

Alexander Mackenzie worked in the Canadian fur trade.

In 1776, when the Americans declared their independence, his father sided with the British and joined a regiment sent to quell the Revolution. Young Alexander fled north—first, in the care of his aunts, to the Mohawk River valley in upstate New York; then, as the Loyalists suffered repeated losses, still farther north, to join the Scottish community in Montreal.

At age fifteen, in that bustling town of 4,000, Alexander Mackenzie began working for a Scottish fur-trading concern that soon became Gregory, MacLeod and Company. It was customary for boys as young as twelve to work, and as the enterprising and ambitious son of a tacksman, Mackenzie excelled. In 1784, after five years of increasing responsibility, he took "a small adventure of goods" west by river to Detroit. These he traded so successfully that his employer offered him a share in the firm's profits on condition that he serve in a post still farther west at Grand Portage, thirty-five miles (60 km) southwest of present-day Thunder Bay.

The following year, as the company expanded to meet competition, Mackenzie took charge of the English (Churchill) River department, based in northern Saskatchewan at Lac Île-à-la-Crosse. In 1787, after his employers joined forces with the North West Company, Mackenzie ventured still farther north and west to a fur-trading post on the Athabasca River.

At this cluster of rough log cabins in the wilderness, before taking nominal control of the surrounding area, Mackenzie spent a winter as second-in-command to veteran fur trader Peter Pond, who was about to retire. Pond believed that at Great Slave Lake, some distance to the north, he had identified the source of a river that flowed to the Pacific coast of the continent, culminating in an estuary recently charted by Captain James Cook.

If Pond proved correct, this river could transform the fur trade. Instead of transporting goods thousands of miles to and from Montreal, the North West Company might be able to conduct business with China and Russia from the far northwest coast of present-day British Columbia, exploiting Cook's Inlet as a fur-trading base the same way its arch-rival, the Hudson's Bay Company, used Hudson Bay.

At age twenty-five, after establishing Fort Chipewyan, a splendid new post on Lake Athabasca, Alexander Mackenzie resolved to investigate the broad river that flowed out of Great Slave Lake. Pond had estimated that, once embarked on the river, paddlers could reach the Pacific in six days. Alexander Mackenzie suspected that the journey might take longer. But on June 3, 1789, when he left Fort Chipewyan with four birchbark canoes, he never dreamed that he was embarking on a four-year quest that would involve two major expeditions.

On this first outing, following conventional practice, Mackenzie took a dozen people: four French Canadian voyageurs, two of their wives, a German who had been a soldier, a renowned Chipewyan guide called the English Chief, two more wives, and two hunters. The women would handle cooking, moccasin sewing, fire building, and campsite maintenance, while the men would paddle, hunt, fish, and erect tents.

Despite bad weather, Mackenzie set a rapid pace. By rising before dawn and paddling until late afternoon, the travellers reached Great Slave Lake in a week. Here they encountered whirling ice floes, and for two weeks, socked in by rain and thick fog, they sheltered in an abandoned trading post. As the ice slowly cleared, they searched for the outlet of the great river, tormented by swarms of mosquitoes. Finally, after twenty days on the lake, they entered the north channel of what is now called the Mackenzie. They found paddling easier, because they were travelling with the current, and they raised their rough sails.

Three days later, the jubilation ended. With the Rocky Mountains looming to the west, the great river changed direction. Instead of flowing northwest towards Cook's Inlet, it veered north. The party began coming upon villages of Dogrib or Slave people. Several times Mackenzie hired local guides, but none proved helpful and, invariably, before long they slipped away home. After passing 61° north, the latitude of Cook's Inlet, Mackenzie wrote in his journal that going farther seemed pointless, "as it is evident that these waters must empty themselves into the Northern Ocean."

His fellow travellers urged him to turn back. Curious and strong-minded, determined to learn the truth of this waterway, Mackenzie persevered. Eventually, rolling hills gave way to flat land and the river split into channels. At last, while encamped on a large island, and after seeing whales, Mackenzie realized that a tide washed the shoreline. He had reached the Arctic Ocean. From Great Slave Lake, in fourteen days, he had travelled 1,020 miles (1,650 km) to the northwest—more than seventy miles (110 km) a day. Among overland explorers, only Samuel Hearne had attained a similar latitude, when eighteen years before he had reached the mouth of the Coppermine River.

By descending this greater river, Mackenzie had situated a second point on the map of the Arctic coast of North America. On July 14, 1789, he erected a wooden post to mark his achievement. The return trip proved an endurance test. But on September 12, after 102 days on the water, the explorer reached Fort Chipewyan. He was exhausted, but besides having discovered the second longest river in North America (after the Mississippi), Alexander Mackenzie had demonstrated his endurance while honing his skills as both traveller and leader.

The expedition had taught the explorer that he lacked crucial navigational skills. In his published journals, Mackenzie explained that, having discovered his deficiencies in this area, he undertook a voyage to London to correct them. In that city, during the winter of 1791–92, he studied astronomy and journals of exploration, and acquired navigational instruments. He remained bent on determining "the practicability of a commercial communication" across the continent between the Atlantic and Pacific Oceans.

In April he sailed back across the Atlantic, and then he travelled, mostly by canoe, from Montreal to Grand Portage and onwards, arriving at Fort Chipewyan in October 1792. From there, he canoed to the junction of the Peace and the Smoky Rivers, where men had begun squaring timbers and cutting stakes for Fort Fork. On December 23, after spending two months in a tent, and with temperatures dropping to well below freezing, Mackenzie moved into a log house.

There he spent the rest of the winter, trading with the local Beaver Indians and gathering what information he could about the rivers and mountains to the west. Thanks to his new instruments and navigational skills, Mackenzie knew that he was at least 500 miles (800 km) from the coast, and possibly twice that by river. He prepared accordingly, and had his men build a large birchbark canoe. Twenty-five feet (7.5 m) long, it could carry almost 3,000 pounds (1,300 kg), yet weighed so little that "two men could carry her on a good road three or four miles without resting."

From Fort Fork, on May 9, 1793, Mackenzie set out with nine men: six French Canadian voyageurs, two Beaver hunters and interpreters, and his Scottish lieutenant, Alexander Mackay. The canoe was so heavily laden, with everything from potential gifts to pemmican and bullets, that it soon began to leak. The men were forced to unload the canoe and repair it with spruce gum, a frustrating process that, during the ensuing journey, they would repeat many times.

Within a few days, Mackenzie saw his first grizzlies—"two grisly and hideous bears"—and then, earlier than expected, the Rocky Mountains. Once into those peaks, the Peace River grew rougher. It swept the men through steep, narrow canyons, or forced them ashore for difficult, miles-long portages. The men hauled their gear over rocky outcroppings, and during one stretch, in the space of two miles (3 km), had to unload the canoe four times and "track" or drag it along by rope. When the terrifying river became "one white sheet of foaming water," several men wanted to abandon the expedition. Mackenzie insisted on making a tough, three-day portage around the rapids.

On May 31, the party arrived at a fork in the Peace River. All the men wanted to take the broad channel northwest, and Mackenzie felt the same way. But he remembered talking with an old warrior at Fort Fork, who had insisted that, when he reached such a place, he must canoe south up the more difficult river. And that was the way he went.

If he had ignored the warrior's advice, Mackenzie would almost certainly have got lost in the twists and turns and been forced to turn back. Instead, he fought his way south against a current so strong that he spent "the greatest part of the afternoon in getting two or three miles—a very tardy and mortifying progress." During the next couple of weeks, at small settlements, he managed to hire local guides—who, after a few days, melted into the forest.

Before he too disappeared, a young Sekani led a portage over a ridge that proved to be the Continental Divide. From here, all rivers flowed not east towards Hudson Bay, but west towards the Pacific, and Mackenzie could travel with the current. This made less difference than he had hoped. At one series of rapids, the men lost control of the canoe, which smashed into rocks, shattering first the stern and then the bow.

With the canoe wrecked and all their bullets lost, the men wanted to abandon the expedition. Mackenzie let them vent their emotions, handed round a bottle of rum, and then appealed to pride, reminding the men of "the disgrace that would attend them on their return home, without having attained the object of the expedition." In response, the voyageurs repaired the damaged canoe well enough to serve until they found materials to build a new one.

On June 17, the expedition emerged from the "Bad River," as Mackenzie called it, and enjoyed "the inexpressible satisfaction of finding ourselves on the bank of a navigable river, on the West side of the first great range of mountains." Yet, before a week had passed, Mackenzie faced another major test. Travelling through Carrier country, accompanied sporadically by local guides, the explorer gleaned that he was heading for a hazardous river-run and an unfriendly people. He pressed on, but the warnings grew ominous. The Carrier described their neighbours, the Shuswap, as a warlike and "very malignant race." If the explorers kept going south, they would "certainly become a sacrifice to the savage spirit of the natives."

Worse, the river ahead sounded daunting—as well it might, given that Mackenzie was on what would become known as the Fraser River, one of the wildest waterways in North America. One Carrier warned that in three places, it was "altogether impassable, from the falls and rapids, which poured along between perpendicular rocks that were much higher, and more rugged, than any we had yet seen, and would not admit of any passage over them." The portages, often narrow paths, ran along cliffs for great distances.

The Carrier recommended an alternative route that ran west through the mountains. They urged Mackenzie to travel overland, following a well-known "grease trail" used to carry fish oil and other trading goods from the coast to the interior. The problem was that this route would mean backtracking for almost 400 miles (640 km). While this sounded daunting, the analytical, tough-minded Mackenzie concluded it was still the best option. Instead of risking a mutiny by simply announcing his decision, however, he gathered the men and praised their "fortitude, patience, and perseverance" before outlining the choices. He insisted that he would go alone along the overland route if necessary, but the men voted unanimously "to follow me wherever I should go."

On June 23, near present-day Alexandria, British Columbia, in the forested wilderness a hundred miles (170 km) south of Prince George, Mackenzie and his men began beating their way back up the torrential Fraser River. Ten days later, after hiding their newly built replacement canoe and caching valuable supplies in the trees, they hiked out of the river valley on a steep track running west. The men carried ninety-pound (40 kg) packs, and even their leader carried seventy pounds (30 kg), plus an awkward telescope. The ensuing trek proved rigorous and terrifying, and included the traversing of a mountain pass at 6,000 feet (1,800 m). But in twelve days, most of them sixteen hours long, the men covered 180 miles (290 km). They emerged from dense forest into an encampment of Bella Coola First Nations, and from them rented two small canoes.

Farther downriver, at present-day Bella Coola, where locals had already encountered European traders arriving from the Pacific, a friendly chief provided a splendid, forty-five-foot (14 m) canoe capable of handing rough, tidal waters, and also four extra paddlers. After passing a few settlements and acquiring a still larger canoe, Mackenzie reached salt water. At a point roughly 300 miles (480 km) north of present-day Vancouver, he emerged from the river into a choppy Dean Channel amid spotted seals, porpoises, and seagulls. He was still some distance from the swells that crash onto the west coast of Vancouver Island, but he had reached the Pacific Ocean.

Two days later and a few miles farther west, the explorer made paint by mixing vermilion with grease and memorialized his accomplishment by writing on a rock: "Alex Mackenzie from Canada by land 22nd July 1793."

Mackenzie had become the first European explorer to cross North America from the Atlantic to the Pacific Ocean north of Mexico. Since leaving Fort Fork on May 9, and not counting the backtracking he did on the Fraser River, in seventy-two days this hard-driving Scot had journeyed 850 miles (1,370 km). He had not discovered a route that would prove useful to the fur trade. Yet his remarkable journey, accomplished a dozen years before Lewis and Clark's comparable trek farther south, would lead directly to the creation of British Columbia—first as a British colony, later as a Canadian province.

Simon Fraser: The Forty-ninth Parallel

In 1805, after settling a violent rivalry with Montreal-based competitors, the partners of the North West Company looked again to expanding their business in the far west. They hoped not only to increase trade but to accomplish what Mackenzie had left undone—to discover a practical canoe route to the Pacific, which would enable them to establish direct trade links with China. To renew this quest, the company chose Simon Fraser, an active, vigorous man, not yet thirty, who had toiled in the fur trade for thirteen years.

Fraser's parents had emigrated from Culbokie, north of Inverness, in 1773, sailing with other Roman Catholic Highlanders to New York on the *Pearl*. They settled on a farm near Bennington, Vermont. There Simon was born, the youngest of nine children, in 1776, just as the American Revolution erupted. His family of Frasers, a cadet branch of the Frasers of Lovat, included two uncles who had served as officers with General James Wolfe at Quebec. In 1777, his father joined the Loyalists in fighting a losing battle at Bennington. Taken prisoner to Albany, New York, he died not long afterwards.

In 1784, with the Loyalists beaten and persecuted, and between 40,000 and 50,000 of them fleeing north, mostly to the Maritimes, Simon Fraser's fifty-year-old mother got the family to the Montreal area, where they had relatives. These included the influential Simon McTavish, the controlling partner in the North West Company, established five years before. At age sixteen, Simon Fraser joined that thriving operation as an apprentice.

During the next seven years, he rose quickly through the ranks. In 1799, he was serving as a clerk in the Athabasca department in the far northwest. Two years later, at age twenty-five, Simon Fraser became a partner. No small achievement, partnership meant he would receive a one-forty-sixth share of all company profits.

At twenty-nine, chosen to lead the expansion into the far west, Fraser accepted a unique mandate. Where Alexander Mackenzie's two expeditions had been purely investigative, Simon Fraser was directed not only to find a useable canoe route but to build trading posts, establish settlements, and take control of the territory west of the Rockies. These orders would have far-reaching consequences—not just for the North West Company but for a future Canada.

In the autumn of 1805, Fraser ascended the Peace River and built a trading post (at present-day Hudson's Hope) to serve as a departure point for westward journeys through the Rockies. He named the surrounding area New Caledonia to honour his ancestral homeland. Fraser intended to retrace Mackenzie's route but, ignoring Native warnings of horrendous canyons and impassable rapids, to continue down the river beyond Alexandria, where his predecessor had turned back. At Trout Lake, Fraser built an advance post (Fort McLeod), the first European settlement west of the Rockies. He built a second post (Fort St. James) farther west at what is now Stuart Lake, which drains into the river he intended to explore.

Late in the spring of 1806, with lieutenant John Stuart and ten paddlers, Fraser again paddled up the Peace River to Trout Lake and beyond. In his journal, he made disparaging remarks about Mackenzie's previous journey, though when he reached the so-called Bad River (James Creek), and struggled through rapids, rocks, and fallen trees, he admitted that his predecessor had described it "with great exactness. It is certainly well named and a most dangerous place."

At Stuart Lake, Fraser met Native people near starvation and, because

This drawing, The Descent of the Fraser River, *by C. W. Jefferys, suggests the skill and daring required to canoe down what was then the wildest river in North America. At the time that Simon Fraser explored it in a light craft, the river was a roaring, canyon-walled succession of rapids, falls, and cascades.*

the salmon run was late, soon faced a similar predicament. The lack of provisions forced him to postpone his journey to the coast. As a new starting point, he established Fort George (now Prince George) near the mouth of the Nechako River. No supplies arrived until autumn 1807, which meant that, with winter closing in, he could not continue downstream until the following spring.

Finally, on May 28, 1808, Fraser left Fort George with two dozen people in four canoes. Warned repeatedly that the river ahead "was but a succession of falls and cascades," the party pressed on, and were soon racing through whitewater rapids in steep-walled canyons. On June 10, just above Lillooet, he accepted that only madmen would remain on the river. Storing the canoes, he proceeded on foot.

Fraser returned to the river whenever possible by borrowing canoes or commandeering them. Villages became numerous, and he encountered Native people in the hundreds, and once in a crowd of 1,200. Near the mouth of the river at present-day Vancouver, he met some Cowichan Indians who proved unenthusiastic about his arrival in their lands. They forced him to turn back before he entered the Strait of Georgia, and made sure he kept retreating.

This resistance continued upriver, and many of his men, fearing for their lives, wished to leave the river and return overland to Fort George. The young Fraser "remonstrated and threatened by turns," and managed to put down the incipient mutiny and get back to Fort George by water. The explorer felt that, though he had accomplished an arduous expedition covering 520 miles (840 km), he had failed. The wild and raging river was clearly impractical as a trade route. Also, having discovered that its mouth was situated at the forty-ninth degree of latitude, he noted, "This river, therefore, is not the Columbia."

In another way, however, Fraser had succeeded beyond his wildest dreams. As a British subject who established permanent settlements in the west, he ensured that when Canada's boundary with the United States of America was established, after the War of 1812, it ran no farther north than the forty-ninth parallel.

Isobel Gunn: Anything Men Can Do

Late in 1807, while in the far northwest Simon Fraser was establishing Fort George, a still more singular event was unfolding in Red River country south of Fort Garry, in what is now Pembina, North Dakota. On December 29, Alexander Henry, the man in charge of the North West Company post at that location, wrote that "an extraordinary affair occurred this morning."

Over Christmas, fur traders in the field would often set aside their rivalry to celebrate together. After he had played host to some Hudson's Bay Company workers, Henry wrote in his journal, "one of the Orkney lads, apparently indisposed, had requested me to allow him to remain in my house for a short time."

Puzzled at this request from young John Fubbister, Henry nevertheless "told him to sit down and warm himself" by the fire. He went upstairs to his own room, but had not been there long when one of his men reported that Fubbister wished to speak with him.

"Accordingly, I stepped down to him," Henry continued, "and was much surprised to find him extended on the hearth, uttering dreadful lamentations. He stretched out his hands towards me, and in piteous tones begged me to be kind to a poor, helpless, abandoned wretch, who was not of the sex I had supposed, but an unfortunate Orkney girl, pregnant and actually in childbirth. In saying this, she opened her jacket and displayed to my view a pair of beautiful round white breasts."

Within an hour, the young woman—whose real name was Isobel Gunn—had given birth to a healthy baby boy. "That same day," Henry wrote, "she was conveyed home in my cariole, where she soon recovered."

Among fur-trade historians, this story is well known. Most accounts identify Isobel Gunn as the daughter of John Fubbister of Tankerness, east of Kirkwall, and say she was born in 1781. However, David Gunn, who worked in Canada for two decades before retiring not long ago to Stromness, has determined otherwise. At the Stromness museum, he produced documents showing that Isobel Gunn was born in nearby Orphir on August 10, 1780, the daughter of John Gunn and Isobel Leask.

In June 1806, at a time when the HBC had a policy of not hiring European women into the fur trade, Isobel disguised herself as a man and, as John Fubbister, signed a three-year contract to work as a labourer. Maybe she was following a man she loved. More likely she sought the steady wages, security, and adventure that drew Orcadian men to join the company.

Based initially at Fort Albany on James Bay, Fubbister worked "willingly and well" and received her annual pay raise. Some details of her service remain unclear, and accounts differ slightly. But Isobel claimed that the father of her child was John Scarth, who had been stationed with her for much of her time in Rupert's Land. With Scarth, apparently, she was posted to Brandon House, west of Winnipeg—roughly 1,000 miles (1,600 km) inland.

While the two were there, according to a plausible, second-hand account published in 1922 in the *Free Press Evening Bulletin* of Winnipeg. Scarth discovered to his astonishment that Isobel was a woman. According to a settler named Donald Murray, he threatened to report her, "but she fell on her knees and begged him not to reveal her identity. After much persuasion, he consented to keep the secret, and they continued to live together under the same conditions as before, and it was not a long time afterwards that she lost her honour."

In summer 1807, Scarth was sent to what is now Grand Forks, North Dakota, while Fubbister was posted to Pembina to serve as a cook. She would have been four months pregnant when she made the canoe trip of 200 miles (320 km).

After giving birth, the young mother resumed her real name: Isobel Gunn. Her son she christened James Gunn. The HBC ordered her back to Fort Albany, where she was not allowed to rejoin the men, but worked as a washerwoman. In September 1809, though she begged to stay, she was sent on a ship back to Orkney. There, she worked as a seamstress and, though often in difficult circumstances, lived to the age of eighty.

Decades would elapse before any other European woman travelled as far west even as York Factory on the coast of Hudson Bay. Isobel Gunn, who canoed hundreds of miles inland with fur-trading brigades, was the first of many bold women to challenge the paternalistic status quo in what eventually became Canada. A pioneering female who lacked only opportunity, she was a harbinger of those countless young women who would demonstrate that the fur trade depended on both sexes for its success.

2

FIRST SETTLERS

The Nova Scotia Beachhead

As the battered, three-masted ship approached the forest that lined the Nova Scotia coast, a kilted piper dug out his bagpipes and went to work, blowing his instrument, according to the earliest account, "with might and main, its thrilling tones for the first time startling the denizens of the endless forest and its echoes resounding through the wild solitude." On September 15, 1773, after a horrific, storm-tossed, ten-week crossing distinguished by rotten food, foul drinking water, dysentery, smallpox, and the deaths of eighteen children, the *Hector* put in at Pictou, opposite Prince Edward Island, with one hundred and seventy-two passengers: men, women, and young people.

These were not the first Scots to arrive bent on settling in these environs. Certain predecessors, having sailed from Kirkcudbright, had tried and failed in 1622, after King James VI of Scotland (James I of England) had changed the name of the area from Acadia to Nova Scotia.

A First Settlement, *by William Henry Bartlett, portrays the wilderness that the early Scottish settlers faced on arrival in Nova Scotia. Today, more than 288,000 Nova Scotians—32 percent of the province's population—claim Scottish heritage.*

And seven years after that, James Stewart, the fourth Lord Ochiltree, had come close to creating a small colony in Cape Breton before being driven off by the French.

More recently, during the French–English wars of the 1750s, the British had supplanted both Mi'kmaqs and Acadians with 8,000 American colonists, who undoubtedly included numerous Scots. So those who waded ashore from the *Hector* were not the first to arrive. But unlike their Scottish brethren in the fur trade, who would soon begin mapping the far northwest, these Scots were intent on putting down roots.

In Great Britain, which ruled the waves but continued to expand its navy, shipbuilders had almost exhausted the forested lands that produced the timber needed for wooden vessels. But in this new world, forested land was astonishingly abundant. By building on this advantage, the new arrivals became the first to establish an enduring Scottish colony, a beachhead, on soil that would one day form part of Canada.

But this achievement did not come easily. Having expected to settle along twenty miles (30 km) of fertile coastal lands, the immigrants learned upon arrival that they were to proceed three miles (5 km) into the heavily wooded interior.

They had landed without the expected provisions or shelter of any kind, and they managed to struggle through the first few weeks thanks only to a scattering of settlers who had arrived previously from the south, and to the existence of a rough store that had brought in goods to serve those people. The newcomers had debarked in mid-September, far too late in the season to plant crops. As a result, more than half of them decided to leave for established settlements like Halifax, Truro, and Windsor, some to purchase more promising lands, others to work as labourers or servants. Seventy-eight settlers remained.

But these did not traipse into the thick forest, as the land agent insisted they should. Instead, recognizing that they needed to fish to survive, they squatted on the promised coastal lands, bounded by rivers and, eventually, any Native land claims notwithstanding, attained legal right to them. From the local store, they seized those goods they needed to survive, keeping careful records so that later they could pay for everything they took—which they did.

Finally, when spring broke, they went to work with a Scottish resolve, chopping down trees and floating them down the rivers. By 1775, just two years after they landed, they had doubled their numbers and shipped their first cargo of squared timber back to Great Britain. They had laid the foundations for a timber trade that would sustain a colony for decades, while acting as a magnet for further settlement.

The early years proved difficult. But in 1776, fifteen families of Scottish immigrants, having suffered through two years of famine in Prince Edward Island, crossed the Northumberland Strait and joined the Pictou settlement. The transformative influx of Scots, however, the decisive, shaping wave of immigration, did not arrive until a few years later. Starting in 1784, following the British defeat in the American Revolution, close to 50,000 Loyalists retreated northwards—more than 30,000 of them flooding into Nova Scotia, New Brunswick, and Prince Edward Island. Of the 19,000 who settled in mainland Nova Scotia, 2,000 were disbanded British soldiers and their families.

One of my own ancestors was among them. Thomas Laffin had served as a junior officer with the 84th Royal Highlands Emigrants Regiment, whose men went into battle in full Highland regalia—kilts, swords, and purses made of raccoon skin. All Loyalist ex-soldiers were offered grants of land—1,000 acres to field officers, 750 to captains, 500 to subalterns, 100 to privates. Laffin received 500 acres near Kennetcook River and added 200 more by purchasing allotments from privates who moved elsewhere.

Many of the disbanded Scots gravitated to Pictou County, heart of the flourishing timber trade. By 1803, when Thomas Douglas, the Earl of Selkirk, visited Nova Scotia to survey Scottish settlements, he could report that each year, twenty 400-ton vessels were leaving Pictou for British ports loaded with timber. Two years later, that number increased to fifty—and many of these ships returned with more Scottish immigrants.

Some were fleeing hard times back home. Others came looking to build a better future—one in which they might hope to own their own lands. By 1803, according to Selkirk, an original *Hector* immigrant named William MacKay had "built a new stone house, exactly a good comfortable farm house in Scotland." He had cleared a hundred acres and kept twelve cows. The "old settled Highlanders," Selkirk added, "have in general cleared as much as they want and do little more— being not ambitious of making money so much as living comfortably."

Visions of prosperity attracted many. Yet even when colonies farther west, notably Upper Canada, began advertising a gentler climate and a still more comfortable future along the St. Lawrence River, many Scottish immigrants preferred Nova Scotia. First, proximity to Europe helped maintain contact with the Old Country. Second, the area was becoming predominantly Scottish—Catholic in some areas, Presbyterian in others. These newcomers wished to retain a collective identity, and to build a life in the New World that closely resembled the one they had left in the old, complete with churches, schoolhouses, and a sense of community.

The descendants of those first settlers remained high in the regard of those who moved farther west. In 1923, for example, when Nova Scotians wrote to the St. Andrew's Society of Toronto indicating that they wished to erect a monument to mark the arrival of the *Hector* 150 years before, the society—appreciative of "the human load that spread into all the provinces and did much valiant work on the upbuilding of the Dominion"—sent a contribution of $500, which today equates to roughly $6,500.

Lord Selkirk: A Rage for Colonization

Today, one-third of the population of Nova Scotia has a Scottish heritage. Or, to be more precise, in the Canadian census of 2006, 32 percent of Nova Scotians indicated that they were of Scottish descent. Only one province exceeds that mark: Prince Edward Island, with 41 percent. As in Nova Scotia, the predominance of Scots in P.E.I.—where Summerside is home to the only year-round Celtic arts school outside of Scotland—can be traced to the province's early history. But unlike its sister province, where many factors and individuals contributed to colonization, P.E.I. is powerfully Scottish thanks largely to a single man, who also played a pivotal role in the Scottish settlement of western Canada.

Thomas Douglas, Lord Selkirk, became a leading champion of Scottish settlement in Canada.

Born in 1771 at Kirkcudbright, the fifth surviving son of an earl, Thomas Douglas never expected to inherit the title and the family estate. At fourteen, with four brothers standing between him and the earldom, he went to the University of Edinburgh to study liberal arts and the law. Arriving into a city still ablaze with the Scottish Enlightenment, home to intellectuals like economist Adam Smith and the late philosopher David Hume, young Douglas co-founded a small group called the Friday Club, which spent a lot of time discussing how to help "the oppressed." With one fellow member, Walter Scott, he became lifelong friends. Later, the great novelist remembered Douglas as "one of the most generous" men he had ever known.

After university, the middle-class Scott joined the Faculty of Advocates, while the wealthy Douglas—reserved, carrot-red-haired, and standing over six feet tall—began travelling. At twenty, he sojourned in post-revolutionary Paris, and the following year he spent several months exploring the north of Scotland, where the Highland Clearances had displaced thousands. Landlords bent on developing hugely profitable sheep farms were still "encouraging" tenant farmers, sometimes forcibly, to abandon their traditional family holdings and move to the coast or to the Lowlands or abroad—anything but remain. Douglas was appalled by the suffering he saw.

Still in his early twenties, still powerless, Douglas finished his education with the extended Grand Tour of Europe typical of his class. He spent a year in Naples under the tutelage of a British ambassador, and in Paris he became friends with Charles de Talleyrand, one of the most versatile diplomats in European history. Then, during a devastating three-year period that began in 1794, all four of his older brothers died—two of yellow fever and two of tuberculosis.

Back in Scotland, heir unexpectedly to the family estate, Douglas prepared himself by acquiring a farm and, to the astonishment of all, working it like a tenant. In 1799, when his father died, the twenty-eight-year-old became one of the wealthiest men in Scotland and the fifth Earl of Selkirk.

Concerned still about the effects of the Highland Clearances, the young earl turned to public affairs—specifically to emigration. Would-be settlers had sailed to Nova Scotia out of Kirkcudbright as early as the 1620s. But the first to establish a permanent Scottish settlement, as Selkirk well knew, were those of 1773, who had sailed from Greenock and Loch Broom in the *Hector*.

Selkirk realized, however, that many of those first settlers had drifted south from Nova Scotia into the now independent United States of America—a pattern repeated all too frequently. Selkirk was fiercely opposed to the Americans as a result of a boyhood experience that arose out of the American Revolution. In 1778, when he was seven, Tommy Douglas had been at home in Kirkcudbright when American privateer John Paul Jones—who had been born not far away—sailed into the harbour that lay off the family estate at St. Mary's Isle.

Hoping initially to kidnap the earl and hold him for ransom, the American sailors had reluctantly settled for plundering the family silver when they discovered he was away on business. They avoided bloodshed and brutality, but looking back decades later, Selkirk remembered that raid as "a momentous event in my life. I was terribly frightened . . . and when I was but a youth I developed an antipathy for the United States due almost solely to the buccaneering of John Paul [Jones]."

As the nineteenth century dawned, Selkirk analyzed the flow of emigration from Great Britain. Precise numbers proved hard to find, but every year, tens of thousands of people were moving to the United

States. Nobody could hope to halt or reverse that flow, but Selkirk wondered if he could channel emigrants towards colonies loyal to Britain, and so provide people with a bright future while strengthening the empire abroad.

Selkirk looked first to Ireland. Not long before, the British government had harshly quelled a rebellion driven by hunger, high rents, and desperation. Selkirk crossed the channel, studied the situation, and returned to propose a radical cure. The solution, he argued, was to offer the Irish rebels a chance to emigrate to the new world, and to assist them in resettling. This the Colonial Office flatly refused, dismissing the Irish rebels as intractable.

Disappointed, Selkirk revised his assistance plan. This time he focused on Highland Scots, who were still being cleared from their lands. As a target area, he proposed Upper Canada, specifically the Falls of St. Mary (Sault Ste. Marie), but the Colonial Office wanted a "maritime situation." Selkirk offered to include Prince Edward Island as part of the scheme. Encouraged by the government, he began recruiting in the Highlands. He signed up one hundred families, almost 800 people, already evicted and bound originally for North Carolina.

But in February 1803, with Napoleon Bonaparte sabre-rattling in France, the Colonial Office withdrew its support for the scheme. Anti-emigration sentiment was growing: if young men departed, where would the government find soldiers? Having already recruited his settlers, and contracted ships and supplies, Selkirk refused to quit, but he needed to reduce expenses. That meant confining this first enterprise to the nearer location, Prince Edward Island.

And so, thirty years to the month after the *Hector*, in July 1803, Selkirk sailed from Scotland with three ships and 800 Highlanders, mostly from the Isle of Skye. He enjoyed a smooth crossing and reached Prince Edward Island early in August. By late September, despite setbacks, disputes, and wrangles over who would get which land, Selkirk had created the colony of Belfast—a settlement that immediately began attracting more emigrants who would otherwise have gone to North Carolina.

From Prince Edward Island, having resolved to write a book advocating emigration as a solution to domestic problems in Scotland, Selkirk set out to gather detailed information on other existing colonies. He sailed to Halifax, then travelled around on horseback to visit Nova Scotia settlers. After proceeding to Boston, Massachusetts, he journeyed by horse and canoe to Newark (Niagara-on-the-Lake). En route, he took detailed notes on everything from land quality and crop prices to local attitudes. He noted the existence of Native peoples, and paid special attention to the adaptations required of Highland immigrants.

Anticipating the development of Canadian multiculturalism by almost two centuries, Selkirk envisioned a series of distinctive "national settlements" that would protect language, culture, and manners, guarding immigrants "from the contagion of American manners." Each would be "inhabited by Colonists of a different nation, keeping up their original peculiarities and all differing in language from their neighbours in the United States."

At York (Toronto), the capital of Upper Canada, Selkirk discovered a "very ragged" ten-year-old town of seventy houses, its "roads called streets infamous & almost impassable." Yet here he happily passed the last six weeks of 1803, analyzing surveys for promising locations in that British colony.

From London, the Colonial Office approved a land grant of 1,200 acres, on condition that Selkirk assume the costs of settlement. Early in January, without visiting the site, Selkirk chose what looked like a promising location on Lake St. Clair, in the southwest corner of Upper Canada. Then, travelling by horse and sleigh to Montreal, he concluded that, unless British immigrants began arriving, these wonderfully fertile lands along the St. Lawrence River would soon be occupied by Americans.

In Montreal, Selkirk discovered not a pioneer settlement like York but a stone-built city of 9,000 people run by fur-trading Scots. Here, in 1779, Simon McTavish had established the North West Company to compete with the London-based Hudson's Bay Company. For decades the most important businessman in the colonies, McTavish was nearing the end of his career. But the fur trade had been good to numerous other Scots, among them James McGill, eventual creator of McGill University; William McGillivray, nephew and successor to McTavish; and the explorer Alexander Mackenzie, who for a while would make common cause with Selkirk.

Initially, while gleaning information about the fur trade, Selkirk moved comfortably among those he described as "grandees, nabobs of the N.W. Co.," colloquially known as "Lords of the North." After a couple of months he returned to York, where he hired a manager for his Lake St. Clair settlement, which he called Baldoon. Having elaborated an ambitious blueprint, Selkirk travelled several hundred miles to visit the site and, with the first settlers on their way from Scotland, watched construction begin. In July, while heading for home, he visited Prince Edward Island, where he saw that his first colony, Belfast, was thriving.

Back in Scotland, Selkirk finished his book and, in 1805, saw it published in London: *Observations on the Present State of the Highlands of Scotland, with a View of the Causes and Probable Consequences of Emigration*. A decade later, Walter Scott would write, in his groundbreaking novel *Waverley*, of changes in Scotland that had been "traced by Lord Selkirk with great precision and accuracy."

Selkirk had received warnings that Baldoon was faring poorly, that swampy ground was giving rise to bad crops, illness, and even death. So he focused in his book on his successes in Prince Edward Island, and his well-written arguments began altering attitudes about emigration.

In 1806, after trying and failing to secure a grant of land in New Brunswick, Selkirk turned his attention to Britain's domestic affairs.

He entered the House of Lords as one of sixteen Scottish peers. Once installed, he supported the abolition of the slave trade but opposed parliamentary reform, mainly because of the horrors that had followed the French Revolution.

At age thirty-six, the handsome but shy and reserved Selkirk married Jean Wedderburn, fifteen years younger. She was strikingly beautiful and also intelligent, resourceful, and brave. The marriage also brought him a powerful ally. Soon, with his wife's brother, Andrew Wedderburn, Selkirk was buying shares in the Hudson's Bay Company, bent on gaining a voice in shaping policy.

Having realized that his Baldoon settlement in Upper Canada had failed, and knowing that the political clique controlling that colony wanted no powerful rivals, Selkirk began casting about for a new settlement area. In *Voyages through the Continent of North America,* by Alexander Mackenzie, he had read that fertile lands existed in the vicinity of Red River (now Winnipeg). Under its charter, the HBC controlled the surrounding region. Selkirk began hoping to attract Scots to that area.

When Andrew Wedderburn joined him on the governing committee of the HBC, Selkirk acted with him to influence company policy. In 1811, dusting off a decades-old proposal to develop Red River as a settlement for retired fur traders, Selkirk put forward plans for a substantial colony.

The partners in the Montreal-based North West Company realized that a settlement like the one Selkirk proposed would interfere with their Athabasca trade route. But they mobilized too late to block the deal. In exchange for founding and financing a settlement, Selkirk gained control of 116,000 square miles (300,000 km^2) of land—a fertile area five times the size of Scotland.

During the next decade, Red River would become the locus of not just an extended brawl between fur-trading companies but an epic struggle in which the past met the future. The old economy, built around the fur trade between Native people and voyageurs, came up against the new economy, which centred on European settlement and farming. Before it ended, the conflict would destroy the North West Company and decimate the Selkirk fortune.

In late summer 1812, about seventy Scots arrived in the Red River Settlement. By autumn, they faced a food shortage. Selkirk had warned the governor he appointed, Miles Macdonell, that the area's political situation remained sensitive. He had told him to proceed with caution, noting that "any violent overstretch of authority would be extremely pernicious to our cause." Forgetting this instruction, Macdonell announced that, because of the shortage, he would have to ban the export of pemmican from the area.

For decades, the fertile lands around Red River had not only provided hunters with an abundance of buffalo but supplied most of the North West Company's pemmican. The canoe brigades needed this lightweight mixture of lean dried meat pounded with melted fat to travel in the far northwest. During the summer of 1814, when the ban came into effect, the two sides managed to achieve a compromise.

But that autumn, while in Scotland, Selkirk learned that senior NWC partners were encouraging locals to rise up against the settlement, which now comprised about 200 people. He tried and failed to get the Colonial Office to provide protection, and arranged to travel himself to Red River. In October 1815, when he reached New York, Selkirk learned that the colony had been destroyed. The Nor' Westers had driven off many settlers, razing houses and destroying crops, and bullied or seduced 140 of them into leaving for Upper Canada. The governor, Miles Macdonell, they had carried off to Lower Canada.

With his wife, Selkirk hurried north to Montreal. During the ensuing winter, he got himself appointed a justice of the peace or magistrate for the Indian territory, and he prepared to travel to Red River in force. He also wrote a polemical pamphlet that appeared later that year—a powerful indictment entitled *A Sketch of the British Fur Trade in North America; With Observations Relative to the North-West Company of Montreal.*

In March 1816, as Selkirk gathered men to go west, a messenger arrived in Montreal with encouraging news. Having travelled 1,800 miles (2,900 km) in the dead of winter, he reported that Scots colonists were rebuilding the Red River Settlement. Some of the original settlers had regrouped, and a second party of Selkirk settlers, led by Robert Semple, had arrived from Scotland, having travelled overland after landing at York Factory on Hudson Bay.

Those who ran the North West Company heard the same news. And so began a race to Red River. Selkirk remained optimistic. Using his powers as a magistrate, he intended to prosecute those who had razed the settlement. He quickly built a powerful fighting force, recruiting ninety ex-soldiers from a recently disbanded British regiment.

The spring brigade of the North West Company, however, left Montreal before Selkirk and his men—and in greater numbers than usual. Also, an advance party of Nor' Westers had slipped away even before that brigade, under orders to put an end to the Red River colony. Selkirk departed Montreal soon after the main brigade, but he and his men proceeded slowly as they were hauling twelve boatloads of supplies for the settlers, including arms.

On July 25, 1816, in the western reaches of Upper Canada, near present-day Sault Ste. Marie, Selkirk learned that, for the second time, the North West Company had razed the Red River Settlement. Not only that, but at a place called Seven Oaks, the fur traders had massacred twenty colonists, at least one of whom had pleaded on his knees for his life.

Selkirk faced a choice. Some of his men, fearing that he might be assassinated, urged him to return to Montreal to seek justice through legal channels. But the Montreal-based Nor' Westers had taken a few prisoners to their secondary headquarters at Fort William, and Selkirk refused to withdraw. After further analysis, and though he was not certain he had brought enough men, he decided to journey westward another 440 miles (700 km) to Fort William. As a legally appointed magistrate backed by a regiment of ex-soldiers, Selkirk intended to arrest the Scottish businessmen who controlled the North West Company—those men ultimately responsible for the massacre at Seven Oaks.

Early in August 1816, when he set out by canoe across Lake Superior, Selkirk was embarking, as biographer John Morgan Gray wrote, "to confront the most formidable set of men the Canadas possessed, on their own doorstep." On arriving at Fort William in the middle of the month, Selkirk took care to ensure that those sheltering behind the walls got a chance to see the size of his regiment. As a result, they offered no armed resistance.

As a magistrate, Selkirk took charge. He conducted preliminary hearings and then arrested nine leading figures, among them William McGillivray, the North West Company's senior partner. After occupying the fort, Selkirk found evidence of complicity in the crimes at Red River, so he sent McGillivray and his partners off to Montreal as prisoners. These had long been the richest, most powerful men in that city, though not everybody loved them. And they would remain controversial: in the 1970s, a laudatory biography of McGillivray prompted one reviewer to decry it as "another failed attempt to manufacture a Canadian hero out of a greedy, selfish, small-minded, unimaginative, disagreeable Scots clerk. . . . The fur traders who rose to become robber barons were distinguished primarily by their ability to rob the Indians, cheat their competitors, and shaft their friends. A more reprehensible lot would be hard to find in any nation's iconography. [McGillivray] owed his success to nepotism; the Northwest Company owed its success primarily to rum."

Soon after reaching their home town, McGillivray and his allies gained their freedom on bail. Yet their ignominious arrival marked a turning point in the protracted war between fur traders and settlers. The North West Company never regained its former eminence: within five years, it was swallowed by the Hudson's Bay Company.

The champion of colonization would appear to have won a victory. Yet the end game dragged on for years. Inevitably, it wound through the courts, where the connections of wealthy men like the Nor' Westers could make a difference. At Fort William, Selkirk had made mistakes. He had made a questionable purchase of property from the sole remaining NWC partner, a notorious drunkard. This opened him up to charges of conflict of interest. He also twice refused to heed warrants from Upper Canada for his own arrest. He had good reason, as these were trumped up by the North West Company—yet even so, these refusals hurt his reputation.

Before returning east, Selkirk spent several weeks at Red River, helping to rebuild the settlement yet again. Fearing an assassination attempt, he travelled through the United States. In 1818, he arrived at Sandwich (Windsor), Upper Canada, to answer the warrants he had previously avoided, and got released on bail. But then, with trials entangled in perjuries and postponements, he saw the leaders of the Seven Oaks massacre slip away unpunished.

After months of legal wrangling, leaving his resourceful wife to safeguard his reputation, Selkirk returned to England to confront the Colonial Office over a ludicrously ill-informed letter that had given rise to the false charges against him. In London, though his health was failing, he wrote and published a book, *A Letter to the Earl of Liverpool*, in which he laid out his account of the past several years.

From his sickbed, Selkirk continued to supervise his settlements, though his finances were running low. Then he suffered a hemorrhage, and by spring 1819, he was reported to be "far advanced in a deep consumption." In June, his wife and two sons arrived from Montreal, and the family retreated to southern France. Selkirk received and rejected an offer for his HBC stock because it came from the North West Company and did not provide for the safety of his settlers at Red River.

After Selkirk died in 1820, the Montreal *Gazette* acknowledged that while his personal endowments and qualifications commanded respect, "perhaps some people would deduct something from his worth on account of his rage for colonization." Some people would, no doubt—like those based in a fur-trading town.

But today, most might be inclined to agree with Lucille H. Campey, who insists that, in the early nineteenth century, nobody understood emigration better than Selkirk. He grasped the concepts of social justice and liberty, she writes, that flowed out of the Scottish Enlightenment: "His liberal views placed him well ahead of his time, and in many respects he would have been far better suited to our own era. . . . He believed that emigration enabled poor people to achieve a better life and that, by moving to British North America, they actually strengthened British interests overseas."

With his Prince Edward Island colony, Selkirk redirected the flow of Scottish emigration. With the Red River Settlement, as biographer John Morgan Gray has noted, he founded a city and staked out a province against American encroachment. Winnipeg, the city that evolved out of Red River, is today home to more than 630,000 people. And the population of Manitoba is 18 percent Scottish.

Cuthbert Grant: The Scottish Métis

In *Canada's Heritage in Scotland,* authors Ged Martin and Jeffrey Simpson rightly describe Lord Selkirk as a visionary nation builder who influenced the course of North American history. His Red River colony, they write, fostered "a Canadian destiny for the northern prairies." Ironically, by inspiring resistance among the fur traders of the North West Company, Selkirk unwittingly played a role in creating the Métis nation—though in this, another figure, half-Scottish, proved pivotal.

The critical year was 1814, when Governor Miles Macdonell, appointed by Selkirk, issued his ill-conceived proclamation forbidding the export of pemmican from around Red River. Two Scots arrived in the colony to lead the opposing Nor' Westers—Alexander Greenfield Macdonell, a second cousin of Miles, and the wily veteran Duncan Cameron, born in Glen Moriston, Scotland, who would later represent Glengarry County in the Upper Canada House of Assembly.

In August 1814, these two rode into the colony "dressed in regimentals," according to an HBC witness. Calling himself a captain and Alexander Macdonell a lieutenant, Cameron declared that Miles Macdonell had no authority there, and that he himself was "Chief of this Country." He announced that he wished to hire all the free men in the neighbourhood, "to prevent them," according to Peter Fidler of the Hudson's Bay Company, "from killing Buffalo for the support of the Settlement."

Cameron and Alexander Macdonell, both NWC partners, had worked out a strategy in consultation with the Montreal McGillivrays, William and his younger brother, Simon. The Selkirk colony, backed by the Hudson's Bay Company, had found allies locally among the Saulteaux Indians. To oust the settlers, the Nor' Westers would need the support of the other people in the area—mainly, the so-called half-breeds of mixed Native and Scottish or French heritage.

This community, according to historian George Woodcock, had taken no position in the dispute between the two groups of Scots represented by the Nor' Westers and the Selkirk settlers. They had not done so because they "as yet lacked a sense of identity and recognized leaders." Led by the astute Cameron, who himself had maintained an

Ojibwa wife and family, the Nor' Westers "proceeded to cultivate, and in fact were the first to voice, the idea of a Métis nation with aboriginal rights to the land and special interests as hunters."

By doing so, Woodcock notes, "they were exploiting ill-defined sentiments of Métis identity and giving them shape and direction." From among the mixed-blood clerks of the North West Company, Cameron chose four who might become leaders able to "channel the energy and provoke the anger of the Métis on behalf of the NWC." By March 1816, one of these four "captains of the Métis," a handsome twenty-three-year-old named Cuthbert Grant, had emerged as notably daring and resourceful. Cameron named him "Captain-General of all the Half-Breeds."

Born in 1793 in a fur-trade post called Fort Tremblant, halfway between Winnipeg and Saskatoon, the fluently bilingual Cuthbert Grant was the son of a Scottish wintering partner, also Cuthbert Grant, and a mother of Cree and French heritage. His uncle Robert Grant had been one of the original Montreal traders who formed the North West Company in 1779. His father, who died when he was six, provided for his education and named William McGillivray his guardian. At age eight, Grant travelled with McGillivray to Montreal, where he was baptized into the Scottish Presbyterian Church.

After a few years attending school in Scotland, Grant returned to Montreal to work for the North West Company. In 1812, when he was nineteen, he travelled west to Fort William with the annual brigade, and then took charge of a small outpost on the Qu'Appelle River. Here the beaver had been virtually eradicated, and the post served mainly to organize the buffalo hunt and provide pemmican for Athabasca country traders. The arrival of the Scottish settlers at Red River not only put additional strain on area resources but also raised questions about how the lands would be used.

In 1814, when the newly arrived Duncan Cameron singled him out as a Métis captain, the twenty-one-year-old Grant took to the work with enthusiasm. Woodcock writes that "there is nothing to suggest that before 1814 he saw the Métis as a nation, or gave any thought to their cause, or even identified himself with them."

During the next couple of years, as a cavalry captain who could inspire a following in both English and French, Grant recruited a large number of Métis to the North West Company cause. In March 1815, after the HBC arrested and charged an ally with assault, Grant led two dozen Métis in taking four colonists hostage—an action that led to a prisoner exchange. That spring, while encamped four miles (6.5 km) from Red River, Grant and his men harried the settlers, stealing horses and plows. By the end of June, he had convinced the settlers to leave the area.

Later that summer, almost incredibly, fifty of the stubborn Scottish colonists returned to try again. Grant had gone back to the Qu'Appelle River valley, and he dismissed overtures from the Hudson's Bay Company. In May 1816, Grant rode out with about sixty horsemen to finish off the Red River Settlement. He ambushed some boats and ransacked a fort belonging to the HBC, and then proceeded through Portage la Prairie with pemmican for North West Company brigades on Lake Winnipeg.

On June 19, while seeking to go around the well-defended Fort Douglas, Grant and his men were confronted at Seven Oaks by Robert Semple, the newly arrived Hudson's Bay Company governor, who rode out, hot-headed and unthinking, with a small group of armed men. Most historians agree that one of Semple's men fired the first shot. Cuthbert Grant fired the second and hit Semple in the thigh, rendering him helpless. Then ensued the battle of Seven Oaks, during which the Métis killed twenty-two men and lost two.

With the colony destroyed, Grant withdrew to Fort Alexander, on Lake Winnipeg. When, a couple of months later, he learned that Selkirk had not only captured the North West Company headquarters at Fort William but revived the Red River Settlement yet again, he could only shake his head at the obstinacy of these bloody-minded Scottish colonizers.

In August 1817, after a new commissioner arrived from Lower Canada to investigate the violence, Grant gave himself up, made his depositions, and was taken back to Montreal to face a trumped-up murder charge. Released on bail, he got wind early in 1818 that he would soon face better-grounded charges relating to the massacre at Seven Oaks. In a light canoe, Grant paddled west out of Montreal.

North West Company officers, influential in both Upper and Lower Canada, eventually got the charges against him shelved. In June 1820, Grant was among those who fought at the last battle between the two Scots-dominated trading companies, when Nor' Westers ambushed a fur-laden HBC brigade returning from Athabasca country.

The following year, on the far side of the Atlantic, pragmatic Scottish businessmen finally contrived an end to the profit-killing war between the rival fur-trading concerns. When they folded the NWC into the HBC, Cuthbert Grant figured as one of the leaders who could not easily be accommodated.

In February 1822, however, when newly appointed governor George Simpson ventured west on his first tour of Rupert's Land, he met the twenty-nine-year-old Grant at Fort Hibernia on the Swan River, just west of Lake Winnipegosis. Simpson was impressed with Grant's historical and geographical knowledge, and realized that the charismatic young man could prove a useful ally. "I am therefore of the opinion," he wrote the London committee, "that it might be policy to overlook the past and if you did not object to it [he] might be smuggled quietly into the Service again."

Cuthbert Grant accompanied Simpson to Red River, where the Métis had become surly and unpredictable. The following July, at Fort Garry, he was made HBC clerk and special constable, but the appointment enraged colonists who remembered his earlier depredations. In 1824, after surviving an assault, Grant "retired" from the HBC.

With the company's blessing, he created a settlement twenty miles (30 km) to the west, where from White Horse Plain on the Assiniboine River he continued to wield influence. With one hundred Métis families, he founded the village of Grantown (now St. François Xavier). Designating himself "Seigneur of White Horse Plain," he put thirty-four acres under cultivation and ran an ostensibly independent fur-trading concern.

In 1828, the HBC made Cuthbert Grant "Warden of the Plains of Red River" and authorized him to prevent "the illicit trade in furs within that district." The Métis community continued to elect him captain of the annual buffalo hunts. In 1835, Grant became a justice of the peace, and four years later, a territorial councillor and sheriff. In 1844, as "Chief of the Half-Breeds and Warden of the Plains," Grant negotiated a peace treaty between the Métis and the Sioux, who had been fighting over buffalo-hunting territories—though a few years later, when the two groups renewed hostilities, Grant could no longer engineer a workable peace.

Among the Métis, a new generation of leaders had emerged. A split developed between Grant's followers in White Horse Plain and the predominantly French element from around the Red River Settlement. But there begins a tale with a different set of actors—one that never could have arisen if Cuthbert Grant, encouraged by his fellow Scots, had not fathered the Métis nation.

Letitia Mactavish Hargrave: No Place for a Lady

To her mother back home in Scotland, Letitia Hargrave wrote in 1843 that she had changed so much during the past three years in Rupert's

Land that "I would shrink from exposing myself to the cool criticism of Mrs. Worsley, who delights in telling me how old people are looking, saying nothing of herself, however." In her next sentence, she changed subject abruptly: "There has been nothing further of John MacLoughlin's murder except that master and men were all drunk, firing at each other till John who was in the condition of a maniac fell dead."

Through the letters she wrote home to Scotland, Letitia Mactavish Hargrave produced a unique picture of life in the fur trade.

Hargrave didn't yet have all the facts, and the victim's father later turned up evidence of premeditation. Yet Hargrave drew some telling conclusions: "The gentlemen here are too apt to thrash and indeed point their guns at their men, and Mr. Anderson who came across from Vancouver last year was so detested that they confessed that if he had fallen into the River, not one would have held out a stick to him. One gentleman actually was drowned, when he might easily have been saved without a man wetting his foot."

These snippets come from *The Letters of Letitia Hargrave,* a work of singular importance to Canadian history. Vivid, radically unselfconscious, addressed mostly to family members back home in Scotland, Hargrave's letters constitute the only extended portrayal we have of life in the fur trade from a woman's point of view.

The writer, born Letitia Mactavish in Edinburgh in 1813, was the granddaughter of the chief of clan Tavish. She was also the eldest child of lawyer Dugald Mactavish, who became sheriff of Argyll when she was a girl. In 1821, she moved with her family to Kilchrist House, just south of Campbeltown near the Mull of Kintyre. She was educated by tutors and then at a finishing school.

Several of her relations, among them Simon McTavish and John George McTavish, had figured prominently in the fur trade. When she was twenty-one, her brother William joined the Hudson's Bay Company and was posted to York Factory, on the western shores of Hudson Bay.

York Factory, like other HBC posts, took its name from the term "factor," which had long been used in Scotland to designate a land agent who acted on behalf of an absentee owner. The hierarchical HBC, London based but Scots dominated, broadened the use of the word, putting "chief factors" in charge of fur-trading posts they logically called factories: Moose Factory, Albany Factory, York Factory. On being made a chief factor, an HBC man ceased to be a salaried employee and became a partner who received a small share of company profits.

At York Factory, the man in charge was James Hargrave. He was still a chief trader, one step below factor, but governor George Simpson had described him as "a Scotchman . . . of good education and of highly correct conduct and character and very useful." Hargrave had a good business head and was "better qualified for a seat in council than 9 out of 10 of our present Chief Factors."

During an 1837 holiday in Scotland, William Mactavish introduced Hargrave to his family. Soon after meeting Letitia—vivacious, sharp-witted and fifteen years younger—the chief trader was summoned back to York Factory on urgent business. He subsequently proposed by letter, and Letitia married him in Scotland in January 1840.

During their extended honeymoon in London, she bought "a 1st-rate square piano, seasoned for any extremes of climate." And in June, when the sea ice melted, she crossed the Atlantic with her husband on the HBC ship *Prince Rupert*. On reaching York Factory in August, she wrote, "my first exploit on being lowered into the yawl, was to turn my back to the company and cry myself sick." But then, looking about, she pulled herself together: "I had no sooner got out of the yawl than I felt better and have ever since got stronger."

Letitia Hargrave would need that resilience. Rupert's Land was famously no place for a lady. In *Many Tender Ties*, Sylvia Van Kirk writes that life there "required considerable physical and psychological adaptation, and the British lady was likely to lack (and would not be encouraged to develop) the bodily strength and mental attitude necessary to make a successful transition." Some young women, she notes, sickened so rapidly that "they soon had to be removed from Indian Country."

For the HBC men, Van Kirk writes, Rupert's Land involved hard work but also camaraderie. "For white women, however, it meant moving to a strange and physically inferior environment" and severing social and family ties. Frances Simpson, wife of HBC governor George Simpson and friend of Letitia Hargrave, "suffered intensely" while living in the Red River Settlement and fled to England, resuming married life only after her husband relocated to Montreal.

Yet Red River, harsh as it could be, was a haven of civilized congeniality compared with bleakly isolated York Factory. True, Letitia Hargrave lived in relative comfort: she had a well-furnished house complete with a piano, and a personal maid as well as an HBC cook and butler. At the birth of her second child, she had a nursery added to the side of the house.

Even so, during the summer, when her husband put in endless hours, often she dined alone. As the only white woman in the area, she proved an object of curiosity, and drew people to her. She writes of "the wee'est girls" coming to visit, wearing their shawls. "Hargrave bought two pounds of peppermint drops at Stromness and they laugh aloud when I give them some. They don't know a word of English or French. When I want flowers or berries I show them a specimen and give them a shove and off they go. It never happens that they fail."

If at times Letitia Hargrave expressed the snobbish attitudes of her class, yet she also empathized across barriers. She castigated a minister at Red River, for example, for keeping Métis children away from mothers who had not been married in a church: "This may be all very right," Hargrave wrote, "but it is fearfully cruel, for the poor unfortunate mothers did not know that there was any distinction & it is only within the last few years that any one was so married."

In 1846, Letitia and her growing family visited Scotland. But, after leaving her eldest son at school in St. Andrews, she returned to York Factory and resumed waiting for her husband's promised transfer. In 1851, she enjoyed another trip to Scotland—though this time, she left her eldest daughter at school with her son. The following year, she rejoined her husband, finally transferred, and established a new family base in Sault Ste. Marie. But in 1854, during a cholera epidemic, she got sick and quickly grew worse. At age forty-three, Letitia Mactavish Hargrave passed away. Behind her, though she did not know it, she left a remarkable legacy: a woman's portrayal of the fur trade.

3

ECHOES OF OLD SCOTIA

The Cape Breton Faithful

During recent decades, Canada has become increasingly secular. Once an avowedly Christian nation, today the country accords all religions equal legal status. But when the Scots were arriving in great numbers, they came from a world segregated between Roman Catholics and Protestants, with the latter further divided (notably among Anglicans, Presbyterians, Methodists, and Baptists). The Presbyterian Church, which would become arguably the most influential in English-speaking Canada, evolved out of the Church of Scotland, the so-called Kirk, whose earliest members, drawing on the teachings of John Knox, put an unprecedented emphasis on literacy and education. They valued Christian morality, thrift, and hard work, and understood that to appreciate the Bible, you had to be able to read.

Presbyterianism came to Canada with the earliest immigrants to Cape Breton Island. By the 1840s, Presbyterian Highlanders were numerous enough in Cape Breton to launch an annual summer tradition of "open-air communion" called the Sacramaid. This five-day religious festival, the social and spiritual highlight of the year, would draw thousands of people, most dressed austerely in black, to key locations around the island. The largest-ever Sacramaid occurred in 1853, when 8,000 people brought 200 boats and 500 horses to a Cape Breton town.

In an essay called "Tabernacles in the Wilderness," historian Laurie Stanley-Blackwell summarizes the usual pattern of events, which reveals much about the religion and values that played such a large role in shaping Canada. Parishioners would spend weeks getting ready: the men ordering their affairs and studying their catechism, the women cleaning house and preparing food. When the time came, families would take visiting Presbyterians into their homes and barns. No musical instruments were allowed, but "precentors" would lead worshippers in chanting psalms.

Opening day, Thursday, focused on fasting and preparation. Friday, also known as the Men's Day, featured open-air testimonials by "old Christian inquirers" who cited scripture and elaborated with commentary. Saturday, the Day of Preparation, brought first communions and separate services in English and Gaelic. Sunday was the climactic day, the Sabbath, when overflowing crowds attended services that lasted four to six hours. It culminated in the ceremonial sacrament, which affirmed the fellowship of those in attendance. Monday, a Day of Thanksgiving, brought a final service at which people said emotional goodbyes.

This five-day schedule followed a grassroots pattern imported from Scotland. "Many of the devout Presbyterians," Stanley-Blackwell writes, "regarded these open-air communions as condensed re-enactments of the drama of the persecuted Covenanters who had sought the safety of secluded glens for their forbidden worship."

In the 1600s, these Covenanters had signed a series of pacts or covenants to maintain Presbyterianism, a bottom-up system of church government that harked back to John Knox and the Scottish Reformation of the previous century. Ironically, because of his emphasis on reading the Bible and thus on literacy, Knox also laid the foundations of the Scottish Enlightenment. And that in turn gave the world such nominal Presbyterians as philosopher David Hume, that prince among godless sceptics, and poet Robert Burns, who satirized the hypocrisy he deplored in the church Knox created.

Robert Burns: A Subversive Rejoinder

Every year in late January, tens of thousands of Canadians gather at often elaborate dinners to celebrate Robert Burns, born in rural Scotland more than 250 years ago. This we have been doing since before Confederation. The St. Andrew's Society of Saint John, New Brunswick, organized in 1798 as the first of many in Canada, sponsored a Burns supper in 1859 to mark the hundredth anniversary of the poet's birth. Annual Burns dinners have been a regular occurrence in this country since at least the 1880s.

Not only that, but statues of Robbie Burns stand vigilant in cities across the country: Halifax, Fredericton, Montreal, Toronto, Windsor, Winnipeg, Edmonton, Vancouver, Victoria. Here in Canada, no other poet, and in fact no other writer of any kind, has inspired anything approaching this level of commemoration in stone. The obvious question is, what gives?

One explanation is that Burns has come to symbolize Scotland itself. All those wishing to wax nostalgic about Old Scotia, even if they've never visited, need only raise a glass to that country's national poet, or sing along with "Auld Lang Syne," his most famous song. Beyond that, one wonders if some Burns fans don't savour the rebellious naughtiness of the "bad boy" poet, who flouted Church teachings and had more than his share of luck with the lassies. Here in Canada, Robbie Burns stands as the archetypal anti-Presbyterian, the subversive rejoinder to the professedly faithful.

Burns was born in 1759 in a cottage built by his father in Alloway, a village just south of Ayr. When he was seven, his father sold the house and became a tenant farmer nearby. Burns, the oldest of seven children, grew up doing hard manual labour on that seventy-acre farm. He learned how to read and write from his Presbyterian, education-oriented father. Then he studied Latin, French, grammar, and mathematics with a schoolmaster who boarded in the area.

Burns wrote his first poem, "O, Once I Lov'd a Bonnie Lass," at age fifteen, to a girl helping him with the harvest. The following summer, while finishing his education with a second tutor, he wrote two songs to another young woman, so confirming a pattern of seduction and commemoration that would endure for the rest of his life.

When he was eighteen, his father moved his large family to a 130-acre farm near Tarbolton, about ten miles (16 km) northeast. Here Robert began to assert his independence, joining a country dancing school over his father's objections and founding the Tarbolton Bachelor's Club. He became a Freemason, wrote poems and songs and, rejected in love, moved a few miles north to Irvine to learn the difficult trade of flax dressing.

In 1782, a New Year's Eve party culminated in a fire that burned the flax shop to the ground, and the poet returned to the farm. Two years later, after the death of his father, Robert moved with the family to yet another farm, this one near Mauchline. When his first illegitimate child was born, to his mother's servant, Burns was compelled to stand penance on a stool in front of the local congregation—a ritual humiliation that did nothing to ease his feelings towards Presbyterian orthodoxy. He endured this rite a second time when Jean Armour, daughter of a local stonemason, bore him twins. But here the situation grew more complex, as her parents, judging him to be a rake without prospects, managed to thwart his efforts to marry the young woman—at least temporarily.

During this period, 1784 to 1786, Burns found his voice as a poet. He produced such works as "Address to the Deil," "The Holy Fair," "The Cotter's Saturday Night," and the fiercely satirical "Holy Willie's Prayer." This last, a hilarious attack on Presbyterian hypocrisy, finds the poet holding forth in the unctuous, prayerful tones of a church elder. The poem remains consistently within the voice of a hypocrite revelling in his supposed moral superiority while revealing (and justifying) various depravities:

Besides, I farther maun allow,
Wi' Leezie's lass, three times I trow—
But Lord, that Friday I was fou [drunk],
When I came near her;
Or else, Thou kens, Thy servant true
Wad never steer her.

Burns wrote much of his work in this Scots-inflected English, the so-called Lallans dialect of the Scottish Lowlands. In this subtly political decision, he followed the poet Robert Fergusson (1750–74)—a debt he acknowledged during his first visit to Edinburgh, when he erected a memorial stone at his forerunner's grave.

Burns undertook that visit after he published *Poems, Chiefly in the Scottish Dialect,* a short book that became a literary sensation. Known now as the Kilmarnock edition, after the location of its publisher, the collection sold out its initial print run of 612 copies within a month. More importantly, influential critics lauded the work.

Critical acclaim culminated in an invitation to Edinburgh to oversee a revised edition of the book, and there the widely read Burns, hailed as a "heaven-taught ploughman" of innocent genius, proved a singular success in intellectual and aristocratic circles. Burns used the voice of an uneducated ploughman as a mask. Yet he was rightly perceived to be an enemy of class constraints and economic injustice, and a champion of free speech and individual freedom.

During these few months in the city, Burns conducted a tragic love affair with an educated, sensitive, and beautiful woman who remained agonizingly out of reach socially. Between December and April, the two traded eighty-two love letters. The affair ended in sadness, but it inspired Burns to compose "Ae Fond Kiss," surely one of the greatest love songs ever written.

In the northeast section of Toronto's Allan Gardens, near the busy downtown intersection of Carlton and Sherbourne Streets, a statue of Robert Burns was unveiled on July 21, 1902—the 106th anniversary of the poet's death. According to reports in the Toronto *Mail and Empire,* the unveiling of the statue, "which is of heroic size," featured the singing, by the male chorus of the 48th Highlanders' Band, of several of Burns's lyrics—among them, "Ae Fond Kiss."

In the early 1960s, this Burns statue became the heart of a well-publicized free speech battle, when a tempestuous poet successfully challenged a Toronto city bylaw prohibiting public speaking in parks except for religious sermons. Today, that statue, like many of its fellows across the country, continues to serve as a rallying point for Scots and Scottish Canadians. Each year, members of the St. Andrew's Society of Toronto gather in Allan Gardens on Robbie Burns Day, often despite freezing winds and blowing snow, to honour the poet while the bagpipes play, and then to adjourn for a suitable libation.

In one of his greatest poems, "A Man's a Man for A' That," Burns displays the egalitarian irreverence that inspires this affection:

Ye see yon birdie cad's a lord,
What struts, and stares, and a' that,
Though hundreds worship at his word,
He's but a coof for a' that.
For a' that, and a' that,
His ribband, star and a' that,
The man of independent mind,
He looks and laughs at a' that.

Sir Walter Scott: The Magic of Pageantry

For English-speaking children growing up around Montreal in the 1950s, the single unmissable public celebration of the year was the St. Patrick's Day parade—an event memorable, oddly enough, for its spectacular Scottish dimension. Come the appropriate Saturday in mid-March, crowds would line Ste. Catherine Street to enjoy a surging procession that lasted for hours. I remember my father lifting me onto his shoulders to listen for the distant sounds of the drums and the bagpipes, and watch for the men wearing kilts and furry black hats. And when at last they arrived, I would ride along on my father's shoulders as he marched, pausing when the pipers paused, marching when they marched. Of course I could not know it, just as children today cannot know it, but we Canadians owe that magical experience, that thrilling to the kilts and the drums and the bagpipes, to an eighteenth-century romantic who found a way to keep Scottish history alive through the ages.

Walter Scott was born in Edinburgh in 1771, the son of a solicitor. At age two, after surviving a bout of polio that left him lame in one leg, Scott went to live in the Border region at his grandparents' farm, near the ruin of Smailholm Tower. Here, besides learning to read, he heard tales and legends that influenced his later work. He returned to the city at age seven and, the following year, began attending the Royal High School of Edinburgh.

Scott read voraciously—poetry, chivalric romances, works of history and travel—and in 1783, at age twelve, he began studying classics at the University of Edinburgh. Three years later, while visiting a friend at the house of professor Adam Ferguson, he met Robert Burns at the height of his fame. A well-known painting illustrates an incident from this meeting. The poet admired a print called *The Justice of the Peace* and asked who had written the poem that inspired it. In the august company of Edinburgh intellectuals, only the bookish young Scott could tell him the name of the author (John Langhorne). Burns gave the youth a nod that later he remembered with pride.

After apprenticing with his father, Scott studied law. As a law clerk he visited the Scottish Highlands during an eviction, and in 1792, he was admitted to the Faculty of Advocates. Along the way, he had learned to read French, Spanish, Italian, and German, and at twenty-five, while practising law, Scott translated and published a collection of rhymed ballads by German romantic Gottfried Bürger. Building on this, and strongly influenced by Burns, who had devoted years to collecting and polishing folk songs, Scott compiled a three-volume collection of old ballads, *The Minstrelsy of the Scottish Border.*

At age twenty-six, after surviving one failed love affair, Walter Scott married Margaret Charpentier, a woman of French descent who would bear him five children. Two years later, he became sheriff deputy of the County of Selkirk, a posting that, together with his wife's income and some money from his father's estate, gave him financial security. In the early 1800s, poetry was regarded as the highest of the literary arts and was also widely read. When, in 1805, Scott published a first book of poems called *The Lay of the Last Minstrel,* he began his climb to celebrity.

During the next few years, he published a series of long narrative poems, among them *Marmion* (1808), *The Lady of the Lake* (1810), *Rokeby* (1813), and *The Lord of the Isles* (1815). The first of these inspired Schubert's *Ave Maria,* and another poem included the oft-quoted lines, "Oh! what a tangled web we weave / When first we practice to deceive!" Though hailed as a major poet, Scott perceived that his work was sliding out of fashion.

In an astute critical biography, *Sir Walter Scott,* writer John Buchan—later governor general of Canada—captured Scott's reaction to the emergence of the younger Lord Byron as a poet: "How could a middle-aged Scottish lawyer compete . . . against a young and handsome lordling, who had about him the glamour of a wild life and a broken heart? How could the homely glens of his own land vie with the glittering cities of the South and the magic of the ancient East?"

Some years earlier, Scott had begun working on a prose narrative set against the Jacobite rebellion of the 1740s, when a Highland uprising against the British king culminated in the disastrous battle of Culloden. He had written the first few chapters of *Waverley,* but when a friend voiced doubts about the work, he set it aside. In 1813, while visiting an attic garret, he chanced upon the manuscript. He decided to finish it—"and thereby," Buchan tells us, "entered into his true kingdom."

The next year, fearful that by publishing a novel, a mere entertainment, he might harm his reputation as a man of letters, not to mention as a sheriff and lawyer, Scott released *Waverley* anonymously. At this time, as Buchan notes, great novels were expected to be studies of contemporary life: "The historical tale was a lifeless thing, smothered in tinsel conventions, something beneath the dignity of literature."

Waverley, however, was clearly serious: entertaining, yes, but also educational, challenging, even provocative. The novel proved a huge popular success. Although he did not realize it, Scott had created a new literary genre with an international future: the realistic historical novel.

The protagonist of his novel, an English Tory named Edward Waverley, is sympathetic to the rebellious Scottish Jacobites, but decides finally to remain loyal to the British king. This position would soon lead to a friendly first meeting between Scott and the prince regent, and ultimately to a spectacular pageant that would reverberate down through the decades and across the Atlantic into Canada.

Following hard on the success of *Waverley,* Scott produced a series of historical novels: *Guy Mannering* (1815), *The Antiquary* (1816), *Rob Roy* (1817), *Ivanhoe* (1819), *Kenilworth* (1821), and *The Pirate* (1822). Most of these works he published anonymously, which caused speculation, and his identity did not become known until after the unknown author had been hailed as "The Wizard of the North."

Early critics of Scott included Mark Twain, who blamed the author's "romanticization of battle" for the American Civil War—a backhanded tribute to Scott's enormous influence. Later, the fastidious novelist E. M. Forster derided Scott for slapdash writing and careless plotting. Scott's reputation rebounded as fashions changed, though few today would argue that he is a novelist of the first rank.

Yet Scott is widely recognized as the father of serious historical fiction—a genre that has an unusually strong presence in Canadian literature. *The Oxford Companion to Canadian Literature* tells us that of foreign authors who influenced early English Canadian writers, "the most important was Sir Walter Scott." Through the late nineteenth and early twentieth centuries, many Canadian home libraries included *Rob Roy, Ivanhoe,* and *The Pirate.*

In recent times, some literary critics have complained that Canadian writers produce far too many historical novels. Certainly, an abridged list of the guilty would include Timothy Findley, Margaret Atwood, Katherine Govier, Lawrence Hill, Joseph Boyden, Anne Michaels, Dennis Bock, Steven Galloway, Karen X. Tulchinsky, Fred Stenson, and Helen Humphreys.

But perhaps the disgruntled critics are using American literature as a yardstick. Canada never staged a revolution. We never severed ties with Scotland, so why wouldn't that country's literary traditions continue to exert influence? Whatever the explanation, here in Canada, the historical novel has remained continuously alive all the way back to its origins in the works of Sir Walter Scott.

If creating that literary tradition had been his sole contribution to Canada, Sir Walter Scott would claim a presence here. But in 1822, Scott organized a pageant that gave Scotland symbols of identity unique in the world—symbols that now play a major role in Canadian life. Four years previously, Scott had led the way in entering the Crown Room in Edinburgh Castle to disinter the ancient honours of Scotland: a crown, a sword of state, and a sceptre that had been locked away since 1707.

For Scott, the occasion was sacramental. When one of the commissioners suggested placing the crown on the head of a young woman present, a mere commoner, an appalled Scott roared, "By God, no!" As John Buchan observes, "That day Edinburgh learned that its genteel antiquarianism was a very different thing from Scott's burning reverence for the past."

When in 1822 King George IV announced that he would make a state visit to Scotland, and so become the first reigning monarch to set foot in the country since 1650, the movers and shakers of Edinburgh realized immediately that the only man who could organize an appropriate national pageant was Sir Walter Scott, recently named a baronet. Scott met the challenge head on, and worked himself to the brink of illness while turning the occasion into an unprecedented celebration of all things Scottish.

During the fourteen days King George spent in Scotland, more than 300,000 people turned out to see him. Great numbers of them wore tartan, as Scott had requested, and marching bands paraded here and there to the skirling of bagpipes. In Canadian terms, the impact of the event could perhaps be compared with that of Expo 67, the Montreal world's fair that gave Canadians a new sense of themselves.

Inevitably, it inspired controversy. Scott's son-in-law and biographer, John Lockhart, praised the extravaganza as "Sir Walter's Celtification of Scotland," while the *Scotsman* complained that the celebration went too far in giving "a Highland complexion to the whole . . . as if nothing were Scottish but what is Highland." Later, in *The King's Jaunt,* author John Prebble took this criticism further, decrying "the Highland dress and spurious tartans" as having little connection with ancient costume, and complaining that no laments were heard "for the evictions, the burnings and the white-sailed ships that were emptying the glens while the men who profited from this disapora formed their highland societies and solemnly debated the correct hang of a kilt and the exact drape of a plaid."

Certainly, Scott's fourteen-day pageant went over the top. But that is why it resonated down through the decades and across oceans. And if the Scottish tartans are shakily grounded, yet they create a sense of continuity and proclaim a respect for history and tradition. Working with a state visit, Walter Scott turned the kilt and the bagpipes into symbols of Scottish identity that continue to colour every major parade in Canada, and today are recognized around the world—and that is no small accomplishment.

Biographer John Buchan tries to put Walter Scott in context: "John Knox gave his land the Reformation, which led to high spiritual exaltations, but also to much blood and tears. . . . [Robert] Burns, with a Greek freedom in his soul, gave Scotland her own French Revolution." And Scott, he writes, "completed what eighteenth-century philosophers had begun and gave [Scotland] her own Renaissance. He is, with Burns, her great liberator and reconciler."

According to Buchan, Scott not only gave his fellow countrymen a new confidence by reconnecting them with their history but also found a way to communicate the distinctiveness of Scotland to the world. Whether that makes him the greatest of all Scots, as Buchan declares, is open to argument. For contemporary Canadians, Scott continues to resonate beyond pageantry because he showed that the future can lie hidden in the past. Scott demonstrated that history can provide a sense of direction, and that the way forward can sometimes be found by looking back at where you came from.

4

ANNALS OF ARRIVAL

Major John Norton: The Cherokee Scot

During the spring of 1814, when Walter Scott was anonymously publishing *Waverley,* he received an excited letter from his brother, mightily impressed with a Mohawk chieftain named John Norton. Thomas Scott, serving in Quebec City as paymaster for Britain's 70th Regiment, asked rhetorically, "What do you think of a man speaking the language of about twelve Indian nations, English, French, German and Spanish, all well, being in possession of all modern literature—having read with delight your *Lady of the Lake,* and translated the same, together with the Scriptures, into Mohawk—having written a history of the five nations, and a journal of his own travels, now in London ready for publication, and being at the same time an Indian Chief, living as they do and following all their fashions."

Although Norton displayed "the most polished manner of civilized life," Thomas Scott continued, he had also adorned himself with war paint and "would not disdain to partake of the blood of his enemy at the banquet of sacrifice. Yet I admire and love the man, and would cheerfully give fifty guineas that you could see him for one half-hour."

While John Norton was indeed a Mohawk chieftain and half Cherokee by blood, he was also half Scottish, and as such a prototype: he embodied the inclusiveness of the earliest Scots to settle in Canada, and anticipated the multicultural reality that, over the next two centuries, would come to characterize the country.

John Norton was born near Dunfermline, north of Edinburgh, in the late 1760s. His Cherokee father had been taken as a boy from Keowee, South Carolina, when British troops destroyed that town during the Anglo–Cherokee War (1758–61). His mother was the daughter of John Anderson, a farmer in the parish of Salen (Saline), outside Dunfermline. After attending school in that vicinity, Norton worked as a printer's apprentice. In 1785, having joined the British army, he arrived in Quebec as a private with the 65th Regiment of Foot.

This portrait of Major John Norton, painted by Mary Ann Knight when he visited England, was shown at the Royal Academy in 1805.

At age eighteen or nineteen, while based at Fort Niagara, young Norton grew restless and deserted (receiving his discharge not long afterwards). He taught school at a Mohawk settlement on the Bay of Quinte, east of Kingston, Upper Canada, but resigned in 1791 and spent four years working in the fur trade. In 1795, he became an interpreter in the Indian Department at Niagara, but soon transferred his services to Mohawk captain Joseph Brant (Thayendanegea), the most celebrated North American Indian of his generation.

In 1799, having adopted Norton as his nephew and successor, Brant named him Teyoninhokovrawen, making him a powerful chief among the Six Nations of the Iroquois. With Brant, and based at Grand River (near present-day Brantford, Ontario), Norton led the land-claims battle for his adopted people, and so made enemies among officials of the Indian Department of Upper Canada. In 1804, Norton sailed to England to negotiate treaties advancing the Iroquois cause. In this his enemies thwarted him.

Yet Norton impressed and became friends with British evangelicals working to abolish the slave trade, among them scientists and politicians led by William Wilberforce. They employed him to begin translating the Bible into Mohawk. His translation of the Book of John became the first foreign publication of the British and Foreign Bible Society. Later, Norton translated the other gospels—though no translation of *Lady of the Lake* has ever been discovered.

Back at Grand River in 1806, he found Joseph Brant (1742/43–1807) in failing health. Norton resumed the struggle against the Indian Department, though personal attacks made him yearn to retire. In 1809, to trace his Cherokee roots, Norton undertook a round-trip journey of about 2,000 miles (3,200 km), travelling through Ohio, Kentucky, and Tennessee to South Carolina. The Cherokee recognized him as one of their own and, as he wrote later in his journal, told him his father "was the brother of the widow of their old Chief Kennitea, who now lived at the Creek Path . . . They thought I had better go there to talk with her, as her great age had prevented her from being present at this meeting."

This Norton did. Arriving at the house of his father's older sister, he met "an old woman of about seventy." She related "the scene in which her brother [his father] was taken from her: she said that she saw the officer rescue him after he had been scorched, on which account he was taken away in a wagon—and they were separated."

Back in Grand River, Norton found conditions depressing, and would have gone "to the westward" except that tensions were escalating between Britain and the United States. In 1812, when war broke out, Norton assumed command of hundreds of fighters from the Six Nations. He played a crucial role in the British victory at Queenston Heights, making a brilliant tactical decision to outflank the Americans. In dispatches, a major-general mentioned the importance of "the judicious position which Norton and the Indians with him had taken."

Pierre Berton, describing Norton as "a strapping six-foot Scot who thinks of himself as an Indian," portrays him even in action as theatrical: "He wears his black hair in a long tail held in place by a scarlet handkerchief into which he has stuck an ostrich feather. Now, brandishing a tomahawk, his face painted for battle, he whoops his way through the woods, terrifying the American militia and confusing the regulars."

One week after Queenston Heights, Norton was made captain of the Confederate Indians, the rank previously held by the late Joseph Brant. He performed heroically throughout the war, leading Iroquois warriors with distinction at Fort George, Burlington Heights, and Chippawa, and also at the climactic battle of Lundy's Lane.

Early in 1814, Norton travelled to Quebec City at the request of Sir George Prevost, governor-in-chief of British North America. It was during this visit that Norton impressed Thomas Scott. The following year, he sailed to Scotland with his wife and son, and remained for more than a year. By then his manuscript journal included not only the story of his journey to Cherokee country and an informed history of the Iroquois but a vivid, first-person account of the War of 1812–14. Norton retired to a farm overlooking the Grand River, but died while travelling in the American south.

His manuscript remained unpublished until 1970, when the Champlain Society released it as *The Journal of Major John Norton, 1816*. In a biographical introduction, editor Carl F. Klinck wrote, "One may sense something truly North American and Canadian in Norton's realistic rejection of medieval-romantic-sentimental fashions in favour of the social current of his time and of his own nature—the humanitarianism of Wilberforce and the Clapham community. The anti-slavery of Britain found its New World equivalent in religious-economic sympathy with the Indians."

John Galt: A Whopping 50,000

Seven years after the death of Lord Selkirk, five after Walter Scott created a Scottish pageant in Edinburgh, and while Cuthbert Grant was still angling to become warden of the plains of Red River, a cultivated Scot, well known in Britain as an author and a friend of Lord Byron, led an eighteen-mile (29 km) march into the forested heart of Upper Canada. There, on April 23, 1827, while four companions watched, forty-eight-year-old John Galt took an axe to a maple tree and set in motion a process that would, at considerable personal cost, change the future of Ontario.

Galt had been born in Irvine, Ayrshire, the son of a naval captain. He would have been nearing his third birthday in January 1782 when a fire in that town ended the flax-dressing career of Robbie Burns. His inquisitive, talkative mother almost certainly took him past the burned-out shed.

Because he was a sickly child, Galt grew up listening to the tales and ballads of old women who lived behind his grandmother's house. At ten, a youth of unusual height, he moved with his family to Greenock, a bustling port town west of Glasgow. His mother encouraged him in active, practical pursuits, and at sixteen, Galt went to work as a clerk, first in the Greenock custom house, then with a local firm. He also began publishing stories and poems in local newspapers, and with two interested fellows created a literary society. In 1804, the young men hosted an event with James Hogg, the celebrated "Ettrick Shepherd" and friend of Walter Scott, who declared their conversation "much above what I had ever been accustomed to hear."

That same year, after the death of a close female friend, Galt moved to London and set up a successful brokerage with a fellow Scot. In 1807, in the *Philosophical Magazine,* he published an essay, "Statistical Account of Upper Canada," that echoed Selkirk in arguing that emigration to the New World might provide the solution to overcrowding in Europe.

A business reversal turned Galt to studying law at Lincoln's Inn, but his health collapsed, and in 1809, he went travelling in Europe. For several months, he rambled around the Mediterranean with George Gordon, Lord Byron, later famous as both rake and romantic poet. And in Greece, Galt helped Lord Elgin, whose son would become governor general of Canada, pack up the controversial "Elgin marbles" from the Parthenon and ship them to England.

Galt returned to London in 1811, married, and turned to writing as a profession. From 1812 onwards, he produced travel memoirs, novels, textbooks, and biographies at an impressive rate. In 1820, he scored a hit with a novel called *The Ayrshire Legatees,* and he followed that with his acclaimed *Annals of the Parish,* which treated the social and industrial changes engulfing Ayrshire. After producing some

In Scotland, author and colonizer John Galt is best known for Annals of the Parish, *but most Canadians view* Bogle Corbet *as the more significant work.*

forgettable historical novels, in the 1830s he built on his early successes, publishing a wildly successful biography of Lord Byron and also such notable political novels as *The Member* and *The Radical.*

A crucial turning point, for those interested in the Canadian connection, came after Galt had gained a reputation as a parliamentary lobbyist during a debate over the building of a canal. In 1824, Upper Canadian Loyalists asked him to serve as their agent in seeking redress for unpaid damages they had suffered during the War of 1812. He accepted, but soon discovered that British parliamentarians had gone deaf on this issue.

In talking with a friend based in Upper Canada—the Roman Catholic priest Alexander McDonell—Galt conceived the idea of using the colony's own resources to acquire the requisite funds. Why not sell off the lands reserved to the Crown and the clergy and use the revenues to reimburse his Loyalist clients? This led to an amended scheme: Galt convinced leading London merchants and bankers to invest in a joint-stock venture, the Canada Company, that would buy reserve lands and sell them to immigrants at a profit.

In spring 1825, Galt visited Upper Canada to evaluate the lands. Inevitably, he came up against the unbending ruling oligarchy, the Family Compact, which was dominated by the Anglican reverend John Strachan, who had been raised in Scotland as a Presbyterian. The Anglicans controlled vast tracts of prime, undeveloped land, all originally set aside for "the support and maintenance of a Protestant clergy." With the help of his former student, attorney general John Beverley Robinson, Strachan kept these lands from the Canada Company. Instead, the company purchased more than one million acres of wilderness (the so-called Huron Tract) to the west of York (present-day Toronto), and another million acres of Crown lands scattered around the colony.

In 1826, as governor of the Canada Company, Galt moved with his family to Upper Canada and established an office at York. The following March, he sent his right-hand man, fellow Scot William "Tiger" Dunlop, officially the "Warden of the Forests," into the Huron Tract to scout a proposed site for a settlement he would call Guelph.

One month later, on April 23, Galt travelled west from York with four men: Tiger Dunlop, his lead surveyor, George Pryor, and two woodsmen. A storm came on and the five got lost in the woods. Finally, after a cold, wet march of about eighteen miles (29 km), they located the giant maple tree that marked the centre of the proposed town.

Galt struck the first blow with an axe. Dunlop and Pryor each took a turn, and then the two local men finished felling the tree. "To me at least," Galt wrote later, "the moment was impressive—the [echoing] silence of the woods . . . was as the sigh of the solemn genius of the wilderness departing forever." Dunlop produced a flask of whisky, "and we drank prosperity to the City of Guelph."

With roads radiating outwards from the heart of town, Guelph impressed everyone as a marvel of imaginative design. But it was not the first Scottish settlement to flourish in Upper Canada. In the southwest corner of Lake St. Clair, after the failure of Selkirk's Baldoon in 1818, Lieutenant Thomas Talbot had established settlers across 65,000 acres of land—a sizable area, but one representing less than 5 percent of the territory controlled by the Canada Company. In the eastern reaches of the colony, starting in the previous century, both Cornwall and Perth had attracted hundreds of Scottish settlers, many of them ex-soldiers, and had developed organically, as part of an evolving network of rivers and roads.

But the town of Guelph came into being largely as a result of the vision and industry of a single man. Inspired by several settlements he had visited in upstate New York, John Galt moved quickly to develop it as a magnet for colonists. He also ventured farther west to Lake Huron, on whose coast, at Goderich, he established a second town—another marvel of imaginative design. By autumn 1828, he and his men had cleared a rough, twelve-foot-wide (3.6 m) roadway from Guelph to Goderich.

Yet all was not right in this little world. Like Selkirk, the cosmopolitan Galt had already clashed with John Strachan and his Family Compact allies. He had shown far too much religious tolerance towards First Nations people; he had snubbed the pretentious lieutenant governor, Sir Peregrine Maitland, both when he hosted a party and failed to invite Lady Maitland to be his hostess and when he failed to toast that potentate during a holiday Maitland had created in honour of the British king.

But Galt went too far—and made himself vulnerable—when he responded humanely to a group of impoverished Scots who had turned up on his doorstep. They had fallen into destitution after failing in an attempt to establish a colony in La Guaira, Venezuela. Galt sold them land without requiring a down payment, and then built houses for them. Because these indigent settlers should have been recognized as wards of the state, Galt covered the costs of housing them by withholding £1,000 that the Canada Company owed the government.

Eventually, the newcomers paid back every cent of their debt. But to their everlasting shame, Maitland and his henchmen refused to accept the fairness of Galt's arrangement. Instead, they accused Galt of mishandling funds. In distant London, worried Canada Company investors decided to send an accountant—ostensibly to assist Galt, really to investigate. Inevitably, given that Galt was far more a visionary than a bookkeeper, this bean counter turned up irregularities. Taking Canada Company records, he decamped to England.

Galt decided to follow. Early in 1829, he was making for London to defend himself when, in New York, he learned that he had been recalled. Soon after he reached the British capital, he was confined to debtors' prison—more like being placed under house arrest—for having failed to pay his sons' school fees. Galt managed to write himself out of this predicament, notably with his bestselling biography of Lord Byron, but also with two popular immigrant novels that drew on his experience in Canada: *Laurie Todd* and *Bogle Corbet*.

By 1834, undaunted, he was spearheading a second colonial venture—the British American Land Company, intended to develop and settle the Eastern Townships outside Montreal. He was serving as company secretary and contemplating permanent emigration to Canada when ill health forced him to resign. His sons did emigrate. All three became highly successful, and one of them, Alexander Tilloch Galt, who began his career as a seventeen-year-old clerk with the British American Land Company, eventually became a leading father of Confederation. In 1834, the ailing Galt and his wife moved to Greenock, and he died there five years later.

John Galt's novel *Bogle Corbet* is still read as a portrait of pioneer life, and literary critic Elizabeth Waterston has rightly called it the "first major work to define Canadianism by reference to an American alternative." Galt's greatest legacy, however, is that by encouraging immigration, he changed the face of Ontario.

In 1812, Upper Canada had a population of just over 75,000. Many of these people had come from the American colonies. Between 5,000 and 10,000 Loyalists had arrived in the 1780s after the American Revolution. During the next couple of decades, the trickle from the south became a stream. Newcomers included Pennsylvania Dutch as well as British and Irish. After the War of 1812, however, most immigrants came from Britain and Ireland. By 1825, Upper Canada had a population of 158,000.

In thirteen years, the population had more than doubled. That was impressive growth. But it cannot compare with the next four years when, assisted mainly by William "Tiger" Dunlop, John Galt attracted more than 50,000 settlers to Upper Canada—the vast majority of them Scottish Protestants. In a colony where traditions and institutions were still being developed, that increase—more than 30 percent in four years—was enough to shape the character of the place.

The process begun, immigrants continued to pour into the colony, a high percentage of them coming from Scotland and Ulster. The population of Upper Canada reached 397,000 in 1837, when political upheaval put an end to the dramatic increase. Today, the province of Ontario has a population of just over twelve million. Thanks partly to the wizardry of John Galt, more than two million of those can claim Scottish ancestry.

The Ulster Variation

The ancestors of many prominent Scottish Canadians, among them scientist Frederick Banting, historian Donald Creighton, business-man Timothy Eaton, judge Emily Murphy, writer W.O. Mitchell, and thinker Marshall McLuhan, emigrated to Canada after a family sojourn in Ulster, that ancient province which made up most of Northern Ireland. And the forebears of many of us who are not so prominent travelled that same route.

Parts of Scotland, notably Argyll and the islands, had been peopled by Gaelic-speaking seafarers for centuries. Then English-speaking Britain became the greatest power in the region, and in the early 1600s, after the Nine Years' War, she gained control of Northern Ireland. The defeated Gaelic leaders there, the O'Neills and the O'Donnells, grew tired of making obeisance to the British king and decamped to Roman Catholic Europe in 1607—an event called the Flight of the Earls.

The British seized the opportunity to "plant" Ulster with more acceptable Protestant settlers from England and Scotland. In 1607, for example, Sir Randall MacDonnell settled 300 Presbyterian Scots families on his lands in Antrim. This marked the beginning of the "Ulster Plantations," and soon Scottish immigrants to Northern Ireland, who lived much nearer, outnumbered English ones by twenty to one. Many North Americans whose ancestors emigrated from Ulster in the eighteenth and nineteenth centuries are descended from these "Scottish planters."

The first waves of Ulster Scots emigrants sailed not to Canada but to the American colonies. A few arrived in the late 1600s, but five successive waves, each of which lasted from one to four years, began in 1718, 1725, 1740, 1754, and 1771. The earliest arrivals settled along the Atlantic seaboard, while later immigrants, seeking farmland, pushed west and south from Pennsylvania.

Of those Ulster Scots who immigrated to the United States, every wave but the last left before the Scottish Enlightenment had begun spreading literacy, scepticism, and tolerance. And these eighteenth-century immigrants arrived in the United States early enough in a sparsely settled land to become a pervasive, shaping influence. In addition to helping create the fundamentalist strain in American culture, Ulster Scots produced seventeen U.S. presidents—more than one in three.

As for Canada, in 1760 a group of Ulster Scots moved to Nova Scotia from New Hampshire, where they had first settled forty years before. They founded the towns of Londonderry, Onslow, and Truro. Then, in the mid-1770s, as the American Revolution slowed immigration from the British Isles to the United States, immigrants began trickling from Ulster directly into the northern colonies.

More came after the Napoleonic Wars ended in 1815, among them the Presbyterian John McGoogan, who arrived in the Eastern Townships of Quebec in 1823 and acquired a farm near the Scottish town of St. John's (now Saint-Jean-sur-Richelieu). He married fellow immigrant Nancy McCormick, and their descendants would gravitate to Scots-dominated Montreal.

The large waves of Ulster immigrants to Canada did not begin arriving until the late 1840s, two decades after John Galt made his major contribution, when a devastating potato famine began driving emigration from all over Ireland. During the fierce winter of 1847, called Black '47, tens of thousands of people perished, either freezing, starving, or succumbing to fever. By the early 1850s, more than 500,000 had died as a result of the famine, and one million people had fled the country. Many of these nominally Irish immigrants were Scottish Presbyterians from Ulster, which explains why demographers believe Canadians of Scottish descent to be more numerous than rough surveys indicate.

Those who escaped Ulster included the wealthier and better educated, all of whom had been influenced by the Scottish Enlightenment. Besides the egalitarianism of Robert Burns and the traditionalism of Walter Scott, these later immigrants also brought a degree of religious scepticism that had not existed in the early to mid-1700s. Because times had changed, they espoused a less Puritanical attitude than those who had migrated to the American colonies in the previous century.

True, the Orange Order had been founded in Ulster in 1795. Strongly anti-Catholic, the Order at inception was also anti-Presbyterian. In Canada, it became a fraternal organization that assisted all Protestant immigrants. Later in the century, it got embroiled in inter-denominational strife in both east and west. It became a political force in Toronto, where in 1942, two-thirds of city councillors were Orangemen. After 1945, however, as Canada became increasingly secular, the Order declined in numbers and influence. Bottom line: although Orangemen sporadically made an impact in Canada, they never became politically dominant.

As for total numbers, the best estimates suggest that by the end of the twentieth century, roughly 500,000 people had migrated to Canada from Ulster. The vast majority arrived after both the American Revolution and the Scottish Enlightenment. Thanks to the relative lateness of their arrival, which coincided with that of many Presbyterians from Scotland, English-speaking Canada became Presbyterian, as well as Anglican and Roman Catholic. But it never became "Orange." The country would remain Christian and conservative well into the twentieth century, yet never would it become evangelical and fundamentalist.

5

THE NORTHWEST PASSAGE

When the Napoleonic wars ended in Europe in 1815, reducing the need for the formidable Royal Navy, Great Britain found itself with a great many half-pay naval officers with nothing to do. The War of 1812 between Canada and the United States was also over. So with Russia growing increasingly active in the Arctic, the British Admiralty decided to renew the search for the Northwest Passage, a navigable trade route across the top of North America.

One of the early beneficiaries of this initiative was naval officer John Franklin. After failing in an attempt to sail north to the pole and beyond from Spitsbergen, that island north of Finland, Franklin was chosen to lead an overland party in charting the Arctic coast of North America.

The expedition proved disastrous. The Royal Navy knew nothing of overland travel. John Franklin lost eleven of his twenty men. He narrowly survived thanks to a Métis guide and some Yellowknife Indians, and he parlayed the debacle into a second expedition thanks only to his second-in-command, a Scottish scientist and doctor who later became one of Britain's leading naturalists.

John Richardson: The Scot behind Franklin

John Richardson was born in Dumfries, Scotland, in 1787, the eldest son of a prosperous brewer and magistrate. The poet Robert Burns was a friend of the family, and Richardson, a precocious boy who learned to read at age four, went to grammar school with Burns's son—all of which may have fostered his interest in knowing how to turn a phrase.

Richardson attended medical school at the University of Edinburgh and then joined the Royal Navy. He served seven years as a shipboard surgeon, including five months during the War of 1812 in Halifax, Montreal, and the Richelieu Valley. At thirty-two, after completing his medical degree and working in private practice, he joined Franklin's first overland expedition as surgeon and naturalist.

John Richardson went on overland expeditions with John Franklin, saving his life and making him famous.

In 1819, the navy men sailed on a Hudson's Bay Company ship to York Factory, then wintered at Cumberland House on the Saskatchewan River. The following year, they journeyed north to Great Bear Lake and spent the winter at Fort Enterprise. In summer 1821, they followed Samuel Hearne's route down the Coppermine River to the Arctic coast. Then, dismissing the warnings of Native guides, and paddling in two leaky canoes, Franklin pushed his party eastwards to Point Turnagain, on the Kent Peninsula, travelling until far too late in the season.

The overland retreat turned desperate. Men began starving. They broke into small groups and, with the whole company in disarray, one of guides resorted to murder and cannibalism. Anticipating more such madness, Richardson conferred with the only other British sailor in his small group, who offered to execute the killer. Richardson accepted his responsibility and shot the madman dead. Had he failed to do so, more men would almost certainly have died—possibly all who eventually survived. This cool-headed execution was one of the pivotal moments of the expedition.

Franklin incorporated the story, attributing it to Richardson, in his published narrative. But he "borrowed" much else without crediting it, as naval conventions dictated that expedition leaders could plagiarize the journals of their subordinates without a second thought. Franklin had lost his own journal on September 14, 1821, when his canoe overturned during the retreat. In writing his book, then, he drew partly on the journal of a murdered midshipman, but mostly on the work of John Richardson.

Besides lifting passages and whole pages verbatim, Franklin reworked some of his subordinate's journal into his own turgid style. Richardson wrote, for example, that it was useless to talk to Canadian voyageurs of going on short allowance: "They prefer running the risk of going entirely without hereafter, that they may have a present belly full." Franklin rendered this more ponderously: "These thoughtless people would, at any time, incur the hazard of absolute starvation, at a future period, for the present gratification of their appetites."

Yet his book proved sufficiently sensational—murder, cannibalism, execution, eleven of twenty men dead—that its apparent author became famous as "the man who ate his boots." Franklin was rewarded with the leadership of a second overland expedition, intended to complete the mapping of the coast. The loyal Richardson—more naturalist than explorer—agreed to serve once more as second-in-command.

During the summer of 1826, after descending the Mackenzie River, the two men parted near the Arctic coast. Franklin led a party westward and charted 374 miles (601 km) of unknown shoreline; Richardson went east to the mouth of the Coppermine and mapped 863 miles (1,389 km)—more than twice the distance. Yet, again following Royal Navy practice, the record books credited Franklin with the whole accomplishment.

Taken together, the two expeditions brought Franklin a knighthood. Without that, he could never have married Jane Griffin, who proved to be one of the most resourceful women in England. But in fact, most of the credit for these explorations should have gone to that talented, self-effacing Scot, John Richardson. He saved the first misadventure from complete catastrophe, and did most of the achieving on the second—not just as a naturalist, though he catalogued many new species, but also as an explorer.

In the 1850s, after Franklin got trapped in the ice and died while seeking the Northwest Passage, the Burns-loving Richardson came up with a few words that, although false, proved so felicitous and inspirational that they ended up on a statue of Franklin in central London: "They forged the last link with their lives."

Thomas Simpson: Clarifying the Riddle

By the 1830s, explorers had charted half the Arctic coast of North America. A gap of 150 miles (240 km) existed in the northwest corner, between Icy Cape, Alaska, visited by ships from the Pacific, and Return Reef, reached by Franklin in 1826 from the mouth of the Mackenzie.

A second gap of 300 miles (480 km) extended east from Point Turnagain, on the Kent Peninsula, to the west coast of Boothia Peninsula.

Such was the situation when another ambitious young Scot arrived in the north, bent on completing the coastal survey—a man as temperamentally different from John Richardson as anyone could be.

Thomas Simpson was born in 1808 in Dingwall, a Highland town fifteen miles (25 km) northwest of Inverness. The son of a schoolmaster, Simpson excelled as a scholar. At twenty he graduated with a master's degree from King's College in Aberdeen, winning a prize for philosophy. In 1829, lacking the money to pursue a medical career, he joined the Hudson's Bay Company as secretary to his cousin George Simpson, who as governor of the HBC was ruling that company with an iron fist.

Thomas accompanied George on a tour of inspection of the HBC territories, and in 1830, he led one hundred recruits from Lachine, near Montreal, to Lake Superior. The following February, he led a second party from York Factory on Hudson Bay to Red River, covering 680 miles (1,100 km) in twenty-eight days and establishing himself as an efficient traveller. By the early 1830s, he was lobbying to lead an expedition north to complete the coastal survey and, possibly, to find the final link in a navigable Northwest Passage.

In 1836, George Simpson approved such an expedition. The HBC would soon be required to renew its licence to monopolize trade in Rupert's Land, and needed to demonstrate that it was fulfilling its mandate to explore the territory. As leader of the expedition, however, the governor chose a veteran chief factor, the stolid Peter Warren Dease. He appointed Thomas Simpson second-in-command—probably because he judged him not only clever and capable but also, and not without reason, arrogant and egotistical.

With Dease and a dozen other men, a disgruntled Thomas Simpson left Fort Confidence on Great Bear Lake in June 1837. The party had orders to chart the 150-mile (240 km) gap on the Alaskan coast between Return Reef and Point Barrow on Icy Cape. Late in July, sixty miles (95 km) from their objective, they encountered impassable ice. Leaving Dease and seven men with the boats, Simpson continued westward on foot with five men.

This group met some Inuit and traded tobacco for temporary use of an *umiak*—a small, light boat well suited to the conditions. On August 4, the travellers reached Point Barrow. In a characteristic outburst, Simpson wrote, "I and I *alone* have the well-earned honour of uniting the Arctic with the great Western Ocean. . . . Dease is an unworthy, indolent, illiterate soul. . . . It is no vanity to say that everything which requires either planning or execution devolves upon me."

The following summer, after a second winter at Fort Confidence, Simpson and Dease descended the Coppermine River and travelled east. Again they were stopped by ice, and again Simpson left his nominal leader and proceeded with a small party on foot, travelling one hundred miles (160 km) beyond Point Turnagain. After a third winter at Fort Confidence, Simpson persuaded Dease to try again. In summer 1839, benefiting from fine weather, the men sailed in small boats all the way to Boothia Peninsula. They erected a cairn at the mouth of a river Simpson named the Castor and Pollux, after his boats. The party explored Queen Maud Gulf and stretches of Victoria Island and King William Island.

Simpson suspected that the final link in the Northwest Passage, a waterway that would connect two navigable channels, one extending to the Pacific, the other to the Atlantic, lay immediately to the north. But with winter looming and ice forming, even the obsessive Simpson felt compelled to retreat to the mainland.

These expeditions had contributed much to the Arctic map. Simpson believed, rightly, that he was within one more foray of solving the riddle of the passage. From Fort Simpson on the Mackenzie River, he wrote seeking permission to resume the search the following summer. His cousin George refused—a decision that would prove a turning point in exploration history. If the so-called Little Emperor had approved one final expedition, Thomas Simpson would almost certainly have discovered the waterway, fourteen miles (22 km) across, that lies open each summer between Boothia and King William Island.

Why did George Simpson refuse to back his cousin? Perhaps he feared that a navigable passage would increase unwanted competition for the HBC. More likely, he believed that Thomas was on the right track, and he wanted to ensure that he himself, as governor of the HBC, received most of the glory for discovering the final link in the Northwest Passage. The governor ordered Thomas to return to Fort Garry and take a year's leave of absence.

Incensed, Thomas decided to go over his cousin's head. He wrote to London requesting approval for one more expedition. He then journeyed to Fort Garry, 1,910 miles away (3,070 km), in just sixty-one days, but was disappointed when the mail arrived in June 1840 without a reply from HBC headquarters.

In fact, the London governors were just then writing to grant his request—and to notify him, as well, that his explorations had already earned him the gold medal of the Royal Geographical Society and a modest pension for life. Unaware of these developments, Thomas Simpson decided to plead his case in London. He started eastward on horseback, riding ultimately with four Métis. While travelling through the Dakota prairies, he died under circumstances that remain controversial to this day.

The official verdict was that he became delusional. He went berserk, shot two of his fellow travellers, and then turned the gun on himself. Most historians agree that this story does not stand up. His brother wrote a book alleging that he was murdered. Perhaps the Métis were avenging an old grudge, or maybe Thomas Simpson said something contemptuous or insulting and the conflict escalated out of control. Another theory is that George Simpson had let it be known that he wished to gain possession of Thomas's journals, and an attempt to steal them ended in bloodshed.

This far-fetched theory lacks supporting evidence, and the mystery remains unresolved. In 1841, George Simpson was knighted by Queen Victoria for assisting in the Arctic explorations of Thomas Simpson—a man whose ambitions he had thwarted. But it was the younger man who did the crucial work. On his last expedition, a model of efficiency in small-boat travel, Thomas Simpson completed the exploration of the coastline between Point Barrow and Boothia Peninsula and clarified the riddle of the Northwest Passage. He showed that if a ship could reach that southern coastal channel from Lancaster Sound, readily accessible from the Atlantic Ocean, then sail west for 2,000 miles (3,200 km), it could emerge into the Pacific Ocean and so complete a Northwest Passage.

The only thing missing was the elusive north–south link.

John Rae: Fate and the Final Link

A surprising number of Scots made their names in Arctic exploration, among them John and James Clark Ross, the Ulster-born Leopold McClintock, and Elisha Kent Kane, an American whose grandfather was a Scottish immigrant from Lanarkshire. These were all post-Enlightenment Protestants blessed with superior education and driven by a sense of duty. The most outstanding figure was the Orcadian John Rae, who solved the two great mysteries of nineteenth-century Arctic exploration. In 1854, after a lifetime of preparation, Rae discovered both the fate of the Franklin expedition and the final link in the Northwest Passage.

Rae emerged onto the international stage thanks to the talented John Richardson, the man who had salvaged the career of John Franklin.

In 1847, at age fifty-nine, Richardson had volunteered to lead an overland search for the lost expedition of John Franklin. By then a sedentary medical officer in the Royal Navy, and also a naturalist of renown, Richardson was sifting through applications at his home in Portsmouth, anxiously seeking a capable second-in-command for his looming adventure, when he read a report in the *Times*.

The author, a Hudson's Bay Company doctor named John Rae, had recently returned to Britain after fourteen years in Rupert's Land. The report described how he had charted one of the last remaining unexplored stretches of North American coastline—an area far to the east of where Thomas Simpson had sailed.

Purists have criticized John Rae for posing in a mishmash of clothing from various aboriginal peoples. But the explorer was expressing solidarity with Native people in general.

Starting from York Factory on Hudson Bay, Rae had led a dozen men in two small boats north of the Arctic Circle (the line of latitude, nearly sixty-seven degrees above the equator, where the sun remains below the horizon for twenty-four straight hours at least once a year). They had wintered over at Repulse Bay, living off the land, with Rae himself serving as principal hunter. The doctor had then mapped 655 miles (1,050 km) of coast, incidentally demonstrating that no Northwest Passage flowed through Boothia Peninsula. On reading this account at his home, Richardson leapt to his feet and cried out to his wife, "I have found my companion!"

Born in Stromness, Orkney, in 1813, the son of a Hudson's Bay Company agent, John Rae grew up hunting, fishing, and sailing. At nineteen, having qualified in Edinburgh as a surgeon, he took a summer job aboard an HBC ship, expecting to return home in the autumn. But the *Prince of Wales* got trapped by ice, and during the ensuing winter, Rae felt drawn to "the wild sort of life to be found in the Hudson's Bay Company service."

During the next fourteen years, while based at Moose Factory, near the bottom of Hudson Bay, Rae applied himself to learning from the Native people who lived in the vicinity: how to handle a canoe, maintain snowshoes, hunt and cache caribou—basically, how to live off the land. By 1846, when he led those dozen men north to Repulse Bay, contemporaries were hailing him not as the greatest rough-country traveller employed by the HBC but as "the greatest of the age."

Rae quickly joined Richardson in seeking Franklin. And when, after a cold dark winter at Fort Confidence, the older Scot retreated to England, the younger one continued the quest. On this expedition, before he was done searching and surveying, Rae charted more than 1,750 miles (2,800 km) of territory, including 1,538 miles (2,475 km) of Arctic coastline (much of Boothia Peninsula and Victoria Island). During subsequent outings, he walked 6,504 miles (10,467 km), mostly on snowshoes, and travelled another 6,634 miles (10,676 km) in canoes and small boats.

By 1854, this peerless explorer had given up hope of finding Franklin. He was surveying a final stretch of Arctic coastline when he learned from some Inuit hunters that the Franklin expedition had ended in disaster, the final survivors resorting to cannibalism. Saddened but not surprised—he had spent most of his adult life in the northern wilds—Rae collected relics and wrote a report detailing what he had learned.

That report, published in the *Times,* shook Victorian England to its foundations. Cannibalism? Among men of the Royal Navy? Impossible! Rae's testimony undermined the campaign, orchestrated by Lady Franklin, to glorify her dead husband as discoverer of the Northwest Passage. That resourceful woman enlisted the aid of Charles Dickens, the most influential writer of the age, to repudiate Rae—and that author did so by arguing from historical precedent and denigrating the explorer's Inuit sources.

The stubborn Scot refused to recant. He defended the integrity of his Inuit informants and the truth of his report. And, a few wishful thinkers to the contrary, he has long since been forensically vindicated. During his lifetime, thanks mainly to the machinations of Lady Franklin, historians and mapmakers ignored many of Rae's achievements and only grudgingly acknowledged those they could not disregard.

The most significant of those accomplishments got lost in the controversy over Franklin. In May 1854, while extending the explorations of Thomas Simpson, and just before he learned the truth about Franklin, John Rae discovered that King William Land was an island, separated from Boothia Peninsula by a channel that remained open for months each year.

John Rae realized that this waterway, which connected points accessible by sailing ship, constituted the missing north–south link in the Northwest Passage. He could not prove it, so he advanced no grand claims in this respect. But when, half a century later, the Norwegian Roald Amundsen became the first explorer to sail through the passage, he not only used that channel but acknowledged its discoverer by naming it Rae Strait.

6

BOUNDARIES YES, BARRIERS NO

In his detailed, seminal work *The Fur Trade in Canada,* published in 1930, Harold Adams Innis demonstrated that Canada "emerged as a political entity with boundaries determined by the fur trade . . . not in spite of geography but because of it." Six decades later, Peter C. Newman refined this idea, arguing in *Company of Adventurers* that the Hudson's Bay Company turned "much of the upper half of North America into a company town writ large."

The HBC started with a few fur-trading posts built in the late 1600s on the shores of Hudson Bay, accessible by a direct sea route from Britain. Driven by competition from the Montreal-based North West Company, the Hudson's Bay Company expanded westwards in 1774, when it built Cumberland House. Along the way, most of those who did the heavy lifting were Scots from Orkney, at times composing almost 80 percent of the workforce.

William Tomison offers a shining example. Born in 1739 on the island of South Ronaldsay, Tomison grew up on a poor farm and received no formal education. At twenty he joined the HBC, whose ships called regularly at Stromness to take on fresh water before crossing the Atlantic. According to local tradition, he learned to read and write during his first voyage.

Tomison spent seven years on Hudson Bay, mostly at York Factory but also at Severn House, where the well-educated Andrew Graham trained him further. In the late 1760s, Tomison spent two winters inland among Aboriginal people. He learned their languages and customs, and forged a reputation as a man "greatly beloved by the natives." In 1776 he left for Cumberland House, recently constructed in response to increasing competition.

Two years later, as the HBC's "inland master," Tomison began setting up posts adjacent to those of the rival North West Company, starting with the immediately profitable Hudson House in present-day Saskatchewan. But then came several terrible years. During the winter of 1781–82, a catastrophic epidemic of smallpox decimated the local Native people. French warships next destroyed both York Factory and Prince of Wales Fort, the HBC's main headquarters on Hudson Bay. Widespread hardship ensued.

Having worked his way up through the HBC's hierarchical structure, which was modelled on the military, Tomison became more egalitarian. He turned Orcadian workers into skilled canoeists and began trading directly with Native peoples who lived farther west, notably the Bloods and the Peigans.

Even after 1786, when he became chief trader at York Factory, Tomison spent most of his time inland, leading the HBC in creating more distant trading posts in tandem with the North West Company: Carlton House, Buckingham House, Manchester House. In 1795, within sight of the Rockies, Tomison established Fort Edmonton. He then endured several difficult years, marked by a stabbing incident that left him walking with a limp.

Yet in 1810, when he retired permanently to Orkney, William Tomison could look back at a chain of trading posts that extended from York Factory in Manitoba, through Cumberland House in Saskatchewan, to the eastern foothills of the Canadian Rockies in Alberta. This Orcadian Scot, while working with the Native peoples there, had laid the foundations of three prairie provinces.

Still, nobody would argue that the rough trading posts established by William Tomison became viable "company towns"—extending credit, exacting deference, and controlling territory—until well into the nineteenth century, after peace came to the violently competitive fur trade. The man who engineered that peace was an altogether different breed.

George Simpson: The Little Emperor

While the Scots who invented Canada were remarkable, not all were admirable, and some, like George Simpson, emerge under scrutiny as closer to detestable. In his history of the Hudson's Bay Company, Peter C. Newman rightly described the HBC governor as "a bastard both by birth and by persuasion."

Simpson managed to erase most details about his background from the public record. But he was born out of wedlock in 1792 to an unknown mother and a lawyer. He was raised in the Highland town of Dingwall, mostly by his aunt Mary. At school, he showed an aptitude for mathematics. When he was sixteen, his aunt prevailed upon a brother to give him a job, and the young man went to London and began working at a sugar brokerage owned by his uncle Geddes Mackenzie Simpson.

In 1812, Andrew Wedderburn, the brother-in-law of Lord Selkirk, became a partner in that concern. Wedderburn, who later changed his name to Andrew Colvile, was also a director of the Hudson's Bay Company. He started using the sharp-eyed George Simpson on matters relating to the fur trade. When the rival North West Company began showing signs of weakness, Colvile looked around for the toughest young businessman he employed. He gave Simpson five days to prepare for the journey of a lifetime.

In March 1820, twenty-eight-year-old George Simpson sailed for North America. He had a mandate to end the murderous competition in the fur trade, preferably by taking over the North West Company. After landing in New York, Simpson travelled to Montreal by steamboat and open cart, and then journeyed west by canoe. At the end of May he reached Fort William (Thunder Bay), inland headquarters of the NWC.

The savvy Simpson knew enough to be guided by experienced Hudson's Bay Company men. Within ten months, he had engineered an apparent merger that was really an HBC takeover. An agreement signed in March 1821 divided fur-trade territory into two departments, northern and southern. Simpson became governor

One of the ironies of Canadian history is that the despicable George Simpson played a crucial role in creating Canada's boundaries.

of the northern department, which comprised the more promising region extending westward from Hudson Bay to the Pacific coast. He ordered an inspection of NWC posts west of the Rockies, and then began reducing "excess personnel" with a view to increasing profits.

So began a new era of cost cutting. At coalition, the HBC had almost 2,000 employees. Within four years, Simpson had reduced that number to 827 and slashed wages by 50 percent. He suppressed bitter rivalries between officers. He got rid of "old and useless men" and withdrew support from their dependants, often the product of "country marriages" to Native women. He brooked no insubordination and kept key officers onside by allowing them to continue sharing in profits. He economized at the expense of the powerless "servants" in the lower ranks.

In 1824, Simpson received orders from London to investigate the far-western Columbia district with a view to ramping up competition with American traders. Here he saw a chance to extend and consolidate his power. On August 15, he left York Factory in a light canoe with eight paddlers and a guide. He drove these men so hard that, six weeks later, he caught up with Dr. John McLoughlin, a veteran trader and medical man who had set out twenty days before him.

On November 8, Simpson reached Fort George (now Astoria, Oregon) after a journey of eighty-four days. By driving his men, he had beaten the previous record by twenty days. With McLoughlin, the newly appointed chief factor of the district, Simpson spent several months devising plans to drive out the competition—both the Russians trading in the far north and the Americans, who conducted an extensive coastal trade.

The following March, he left Fort Vancouver (now Vancouver, Washington) and, travelling again at record speed, reached Red River in ten weeks. In the autumn, he proceeded to York Factory and sailed for London. There, at HBC headquarters, he delivered an impressive report. Simpson had introduced economies, increased profits, and begun consolidating the Pacific coast trade. In February 1826, while still in London, he witnessed the recall of his rival department head. He himself took control of both the northern and southern departments. As governor-in-chief of all Rupert's Land, he now controlled more than half the territory of what would eventually become Canada.

For four decades, while based at York Factory, Red River, and finally Lachine, just west of Montreal, George Simpson ruled the HBC with an iron fist. Efficient and relentless, a fur-trading Machiavelli, he proved devious, manipulative, misogynistic, mean spirited, and racist. Chief factor John McLean, who became one of many enemies, wrote that Simpson combined "the despotism of military rule with the strict surveillance and mean parsimony of the avaricious trader." French Canadian voyageurs spoke of him as having "une âme de glace"—a soul of ice.

At one point, even head office felt compelled to remind Simpson "that considerations of humanity must colour the company's policy." By that time, referring to his autocratic manner, his short stature (at most, five foot seven), and his well-known admiration for Napoleon Bonaparte, HBC men had taken to calling him "the Little Emperor"—though never to his face.

To most of his underlings, Simpson was the boss from hell. While micromanaging the fur trade and keeping a "Character Book" of word portraits of his employees, Simpson criss-crossed North America by canoe almost annually, often at record-breaking speed. In 1841, for example, he crossed North America from Halifax to the west coast, mainly by canoe, covering 1,900 miles (3,000 km) in forty-seven days.

Simpson himself never lifted a paddle. For that, he relied on his minions. Approaching his wilderness outposts, he would change his clothes, don his top hat and, bent on arriving in style, start his voyageurs singing. Early on, judging this to be insufficiently grand, Simpson had gone looking for a bagpiper. He wrote to John Rae, the HBC agent in Orkney and father of the peerless Arctic explorer, and asked if he could find a qualified man willing to play the pipes for thirty pounds a year.

Eventually, Simpson located one Colin Fraser, probably a distant relative, and told Rae to send him to York Factory "to winter there and obtain a little insight of the Service" before Simpson arrived the following spring. From that time forward, with Fraser in tow, the top-hatted governor would announce his imminent arrival at garrisons and company towns with a skirling of bagpipes.

Yet this "pompous little stump of a man," as biographer James Raffan describes him, also understood where he was. As early as February 1821, when John Franklin was about to embark on his first overland expedition, Simpson judged the mission disorganized and ill prepared. Franklin, he declared, "has not the physical powers required for the labour of moderate voyaging in this country. He must have three meals per diem, Tea is indispensable, and with the utmost exertion he cannot walk above *eight* miles in one day, so that it does not follow if those Gentlemen are unsuccessful that the difficulties are insurmountable." Franklin proved Simpson prescient by disregarding the advice of Native guides and, on this first overland expedition, losing eleven of his twenty men.

Also from early on, while based in Red River and York Factory, and having already fathered two illegitimate children in Britain, Simpson began taking and discarding country wives. In letters, he referred to these Native women as his "articles," his "commodities," and his "bits of brown." He fathered children with eight or more of them, and disposed of at least two in cavalier fashion. In 1822, for example, Simpson had one of his chief factors oust his country wife from their home.

Betsey Sinclair had become an "unnecessary and expensive appendage," he wrote, as she was due to give birth within weeks: "I see no fun in keeping a woman without enjoying her charms, which my present rambling life does not enable me to do. If my Article requires anything previous to her departure for [Rock Depot, a tiny outpost] pray let her be supplied (to my account) and if you will solace her with a little tea and sugar or any other necessary it will be obliging."

A few years later, while visiting London in 1829, Simpson received a letter from John Stuart, chief factor at Fort Alexander. He wrote that a later wife, Margaret (Peggy) Taylor, had recently given birth to a second child. Along with his two-year-old son, she looked forward to his return:

"A little while ago, when at supper I was telling Geordie that in two months and ten days he would see his father, Peggy smiled and remarked to her sister that seventy days was a long time and she wished it was over." Her waiting ended soon enough. When Simpson arrived back in fur-trade country, he brought an unwitting white wife, and hurried her past Fort Alexander without stopping to lay his eyes on this months-old son.

Two years before, George Simpson had revisited the Pacific coast to assess the fur-trade potential of the area west of the Rockies, and also the viability (non-existent) of using the terrifying Fraser River as a trade route. The following spring, he had returned east and proceeded to London. He went to seek medical advice—"exertions which were formerly but exercise for me are now fatiguing"—and also to find a white wife.

By now, the daughter of his London-based uncle Geddes Simpson, the man who had given him his first job, had turned eighteen. In 1830, Simpson married her. With Frances Simpson, he returned across the Atlantic to Montreal, canoed west (past Fort Alexander) and took up residence at Red River.

For young Frances, who had grown up in London, the change proved traumatic. In 1833, having produced two of an eventual five children, she returned with Simpson to England—and stayed there for the next five years. Not until 1838, after the governor had built a mansion at Lachine, did she rejoin him in North America.

Crucially, from the mid-1830s onwards, Simpson had begun producing annual profits ranging from 10 to 25 percent. Who could argue with that? Only those he exploited or drove to the limits of human endurance, all of whom were powerless.

And so Simpson amassed a private fortune. He joined the boards of steamships and railroads. He hired lobbyists and bribed legislators. He arranged to give "10,000 golden reasons," for example, to powerful Upper Canadian politicians to secure their help in gaining government contracts for a steamship line.

With HBC employees, Simpson took a less generous line. In a letter to James Hargrave, who was in charge of York Factory, he complained, "I consider it quite unnecessary to indent [requisition] for Sauces & Pickles on public account. . . . I never use fish sauce in the country, and never saw anyone use it or pickles either. From the quantity of Mustard indented for, one would suppose it is now issued as an article of trade with the Indians!"

Again, while putting the supremely capable John Rae in charge of Rupert's River district, he wrote to the outgoing chief factor that "a little lecture on economy will not be lost on him. I have no doubt that he would be very popular with Indians as well as the officers and servants, but am aware that he is over liberal in all payments to Indians on his private account and might be disposed to go a little beyond the mark in Company dealings."

George Simpson even became the author of a book by hiring a ghost writer, and he achieved a knighthood by taking credit for the explorations of Thomas Simpson and Peter Warren Dease. In summer 1860, his health in decline, Simpson orchestrated a grandiose visit to Montreal by the Prince of Wales. Shortly afterwards, he died and was buried in Mount Royal Cemetery next to Frances, who had preceded him by seven years.

Simpson left an estate worth more than £100,000, the equivalent today of roughly $15 million. In his will, he named only one of his illegitimate children, his Scottish daughter Maria Mactavish, leaving her a pittance. To his numerous children by Native women, he left nothing.

In the history of Canada, few figures evoke less sympathy than George Simpson. Yet this dislikeable "bastard" Scot proved crucially important to the invention of the country. By establishing and sustaining a fur-trade monopoly, Simpson ensured that the vast territories controlled by the Hudson's Bay Company remained first in British and then in Canadian hands. Of the many ironies that mark our past, this stands as one of the bitterest: that the despicable Simpson did so much to create Canada's boundaries.

James Douglas: The Scotch West Indian

According to its 1670 charter, drawn up in London, the Hudson's Bay Company controlled all those lands drained by rivers flowing into Hudson Bay. The charter said nothing about territories drained by rivers flowing north to the Arctic coast, like the Coppermine and the Mackenzie, or west to the Pacific Ocean, like the Columbia and the Fraser. In other words, it said nothing about the northwest or the contemporary province of British Columbia.

If the HBC had not acquired control of that territory, present-day Canada would not exist. Economic historian Irene Spry has put this succinctly: "There is little doubt that the forces of American manifest destiny would have taken the West into continental orbit, and if Canada had not been coast to coast, the pitiful little settlements in the St. Lawrence Valley would have been absorbed by the Americans long ago."

George Simpson played an important role in gaining control of the lands in question. But he had the help of a pivotal figure who, because communications in the nineteenth century were so slow, often had to act alone. That individual was a Scot as different from Simpson as can be imagined—a man known in the fur trade as a "Scotch West Indian."

Born in 1803 in British Guiana, now Guyana, James Douglas was the son of a wealthy Glasgow merchant, John Douglas, and a free Creole woman, Martha Ann Ritchie, originally from Barbados. As a boy, Douglas was sent to preparatory school in Lanark, Scotland, where he excelled as a scholar while learning to fight his way, he said later, "with all sorts of boys, and to get on by dint of whip and spur."

Douglas received additional education from a French tutor at

Chester, England, and people in later years would remark on his fluency in French, both oral and written. At sixteen, he joined the North West Company as an apprentice. He sailed from Liverpool to Quebec, proceeded to Fort William, and spent the winter learning the fur trade. The following summer, he was transferred to Île-à-la-Crosse, where he fought a duel and sparked a warning from the Hudson's Bay Company to cease parading around provocatively with "Guns, Swords, Flags, Drums, Fifes, etc., etc."

Later that year, when George Simpson merged the competing companies, young Douglas made a smooth transition, joining the HBC as a second-class clerk. His older brother, Alexander, had joined before him, but did not last. Simpson judged him "stupid and inactive, deficient in education, not adapted for the country," and quickly dismissed him. James Douglas, in contrast, impressed Simpson and everyone else who met him, and in 1825, he travelled north to take charge of Fort Vermilion.

With him he carried a library of books from Scotland, among them forty-five volumes of what he called "British classics," as well as a history of England, a French dictionary, and textbooks in geometry, arithmetic, and grammar. In this rugged world, his bookishness set him apart, and Douglas could be both superior and pedantic. Later in life, he would complain that slang was "essentially vulgar and to me unbearable," and edit letters from his young-adult daughter: "Observe how it is improved by the process."

After one winter at Fort Vermilion, Douglas crossed the Rockies to Fort St. James, fording flooding rivers and traversing cliffside mountain passes on a journey he would describe as perilous, exhausting, and exciting. From that outpost, headquarters of the New Caledonia district, Douglas travelled 2,000 miles (3,200 km) while leading a pack-horse brigade in a return journey to Fort Vancouver on the Pacific coast—present-day Vancouver, Washington.

In 1827, having established Fort Connolly on Bear Lake, Douglas resolved to retire from the fur trade when his three-year contract expired. He pronounced himself tired of the isolation, of the lack of good books and companionship, of the hostility of some Native peoples, and of the hunger that ensued when the salmon run failed. He was "bent on leaving the country."

The chief factor at Fort St. James, William Connolly, responded with alacrity. Soon after meeting Douglas, he had judged him a "fine steady active fellow good clerk & trader, well adapted for a new country." Now, rather than lose him, Connolly not only increased his salary by two-thirds but allowed him to marry, according to the custom of the country, his beautiful half-Native daughter. Amelia Connolly was a "shy, sweet and lovable girl," not yet sixteen, known as the "little snowbird." She would give Douglas thirteen children, five of whom did not survive infancy.

In 1828, while in charge of Fort St. James, Douglas—"furiously violent when aroused"—seized and executed a Carrier man who had been involved in murdering an HBC man five years before. This prompted a couple of attempts on his life, and Connolly wrote to George Simpson that "Douglas's life is much exposed among these Carriers." Douglas "would readily face a hundred of them," he reported, "but he does not like the idea of being assassinated." Connolly recommended that the young man be transferred to Fort Vancouver and the expanding coastal trade.

Already, after two meetings, Douglas had impressed George Simpson, who had described him at length: "a stout, powerful, active man of good conduct and respectable abilities—tolerably well-educated, expresses himself clearly on paper, understands our Counting House business and is an excellent trader. Well qualified for any service requiring bodily exertion, firmness of mind, and the exercise of sound judgment. . . . Has every reason to look forward to early promotion and is a likely man to fill a place at our Council board in the course of time."

In January 1830, accompanied by his wife and lugging his library, James Douglas travelled south to become chief accountant under yet another formidable Scot—Dr. John McLoughlin, "the white-headed eagle" in charge of the HBC's Columbia department.

Nestled on the north side of the Columbia River, Fort Vancouver comprised a wooden palisade enclosing eight substantial buildings. In these, about one hundred HBC employees lived and worked. A number of smaller buildings lay beyond the walls, where 300 Native people had settled. In addition to trading in furs, this district centre included a farm that grew food for export to Alaska. A small shipyard, a lumber mill, and an active salmon fishery completed the picture. By the time the Scotch West Indian arrived, Fort Vancouver was a thriving company town.

Within a year, a fellow fur trader reported that "James Douglas is at Vancouver and is rising fast in favour." Two years in a row, Douglas was entrusted with carrying considerable coastal revenues to York Factory. And in 1835, while still serving as McLoughlin's right-hand man, he travelled to Red River and received his commission as chief trader. Three years later, with McLoughlin on leave, Douglas ran Fort Vancouver for a year, and in 1839 he became a chief factor—a promotion that doubled his income and brought financial security.

During McLoughlin's absence, Douglas sought to eradicate slavery. "With the Natives," he wrote, "I have hitherto endeavoured to discourage the practice by the exertion of moral influence alone. Against our own people I took a more active part, and denounced slavery as a state contrary to law; tendering to all unfortunate persons held as slaves, by British subjects, the fullest protection in the enjoyment of their natural rights."

In 1840, with McLoughlin battling American competition and

Simpson seeking to expand trade generally throughout the Pacific, Douglas sailed north to Sitka, Alaska, where he dealt with Russian authorities and established Fort Taku. Then he travelled south to California and negotiated a trading arrangement with Mexican officials. The following year, this time with Simpson, Douglas again journeyed to Sitka to deal with the Russians.

During this trip, rejecting McLoughlin's territorial approach, Simpson decided to abandon the HBC's far northern outposts. Instead, he opted to expand the steamboat-based trade along the coast and, in response to American pressure around Fort Vancouver, to establish a new port farther north, on Vancouver Island. In 1842, James Douglas explored that island and chose a site. The following March, with the help of friendly Songhee people, he began to construct Fort Victoria.

By now, Douglas wrote, countless people "of a class hostile to British interests" were pouring into Oregon. Also, the U.S. government was seeking seaports on the Pacific coast. Douglas worried that every port would "be converted into a naval arsenal and the Pacific covered with swarms of Privateers, to the destruction of British commerce in those seas." He warned Simpson that "an American population will never willingly submit to British domination, and it would be ruinous and hopeless to enforce obedience, on a disaffected people; our Government would not attempt it, and the consequence will be the accession of a new State to the Union."

In 1845, with 6,000 settlers in Oregon, the provisional U.S. government extended its jurisdiction north of the Columbia River over territory that included Fort Vancouver. Faced with an imminent crisis just as John McLoughlin was about to retire, the HBC appointed a board of management, and in 1846 made Douglas the senior member. McLoughlin threw in with the Americans, partly because of his antipathy towards George Simpson, who, on top of everything else, had slandered his son.

Later that year, when Britain accepted the forty-ninth parallel as the U.S. border, James Douglas orchestrated the HBC's northward retreat. He reorganized canoe routes and, in 1849, moved the company's west coast headquarters to Fort Victoria. By agreement with Britain, the HBC was to establish a colony there within five years. In 1851, while remaining a chief factor, Douglas became governor and vice-admiral of Vancouver Island and its dependencies.

Given a free rein, James Douglas would have ensured that the San Juan Islands became Canadian rather than American. This Scotch West Indian was credited as "the father of British Columbia."

Not surprisingly, given that his wife was half Native, Douglas devoted considerable attention to Aboriginal policy. From the outset, he aimed "to conciliate the goodwill of the native Indian tribes by treating them with justice and forbearance, and by rigorously protecting their civil and agrarian rights." He not only allowed Native peoples to choose their own reserves of land but ordered surveyors to include fishing stations, burial grounds, cultivated land, and "all the favourite resorts of the Tribes, and in short to include every piece of ground to which they had acquired an equitable title through continuous occupation, tillage or other investment of labour." He also allowed Aboriginal individuals to buy property on the same terms as everyone else.

To develop the colony, Douglas had recommended free land grants of 200 to 300 acres. Both the HBC and the Colonial Office rejected this. But where some HBC men bridled at the high land prices, Douglas bought lands at the going rate, the most valuable of which were situated near the government reserve at James Bay.

In 1856, the Colonial Office ordered Douglas to establish an assembly. He complied, though he lacked experience or expertise as a legislator. He also actively developed Vancouver Island, building roads and schools and encouraging farming, sawmills, coal mines, and salmon fishing.

Late in 1857, following the discovery of gold along the Fraser and Thompson Rivers, large numbers of Americans began pouring into the country. Acting without instructions from London, the decisive Douglas proclaimed British control of mineral rights and announced that all miners required licences. The following April, with Californians streaming into Victoria and heading for the mainland, Douglas put a gunboat at the mouth of the Fraser River to collect licensing fees. More than 8,000 miners made their way up the Okanagan Valley. On the mainland as a whole, the influx approached 25,000. This tidal wave worried Native people and threatened the region with lawlessness.

Twice that summer, Douglas went upriver to assess the situation. To the Colonial Office, after the first visit, he reported that he "spoke with great plainness of speech to the white miners who were nearly all foreigners representing almost every nation in Europe. I refused to grant them any rights of occupation to the soil and told them distinctly that Her Majesty's Government ignored their very existence in that part of the country, which was not open for the purpose of settlement, and they were permitted to remain there merely on sufferance, that no abuses would be tolerated, and that the Laws would protect the rights of the Indians no less than those of the white men."

In August, Douglas made a second visit. Accompanied by twenty sailors and sixteen Royal Engineers, he relied for order primarily on the force of his personality. He drew up mining regulations, hired constables, and put Native men in charge of policing their own peoples. He raised volunteers to build a road to Lillooet and a mule track from Yale to Lytton. And he not only outlawed squatting but surveyed the land near Langley and Hope and put lots up for sale—though only to British subjects. "If the majority of the immigrants be American," he wrote, "there will always be a hankering in their minds after annexation to the United States . . . They will never cordially submit to English rule, nor possess the loyal feelings of British subjects."

Douglas could not hope to check immigration, but he wanted settlers loyal to the Crown, and he offered naturalization to anyone who sought it. Meanwhile, with affairs growing increasingly complex, the Colonial Office and the Hudson's Bay Company found themselves occasionally at odds. Late in 1858, when mainland British Columbia became a colony, Douglas resigned from the HBC to become governor.

The following year, when Vancouver Island changed from a company-run to a Crown colony, he added a second governorship. Simpson knew him to be easily the best man for either office, yet opposed his request that the HBC pay him a retirement allowance, arguing that his government salary would be sufficient "to carry him through his difficulties, aided by personal vanity of which he has a fair store combined however with a good deal of determination and tact."

In July 1859, an American military force landed on San Juan Island, the second largest of a group of islands situated between southern Vancouver Island and the mainland. Douglas wanted to expel the occupation by force. He was prevented by the joint opposition of the legislative assembly of Vancouver Island and a British rear-admiral who arrived to overrule him on this naval matter. The island was placed under joint military occupation and, with a number of others nearby, eventually ceded to the United States.

A son-in-law of Douglas later insisted that if the Scotch West Indian "had had his way, the affair would have been quickly settled, the Island occupied by the British, and the diplomacy would have settled the matter—he thought possession of great importance." In short, if James Douglas had carried the day, the American San Juan Islands would today be part of Canada.

In 1862, prospectors found gold in the Cariboo region, which extends north from the Fraser River canyon at the heart of the earlier discovery. With 5,000 miners pouring into the area, Douglas planned a major wagon road to run 400 miles (640 km) from Yale to Quesnel and Williams Creek. This Great North Road would end the threat of economic incursion from the south by making the Fraser River the main commercial artery of British Columbia.

Douglas advocated extending this road through the mountains to Edmonton and Fort Garry. If this were done, he wrote, "trade would find an outlet, population and settlement would follow." In 1863, Douglas envisaged the development, within the decade, of "an over-land Telegraph, *surely,* and a Railroad on British Territory, *probably,* the whole way from the Gulf of Georgia to the Atlantic."

Douglas was widely recognized as a man of vision, though some considered him pompous. As governor, he refused "to represent her Majesty in a shabby way." And some of his refinements—he affected "lordly dress" and kept a piano—struck less educated settlers and immigrants as pretentious. On the other hand, he impressed visitors like Lady Jane Franklin and her niece Sophy Cracroft, who wrote that Douglas had acquired "not merely immense local information, but general also, by reading. He has read enormously . . . and is in fact a self-educated man to a point very seldom attained."

More significantly, Douglas remained an authoritarian. Increasingly, he found himself at odds with a citizenry that wanted responsible gov-ernment, which he regarded as "associated with revolution" and ultimately menacing. Though he would have preferred "wise and good despotism," he did introduce representative government in 1862. The following year, faced with mounting unrest, the Colonial Office urged Douglas to accept a knighthood and retire from both governorships.

Douglas did so the following spring. He then set out alone on a voyage to the Auld Sod, enjoying a once-in-a-lifetime holiday that found him visiting also the great cities of Europe. Here and there he saw relatives, but most poignantly, he went to Lanark—the schoolboy home he had not seen in fifty years. He reported that the town had grown in size, and that the old houses were "not improved by age. The old people are all gone . . . and their very memory has perished. . . . As it is with them, so it will be with us." Douglas found the visit "after so long an absence more painful than agreeable—the face of nature remains the same, but everything else is changed. I was advised of these changes; deaths and departures were duly reported; but it was only upon my return that I felt the stern reality."

James Douglas had spent his life in the New World. He had laid out towns, built a unifying highway, and established order in rough country. During the Cariboo gold rush, he had seen farmers and settlers arrive from Canada, bringing "the British element"—much of it Scottish—of which he so approved. The man had transformed Victoria from a muddy settlement into a city of 6,000.

In 1871, Sir James Douglas saw British Columbia enter Confederation. This Scotch West Indian, remembered in such names as Port Douglas, Douglas College, and the Douglas Ranges, had retained the Pacific seaboard for the British Crown. And when, in 1877, he passed away, more than 3,000 people attended his funeral. Already they were calling James Douglas the father of British Columbia.

Jennie Gowanlock Trout: First Woman Doctor

In 1841, when Letitia Hargrave was settling into life at York Factory, George Simpson was reorganizing the fur trade on the Pacific Coast, and James Douglas was wondering where to build a new HBC head-quarters on Vancouver Island, a girl was born in the heart of Walter Scott country who would one day feature on a Canadian postage stamp. After a late start, Jennie Kidd Gowanlock Trout would become the first woman licensed to practise medicine in Canada.

Born near Melrose in the parish of Kelso, where as a boy Scott had spent many summers, Jennie (sometimes spelled Jenny) Gowanlock was descended from a persecuted Swiss Hugue-not preacher who had escaped to Scotland, and a family of Protestant reformers based in Glasgow. She came to Canada at age six with her parents, and grew up on a thriving, ten-acre farm just north of Stratford, Ontario.

With her family, young Jennie attended the Knox Presbyterian Church. At nineteen, after graduating from high school, she moved to Toronto to train as a teacher at that city's Normal School. While there, acting on her reformist heritage, she joined the evangelical restoration movement and got baptized into the Shuter Street Church of Christ.

Jennie Kidd Gowanlock Trout, honoured with this postage stamp in 1991, was the first woman licensed to practise medicine in Canada.

Having qualified as a teacher, Jennie Gowanlock taught school in the Stratford area for four years. In 1865, after a long courtship, she married Edward Trout, an ambitious young man who sold advertising for the *Toronto Leader* newspaper. Her husband helped to create, and then became the sole owner of, a profitable financial weekly called the *Monetary Times*.

During the early years of her marriage, while living in Toronto, Jennie Gowanlock Trout suffered from a "nervous disorder" that rendered her a semi-invalid. In her late twenties, probably at the urging of Emily Howard Stowe, a suffragist friend, she tried newly developed electrotherapy treatments. These proved so successful that, in keeping with her Christian faith, she decided to become a doctor.

Women were still excluded from that profession. But in 1871, Gowanlock Trout began a one-year qualifying course at the Toronto School of Medicine. Both she and Emily Stowe, her sole female classmate, faced crude practical jokes and lewd remarks from male students and professors, most of whom did not want women in medicine. No Canadian medical college would accept females as full-time students, so Gowanlock Trout went to Philadelphia and attended the Christian-oriented Women's Medical College.

She graduated early in 1875 and, that spring, passed the licensing exams of the College of Physicians and Surgeons of Ontario—the first woman to do so. With another woman doctor she had met in Philadelphia, she opened a Toronto practice that offered "treatments to ladies by galvanic baths or electricity." For six months, Gowanlock Trout also ran a free dispensary for the poor, trying to cover costs by giving lectures on medicine in Toronto, Brantford, and Hamilton.

This proved impractical, and in 1877, having closed the dispensary, Gowanlock Trout launched the Medical and Electro-Therapeutic Institute, which comprised several adjoining houses just north of her Jarvis Street home and could accommodate sixty women. This proved immensely popular. But after adding branches in Hamilton and Brantford, Jennie Gowanlock Trout, never robust, began suffering from fatigue. At age forty-one, again a semi-invalid, she had to retire from active practice.

Yet she was not finished breaking down barriers. In 1883, Gowanlock Trout joined an initiative led by Dr. Michael Barrett to establish a women's medical college in Toronto. When Barrett opposed the notion of having women trustees, she split with him to help create a similar institution at Queen's College in Kingston.

She was stunned when she learned that Barrett had changed his mind. By accepting women as trustees and faculty, he had gained the support of her old friend Emily Howard Stowe and the Canadian Women's Suffrage Association. Both medical colleges opened in October 1883. With Gowanlock Trout serving as both trustee and financial patron, the Kingston College competed with the Toronto one until 1894, when the two joined forces to form the Ontario Medical College for Women.

By then, Gowanlock Trout had become increasingly involved in the work of Christian foreign missions, as well as the temperance movement and the Association for the Advancement of Women. When her portrait appeared on a forty-cent Canada Post stamp in 1991, however, Jennie Gowanlock Trout was being recognized primarily as the first female licensed physician to practise medicine in Canada.

Book Two
THE BUILDERS

Prologue

THE VIEW FROM BLACK CREEK VILLAGE

In Black Creek Pioneer Village on the outskirts of Toronto, if today you go looking, you can learn a lot about the Scottish Protestants who settled so much of Upper Canada in the 1800s. In this historical village, a typical crossroads settlement, you will come upon Mackenzie House, built as a log cabin around 1830. Two decades later, it was expanded into a one-and-a-half-storey abode, complete with a "town barn" for the horse and buggy. This was the ancestral home of Major Addison Alexander Mackenzie, a doctor who, after being wounded and decorated in the First World War, resumed living in it while serving as a member of the Ontario legislature.

Around the corner from Mackenzie House, you can visit Dickson's Hill School, a one-room schoolhouse built in 1860. It features separate entrances for boys and girls, and hard benches that were shared by two or more students. The "central heating system" consists of a

The Fisherville Presbyterian Church in Black Creek Pioneer Village testi-
fies to the Protestant spirit of nineteenth-century Ontario. This austere house
of worship contains no statues, paintings, or ornamentation of any kind.

box stove at the back of the room with a stovepipe running along the
ceiling to the chimney at the front. This is typical of the schools built
in the second half of the nineteenth century. Most children in what is
now Ontario grew up on farms and attended schools like this until well
into the twentieth century.

The most evocative building in Black Creek Village has to be the
Fisherville Presbyterian Church, built in 1856 to serve an active congregation of a few dozen. In this Protestant house of worship, you find
no statues, no paintings, no ornamentation of any kind. The pews are
hard, straight-backed benches with a swinging aisle door at each end.
The backs of the benches include no holders for hymnals or prayer
books—nothing. The pews face a circular raised pulpit for the preacher.
Candles provide the only light except for three unadorned windows on
each side of the church. Everything is painted black or grey.

This austere, Spartan building is typical of the country churches that responded to the spiritual needs, and shaped the values, of generations of Scottish Canadian Protestants. Its message is radically different from the one voiced by the magnificent cathedrals of Roman Catholicism. Fisherville Church and hundreds like it transmitted the Protestant work ethic that had evolved from the teachings of John Knox.

Starting from Nova Scotia in the 1770s, with early settlements of both Catholics and Protestants on Cape Breton Island, Scottish colonists had multiplied westwards, the Protestants becoming more numerous. While competing against Roman Catholicism and the Church of England, the Presbyterian Church of Scotland spawned the Free Church of Scotland in 1843—which was also Presbyterian but more evangelical. Other Protestant denominations also made inroads in Upper Canada: Methodists, Congregationalists, Baptists, Plymouth Brethren.

The intricate dance of religion-based politics need not detain us here. The Protestant churches had more in common than they appreciated. All of them highlighted the New Testament and taught people to seek salvation through Christ. Some emphasized the doctrine of predestination, while others focused more on making converts. But all of them had roots in the Protestant Reformation, and preached austerity, morality, discipline, duty, self-sacrifice, thrift, and hard work. These were the values that shaped the character of the Scottish Protestants who multiplied across the country.

In *The Scottish Tradition in Canada,* W. Stanford Reid argues that the most important event in the history of Scotland was not the Highland Clearances or the battle of Culloden, but the Protestant Reformation of the sixteenth century. That is the moment, he notes, that "set the Scots apart as different from all other peoples." Elsewhere in Europe, the upper classes drove the Reformation. But in Scotland, Reid writes, Protestantism developed "from the grass roots in spite of much opposition at the higher levels of society."

This spawned a fiercely independent mindset—one that would remain characteristic of Scottish Protestants, who represented a tough-minded of strain of the Calvinism that John Knox introduced after studying with Protestant reformer John Calvin. More than four centuries after Knox, when in 1923 Scottish Canadian clergymen tried to enforce conformity throughout the Presbyterian Church, one of the so-called rebels reminded those assembled of the recalcitrance of the Covenanters, and warned that "Scottish Presbyterians have not changed overmuch since then."

Reid argues that the Calvinist emphasis on personal responsibility, closely identified with the Protestant work ethic, fosters initiative and risk taking, but also a sense of duty. An individual has a responsibility to use his or her gifts to benefit others. This credo has often produced a hard-working people, tight fisted yet capable of surprising generosity, "independent, sometimes irascible, argumentative and often very sure of their own correctness of vision and action." The Protestant Scot, Reid writes, "by no means always a 'lovable' character, has very often been a person possessing the necessary drive and self-assurance to make a good colonist."

Whatever their walk of life, those Scots who came to Canada brought similar values and perspectives. They came of a tradition that rejected class distinctions and encouraged social mobility. They viewed education as essential and self-improvement as a duty. Given the relatively open, undeveloped nature of Canada, farming families began to produce ministers, doctors, lawyers, nurses, teachers, economists, and newspaper magnates.

The emphasis on education began in the home. Reid's father, for example, raised on a farm in the Eastern Townships, grew up in a family that gathered "every Sunday night to recite the Catechism, one-half one evening the other half the next." This was the Westminster Shorter Catechism, a series of 107 questions and answers that teach

Calvinist doctrine (God, Christ, original sin, baptism, communion). Among Scottish Canadian Protestants of the nineteenth and early twentieth centuries, these exercises were the rule, not the exception.

The family of George Brown, who founded the Toronto *Globe* (precursor of the *Globe and Mail*) and became a father of Confederation, were staunch members of the Presbyterian Church of Scotland. According to biographer J.M.S. Careless, "Family prayers, Sunday-school teaching for George, charitable work among the poor for his mother and elder sisters, all were an essential part of their lives."

John A. Macdonald, Brown's great contemporary, arrived in Canada from Scotland at an early age. Once settled, he experienced much the same upbringing. He was a great reader from an early age, according to biographer Donald Creighton, "and he would sit for hours deep in a book, almost oblivious to what was going on." At age fourteen, after attending a one-room schoolhouse, Macdonald switched to a school for "general and classical education" founded by a newly arrived Presbyterian minister from Scotland. This implied the usual rituals and question-and-answer sessions—though Macdonald left school after one year.

Novelist Hugh MacLennan, who grew up in Halifax early in the twentieth century, described his doctor father as "a formidable keeper of the Sabbath." Twice each Sunday, the family attended St. Matthew's Presbyterian Church. This upper-class church was much grander than the vast majority of those located in the countryside. It had a rose window copied from Chartres, and in addition to a high pulpit, a special pew for the lieutenant governor of the province. Yet in tone and teachings, it resembled the others.

On the Sabbath day, before going to church, young Hugh attended Sunday school. According to biographer Elspeth Cameron, "The combination of this school, the Presbyterian sermons, [his mother's] prominence in the choir, and their own informal gatherings for religious song at home meant that Hugh was thoroughly indoctrinated with Christian principles in general and Calvinist doctrines in particular."

MacLennan's contemporary, John Kenneth Galbraith, became a famous economist and forged a spectacular career outside Canada. But like Harold Adams Innis and Frederick Banting, to whom we will return, he grew up Scottish Protestant on an Ontario farm. In a wry memoir called *The Scotch,* Galbraith painted a vivid picture of "the uncompromising Calvinism of our upbringing" near Wallacetown in the southwest of the province.

The local school "was a plain rectangular structure of white brick and consisted of one small room together with a very small entry where we hung our coats on hooks and stowed our lunch boxes on a shelf above." At the back of the room was a large wood stove, and as in the Dickson's Hill School at Black Creek Village, a stovepipe ran to the front: "In the winter, one of the larger boys went early to the school and lit the fire, and it was his responsibility to stoke it during the day."

Here Galbraith learned to read and write—mostly, he suggests, despite his teachers. As for the Baptist church he attended, it was "completely accommodated" to the "the rural Scotch," as he called them. "This became evident the moment one stepped inside the church. For it contained nothing, literally nothing, but square oaken pews and a plain wooden pulpit. Church doctrine forbade a choir, organ—in fact music of any kind. The singing of Psalms was allowed." Galbraith found the austerity hard to bear and the sermons worse. "My recollection of these exercises," he writes, "is of the most acute pain. For thirty years I have not been in a church for other than architectural reasons or to witness a marriage or funeral, and it is partly because I associate them to this day with torture."

Before he was done, this sardonic ex-Baptist would serve as an adviser to three U.S. presidents and as the American ambassador to India—all while writing and publishing fifty books and more than a thousand articles. The question becomes: what made Galbraith run? As early as the 1970s, W. Stanford Reid could see that secularism was eroding the religious foundations of the Scottish Protestant tradition. "The ethical and moral principles, however, have been so embedded in the individual's personality that they are still operating automatically."

Because he defected from both Canada and Christianity, John Kenneth Galbraith can be viewed as the perfect poster boy for Scottish Canadian Protestantism. Independent, educated, duty-driven, overachieving, Galbraith demonstrates that the Protestant work ethic could drive infidels of the mid-to-late twentieth century just as effectively as it motivated the faithful and the unconvinced of the early nineteenth. Down through the decades, the influence of Scottish Protestantism has been pervasive and profound. Looking out from Black Creek Village, a visitor cannot help but realize that it played a significant role in shaping Canada.

7

Makers of 1867

John A. Macdonald: A Perfect Rascal

Twenty years after Confederation, in the midst of a treaty negotiation in Washington, the wife of a U.S. senator found herself talking with a Canadian delegate. She said, "I guess you come from Canada."

"Indeed, I do."

"You've got a smart man there, the Honourable John A. Macdonald."

"Yes, ma'am, he is very smart."

"But they say he is a perfect rascal."

"Yes, ma'am, he is a perfect rascal."

"But why do they keep such a man in power?"

"Well, you see, they cannot get along without him."

Just then the woman's husband arrived, the senator himself, and said, "My dear, let me introduce you to the Honourable John A. Macdonald."

This anecdote is one of many used to illustrate the witty style of Canada's first prime minister. Years before this, when he was serving as the member of Parliament for Kingston, Macdonald had turned to George Monro Grant, the influential principal of Queen's University, and asked him, "Do I have your support?"

No slouch with a quip, Grant responded, "You always have my support when you're right."

"That I can get from anyone," Macdonald answered. "I need people who will support me when I'm wrong."

Then there was the occasion when Macdonald listened while a governor general spoke to a university audience

The earliest portrait of Sir John A. Macdonald, painted by an unknown artist around 1842, suggests energy, ambition, and a twinkle in the eye.

in ancient Greek. Afterwards, he told a newspaper reporter, "His Lordship spoke in the purest ancient Greek without mispronouncing a word or making the slightest grammatical solecism." A colleague who overheard this exchange later expressed surprise: "So you know Greek?"

Macdonald looked over at him: "No, but I know politics."

As Pierre Berton put it, "the twinkling eyes, the sardonic smile, the easy tolerance, the quick wit, and the general lack of malice made Macdonald an attractive figure in and out of Parliament." This remained true even though Macdonald was also a binge drinker with a fiery temper who at one point was driven from office by a bribery scandal. How is it, then, that when we turn to the act of Confederation, that crucial first step towards creating the Dominion of Canada, this self-confessed "perfect rascal" proves to be what Richard Gwyn calls the one "irreplaceable man."

John Alexander Macdonald, the son of an ambitious young man from the Highland town of Dornoch, was born in Glasgow in 1815. At age five, with his family, he moved to Kingston, Upper Canada, a bustling market town of 4,000 controlled by immigrant Scots. His father operated a series of shops and businesses around Kingston and in nearby Prince Edward County, and in 1829 became a local magistrate.

As a boy, Macdonald attended private schools and studied Latin, Greek, arithmetic, geography, and English (reading, grammar, and rhetoric). At fourteen, he switched to a coeducational school founded by a Presbyterian minister recently arrived from Scotland. In those days, the law profession required no special education but hands-on experience, and at fifteen, Macdonald went to work as an apprentice in the office of a Kingston lawyer, George Mackenzie. Five years later, in August 1835, he opened his own Kingston law office.

Macdonald made a name by taking on difficult cases, including one involving rebels from the Rebellion of 1837–38. Having served (without firing a shot) in the militia that quelled the Toronto uprising during that rebellion, Macdonald nevertheless believed that the rebels, many of them Scots, deserved a competent defence. His principal client, a rebel leader named Nils von Schoultz, rejected his advice and pleaded guilty to offending against a statute forbidding foreign nationals from assisting "traitorous and rebellious British subjects" in making war against the crown. For that, to Macdonald's lasting sorrow, he got himself hanged.

At age twenty-four, Macdonald began focusing on lucrative corporate law. His clients included Kingston's two main financial institutions, the Commercial Bank and, from 1843, the Trust and Loan Company of Upper Canada. From that time, too, he practised law with a series of partners: Alexander Campbell, Archibald John Macdonell, and Robert Mortimer Wilkinson.

From the 1840s onward, active as a businessman, Macdonald bought and sold property in Kingston, Guelph, and boom-town Toronto. He became a director of a dozen Canadian companies and sat on two British boards. In the late 1850s and 1860s, he suffered reverses as a result of bad investments, the collapse of the Commercial Bank, and the death of one of his legal partners. Thanks to his law practice, he avoided bankruptcy.

Meanwhile, starting in the 1830s, Macdonald had become active politically. At nineteen, he served as secretary of the Prince Edward District Board of Education. In Kingston, he became recording secretary of the Celtic Society, president of the Young Men's Society, vice-president of the St. Andrew's Society, and a prominent member of the Presbyterian community.

In March 1843, he easily won election as a Kingston alderman. The following year, at age twenty-nine, after a campaign championing the maintenance of close ties with Britain, he was elected as a Conservative to the legislative assembly of the United Province of Canada. That province had been created in 1841, when Upper and Lower Canada, renamed Canada West and Canada East, were brought into a single legislature that gave each of them forty-two seats.

Over the next thirty years, based in Kingston, Macdonald would win ten consecutive elections—seven to that legislature and three, beginning in 1867, to the confederated Parliament. He became a chameleon, an elusive, magpie politician who took whatever he needed from wherever he found it and made it serve his own ends—and, happily, those of his emerging country.

During his first decade as an elected politician, Macdonald remained staunchly Conservative. He opposed any initiative that might weaken ties with Great Britain or undercut the propertied interests he represented. This meant resisting any extension of the right to vote to property-less men, and even responsible government—the notion that the prime minister and his cabinet were responsible not to the governor general (who represented the British monarch) but to the legislative assembly elected by the people.

Yet from the outset, Macdonald proved pragmatic. As early as 1844, he declared that he did not want "to waste the time of the legislature, and the money of the people, in fruitless discussions of abstract and theoretical questions of government." He served as a junior cabinet minister for several months until 1848, when Reformers took over the government. For the next six years, while sitting in opposition, Macdonald focused on Kingston-area issues and business, mindful always of his own interests.

In 1854, with more than ten years as a politician behind him, Macdonald became attorney general for Canada West in a French–English coalition government that emerged, according to historian John Charles Dent, from negotiations in which "his was the hand that shaped the course." Others argue that he made no special contribution. However, the changing Conservative Party clearly reflected his declared intention to "enlarge the bounds of our party" and maintain "friendly relations with the French."

For thirteen years, except for brief periods when the Conservatives lost power, John A. Macdonald served as attorney general of Canada West. Early on, he pushed through a controversial bill on private schools that formed the basis for the existing system in Ontario, defending the right of Roman Catholics "to educate their children according to their own principles."

This opened his government to charges of "French domination" from Reform leader George Brown, a Scottish immigrant who in 1844 had founded the *Globe* newspaper in Toronto. Soon enough, Brown was advocating representation by population, a system that would have given Canada West (now Ontario) more seats than Canada East (Quebec) in the legislature they shared.

In 1856, after some deft political infighting, Macdonald became co-premier of the Province of Canada, representing Canada West. The following November, when George-Étienne Cartier gained control of Canada East, Macdonald acquired a long-standing French Canadian partner. He controlled the Conservative Party tightly, intervening even at the riding level, and sought allies among the leaders of large blocs of voters, including the Methodist and Catholic Churches and the Orange Order.

Socially, Macdonald's instincts were progressive—prototypically "Red Tory." Already, as leader of the government, he had laid the foundations for Canada's social-welfare system, setting standards for asylums, reformatories, and correctional institutions. He had reformed the judicial system, improved roads and transportation, and created a department of finance. In 1857, with Alexander Tilloch Galt, he also acted to protect Canadian industry, introducing a tariff system that foreshadowed the National Policy of the 1870s. Indeed, he did much to encourage businesses involved in transportation, insurance, finance, mining, and resources, including many in which he and his colleagues had a personal stake.

As a strategic pragmatist, Macdonald had no rivals. On one occasion, faced with deciding where to locate the permanent seat of government—a difficult decision given French–English tensions—he adroitly referred the matter to Queen Victoria. In the early 1860s, after she "chose" Ottawa, on the border between Canada East and Canada West, he steered the government through the onset of the American Civil War. And while meeting these and other challenges, he held together a fragile coalition of Conservatives and moderate Reformers—mainly by developing and controlling a patronage system.

Along the way, of course, he drank. Yet his binge drinking did not become a serious public problem until spring 1862. Then he had "one of his old attacks," as the *Globe* reported, during an extended debate over expanding the militia. Defeated on the Militia Bill, the government resigned. Macdonald would spend the next two years in opposition.

Those who claim that alcoholism is not genetic, but arises out of an unhappy personal history, could make a case with Macdonald. When he was seven, he saw a drunken servant kill a younger brother, probably accidentally. His own first son died from a fall at age two—and decades later, he still had the child's toys. In his early forties, Macdonald watched his first wife, Isabella, die a lingering death. His second wife, Agnes, gave birth to a hydrocephalic daughter, and she wrote of realizing this as "one of the saddest times of my life."

Some men might have resorted to religion. But as a Presbyterian, Macdonald proved far more Robbie Burns than John Knox. At moments of crisis, he sometimes went missing. Yet even strong drink failed to dull his wit. On one occasion, when he was serving as attorney general, the governor general sent an aide-de-camp to look for him. The young man found the lawmaker lying in bed with a French novel and a decanter of sherry. "If you are here in your official capacity," Macdonald told him, "give my compliments to the governor general and tell him to go to hell. If you are here as a private individual, you can go there yourself."

Some years later, an election campaign produced several versions of another anecdote. During an onstage debate, according to the most cogent formulation, an inebriated Macdonald turned away and discreetly vomited. His opponent cried, "Is this the man you want running your country? A drunk?" Macdonald pulled himself together: "I got sick not because I'm a drunk but because I have been listening to the ranting of my honourable opponent."

Even drunk, Macdonald could be lethal. And at his best, he was inspirational, though you could not believe every word he said. Certainly in Halifax in 1864, people must have found it hard to imagine that this wily old politician had ever been bored. Yet while speaking at one fancy dinner, he insisted that "for twenty long years, I have been dragging myself through the dreary wastes of Colonial politics."

This was in September, immediately following the inaugural Charlottetown Conference, which had been called to discuss the unification of four British colonies. "I thought there was no end, nothing worthy of ambition," Macdonald told the delegates. "But now I see something which is worthy of all I have suffered in the cause of my little country."

Macdonald was speaking of Confederation, the first step in creating a unified political entity, the Dominion of Canada, by bringing together Quebec, Ontario, New Brunswick, and Nova Scotia. Eventually, the other provinces and territories would join these four, each in its own good time (starting with Manitoba and the Northwest Territories in 1870, British Columbia in 1871, and Prince Edward Island in 1873). But Confederation had to happen first. And even his critics agree that Confederation could not have happened without Sir John A. Macdonald.

This transplanted Scottish Presbyterian did not succeed alone. Two radically different Scots—William Lyon Mackenzie and James Bruce, Lord Elgin—had done crucial preliminary work, and to them we shall return. Also, during the thrust and parry of extended argument, Macdonald would receive crucial help from a powerful French Canadian, George-Étienne Cartier, and two fellow Scots: Alexander Tilloch Galt and, especially, his sometime nemesis George Brown.

Yet of these last "Big Four" figures, as Richard Gwyn demonstrates in *John A: The Man Who Made Us,* Macdonald was the one irreplaceable man, the nuts-and-bolts politician who hammered disparate dreams and aspirations into a shared vision of a British North American state reaching from coast to coast to coast. Opportunity arose as a result of the American Civil War, which began in 1861. Macdonald turned a blind eye to the Underground Railroad, which carried tens of thousands of escaped slaves into the northern colonies. But border incidents and the crisis atmosphere led George Brown to call for a coalition government that would look at creating a more flexible, federal union of Canada East and Canada West.

Macdonald proposed a broader federation involving all the British

North American colonies, and he carried the day. The Maritime provinces of Nova Scotia, New Brunswick, and Prince Edward Island had already planned a regional conference at Charlottetown to discuss legislative union. They agreed to allow representatives of the two Canadas to join the discussion, and to make their case first. So began the process that led to Confederation.

After meeting in Charlottetown, provincial delegates gathered again in Quebec City. Drawing attention to American expressions of Manifest Destiny, the idea that the United States was destined to control all of North America, Macdonald argued in favour of retaining close ties with Great Britain, and stressed that a larger, more comprehensive union would prove more sustainable.

As early as 1858, Alexander Tilloch Galt, son of the colonizer John Galt, had developed a plan to unite the two Canadas and the Maritimes. In 1864, Macdonald realized, Why not go farther? Why not create a nation extending from the Atlantic to the Pacific by incorporating the colonies of British Columbia and Vancouver Island?

And so, drawing on his legal background, Macdonald applied himself to drafting a constitutional framework. Later, his friend and colleague Thomas D'Arcy McGee declared that Macdonald wrote fifty of the seventy-two resolutions passed at the Quebec conference.

Certainly, Galt worked out the financial arrangements and also the separate schools system. Cartier contributed the provisions relating to the French language and the continued use in Quebec of a distinctive legal system, the *Code civil*. For the rest, Macdonald borrowed freely. From Brown, he took the idea of extending Canadian jurisdiction into the northwest; and in response to Maritime delegates, he added a clause providing for the building of an intercolonial railway—an objective that, before long, he would make a priority.

Given a free hand, Macdonald would have established a stronger central government. But as he told a friend, "of course it does not do to adopt that point of view in discussing the subject in Lower Canada." To the federal government, Macdonald reserved control over national defence, finance, trade and commerce, taxation, currency, and banking—and also the power to disallow provincial legislation. He believed the provincial governments so weak they would wither and die. Nor was that his only miscalculation. He failed to provide a mechanism for amending the constitution. He gave no thought to the importance of resources, or to providing for cities or Native peoples. Also, at a time when only 15 percent of adults had the right to vote, he sidestepped what he regarded as the chief weakness of the U.S. system: universal suffrage.

Of the thirty-six original fathers of Confederation, more than half were Scottish Canadians. In time, other Scots and descendants of Scots, figures as different as Nellie McClung and Pierre Elliott Trudeau, would improve upon Macdonald's foundational handiwork, all of them displaying a characteristically Scottish faith in institutions as guardians of individual rights and freedoms. Of the twenty-two politicians who have served as the country's prime minister, thirteen have been Canadians of Scottish descent—almost 60 percent (see Appendix 3).

But in the early days, quite apart from drawing up the constitution, Macdonald proved irreplaceable as a savvy political animal. In 1865, when Confederation looked like a done deal, opposition arose in both New Brunswick and Nova Scotia—the latter led by the formidable Joseph Howe. Macdonald assessed the situation, spent money where he had to spend it, and then delivered a master stroke. He led the "Big Four" delegation to Britain—Galt, Brown, Cartier, and himself—and obtained loan guarantees from the British government. By doing so, he achieved something more crucial to Atlantic Canadians than the promise of money: London's approval. At Macdonald's urging, the British had signalled that they wanted Confederation. In New Brunswick and Nova Scotia, where loyalty was paramount, that closed the deal.

In December 1866, when Macdonald returned to London to lead one final Confederation conference, and to see the British North America Act through the British Parliament, he led representatives from all the colonies involved. At a time when the United States was buying Alaska from the Russians, and the foremost American representative in Canada was arguing that Britain should cede Vancouver Island and British Columbia to the United States as payment for damages during the Civil War, Macdonald was being hailed in London as "the ruling genius" of Confederation.

During the conference, Richard Gwyn tells us, Macdonald did once "spectacularly" succumb to his particular vice. Having returned to London after spending a weekend at a country estate, he lay down to drink, smoke, and read the newspapers. Later, he awoke to discover his "bed, bed clothes & curtains all on fire." With the help of George-Étienne Cartier, who came running, Macdonald managed to douse the curtains and put out the blaze. But he had scorched his hair, forehead, and hands, and he wrote his wife that if he had not been wearing a thick flannel shirt under his nightshirt, he "would have been burned to death."

Despite this incident, Macdonald prevailed. British journalist Goldwin Smith marvelled at the time that Macdonald had been able to "hold together a set of elements, national, religious, sectional and personal, as motley as the component patches of any 'crazy quilt,' and actuated each of them by paramount regard for its own interest." In February 1867, with four other Canadian delegates, Macdonald met privately with Queen Victoria, who thanked him for his loyalty.

By March 29, when she gave royal assent to the British North America Act, stipulating July 1 as its effective date, Macdonald was back in Canada. That act signalled the beginning of a new era and, if not the birth, then certainly the conception of a nation—one that could not have emerged but for the political leadership of that perfect rascal, John A. Macdonald.

William Lyon Mackenzie: Necessary Iconoclast

Thirty years before Confederation, in a farmhouse overlooking the Niagara River, a radically different Scottish Canadian politician felt a premonition. Late one morning in December 1837, before sitting down to breakfast, William Lyon Mackenzie—volatile, idealistic, erratic, and currently a fugitive on the run—stepped outside to scan the dirt road that wound to this farmhouse through the tree-dotted countryside. To his shock, at a distance of a few hundred yards, Mackenzie spotted a posse of green-coated dragoons riding towards him, carbines at the ready.

Having spent the past several days making his way here from Toronto, with nobody turning him in despite the offer of a huge reward, the forty-two-year-old firebrand had no intention of getting caught now. With his host, Captain McAfee, and a local volunteer, Mackenzie raced to the shore, jumped into a boat and rowed furiously for the other side of the river, bent on reaching the safety of American soil. He and his two allies had scarcely departed when the troops arrived and dismounted. Mrs. McAfee and her daughters rushed out to greet them and, while several dragoons pretended not to notice the departing rowers, talked with sufficient animation to distract the officer in charge until Mackenzie and his friends had disappeared around a nearby island.

William Lyon Mackenzie (1795–1861) is one of the most significant and controversial figures in Canadian history. He is best known as the driving force behind the 1837 Rebellion in Upper Canada, an uprising against the British colonial government inspired mainly by land allocations. Leading members of the Anglican Church, having beaten back settlement attempts by Lord Selkirk and John Galt, retained control of the extensive lands set aside as "clergy reserves." But they lacked enough Anglicans to develop them and refused to sell their holdings to non-Anglicans.

Because these great, undeveloped tracts were scattered throughout the countryside, many farms remained isolated and less viable than they might have been. Roman Catholic, Presbyterian, and other Protestant churches protested. The Methodist Church, which had broken away from the Anglican Church in Britain, proved especially vocal. Many Methodists in Upper Canada were descendants of "late Loyalists" who had flocked north just before the War of 1812. These included travelling "saddlebag preachers," who had won many converts in frontier conditions. In 1828, Upper Canadian Methodists—who held camp meetings reminiscent of the Sacramaids of Cape Breton—sought to become more acceptable locally by cutting ties with American Methodism.

The Anglican oligarchy refused to budge. Here was a popular cause looking for a champion, and William Lyon Mackenzie filled the bill. He labelled the elite Anglican Tories "the Family Compact" and became prominent as a crusading journalist. Years before John A. Macdonald emerged onto the political stage, Mackenzie tried to bring about political and social reforms. He got himself elected to the provincial assembly five times, only to be repeatedly expelled. He travelled to London, found allies among prominent British Reformers, and convinced one colonial secretary to make significant changes—only to see that crucial decision reversed by the man's successor. Finally, he despaired of the political process. Acting roughly in concert with the better prepared *patriotes* of Lower Canada, Mackenzie orchestrated an uprising that ended in debacle.

And so we enter the realm of controversy. In *Eminent Canadians*, writer John Fraser calls Mackenzie a "dysfunctional rabble-rouser" and complains that he "has generally been served up to us as an idealized democrat ahead of his time, rather than the intemperate and malignant nincompoop that he truly was." Yet even if Mackenzie was "a melodramatic asshole," as Fraser contends, he accomplished certain necessary destructions. He was a political John the Baptist figure who cleared the way for the constructive work of John A. Macdonald.

Born in Dundee, Scotland, in 1795, William Lyon Mackenzie entered school at age five. From the start, he proved boisterous yet meticulous. Between the ages of eleven and twenty-five, he read 958 books, listing them as he proceeded by year and genre. At fifteen, young Willie went to work in the newsroom of a local newspaper. Also, he joined a scientific society, where he met Edward and James Lesslie, father and son, who would become lifelong patrons.

In the context of Canadian political history, William Lyon Mackenzie was an icon-smashing figure who cleared the way for nation builders.

For a while, with the backing of Edward Lesslie, Mackenzie and his widowed mother operated a general store and circulating library at Alyth, twenty miles (30 km) north of Dundee. That business failed during a depression, and for four years, starting from age seventeen, Mackenzie shuttled between London and Paris, living what he later described as a dissipated life of gambling and drinking. In 1814, he fathered an illegitimate son named James, and his mother undertook to raise the child.

At twenty-five, with John Lesslie, another son of Edward, Mackenzie sailed to Canada. He helped to build the Lachine Canal and wrote for the *Montreal Herald,* then moved to York (Toronto) to join Lesslie in working for a book and drug company. Soon he was writing for the *York Observer* under the name "Mercator." In summer 1822, Mackenzie's mother arrived with a seventeen-year-old Dundee woman, Isabel Baxter, she had brought to marry her son. With Isabel, Mackenzie would father and raise thirteen children.

In May 1824, while running a general store in Queenston, near Niagara Falls, Mackenzie launched the *Colonial Advocate,* his most famous newspaper. The following November, he moved that unprofitable journal to York, where he used it to attack wealthy members of the Family Compact for discriminating against non-Anglicans.

This provoked threats, and in May 1826, the rabble-rousing journalist fled to Lewiston, New York, to avoid retribution. Early the following month, fifteen young Tories ransacked his newspaper office. They smashed his press and threw his type into the harbour. Mackenzie sued them, won a settlement large enough to pay off a mountain of debts, and re-established the *Colonial Advocate.*

During the War of 1812, American troops had invaded Canada and taken York. Memories remained vivid, and American settlers faced discrimination from the tight-knit Family Compact. As a Scot, Mackenzie had grown up an underdog in Britain, and he felt drawn to the settlers' cause. In 1827, when John A. Macdonald was just twelve years old, Mackenzie helped win concessions in London that extended full rights to U.S.-born settlers.

The following year, faced with a land grab on behalf of the Church of England, Mackenzie stood for election in the two-member county of York (which extended northward from Queen Street in present-day Toronto). In those days, elections could be tumultuous affairs. Farmers came from miles around and met at polling stations, anxious to eat and especially drink at the expense of candidates seeking election. Voters would loudly proclaim their allegiances, and groups of thugs tried to prevent opponents from reaching the polls. Votes were bought and sold, fist fights erupted, and the election process frequently produced broken heads and bloody noses.

William Lyon Mackenzie and fellow Reformer Jesse Ketchum won a landslide victory. After taking his seat in January 1829, Mackenzie organized committees and pressed for reforms in agriculture, commerce, and postal services. He offered detailed critiques of the Bank of Upper Canada and the Welland Canal Company. In March, having visited the United States to buy books for resale, he studied the workings of the U.S. government and recognized that the "spoils system"—giving government jobs to loyal party workers after winning an election—could provide a way to remove Family Compact officials. He returned home an admirer of U.S. institutions, and in the early 1830s escalated his verbal attacks on the Tories.

When he called the entire assembly a "sycophantic office," the Tory majority expelled him by a vote of twenty-four to fifteen—and so helped create his image as an iconic martyr. In York, a mob of several hundred forcibly entered the assembly and demanded (unsuccessfully) that the lieutenant governor, Sir John Colborne, dissolve parliament. In the ensuing by-election, Mackenzie won a landslide victory. Supporters presented him with a gold medal and accompanied him, with skirling bagpipes and 134 sleighs, all the way down Yonge Street.

Almost immediately, in response to another strident speech, Mackenzie was expelled. Again he was re-elected. He then disrupted a meeting called by Bishop Alexander McDonell to support the government, and was subsequently lured out of his hotel and beaten by thugs. Riots ensued, and Mackenzie went into hiding until April 1832, when he left to seek justice in Britain. There, he met Reformers Joseph Hume and John Arthur Roebuck and presented the moderate Whig colonial secretary, Lord Goderich, with a long list of grievances. He argued that an insolent and autocratic Family Compact refused to relinquish control of the "clergy reserves" and discriminated relentlessly against non-English farmers.

Goderich tried to straighten out the political situation, but in 1833, he was replaced by an arch-conservative. Lord Stanley restored key Tories to high office—a setback that, for Mackenzie, proved decisive. He lost faith in appealing to Great Britain. Back home in December, and excluded from the assembly, he changed the title of his newspaper to the *Advocate,* dropping the word "Colonial."

In March 1834, York was renamed Toronto and held its first municipal elections. Reformers won a majority on council and chose their most outspoken alderman to serve as the city's first mayor. Mackenzie sold the *Advocate* and got rid of Tory officials but proved weak as an administrator. The following year, the Tories gained control of city council, and Mackenzie lost his aldermanic seat. In response to further political setbacks, Mackenzie launched a newspaper whose name, the *Constitution,* attested to his growing interest in American constitutional practices.

Early in 1837, Great Britain acted to make the executive branch in Lower Canada supreme over the elected assembly, and Mackenzie lost all remaining hope in the imperial centre. The *Constitution* began alluding to possible armed resistance. By summer, Mackenzie was organizing committees and unions, and calling for a convention of delegates from both Upper and Lower Canada—though he remained ambivalent about resorting to arms.

Despite the fierce opposition of Protestant Orangemen, who abused and physically attacked him and his supporters, Mackenzie drew large, enthusiastic crowds. Finally, he concluded that the only way to effect change would be to inspire his relatively mild-mannered enthusiasts to march on Toronto from the outskirts of town.

In mid-October 1837, rebellion erupted in Lower Canada, where the Chateau Clique, which included French Canadian seigneurs, had been playing the role of the Family Compact. Learning that Upper Canada's lieutenant governor, Sir Francis Bond Head, had sent virtually all of his British regulars to put down that uprising, Mackenzie tried to seize the moment. He called a meeting to persuade his fellow leaders that Toronto was theirs for the taking. If they moved quickly, they could use "Dutcher's foundry-men and Armstrong's axemakers," employees of wealthy Reformers, to seize control of the city and, indeed, the colony.

Mackenzie was almost certainly right. But the Reform leaders, most of them businessmen, were not prepared personally to commit treason, and so the moment passed—a historical turning point. A frustrated Mackenzie proposed that the farmers be organized to overthrow the government. He claimed, falsely, that the Lower Canadian rebels had requested a diversionary action to draw off British troops. In the third week of November, he called a meeting of leaders from the staunch Reform territory north of Toronto, and convinced them that, with a show of force, they could succeed in ousting the government. He also set a date for action: December 7, 1837.

Back in Toronto, Mackenzie convinced other leaders to accept this plan. He appointed Colonel Anthony Van Egmond, a man of extensive military experience, to command the rebel forces. On November 15, Mackenzie published a draft constitution based on the U.S. model but incorporating radical English Reform ideas. The uprising in Lower Canada had already begun, and Mackenzie sought frantically to organize his supporters, urging friends to recruit their neighbours.

On Saturday, December 2, north of Toronto at Stoufferville (now Stouffville), he urged a large meeting to stage an armed demonstration, promising that a provisional government would confiscate clergy reserves and distribute the land among participants. He prepared a declaration of independence to be distributed before the march. The next day, while riding back to Toronto, Mackenzie learned that Samuel Lount, a Reform leader from north of the city, had been asked to act with a few hundred men—a party now marching to Montgomery's Tavern on Yonge Street, just north of the city.

On Monday night, as men began to arrive, the leaders debated whether to proceed immediately into the city. Mackenzie led a scouting party south and, in a skirmish involving prisoners, lost Anthony Anderson, the only Reformer in the vicinity with military experience. Next day, an overwrought Mackenzie, still awaiting military leaders, began behaving erratically. That evening, he pulled himself together and approached the city, but a small party of Loyalist guards managed to disperse the marchers. Those who had come merely to demonstrate turned around and headed for home.

On Wednesday, Mackenzie seized the mail coach that ran west out of Toronto, while the main rebel force waited at Montgomery's Tavern. Next day, December 7, militiamen armed by the government marched out of the city and routed the poorly armed rebels. The military man Van Egmond, having arrived just a few hours before, warned that the situation was hopeless. Historian William Kilbourn writes that Mackenzie "threatened to have the old gentleman taken out and shot," while the *Dictionary of Canadian Biography* declares that an agitated Mackenzie had "put a pistol to his head" and ordered him to fight.

The leaders of the rebellion fled to the United States—Mackenzie halting briefly at that farmhouse on the Niagara River. He reached American soil on December 11, and gave the first of many speeches the following day, telling supportive audiences of the widespread yearning for freedom among Upper Canadians. Soon, installed on Navy Island in the Niagara River, and with the help of sympathetic Americans, Mackenzie began organizing an invasion. Despite the arrival of arms, supplies, and several hundred volunteers, Mackenzie and his rebels were outgunned and forced to retreat to U.S. territory.

The rebellion proved to be the climactic moment of his career, though Mackenzie would remain a political force for another two decades. Having escaped, he lived for a while in New York City, where he launched yet another newspaper. Meanwhile, several rebel leaders were hanged, and others were banished to Van Diemen's Land, that wretched island penal colony south of Australia.

Gradually, Mackenzie realized that law-abiding Upper Canadians would never overthrow the government. In June 1839, he insisted, foolishly, on defending himself against charges of breaking neutrality laws.

Found guilty and sentenced to eighteen months in jail, he served less than a year before gaining a pardon and retreating to the United States.

Mercurial as ever, Mackenzie called for "shrewd and daring fellows" to burn English ships, barracks, and warehouses in Canada. He changed his mind, however, after learning that the British had begun granting amnesty to rebel leaders. He admitted that the rebellion had been an error and, as Reformers less radical than himself started coming to power, lobbied for a general amnesty. By September 1841, Mackenzie would write that "the more I see of this country, the more bitterly I regret the attempt at revolution at Toronto."

Mackenzie spent the next eight years in the United States, working mainly in newspapers. Early in 1849, the Reform administration of Robert Baldwin and Louis-Hippolyte LaFontaine finally announced an amnesty that included Mackenzie. By May of 1850, the firebrand had moved back to Toronto.

The following spring, almost incredibly, Mackenzie was elected back to parliament. Fiercely independent, he backed "true reform" measures, fretted about overspending, and opposed government assistance to monopolistic railways. He also conducted a damning investigation into a court reorganization that benefited close allies of Baldwin, who had helped bring about the broad pardon, so forcing him to resign as premier.

Gradually, by taking uncompromising positions, Mackenzie alienated potential allies and lost influence. By 1858, he was calling for independence from Britain, while suggesting that annexation to the United States would inevitably follow—precisely the opposite position to the one taken by John A. Macdonald. By 1861, Mackenzie had abandoned that idea. He was envisaging some larger political union, perhaps involving Great Britain, the United States, Canada, and Ireland, when towards the end of August, he suffered an "apoplectic seizure" and died.

Capricious, volatile, uncompromising: William Lyon Mackenzie was the polar opposite of John A. Macdonald. Yet without this sometime revolutionary, whose rebellion finally drove home to Great Britain that the political status quo was no longer viable, it is hard to see how the other, the wily pragmatist, could ever have succeeded in bringing about Confederation. The system had to be broken, and also be seen to be broken, before it could be put back together in a new form.

Lord Elgin: The Middle Man

The Rebellions in Upper and Lower Canada demonstrated that the colonial system of government, with crucial decisions being made thousands of miles away, had become dysfunctional. Thirty years later, Confederation would unite four colonies and create the foundation for an evolving political entity that has endured to the present day.

James Bruce, Lord Elgin, showed his Scottish backbone by recognizing responsible government and approving the controversial Rebellion Losses Bill.

Between the rebellions and Confederation came one necessary step: responsible government. And it, too, emerged courtesy of a Scot—an expatriate, this time, rather than an immigrant.

Born in London in 1811, James Bruce, a direct descendant of Robert the Bruce, the legendary Scottish hero, was the son of the seventh Earl of Elgin, the man who "collected" the so-called Elgin marbles from the Parthenon in Greece. After attending Eton, young James went to Oxford University, where he emerged as a leading intellectual. Influenced by the poet Samuel Taylor

Coleridge, he came to believe that society is essentially organic, that it grows and develops along natural lines. After graduating at age twenty-one, he helped manage the family estate in Fife, ten miles (16 km) south of St. Andrews, while reading, writing, and preparing for a political career.

In 1840, he won election to the House of Commons. He resigned the following year when, at the death of his father, he became a Scottish peer: the eighth Earl of Elgin. For four years ending in 1846, he served as governor of Jamaica. He then accepted the more challenging post of governor general of the United Province of Canada, which then comprised Canada East and Canada West.

As a direct result of the recent rebellions, progressive British parliamentarians wanted to ensure that those colonies were not annexed by the expansionist United States of America, where the term "Manifest Destiny" had begun appearing in print in 1839. Before he left London, Lord Elgin undertook to advance responsible government in British North America. This meant that the prime minister and his cabinet would become accountable not to the governor general but to the elected House of Commons.

Unlike in the United States, where the president is elected directly by the people, the executive branch under the British system is responsible to the legislative branch, which is made up of representatives elected by the people. As in Britain, the colonial government would have to retain the confidence of a majority in the House of Commons, or else resign. At that point the governor general could either call an election or seek a political configuration that commanded the confidence of the House.

Lord Elgin, nominally a Tory, had been appointed by a Whig (Liberal) administration. Given this circumstance, even before reaching Canada in January 1847, he decided against acting as "a partisan governor." He intended to remain neutral "as regards mere Party contests," and so to ensure the development of what he called "constitutional government" in Canada, a system that would function according to established conventions.

Later that year, when the Reform Party won the election, Elgin broke from the traditional practice of merely adding a few new ministers to the existing cabinet. Instead, he invited Louis-Hippolyte LaFontaine, leader of the largest block of Reformers, to organize a government.

Elgin was deliberately stepping back and, for the first time, placing power in the hands of the elected party. While retaining a voice in defence and foreign relations, he was relinquishing control of most levers of power, including patronage appointments. The new Reform ministry, which took office in March 1848, faced a number of problems, including the recent famine migration, termed Black '47, that had brought 70,000 immigrants from Ireland. Also, Louis-Joseph Papineau, a leader of the 1837 Rebellion in Lower Canada, had returned from exile in France and was denouncing responsible government as a sham.

Papineau was threatening to regain his former influence when Elgin got an opportunity to demonstrate that responsible government was no sham, later that year. Quelling the two rebellions had resulted in considerable property damage. In Canada West, property owners had already been indemnified. Now, LaFontaine and his Reform allies, led by Robert Baldwin, passed the Rebellion Losses Bill, which mandated similar reimbursements in Canada East.

The Tories, led by Sir Allan Napier MacNab, denounced the "paying of rebels" and urged the governor general to follow the usual practice and refer the controversial legislation to the imperial government. Elgin himself detested the bill, but he had resolved to establish responsible government in these colonies. This was a local matter to be decided locally, and the elected legislature had rendered its majority verdict.

On April 25, 1849, in Montreal, Lord Elgin acted on principle. He drove down to the House of Assembly and, as representative of the British monarch, gave royal assent to the Rebellion Losses Bill. The gallery was packed with spectators. They rushed outside and, when Elgin emerged, pelted him with rocks and garbage. He managed to get into his enclosed carriage and drive off.

Since 1831, English speakers had formed a majority in Montreal. Evening brought about 1,500 of them into the streets. They broke into the House of Assembly and vandalized it, taking an axe to the throne and stealing the mace. When fire broke out as a result of smashed lighting-gas mains, they surrounded the House, hooting and hollering, and prevented firefighters from saving it.

Elgin remained unfazed. One month later, when he returned to meet the parliament, a mob welcomed him with more shouted abuse and more stones—one of which, a two-pounder, he took away in his carriage. He responded with restraint, and by October, had guided the protests into more peaceful channels. Tory Montrealers, still denouncing "French domination," produced an Annexation Manifesto advocating economic and political union with the United States. The result was that legislators declared Montreal unfit to be the seat of government and began the process of moving the parliament to Ottawa.

By 1850, the furore had ended. Much later, historian W. L. Morton summarized succinctly: "Responsible government and all it implied—French Canadians in office, British, not American conventions of government, efficiency in public finance and the civil service, local decision-making and local control of patronage—had been tested in the fires of riot and the threat of annexation."

Having arrived in the aftermath of the 1837 Rebellions, and when William Lyon Mackenzie was an ebbing force in Canada West, Lord Elgin left Canada in 1854, just as John A. Macdonald was emerging from the political shadows to serve as attorney general in a coalition government.

In the judgment of the St. Andrew's Society of Toronto, which welcomed him as an honorary member, Elgin's principled stand against the threatening Montreal mob was a turning point that "established firmly and finally the principle that the government of Canada was responsible to the representatives of the Canadian people." Yet nothing he ever did, we read in the society's *One Hundred Years of History,* "entitles him to greater gratitude from the Canadian people than his courageous and far-sighted stand at the time of the burning of the Parliament Buildings in Montreal." The system of responsible government Elgin introduced served Canada for nearly two decades. In 1864, it culminated in the political deadlock that, once broken, inspired Confederation.

What does it all mean? William Lyon Mackenzie, remembered in Toronto at Mackenzie House, shattered the illusion that these settler-colonies could be governed from afar. Lord Elgin, commemorated in Ottawa by Elgin Street and the Lord Elgin Hotel, showed that to remain viable the colonies had to be governed by elected representatives responsible to the people. And John A. Macdonald, whose Kingston family home is now a museum, launched the process that would see Canada become an autonomous country.

8

STEEL RIBBON BLUES

The historic day had dawned dreary and dismal. But as the train rolled west, Donald Alexander Smith later recalled, "we soon got out into the open country, and presently it was one of those bright, pleasant, bracing days of the autumn summer." Smith, a driving force in creating the railway he was on, had boarded the train eleven days before in Montreal. Rainy weather had caused delays. But now, on Saturday, November 7, 1885, Smith was rattling through the Rocky Mountains to drive home the last spike in the Canadian Pacific Railway—"the great symbolic act," as Pierre Berton would call it, "of Canada's first century."

That act would be captured in a legendary image. For some of those present at Craigellachie, the central figure in the now-famous photo evoked the first wave of Scots who had traversed, explored, and mapped this rugged country, among them Mackenzies, McTavishes, Frasers,

Stuarts, Simpsons, and McLaughlins. Surveyor Sandford Fleming, who made this observation, might have added that Smith himself represented a second wave, one comprising those Scots who had proven crucial to building this extraordinary railway. In fact, Smith was one of three irreplaceable Scots without whom the Canadian Pacific Railway would never have been built.

Donald Smith: All Bets Are Off

Donald Alexander Smith is remembered today as Lord Strathcona, a Scottish-born financier and philanthropist. He gave huge sums of money to McGill University to establish a school for women; with his cousin George Stephen, he donated the funds to set up the Royal Victoria Hospital; and during the Second Boer War (1899–1902), he created a Canadian regiment, Lord Strathcona's Horse. But his greatest achievement, because it unified the country when it might have fallen apart, emerged directly out of his long career with the Hudson's Bay Company.

Born in the town of Forres on the northeast coast of Scotland in 1820, Donald Smith grew up hearing stories of his mother's brother, John Stuart, a veteran fur trader regarded by George Simpson as "the father or founder of New Caledonia [northern B.C.]." Stuart had spent twenty years dealing with "all the misery and privation which that inhospitable region could bring forth," and had also canoed down the Fraser River with the explorer who gave it his name.

At age seventeen, enchanted by these tales, and after apprenticing with the Forres town clerk, Smith wangled passage to Montreal. He called on Simpson, governor of the HBC, who had an opening in the company's eastern district. In spring 1838, after serving briefly at the headquarters in Lachine, Smith joined the HBC post at Tadoussac, on the north shore of the St. Lawrence River some 125 miles (200 km) northeast of Quebec City.

So began an affiliation that would last seventy-five years.

After five years at Tadoussac, Smith took charge of Mingan, the HBC territory that extended east to the Labrador coast. In 1846, the Mingan post burned down, and Smith hurt his eyes in the blaze. The following year, not yet fully healed, he travelled to Montreal to seek treatment, thinking also to tender his resignation. George Simpson convinced him to renew his contract, but almost immediately, and despite severe weather conditions, ordered him to return to his post. Later, when people said they would have told Simpson what he could do with his contract, Smith remarked, "I too felt like that for a moment. Then I said to myself, 'If Governor Simpson can bring himself to give such an order as that, I can bring myself to carry it out.' And I went."

By 1853, while based at Rigolet on the Atlantic coast, Smith had gained promotion to chief trader. Also, he had married, *à la façon du pays*, Isabella Hardisty, whose mother was half Scottish and half Cree. This enduring marriage would foster in Smith a tolerance for cultural differences that was far ahead of its time. "I am a Presbyterian because I was born one," he would write. "I was born in a Presbyterian environment. Suppose, however, I had been born in India—I would have been a Hindu or a Mohammedan. A mere accident you see. Should this consideration not make us tolerant of those who differ from us, seeing that it is simply accident, birth and environment which make up what we are?"

During the 1850s, in an area regarded by most as inhospitable, Smith created a flourishing farm. In 1860, a visitor from the Smithsonian Institution in Washington turned up to view an eclipse. On arrival, he reported, "the astonished ear is greeted with the lowing of cattle and the bleating of sheep on shore; and in the rear of the agent's house are veritable barns, from whose open windows hangs fragrant new-mown hay; and a noisy cackle within is ominous of fresh-laid eggs. Surely Nature has been remarkably lavish here, or some presiding genius, of no ordinary enterprise and taste, has redeemed the place from its wilderness desolation!"

Later that same year, Arctic explorer Leopold McClintock visited while taking soundings for a transatlantic cable. He described Smith as "about forty years old, some five feet ten inches high, with long sandy hair, a bushy red beard, and very thick red eyebrows. He was dressed in a black swallowtail coat, not at all according to the fashion of the country, and wore a white linen shirt. Although the Factor's countenance could hardly be called handsome, it was distinguished, and his manners were irreproachable. His talk showed him to be a man of superior intelligence." Smith invited McClintock into the parlour, which the explorer described as "very well, even tastefully, furnished. There were several pictures on the wall, prominent amongst them a large engraving of the coronation of Queen Victoria."

When McClintock visited, Smith was not yet a chief factor—though he became one in 1862. By then he had shown himself to be such a shrewd investor that other HBC men relied on him to manage their unspent earnings. Smith kept an eye out

Donald Alexander Smith survived the tyranny of fellow Scot George Simpson to become a driving force in the creation of the Canadian Pacific Railway.

for opportunities, and in 1865, while visiting Montreal on company business, Smith paid a surprise visit to George Stephen, a businessman cousin he had never met (son of his father's sister, Elspeth Smith).

This meeting proved serendipitous. Soon the cousins were sharing in a profitable sideline, with Smith selling Stephen-made woollens to the HBC. This partnership would thrive and evolve, culminating eventually in the building of the Canadian Pacific Railway.

Now Smith travelled to London, where he impressed newly appointed administrators with his knowledge of HBC operations and opportunities. Most wintering partners, who stayed year round at fur trade outposts, believed settlement to be incompatible with the fur trade. But Smith perceived the potential in land development. In 1868, promoted to commissioner of the Montreal department, he took control of the HBC's eastern operations. That year, too, with George Stephen, Hugh Allan, and other Montreal business leaders, Smith became a partner in the Canada Rolling Stock Company, which leased railway cars.

In 1869, as the two-year-old government of Canada began taking official control of HBC territories in the west, Smith perceived a crisis building. Those opposed to the transfer were rallying behind Métis leader Louis Riel, resisting surveys and demanding compensation for traditional lands they had never relinquished. In November, a worried Smith got George Stephen to introduce him to Prime Minister John A. Macdonald.

While Macdonald hoped that opposition to settlement in the west would wither and fade, Smith argued that he should dispatch a respected "man of business" to quell the simmering insurrection. To Stephen, Macdonald wrote, "I was very glad to see Mr. Smith, who seems a clever man; at the same time I am exceedingly disappointed at the apparent helplessness of the Hudson's Bay authorities."

Smith had suggested sending Stephen westward, but probably knew that his business partner would decline. As expected, Macdonald then made Smith himself a special commissioner and sent him west. At Upper Fort Garry (Winnipeg), Smith used all his influence and negotiating skills—and also a $1,000 bribe authorized by Macdonald—to free three men Riel had jailed. During these discussions, Smith gained ground by noting that he was related to Cuthbert Grant, who several decades before, in 1816, had led the Métis at the battle of Seven Oaks.

In January 1870, Smith conducted tumultuous public meetings during which he reiterated the government promise to recognize land titles and create a territorial council. Not long afterwards, and as he had intended all along, he invited Louis Riel to send a delegation to Ottawa to negotiate terms. Meanwhile, a group of volunteers had organized to overthrow Riel. They were captured and four were sentenced to death. Smith managed to get three of them released. But on March 4, at the last moment, he learned that the fourth, Thomas Scott, was about to be executed. He hurried to Riel and pleaded for clemency, warning that such action would have dire consequences—but to no avail.

Two weeks later, in the midst of a near blizzard, Smith set out eastward with a dog train to report to Macdonald and recommend sending a military force to keep the peace. He hadn't travelled far when, to his utter amazement, he encountered a dog team coming in the opposite direction through the blowing snow. It was driven by James Jerome Hill, a sharp-eyed young colleague of the Hudson's Bay Company agent in Saint Paul, Minnesota.

Darkness was falling and together the men set up camp. All through the evening, they talked—Smith, nearing fifty, an old HBC hand, and Hill, a rugged thirty-two-year-old with an eye for the main chance. The younger man had ventured north to see if the rumoured political unrest might not give rise to business opportunities in transportation. "I liked him then," Smith remembered twenty-five years later, "and I have never had reason to change my opinion."

In 1872, while shuttling between Montreal, Ottawa, and Red River, and acting unofficially for the Conservative government, Smith spent $3,000 in HBC funds to keep Louis Riel out of the country—essentially, another bribe. This quickly became contentious, as HBC directors wanted the money repaid, and Old Tomorrow, as Macdonald was called, waffled while he sought a way to conceal this expenditure in the aftermath of a difficult election.

British Columbia had joined Confederation on July 20, 1871—but only on condition that a railway would be built to unite it with the eastern colonies. Macdonald had promised to build the Canadian Pacific Railway. But during the election of 1872, Macdonald and key allies, notably George-Étienne Cartier, had solicited funds—also in effect bribes—from a group of railway promoters led by Sir Hugh Allan.

Without Macdonald knowing, Allan had advanced funds he had obtained from secret American partners, who believed they would become involved in building the promised railway. This action might have gone undetected, but the Liberal opposition pulled a Watergate-style office break-in. They acquired and publicized damaging letters and cables, creating a political conflagration that came to be called the Pacific Scandal.

In 1873, with a select committee asking embarrassing questions about all this, Macdonald tried and failed to prorogue Parliament. By now, while still directing the HBC, Donald Smith had been elected as a Conservative to both the Manitoba legislature and the federal Parliament. He had become influential enough that, with a crucial vote of confidence looming in the House, his fellow Conservatives implored Smith to meet privately with the prime minister.

As requested, Smith called on Macdonald. But the prime minister, not surprisingly, had been drinking heavily, and when Smith mentioned the $3,000 Riel bribe still owing to the HBC, the usually unflappable prevaricator lost his temper. Coldly furious, Donald Smith, member of Parliament for Selkirk, turned on his heel and walked out. The next day, with the projected vote too close to call and the Conservatives hoping to retain power, Smith rose to speak in the House of Commons.

When he had finished speaking, Macdonald and his colleagues knew they were done.

"For two days and two nights," the Presbyterian Smith wrote later, "I struggled with myself over the course I should take. On the one hand my admiration for Sir John Macdonald, my grateful sense of his services to the country, my confidence in his ability and statesmanship.

On the other hand was a clear perception of the terrible political mistake which had been committed [the bribery] and the evil effect which it might have on the community. But the chief reflection which led me to vote as I did was that I had been sent into Parliament to represent my constituents, and I soon had ample reason to know how they regarded the affair. I had therefore only one course to take; it was a severe wrench to my personal feelings, but I took that course, let the cost be what it might."

The day after Smith spoke, Macdonald resigned.

In the ensuing election, the Liberals won a majority and took power under yet another Scot, Alexander Mackenzie, who had long been sceptical of building a national railway. Donald Smith crossed the floor to become a Liberal. He and Macdonald ceased speaking to each other. Sir Hugh Allan's clandestine deal to finance the Canadian Pacific Railway with American allies and funds had disappeared into oblivion—and with it, all hope of creating that all-important railway any time soon.

George Stephen: "Stand fast, Craigellachie!"

On the first page of *The Last Spike,* his classic history of the Canadian Pacific Railway, Pierre Berton wrote that "George Stephen ought to have been driving the final spike" instead of Donald Smith. He added that Stephen was nowhere near Craigellachie, however, but rather 8,000 miles (12,875 km) away in London, "resting briefly after his four-year battle to keep the railway solvent." Stephen would never have got involved with the CPR if Donald Smith, his first cousin, had not introduced him to James Jerome Hill. Yet nobody can doubt that this Scottish financial wizard played a crucial role in making the railway a reality.

Born in 1829 in Banffshire, the son of a carpenter and a crofter's daughter, Stephen moved to Dufftown as an infant. He attended the local parish school to age fourteen and then worked for four years in Aberdeen as an apprentice to a silk merchant. In 1850, after spending two years in London with a dry-goods firm, Stephen followed his father and sister to Montreal. He worked with an older cousin, an importer of dry goods, and soon became chief buyer.

As such, he began showing the acumen and daring that would make him the foremost businessman of his time and place. When his cousin died in 1862, George Stephen took control of the business. Within two years, he had been elected to the Montreal Board of Trade. In 1866, he established George Stephen and Company, which made and sold woollens and other cloths. He also began investing in other ventures, like a brother's tweed mill in Upper Canada.

The previous year, on meeting his cousin Donald Smith, he had recognized a kindred spirit. By the late 1860s, with the backing of Smith, who invested for both himself and other HBC men, Stephen had become one of Montreal's leading financiers, with interests in life insurance and the manufacturing of nails, iron bars, and cotton. In 1870, having formed the Canada Rolling Stock Company, Stephen found himself analyzing proposals to build a railway line to Fort Garry (Winnipeg)—an idea he judged premature.

George Stephen didn't catch the railway bug until later that decade, after Donald Smith introduced him to James Jerome Hill. An American born in Rockwood, Upper Canada, of Ulster Scottish parents, Hill ran a profitable steamboat line on the Red River between Minnesota and present-day Manitoba. In November 1871, Hill had sent Smith a letter outlining a brilliant plan to amalgamate shipping on the Red River, where a paddle-wheeler owned by the HBC was competing with an American steamboat. Not long afterwards, while passing through St. Paul, Smith had conferred with the younger man.

They had drafted a confidential agreement and the Red River Transportation Company was born—an instantly profitable monopoly.

Obsessed with elaborating a grand transportation system involving railways and steamboats, Hill was garrulous, practical, and detail-oriented. George Stephen, in contrast, was a sophisticated, courtly individual, elegant and flawlessly tailored, who was emerging as the savviest businessman in Canada. And he thought of Minnesota, Donald Smith claimed, "as many others did, that it was at the North Pole somewhere."

Yet Stephen was also a visionary. And in 1877, Smith convinced him and his right-hand man, Richard Angus, to take a short ride on Hill's unfinished railway line, operated by the Red River Transportation Company. On September 1, as the businessmen rolled out over the hot, dusty prairie, Stephen remained unimpressed. But when the train reached a small town called De Graff, where he saw scores of settlers heading out in wagons and Red River carts to attend mass, he grew curious.

Hill explained that a churchman had been "planting colonies" and had brought these colonists from Ireland the previous year. George Stephen the visionary needed no more convincing: in a flash, he realized that colonization would turn this incomplete railway line into a goldmine. According to Donald Smith, Stephen and his senior aides "were looked upon at home as sober, serious men, but when they returned from the West, they were almost beside themselves, and advised everyone to 'go west.'"

Back in Montreal, Stephen set up one of the most profitable partnerships in railway history. Besides himself, Smith, and Hill, it included Norman Wolfred Kittson, Hill's steamboat partner—the son of a Scottish fur trader and a Métis woman—and John Stewart Kennedy, a Scotland-born New York investment banker. These five purchased Hill's existing line for $5.5 million in cash and bonds, and renamed it the St. Paul, Minneapolis and Manitoba Railroad, installing Stephen as president.

The deal proved controversial, with critics charging that Stephen had used his position as president of the Bank of Montreal to obtain loans on special terms. Scorning these "ink-slingers," Stephen and his partners transformed the St. Paul–Manitoba railroad into a money-making machine. Eventually, Hill would develop this line into the Great Northern Railroad and turn it into a transcontinental network.

By 1880, with St. Paul–Manitoba railway profits rolling in, John A. Macdonald back in office, and the Pacific Scandal of 1873 a distant memory, George Stephen began negotiating for the contract to build the Canadian Pacific Railway, which, except for a short section in British Columbia, reached with gaps only as far west as Winnipeg. Using yet another Scottish businessman as a front man, Duncan McIntyre of the Canada Central Railway, he secured an extraordinary deal in October 1880.

To build the CPR, Stephen's Scottish Canadian syndicate would receive $25 million in cash, 25 million acres of land west of Winnipeg, and more than 700 miles (1,100 km) of finished railway lines. Stephen also won concessions on taxes and duties, and a twenty-year prohibition on railway lines south of the CPR line in western Canada.

Besides Stephen and McIntyre, syndicate signatories included Angus, Hill, and Kennedy. Donald Smith remained a major stakeholder, but because he was in London at the time of signing, and also because he and Macdonald were still not speaking, Stephen left his name off the contract. Smith was outraged. He viewed the building of the CPR as the most important national undertaking since Confederation, and to remain invisible? He made his fury known.

"I have had a terrible bother with D. Smith," Stephen wrote to a close colleague, "because his name is not printed in the papers submitted to the House. It was not necessary to have it then . . . and I thought we were doing him a good turn by keeping him out. He has been like a baby over the thing." To Macdonald, he wrote, "He is excited almost to a craze and so troublesome that I do not care if he does withdraw, though his money and cooperation would be useful, so would his knowledge of and influence in the Nor West."

In February 1881, when George Stephen became president of the newly incorporated Canadian Pacific Railway, he resigned from the board of the Bank of Montreal. By November, he could see that the CPR was "assuming dimensions far beyond my calculations." To handle the workload, he withdrew from managing the St. Paul–Manitoba railway and recalled Richard Angus, its vice-president, to assist him. Acting on the advice of James Jerome Hill, he hired the hard-driving William Cornelius Van Horne as construction manager—an important addition.

At the same time, despite Hill's urgings, Stephen refused to cut costs by abandoning plans to send the railway north around Lake Superior. He saw that a more southerly route would connect with American railways, and so prove cheaper. But it would also turn Canada's national railway into a feeder line, a prospect that, influenced by Macdonald, he had come to view with distaste. Partly as a result, cost overruns created a need for additional funding—a challenge as large as laying track across 2,000 miles (3,200 km) of mountainous, canyon-scarred country.

While estimating total costs at $100 million, Stephen hoped to apply the Manitoba railway model and to finance the building of the CPR from current profits, land sales to settlers, and government loans based on miles of completed track. But speculators drove up land prices and immigrants proved hard to attract, most of them preferring the more settled and established eastern regions. In Ontario and Quebec, Stephen fared better. He acquired complementary railway lines and built extensions between them—expansions that brought the CPR into competition with the American Grand Trunk Railway.

In 1883, having found few investors in London or New York, Stephen had to borrow money using his Manitoba stock and his Montreal mansion as collateral. To meet expenses, he and Smith sold shares in the highly profitable Manitoba railway. In May, realizing that he was competing against himself, James Hill resigned from the CPR board and sold half his shares. Then Kennedy bailed out, making investors still more difficult to attract, and in 1884, McIntyre followed. In March, to maintain share prices, Stephen got the Macdonald government to guarantee the CPR dividends that would become payable later that year.

Then he travelled to Britain to find investors. In Scotland, by pledging bonds owned by himself, Smith, and Angus, he raised roughly a quarter of a million dollars—the equivalent today of around $300 million. And that is why, from Edinburgh, as the deal came together, a jubilant Stephen cabled Smith the rallying cry of their Grant-clan ancestors, with its allusion to the great stone bluff that overlooks the town of Aviemore: "Stand fast, Craigellachie!"

The reduced, three-man syndicate had exhausted all their collateral. Stephen told Macdonald that the CPR could get no more credit abroad, "and the ability of Smith and myself to sustain it is about exhausted." Later, Stephen wrote that what he and Smith had done was "simply absurd on any kind of business grounds. I venture to say there is not a business man in all Canada, knowing the facts, but will say we were a couple of fools for our pains. . . . Personal interests have become quite a secondary affair with either of us."

With work progressing—thousands of workers, hundreds of miles of track—expenses soared. Stephen had to approach the government yet again. In Ottawa, according to one observer, while awaiting a response from Macdonald, Stephen was "a man torn with anguish and remorse whose heart seemed to be breaking with compassion for friends whose downfall he felt himself responsible for." As navvies clamoured to be paid for work they had already done on the railway, and having no money to send them, Stephen came close to what today we would call a nervous breakdown. To Macdonald, he wrote that "it is impossible for me to carry on this struggle." Government waffling had finished him: "I am utterly unfit for further work."

In summer 1884, George Stephen retreated to his home in Montreal.

Macdonald Again: Old Tomorrow Wins Today

"In the whole annals of railway construction," Sir John A. Macdonald told an admiring audience of several hundred, "there has been nothing to equal it." The prime minister was toasting the almost finished Canadian Pacific Railway while celebrating his seventieth birthday at an Ottawa banquet in his honour. Macdonald, of course, was the third irreplaceable figure without whom the CPR would never have been built.

Even as he spoke, on January 12, 1885, the project stood in jeopardy. The previous Friday, George Stephen had wired Macdonald: "Imminent danger of sudden crisis unless we can find means to meet pressing demands. Smaller class creditors getting alarmed about their money. Hope Council will deal today with questions of advancing on supplies." The Privy Council did not immediately act, and within two weeks, CPR stock reached a new low.

Stephen had presented an ingenious scheme to keep the company solvent. He wanted the Macdonald government to guarantee a bond issue. Then, he would use half the cash acquired from the sale of bonds to pay off a loan from the previous year. While admiring the brilliance of the scheme, Macdonald dithered and delayed. To present this plan to Parliament would invite political disaster. Last year, when he had pushed through a government loan, the opposition had warned, "Don't call it a loan. You know we shall never see a penny of this money again."

To return now to the House, cap in hand, would be to invite opposition leader Edward Blake to an eloquent and damaging "I told you so." Macdonald hoped the CPR could stay afloat until the following year. But from Montreal, Stephen responded with a one-word cable: "Impossible." He returned to Ottawa, though to no avail, and not long thereafter, staring bankruptcy in the face, told Donald Smith, "If we fail, [then] you and I, Donald, must not be left with a dollar of personal fortune."

From the outset, fifteen years previously, Macdonald had viewed the Canadian Pacific Railway as a way to unite the emerging dominion and to bring the northwest and British Columbia into the fold. He had believed that the sale of prairie lands could underwrite the cost of building the CPR, and he had battled to keep the project Canadian. If American money entered the equation, American immigrants might insist on following. Four years earlier, Macdonald had convinced Stephen that the line had to run from the Atlantic to the Pacific to reach its full potential. Now Stephen praised his tenacity on this point: "Events have shown you were right and all the rest wrong.".

Stephen had also acted to end the breach between his two closest allies, which had lasted now for more than a decade. Early in 1884, he arranged for Smith to call on Macdonald. The next day, he thanked the prime minister for his cordial reception of Smith, reporting that his partner said nothing, "but I know he *felt* a good deal and I know without saying it that he is today a much happier man. The pluck with which he has stood by me in my efforts to sustain the credit of the CPR made it almost a duty on my part to try and restore friendly relations between one who has stood so courageously by the company in time of trouble and you to whom alone the CPR owes its existence as a *real Canadian* Railway. I hope some day this fact will become more generally known than it is now."

Yet within a couple of months, with costs soaring and stock prices falling, Stephen was warning that the CPR again faced bankruptcy. He told the prime minister that "you must not blame me if I fail. I do not, at the moment, see how we are going to get the money to keep the work going . . . If I find we cannot go on I suppose the only thing to do will be to put in a Receiver. If that has to be done the quicker it is done the better."

By July 1884, Macdonald could tell one of his cabinet members, "I would leave the Govt. tomorrow if it were not that I really think George Stephen would throw up the sponge if I did. He was so worried & sleepless that his wife became alarmed." Stephen did not fret alone. Early in March 1885, his general manager, the irrepressible Cornelius Van Horne, intercepted Macdonald in the lobby of the House of Commons. "Sir John," he said, "we and you are dangling over the brink of Hell."

"Well, Van Horne," Macdonald replied, "I hope it will be delayed a while. I don't want to go just yet."

On March 18, George Stephen submitted yet another brilliant application for a government loan, this time for $5 million. After due consideration, the Privy Council rejected it. Stephen vowed to leave Ottawa and never return. As far as he could tell, the CPR was finished. Clamorous creditors would soon drive it into bankruptcy.

Then, just five days later, newspapers carried the first intimations of an insurrection that would, ironically, give Macdonald the opening for which he had been waiting. By March 27, all Canada knew that rebellion had erupted in the northwest. At a place called Duck Lake, rebels under Métis leader Gabriel Dumont, determined to preserve a traditional way of life based on buffalo hunting, had killed ten soldiers and volunteers, some of them related to prominent figures. They had wounded another thirteen men, two of them mortally.

That day, several militia regiments were ordered west. But how were they to travel? In 1870, during the last bout of unrest, soldiers had taken weeks to reach Red River. But this latest rebellion, unless quickly stifled, would probably spread. If the Canadian soldiers travelled west via the Grand Trunk through the United States, they would have to disarm at the border, pack their rifles and ammunition into boxes, and ride as civilians.

That left only one option: the Canadian Pacific Railway. Troops began piling into passenger cars to rumble west. Within seven days, despite having to march eighty-six miles (138 km) over four stretches of incomplete track, the first troops arrived in Winnipeg. Soon enough, they had quashed the rebellion and arrested its leaders, notably Poundmaker and Louis Riel.

The Northwest Rebellion can still excite controversy. Yet this much is agreed: virtually overnight, Canadians realized that the CPR could serve a national purpose. For Old Tomorrow, as Sir John A. was called, the waiting game had paid off. The political climate had shifted. As one biographer wrote, the CPR had become "a steel ribbon binding the nation together instead of a leech sucking the country's treasury dry." Macdonald immediately asked Parliament to reverse the Privy Council decision and approve the loan Stephen had requested.

A single bit of drama remained. One creditor, owed $400,000, had vowed that, if he were not paid by July 10, he would force the CPR into receivership. The money came due at 3:00 p.m., and the House did not sit until 1:30 p.m. At 2:00 p.m., Macdonald got the vote and the result he needed, and that proved sufficient to satisfy the creditor.

Smith Again: The Last Spike

On arriving at Craigellachie, thirty miles (50 km) west of present-day Revelstoke, Donald Smith and a few other dignitaries alighted from two special cars at the end of the train. Some weeks before, the governor general of Canada, Lord Lansdowne, had started west to perform the ceremonial spike-driving that would signal the unification of a North American nation extending from the Atlantic to the Pacific.

But track-building delays had halted his progress, and a disappointed Lansdowne had been compelled to return to Ottawa to reopen Parliament. In his briefcase he had been carrying a specially made silver spike. As a result, the last spike would be, in the words of the no-nonsense general manager of the CPR, "just as good an iron one as there is between Montreal and Vancouver."

With George Stephen in Great Britain, the honour of driving

Donald Smith, who grew up in Scotland not far from the Rock of Craigellachie, pounds home "the Last Spike" in the Canadian Pacific Railway at Craigellachie, British Columbia.

home the last spike had fallen to Smith. Two days before, with stock prices rising, he had received a welcome cable from London: "Railway now out of danger." Emerging from the parlour car, white-bearded and nattily attired, Smith greeted the motley gathering of CPR workers and engineers with a tip of his top hat. Handed a sledge, and after posing for a first photograph, Smith swung, missed and bent the iron spike. Someone tossed it aside and replaced it, and Smith raised the hammer to try again.

On his second attempt, Donald Smith drove home the iron spike. According to Sandford Fleming, who had surveyed most of the route, "the engineers, the workmen, every one present, appeared deeply impressed by what was taking place. It was felt by all to be the moment of triumph."

That moment would resonate down through the decades. Thanks to the deals cut by a few Scots, suddenly the CPR owned twenty-five million acres of prime prairie land. Because those same Scots were canny businessmen, they hired agents in Europe and began offering potential immigrants package deals that included a voyage to Canada, a train ride across the country, and good farmland waiting at the other end. Tens of thousands of people took them up on this offer, and the CPR became a driving force in the development of western Canada.

9

POLITICAL PERSONS

Where were the women? The immigrant Scotsmen who fathered Confederation and built the Canadian Pacific Railway may have launched Canada as an evolving political entity, but they did not do much for the lasses. Fortunately, because this country could not come of age until women became equal partners within it, the lasses were ready to do for themselves. Here again, those of Scottish heritage led the way.

Through the 1800s, the "cult of domesticity" remained firmly entrenched throughout British North America, especially in farming areas. The colonists believed that woman's god-given role was to become wife, mother, housekeeper, and guardian of morality. Of married women, more than 90 percent remained at home, their lives tied to child rearing and unpaid drudgery. Women risked death every time they gave birth, and infant mortality rates were high.

With little opportunity to gain wide experience and education, women did get together at church. In the later decades of the nineteenth century, as alcoholism became a countrywide scourge, church-based auxiliary groups gave rise to broader-based organizations like the Woman's Christian Temperance Union and the National Council of Women. Initially, these organizations focused on helping needy women and children. Then, they sought to eradicate alcoholism and prostitution in urban areas, while reducing isolation and fostering education in rural ones. Eventually, they sought to reform the state through legislation, launching a decades-long struggle to gain women equal status with men.

Nellie McClung: The Right to Vote

In 1889, four years after Donald Smith drove the last spike of the Canadian Pacific Railway, an ambitious sixteen-year-old farm girl spent five months at a Winnipeg Normal School training to be a teacher. The following year, forty miles (65 km) east, young Nellie Mooney taught all eight grades in a one-room schoolhouse in the town of Hazel. Here she met Annie McClung, wife of the Methodist minister. Nellie later described the older woman as graceful and square-faced, and insisted that she knew from their first meeting that she wanted "to have her as a mother-in-law."

Annie McClung was a strong woman who, as provincial president of the Woman's Christian Temperance Union, led struggles for prohibition and universal suffrage. Her son, Robert Wesley McClung, worked as a pharmacist at the local drugstore. Nellie felt certain that "Mrs McClung's son must be the sort of man I would like. She had all the sweetness, charm and beauty of the old-fashioned woman, and in addition to this had a fearless, and even radical, mind."

By radical, she meant that "her one girl, Nellie, who was my age, did no more than one share of the work; being a girl did not sentence her to all the dishwashing and bedmaking." The pharmacist son never stood a chance. "I made no pretence," Nellie would write, "of being the Victorian maiden who sits on the shore waiting for a kindly tide to wash something up at her feet—not at all! Having seen something that looked like a treasure, I plunged boldly in and swam out for it!"

What's more, Wes McClung assured her that "I would not have to lay aside my ambitions if I married him." In 1896, Nellie did just that. The following year, she gave birth to the first of five children. While raising them to adulthood, Nellie McClung would make her mark as a writer. Not only that, but she would help turn women into "persons" and get them the vote.

Nellie McClung, who came from a long line of strong women, shone as a mother, a bestselling author, and a pioneering women's rights activist.

Nellie McClung came from a long line of strong Scottish women. Her grandmother, Margaret Fullerton McCurdy, was living in Dundee when she lost her husband to a cholera epidemic. In 1857, she packed up two of her three daughters—the eldest had already married—and sailed to Canada, where she settled in Grey County, Ontario, near extended family. Nellie's mother, Letitia McCurdy, was a strict Presbyterian who married John Mooney, an easy-going Irish immigrant twenty years her senior.

Born in 1873 on a hardscrabble farm in Chatsworth, Nellie Letitia Mooney was the youngest of six children. A lively, talented girl, she showed a gift for mimicry, annoying her straitlaced mother by impersonating her two aunts. When Nellie was six, her oldest brother, nineteen-year-old William, after reading glowing newspaper reports about better lands in the west, set off for Manitoba.

Their sixty-seven-year-old father "was less enthusiastic," historian Charlotte Gray writes, "about leaving the 150 acres he had cleared himself." But when William wrote describing the homestead he had staked out on the Souris River, their mother carried the day.

The family packed up and spent days travelling west—first by steamship from Owen Sound to Duluth, Minnesota; then by train to St. Boniface, Manitoba; and finally, for another 130 miles (210 km), in two heavy-laden wagons pulled by oxen, to a spot near present-day Wawanesa in that same province.

After surviving a tough winter in a log cabin with a single window, the family welcomed spring. Later, McClung would recall walking "proudly behind my father in the clean new furrows in my bare feet, as he broke the new sod on our farm. . . . I knew that he was doing something more than just plowing a field. I knew there was a significance in what he was doing, though I had no words to express it."

Within two years of arrival, Nellie's father and brothers had built the family a sturdy house with three bedrooms. Growing up under the wide prairie sky, Nellie learned self-reliance, hard work, and Christian faith, taking a belief in a well-disposed deity from her Methodist father, and strong convictions about right and wrong from her Presbyterian mother.

She learned early to assert her rights, and wanted to know why a brother only four years older had so much more freedom. At a community picnic, to race against boys, she wanted to remove her long skirt and run in her underwear. When her mother refused, she demanded to know why and met "a stone wall . . . that baffled me."

Because of the absence of a nearby school, Nellie did not begin her formal education until she was ten. But already she listened avidly to the adults around her. Later she wrote, "The fires of rebellion in my heart were fanned by the agitation going on now about the railways, and the men at Ottawa giving away our railway rights without consulting the people of Manitoba. . . . It was our country! We were doing the work, but we were powerless! We were the common people! I grew indignant as I read the history and saw how little the people ever counted, and longed for the time when I would be old enough to say something. But my business was to acquire knowledge. Knowledge unlocked doors and gave liberty. I had to plug at these books, snatch every minute I could and let nothing to divert me."

From at least 1892, when she moved into the bustling town of Manitou to teach in a larger school, Nellie dreamed of becoming a writer. After marrying, she began churning out articles, stories, and poems for local newspapers, prompting one editor to tell her, "I have enough on hand for some time."

In 1902, when Nellie had four children underfoot, her mother-in-law drew her attention to a short story contest in *Collier's Weekly* and told her, "If you wait until you are ready to write, you will never write." Nellie submitted a story about a girl named Pearlie Watson, and when it failed to win, she sent it to the editor of the Canadian Methodist Sunday School paper.

Three years later, from Toronto, she received a letter from the editor of a Methodist book publisher, who praised the story's "vitality, humour and originality," and told her to "go ahead with this and make it into a book." Nellie did as suggested, and soon the editor was exclaiming, "I don't know when a story moved me more. . . . And yet, through my tears, I found myself bursting into a chuckle over some of your inimitable touches of humour."

Nellie was thirty-five when that first book, *Sowing Seeds in Danny*, appeared in both Canada and the United States, and quickly became a bestseller in both. By then, the author had published short stories in several magazines, among them *Saturday Night*, the *Canadian Home Journal*, and the *Ladies' Home Journal*.

The highly original Pearlie Watson would dominate two more novels—though she would never really compete with Anne of Green Gables, who appeared for the first time in the same year. Nellie's fiction, as one editor observed, was "too loaded with nineteenth-century sentimentality to hold the attention of a modern reader."

Her later novels, as Charlotte Gray has noted, "often slid into propaganda for one of her causes—Prohibition, women's rights, pacifism, welfare programs." Yet McClung insisted that "a writer must have a vision of a better world if his work is to live." And she produced sixteen books, mostly uplifting tales featuring brave women shaming weak-willed men into behaving better, but also including three acclaimed memoirs.

With sales of 100,000 copies, Nellie McClung's first book proved a massive bestseller. Three years after it appeared, the author used the proceeds to move the family to Winnipeg, by far the largest settlement on the prairies. Within a year, she had helped organize the Political Equality League, and after struggling initially, she became an entertaining platform speaker.

During the 1914 provincial election, McClung led Manitoba premier Rodmond Roblin through Winnipeg sweatshops, showing him the appalling conditions in which some women worked. When he suggested that "nice women" did not want the vote, she told him, "By nice women . . . you probably mean selfish women who have no more thought for the underprivileged, overworked women than a pussycat in a sunny window for the starving kitten in the street."

With colleagues from the Winnipeg Political Equality League and the Canadian Women's Press Club, she staged a play called *The Women's Parliament* that satirized and ridiculed the government position on women's suffrage. Nellie herself played Roblin to uproarious laughter. Roblin won the election anyway—though he soon fell as a result of a scandal involving the construction of the new legislative building.

In 1916, thanks to McClung's campaign, the new Liberal government gave Manitoba women the right to vote in provincial elections. Alberta, British Columbia, and Saskatchewan did the same soon afterwards. Other provinces followed, and in 1918 women (except servicewomen) gained the right to vote in federal elections. Even so, women in Quebec, where Scottish influence had waned, did not achieve the vote until 1940; and across the country, women of Asian and First Nations descent had to wait until after the Second World War.

Also in 1916, McClung and her family had moved to Edmonton. She joined the Edmonton Equal Franchise League and fought for women's rights, prohibition, and factory safety laws. When the First World War broke out, McClung aggressively supported the war effort. In 1921, she was elected to the Alberta legislature, where by championing mothers' allowances, free medical and dental care for children, liberalized birth control, divorce laws, and better property rights for married women, as well as the sterilization of the mentally unfit, she cemented her reputation as a radical.

That November, when the Canadian Authors Association launched the first Canadian Book Week, McClung was guest of honour at a dinner at the Toronto Arts and Letters Club. McClung sat next to Lucy Maud Montgomery, who later, perhaps a bit jealous, professed herself unimpressed: "Nellie is a handsome woman in a stunning dress, glib of tongue. She made a speech full of obvious platitudes and amusing little stories which made everyone laugh and deluded us into thinking it was quite a fine thing—until we began to think it over."

Nellie McClung lost her Alberta seat in 1926, mainly because of her stubborn fight for prohibition. But now she joined a struggle led by Emily Ferguson Murphy to make women eligible to hold seats in the Senate. The existing law allowed women to vote and run for office, but not to become senators because the British North America Act interpreted the word "persons" as referring only to men.

McClung joined Murphy and three other prominent prairie women—

together known as the "Famous Five"—and stumped around the west lobbying to have women recognized as "persons" equal before the law to men. The fight went all the way to the British Privy Council. On October 18, 1929, a British lord, speaking for the Privy Council, declared that under the British North America Act, "the word 'persons' includes members of the male and female sex, and that therefore . . . women are eligible to . . . become members of the Senate of Canada."

Nine years later, on a hot, sticky day in June 1938, a sixty-five-year-old crusader climbed the steps of Ottawa's Parliament Hill and made her way to the Hall of Remembrance. She wore a dark, elegant evening dress belted with a silver buckle, and she greeted the formally dressed Prime Minister William Lyon Mackenzie King, grandson of the Upper Canadian rebel of 1837, in a forthright, friendly manner.

Nellie McClung, the most famous women's rights activist in Canada, had crossed the country by train to attend the placing of a plaque commemorating the "Persons Case." Three of the Famous Five had died, and the fourth had not felt healthy enough to journey from her Alberta farm. So on that historic Ottawa afternoon, in front of 300 people, McClung alone watched proudly as the prime minister unveiled the plaque. King gave a stiff, predictable speech, and then she took the microphone.

Years before, soon after the Privy Council judgment, McClung had written in the *Canadian Home Journal,* "Sex prejudice and the male superiority complex, built up since time began, will not go out in one generation." Taking up this theme, she spoke now of the long struggle women had undertaken to "convince the world they had souls, and then that they had minds"—and then that they had the right to political office.

Aware that much work on behalf of women needed still to be done, if not precisely that a second and then a third wave of what would come to be called feminism would be required, McClung ended by looking to the future: "The end is not yet."

Emily Ferguson Murphy: Janey Canuck

The struggle of Canadian women to be recognized as "persons" under the law, and so as full partners in the national enterprise, did not begin with Nellie McClung. It began with Emily Ferguson Murphy, a feisty, larger-than-life figure whose legacy remains controversial.

Born in Cookstown, Ontario, in 1868, the daughter of a wealthy businessman, Emily Ferguson came from a prominent family of Ulster Scottish immigrants. Her maternal grandfather, Ogle R. Gowan, had founded a local branch of the Orange Order. One uncle was a Supreme Court justice and another was a senator. One of her brothers would also become a member of the Supreme Court.

Emily Ferguson Murphy, a descendant of leading Ulster Scottish immigrants, spearheaded Canadian women's political and legal struggle to be recognized as "persons."

Later in life, she alluded to this background in describing how, while learning to ride and getting bucked off a horse, she decided to get back on and try again: "Yes, I would do it; else where is the use of belonging to the pick of the Scots who fought their way to Canada by the north of Ireland?"

As a young woman, Emily Ferguson attended Bishop Strachan School in Toronto, an elite Anglican private school for girls. At nineteen, lacking any burning desire to become a schoolteacher, and with no other careers available, she married Arthur Murphy, an Anglican priest eleven years older.

Soon they had four daughters. Starting in 1898, the family spent three years in England, and there Emily Ferguson Murphy began writing nostalgic sketches under the pseudonym "Janey Canuck." In 1901, she published her first collection: *The Impressions of Janey Canuck Abroad*. Back in Canada, one of Emily's daughters died of diphtheria. The family sought a change by moving west—first to Swan River, Manitoba, and then, four years later, to Edmonton.

In 1908, at age forty, with her daughters growing up, Emily Ferguson Murphy looked around and saw women living in poverty and isolation. True to the Calvinism in which she had been raised, she began organizing women's groups and giving talks about the socially disadvantaged.

A turning point came when she learned of an Albertan farmer who had sold the family farm, pocketed the proceeds and abandoned his wife and children, leaving them homeless and penniless. About such a case, existing property law said nothing. Outraged, Emily Murphy launched a campaign to assure the property rights of married women. In this, along with her ally Nellie McClung, she proved successful. In 1916, the Alberta legislature passed the Dower Act, which granted a woman legal rights to one-third of her husband's property.

That same year, Murphy and a few friends sought to observe the trial of several women charged with illegal prostitution. They were barred on the grounds that the evidence was not "fit for mixed company." Murphy protested to the provincial attorney general, arguing that if this were true, "then the government must set up a special court presided over by women, to try other women."

Despite the protests of many, the attorney general not only accepted this argument but offered to make Emily Ferguson Murphy a police magistrate for the city of Edmonton. She accepted and, in 1916, became the first female judge in the British Empire.

On the bench, Murphy earned a reputation as stern but compassionate. She preferred rehabilitation to punishment. But political enemies began to argue that she had no right to serve as a magistrate because under the British North America Act—which governed Canada until 1982—women were not recognized as "persons." So began the long struggle to gain legal recognition of women as "persons" eligible to become judges or to be appointed to such bodies as the Canadian Senate.

In 1927, Murphy gained the backing of four other prominent Alberta women, including Nellie McClung. Together, the Famous Five signed a petition to the Supreme Court of Canada. After that court ruled against them, the women could appeal to only one higher authority: the Privy Council in Britain.

On October 18, 1929, the Judicial Committee of the Privy Council unanimously ruled that women were "persons" under the BNA Act. One year later, the fluently bilingual Cairine Mackay Wilson—daughter of a liberal senator born in Caithness, Scotland—became Canada's first female senator.

Today, while recognizing her achievements, most commentators believe that Emily Ferguson Murphy made serious errors of judgment in two areas. First, in a book called *The Black Candle*, which she published as "Judge Emily F. Murphy/Janey Canuck," Murphy encouraged a "war on drugs" mentality that went racial.

She wrote that her concern arose out of her experience in the courtroom, where she had come into "disproportionate contact with Chinese people." Police in Vancouver had taken her on a tour of that city's opium dens. Murphy's writings had a dubious undertone, reached a broad audience, and contributed to the passing of the Chinese Immigration Act of 1923, a racist bill that banned most Chinese immigrants, and which finally inspired a federal government apology in 2006.

Second, Murphy joined the legions who, in the early 1930s, got on the "eugenics" bandwagon. They attributed alcoholism, drug abuse, crime, and other social problems to genetically transmitted defects and deficiencies. And they believed that science and technology had found the answer: selective breeding.

Along with most progressive thinkers, Murphy supported the compulsory sterilization of individuals considered mentally defective. In Alberta, her advocacy helped produce the Sexual Sterilization Act of 1928. Between that date and 1971, when the act was repealed, more than 2,800 people were unknowingly sterilized.

On the negative side of the ledger, then, Emily Ferguson Murphy encouraged racist and reactionary attitudes—though obviously these would have gained ascendancy without her. On the positive side, she led a transformative advance in the status of women. And in that struggle, she played a galvanizing role.

Agnes Macphail: Into the Commons

Canada's first female member of Parliament, Agnes Macphail, experienced a life-changing moment when she visited the church frequented by her ancestors in Kilmartin, Scotland.

As an adult, after visiting Scotland, she would change the way she spelled her surname. But she was born Agnes Campbell McPhail in 1890 on a small Ontario farm in Grey County, southwest of Georgian Bay, a region settled by Scottish immigrants. With her two younger sisters, she grew up in a log house that was cold and dark in winter, though "the kitchen was big and attractive, and we children loved it."

When Agnes was twelve, the family moved to a larger farm with a brick farmhouse in nearby Artemesia. As a girl, she preferred tending animals to housework, and talk of politics and current affairs to that of domestic events. This was a period when women were expected to stay at home, but Agnes resolved early that she would make a contribution "in addition [to], or in place of, having children." She wanted to do "some work as a person."

She especially admired her maternal grandmother, Jean Black, a progressive thinker, Agnes wrote later, who had enjoyed "few worldly advantages." She described her thrifty, hard-working mother, Henrietta Campbell, as having had "the sterling quality of standing by her beliefs no matter what the cost." From her father, Dugald McPhail, a sociable man who never realized his potential, she felt she had gleaned wit and insight: "Perhaps if I owed him the ability to get into Parliament," Macphail wrote, "I owed her the ability to stand it when I got there."

At fourteen, having gone to grade school in one-room schoolhouses, Agnes McPhail passed her high school entrance exam and looked forward to becoming a teacher. But further education would require moving away, and because of her youth, her parents kept her at home. At sixteen, away she went to Owen Sound Collegiate Institute, where she excelled. Two years later, she enrolled at the Normal School for teachers in Stratford, Ontario, where she roomed with an aunt and uncle.

After graduating in 1910, the twenty-year-old began teaching in one-room schoolhouses in western Ontario, first near Port Elgin, then at Kinloss, southwest of Walkerton. At Kinloss, when farmers gathered to talk politics at the local hardware store, she began voicing political opinions—and began to think of entering politics. After spending a few months in Alberta, she returned to Ontario and took a teaching position at Pegg's School near Sharon, thirty-five miles (55 km) north of Toronto.

As she neared thirty, McPhail became politically active. Still working as a teacher, she joined the United Farm Women of Ontario and began attending meetings of the United Farmers of Ontario. She also began writing a column for the *Farmers' Sun,* where her education enabled her to voice pro-farmer positions on contemporary issues. She opposed tariffs, which benefited industry at the expense of farmers, and she fought forced recruitment or conscription into the armed forces.

In 1921, for the first time, and after a long struggle led by Nellie McClung and others, Canadian women would be allowed to vote in a federal election. Despite the misgivings of friends and even family, Agnes McPhail decided to run for the joint United Farmer–Independent Labour nomination to represent South-East Grey County.

Two dozen candidates sought this opportunity. Well known as a result of her newspaper column, McPhail gained enough support among farmers that she carried the day. A backlash arose and the party asked her to resign, but she refused. Now came the election campaign. Battling an incumbent, McPhail toured the countryside in her broken-down old car, and was forced to finish more than one outing by walking to her destination. Her hard work paid off, and on December 6, 1921, the farmers of Grey County elected Agnes McPhail to be Canada's first female member of Parliament.

When first she entered the House of Commons, in March 1922, McPhail found a bouquet of roses on her desk. Initially delighted with this welcoming gesture, she soon learned that the roses had been sent to pay off a bet. The MP who sent them had bet she would lose the election.

"These ironical roses," she later told a Montreal *Gazette* reporter, "were emblematic of my reception to a House hitherto sacred to me. I was intensely unhappy. Some of the members resented my intrusion. Others jeered at me. Everything I said was wrong, everything I wore was wrong, everything I did was wrong. . . . The men did not want me in Parliament and the women had not put me there."

After the House recessed, Agnes McPhail sailed to Glasgow, journeyed west to the town of Oban, and then travelled south to the village of Kilmartin in Argyll. "Progress has passed it by," she wrote later, in a family history called *My Ain Folk*. "The little stone church is still lit by the great hanging sconces of oil lamps. A quarter of the gravestones are moss-grown and scoured . . . to illegibility. But inside the building the brass plaques commemorating the famous dead are kept gleaming, and the stained-glass windows throw rainbows on the pavement."

She continued, "My Macphail ancestors came from Kilmartin, and standing in the doorway which they must so often have entered, I thought how like the church is the family tradition. No one generation built that church or gave all that stained glass or put up all those plaques. But each had its part in something which by its very age and continuity became more than the sum of all of them."

This awareness hit with the force of revelation. And soon after she got back to Canada, the thirty-two-year-old member of Parliament expressed her sense of continuity with her Scottish forebears by changing the spelling of her surname to accord with the way they had spelled it: from McPhail to Macphail.

Agnes Macphail would spend twenty years as a politician, even though, as she said, people pointed her out in crowds as a woman in politics, often making her feel like a bearded lady in a circus sideshow. She was called "mannish" and ridiculed as a spinster schoolmarm in sensible shoes and horn-rimmed glasses. When Agnes Macphail spoke, however, people felt compelled to listen. A *Toronto Telegram* reporter once wrote that her voice "had the quality of a viola, deep and compassionate and heart-catching." When she stood up "to denounce injustice or deride pettiness from her place in the Commons of Canada, [she] spoke in tones that echo unforgotten across the years."

Macphail championed farm and labour issues, but also peace activism and prison reform. She battled the subjugation of women, and fought to award pensions to the old, the blind, the disabled, and the unemployed. She also founded the Canadian branch of the Elizabeth

Fry Society, which assisted women recently released from prison.

During the 1920s, she attended several international peace confer-ences and became one of the first female delegates to the League of Nations. Through the 1930s, with the Second World War looming, Macphail took a pacifist position, urging Canada to remain neutral.

In 1940, when a blizzard prevented rural voters from reaching polling booths, Macphail lost her seat in the federal House. Three years later, having supported herself mainly by writing an agricultural column in the *Globe,* she ran in the Ontario election for the Co-operative Com-monwealth Federation (CCF), forerunner of the NDP. She won and so became one of the first two women to serve in the Ontario legislature. In 1951, she introduced the province's first equal-pay legislation. Later that year, she lost her seat.

In 1954, after visiting Scotland for the second time, and just as she was about to be appointed to the Canadian Senate, Agnes Macphail died of a heart attack. Fortunately, she had done her work. With Agnes Macphail, Canadian women became fully functioning members of the political process.

10

BANKERS AND EDUCATORS

Late in 2008, when the global financial crisis hit the headlines, banks were collapsing in countries around the world. In the United States, twenty-five banks had failed by the end of the year. This compared with three in 2007, and none in the two years before that. The United States has over 8,000 banks, so the percentage remained small. But in 2009, the number of bank failures in the United States skyrocketed to 140, and only government action halted the trend.

As a result of the American-centred crisis, and because Canada does so much trade with the United States, this country entered a recession. Yet here not a single bank failed. Indeed, the World Economic Forum declared the Canadian banking system the soundest in the world. That system was built by nineteenth-century Scots. It flourished because the fathers of Confederation, the majority of them Scots, insisted that banking was a national concern, not a provincial one—a judgment that encouraged the emergence of large banks with many branches.

By the end of the nineteenth century, building on the successes of the Hudson's Bay Company and the Canadian Pacific Railway, Scottish immigrants had invented a British colony that extended from the Atlantic to the Pacific. Within that countrywide framework, they had also begun creating most of the networks any modern society needs: educational, social, communication, and financial.

If there was a blueprint for Canada's financial institutions, historian Duncan McDowall tells us, "it was drawn up in Scotland." In *Quick to the Frontier: Canada's Royal Bank,* McDowall describes how, early in the nineteenth century, stimulated by the Industrial Revolution, Scottish businessmen began displaying remarkable initiative. By 1810, merchants had created the "joint-stock bank," which promoted stability by sharing ownership and developing branches.

Despite setbacks and failures, Scottish bankers then introduced a uniform Canadian currency while steadily expanding westward. By the 1850s, they had reached a consensus on common procedures. By 1900, the major banks they built in Canada had become so large, cautious, and strictly managed that, according to McDowall, "none was ever threatened with liquidity problems."

Scottish bankers built their branch-banking system on a foundation of standardized procedures and staffing. Working from centralized head offices, they introduced clearing houses, overdrafts, limited liability for shareholders, and internal inspections. They became sticklers for on-the-job training, precise job descriptions, and hierarchies.

At the top stood the "cashier" or general manager, who evolved by century's end into a chief strategist. Theoretically responsible to a chairman and board of directors, he was in reality all-powerful, like the captain of a ship at sea. Beneath him came an all-male head-office staff: accountant, inspectors, secretary, and clerk trainees, and also a superintendent of branches responsible for branch managers, tellers, and clerks.

This Scottish system offered job security and steady advancement. While it also brought low pay, little prestige, and stiff discipline, it was expressly designed to build character: accuracy, honesty, and loyalty. Certainly it worked well enough that Canadian banks not only used it but imported Scottish bank clerks until well into the twentieth century, on the grounds that they brought an attitude of frugality and industry.

Often, in the past, they brought those qualities first to Montreal, where on the southern slopes of Mount Royal—an area dominated today by McGill University—Scottish immigrants built a "Golden Square Mile" of spectacular mansions. The richest men in Canada, financiers who controlled two-thirds of the nation's wealth, lived in these splendiferous castles—among them Simon McTavish, Hugh Allan, George Stephen, Donald Smith, and James McGill.

In *The Square Mile: Merchant Princes of Montreal,* historian Donald MacKay writes that the Canadian millionaire was almost invariably "a Scottish Presbyterian who had left school at the legal age of fourteen, apprenticed himself to a business house, invested in new railways and shipping, and served on the board of the Bank of Montreal, which became something of a finishing school for commercial talent." MacKay exaggerates for effect. Yet he is not far wrong when he writes that the nineteenth-century figure most "archetypical of the Scots who dominated Montreal commerce"—and so that of Canada as a whole—was a man who spent more than two decades as president of the Bank of Montreal.

Peter McCutcheon McGill: Old Country Principles

In 1809, an ambitious twenty-year-old named Peter McCutcheon arrived in Montreal from Scotland. He got a job in the fur trade, branched out into exporting timber and grain, bought real estate, and entered politics. Eventually, he would be mayor of Montreal, a member of the legislative assembly, president of the board of trade, a governor of the Montreal General Hospital, and a founder of the city's St. Andrew's Society.

Peter McCutcheon McGill was one of the early Scots who shaped the Canadian banking system.

But most significantly of all, for twenty-six years this Scottish immigrant would preside as president over the Bank of Montreal. He was a hands-on business-man who applied financial principles developed in Auld Scotia to create the Canadian banking system—the very system that the World Economic Forum recently declared the best in the world.

Peter McCutcheon was born in 1789 in Creebridge, southwest Scotland, and arrived in Montreal as an ambitious nineteen-year-old. After serving an apprenticeship with a mercantile firm called Parker, Gerrard, Ogilvy and Company, he became a junior partner in an importing concern. Then, in 1820, he moved into the timber trade as it entered a boom period.

He changed his surname the following year to honour an uncle, John McGill, who was assisting his career. Probably, following a practice that was not unusual at the time, the older McGill found himself with no heir to carry on his name and offered his nephew a bequest to make the change. The young man had a head for figures. By 1823, he was running Peter McGill and Company, an increasingly diversified and profitable concern.

For four years beginning in 1825, when the first worldwide crash of capitalism occurred, McGill served frequently as a trustee in bankruptcy proceedings—public recognition of his financial expertise. As profits from both importing and the wood trade grew, McGill began buying real estate, starting with the firm's two-storey stone headquarters next door to the Bonsecours Market in what is now called Old Montreal.

As early as 1819, McGill had become a member of the board of directors of the Bank of Montreal, which had been founded just two years before. As an emerging business leader, McGill was elected vice-president in 1830 and president in 1834. In that capacity, essentially chairman of the board of the most important financial institution in the colonies, McGill served for more than a quarter-century.

In the 1840s, the Bank of Montreal expanded by building branches in Upper Canada. Because Peter McGill did not guide the necessary amendments through the legislative assembly, some historians have wondered how large a role he played in this crucial development. But it is hard to see how, without his support as president, the initiative could have gone forward. Thanks to Peter McGill and men like him, Canadian bankers rejected the model provided by the older colonies to the south, which featured a multitude of small, privately owned banks. Instead, they chose the Scottish model, and built a system comprising a few national banks with branches from coast to coast.

James McGill: From Glasgow to Glory

As it was with the banks, so it was with the universities. Across the country, almost without exception, Canadian universities share a Scottish heritage. In Atlantic Canada, the University of New Brunswick evolved out of the Academy of Arts and Science, founded in Fredericton in 1785 and expressly modelled on the early Scottish universities of Edinburgh and St. Andrews. In Nova Scotia, George Ramsay, the Scottish Earl of Dalhousie, founded Dalhousie University in 1818 while serving as the province's lieutenant governor.

In 1841, the Church of Scotland established Queen's College in Kingston, modelling it after the University of Edinburgh, with its traditions of academic freedom, authority, and moral responsibility. While evolving into a university, Queen's became the first degree-granting institution in the United Province of Canada, and the first west of the Maritimes to admit women.

On the prairies, Alexander Cameron Rutherford—the Ontario-born son of Scottish immigrants—established the University of Alberta. That institution spawned the University of Calgary, which takes its name from a gorgeous bay on the Scottish Isle of Mull. In Vancouver, Simon Fraser University celebrates a Scottish explorer we have already encountered. And the University of British Columbia evolved out of a relationship with McGill University, which was founded by James McGill.

In 1809, when twenty-year-old Peter McCutcheon arrived in Montreal, James McGill was already a leading citizen—a wealthy sixty-five-year-old contemplating a decision that would shape the future of higher education in Canada. McGill had lost three siblings in the past dozen years. In January 1811, he drew up a last will and testament leaving £10,000 and a centrally located, forty-six-acre estate for the creation of a college or a university that would bear his name.

McGill's early years remain obscure. Born in Glasgow in 1744 to a family originally from Robbie Burns country, the precocious McGill matriculated into the University of Glasgow at age twelve. He might conceivably have been among the British soldiers who fought and won the battle of the Plains of Abraham in 1759—a pivotal event in the making of Canada. More likely, because he was just fifteen then, he arrived in the early 1760s as part of a surge of Scottish settlement that followed the Conquest.

In 1766, certainly, he was travelling from Montreal to the *pays d'en haut* as deputy to William Grant, a Highland Scot of his own age who was emerging as a leading Quebec merchant. In the fur-trade

McGill University owes its existence to philanthropist James McGill, who made his home a Loyalist rendezvous during the 1776 American occupation of Montreal.

hinterland of the Great Lakes, McGill began trading on his own account. By 1775, he was residing in Montreal, and that November, when American forces invaded during the Revolutionary War, he negotiated the capitulation of the city. During the ensuing occupation, his house became a Loyalist rendezvous, and the following May, British reinforcements drove off the Americans.

That December, McGill married the widow Charlotte Desrivières, acquiring two sons and an extended family. He fathered a third son and for the rest of his life remained solicitous of all three. Also in 1776, at thirty-three, McGill became a justice of the peace, the first of ten public appointments. The previous year, with several partners, he had sent a dozen canoes to Grand Portage with a shipment that, according to historian Harold Adams Innis, "appears to mark the beginning of large-scale trade to the Northwest . . . and of the Northwest Company."

By 1779, McGill was one of the largest shareholders in the North West Company, though he soon dropped out to function independently. Through the 1780s and '90s, while continuing to import and export, McGill acquired considerable real estate in Lower Canada. In 1801, he began buying land more methodically: 10,000 acres northeast of Montreal, 32,400 acres southeast of the city, and smaller parcels in Upper Canada near Kingston and York. In 1803, Lord Selkirk observed that while McGill had withdrawn from the fur trade, he remained active in "the ordinary Colonial trade."

A decade before that, the fluently bilingual McGill had been elected a member of the newly created Legislative Assembly of Lower Canada. He did not stand in the next election, but served two more terms (eight years in total) beginning in 1800. In 1810, he became the senior militia officer in Montreal, and was serving as such in 1812, when again the Americans and the British went to war. In the midst of that conflagration, in December 1813, he died suddenly, either of a stroke or a heart attack, having had, according to one contemporary, "no idea of going off half an hour [before] he died."

Still, McGill did not die unprepared. Two years before, he had written a will detailing bequests to family members, old friends, the Montreal poor, several local hospitals, and two Glasgow charities. He also gave to churches of various denominations: Anglican, Roman Catholic, and Presbyterian. Most significantly, he left both land and money to establish a college or university. A businessman of foresight, he stipulated that the Royal Institution for the Advancement of Learning, the provincial agency responsible for education, had to open the college on site before the bequest became operative.

Formally established in 1821, McGill College began holding classes eight years later in what had once been James McGill's country house. The college awarded its first degree in 1833, and then began construction of an arts building. Starting in 1855, principal John William Dawson—a Nova Scotia Scot who had completed his education in Edinburgh—turned the college into a university with the financial aid of those who lived in the Golden Square Mile around McGill. Mostly Scots, these donors left their names on various university buildings: the Redpath Museum, the Macdonald Physics Building, the Strathcona Medical Building, and so on. McGill became a university in 1885.

The previous year, Lord Strathcona—Donald Smith of the last spike—had started funding separate classes for women. McGill granted its first degrees to females in 1888, and the next year, thanks again to

Along with golf, which they began playing in the twelfth century, the Scots brought curling to Canada. Curling Match, Montreal (1855), by artist W. S. Hatton, depicts the Royal Montreal Curling Club in action beneath the Union Jack on the frozen St. Lawrence River. Modest Mount Royal is visible in the middle distance.

Smith, it opened Royal Victoria College as a residential college for women. Until the 1970s, all female undergraduates were called "Donaldas" and considered members of that college.

Other Scots kept the institution growing: first came the McLennan Travelling Library in 1900, and then, in 1905, a second campus west of the city: Macdonald College. Meanwhile, in 1903, McGill had established Victoria College, the first post-secondary institution in British Columbia, and the precursor to the University of Victoria. In 1908, it spawned the McGill University College of British Columbia in Vancouver, which granted McGill degrees until 1915, when it became independent as the University of British Columbia.

Today, McGill is recognized around the world as a leading university. Its twenty-one faculties and professional schools offer more than 300 programs to 30,000 students at the undergraduate and graduate levels. The main language of instruction is English, though students have been allowed to write graduation theses in French since as early as 1935. Of the student population, 57 percent come from Quebec, 24 percent from elsewhere in Canada, and 19 percent from 160 different countries. The mother tongue breakdown is 53 percent English, 18 percent French, and 29 percent other.

The progressive, outward-looking James McGill would have approved.

John Strachan: Alias John Toronto

Early in 1807, an ambitious Scottish immigrant who had founded a grammar school in Cornwall, seventy miles (110 km) west of Montreal, entered the family circle of the aging James McGill by marrying the widow of his late brother. Twenty-nine-year-old John Strachan almost certainly persuaded McGill to establish a university in Montreal, arguing that by doing so, he would extend his name far into the future. To ensure that this purpose would be served, McGill made Strachan one of the four trustees of his will.

Less than two decades later, Strachan would take a far more prominent role in establishing a different university—not in Montreal but in muddy York, 340 miles (550 km) to the west. By that time, he would be residing in a grand, two-storey edifice on Front Street popularly called "The Palace," and signing official letters as "John Toronto."

Born in Aberdeen in 1778, the youngest son of an overseer in a granite quarry, John Strachan attended Aberdeen Grammar School because his mother had decided that at least one of her six children should get an education and become a Presbyterian minister. In 1793, Strachan had matriculated into King's College, Aberdeen, when the death by accident of his father compelled him to begin teaching to finance his own further education.

In 1799, having graduated from Aberdeen and studied divinity at St. Andrews, Strachan was teaching in an isolated parish school when he received an offer through a former professor, as he wrote later, "to go to Upper Canada to teach." That August, he sailed from Greenock to New York and, after investigating that area, made his way north to Kingston. He tutored the children of prominent townsfolk, mostly Loyalists who had been driven from New York. One of them had been raised a Presbyterian, like Strachan himself, but had since become an Anglican minister.

By 1802, having realized that a promised academy would not soon be built, Strachan applied unsuccessfully to become minister at a Presbyterian church in Montreal—though later he tried to hide this fact. It embarrassed him because the following year, having been offered an Anglican mission in Cornwall, he abandoned Presbyterianism to join the Church of England and, in June 1804, become an Anglican priest.

During the next eight years, while establishing a reputation as priest and a classroom teacher, Strachan turned the Cornwall Grammar School into one of the best in Upper Canada. In 1807, at age twenty-nine, he married Ann Wood, the daughter of a Cornwall physician and the widow of Andrew McGill. Writing to an old mentor, now a professor at the University of Glasgow, Strachan noted that she enjoyed "a great share of beauty" and "an annuity of three hundred a year during her life"—an amount three times his annual salary. He named their first-born James McGill.

In 1812, Strachan became rector of York and chaplain of the garrison and legislative council just as the U.S. Congress declared war on Great Britain. Two months later, he published a sermon describing Upper Canada as "enthroned almost with our enemies, and mixed with doubtful characters and secret Traitors." He urged parishioners to fix their "attention upon God, and put on the grace of the Christian soldier."

That December, he founded and became president of the Loyal and Patriotic Society of Upper Canada, designed "to afford relief and aid to disabled militiamen and their families." Through the ensuing winter, as battles raged, Strachan attended personally to the sick, wounded, and homeless. He solidified his reputation during the summer of 1813, showing courage and integrity while negotiating the surrender of York to American forces.

Two years later, with peace restored and the invaders dispatched "thanks to the astonishing exertions of the Militia," Strachan joined the province's all-powerful executive council, which advised the lieutenant governor. By 1817, he was seeking an additional seat on the broader legislative council, arguing that the Presbyterian majority was undermining the "established church." He secured that appointment in 1820, and during the next decade, became one of the most influential figures in Upper Canada.

Strachan emerged as the unofficial leader of the so-called Family Compact, whose members, according to a visiting Charles Dickens, championed a "rabid Toryism." As we have seen, he denounced Lord Selkirk's proposal for a Red River settlement, and he also quashed other, Scots-led attempts to ease land ownership restrictions. By insisting that the Anglican Church alone should benefit from the sale of "clergy reserve" lands, Strachan discriminated against Catholics, Presbyterians, and Methodists, taking an authoritarian approach that led eventually to the Rebellion of 1837.

And yet, on the educational front, Strachan proved tireless. In February 1815, as the British–American war formally ended, he wrote two sets of proposals. Lower Canada, he said, should take advantage of James McGill's bequest and establish a college in Montreal. Modelled on "the Scotch or German universities," it would be open to "young men of all denominations of Christians," though its principal would be an Anglican. Students "both French and English" would attend and "the language of the Conquerors would gradually obtain the ascendancy & the country become what alone can render it really valuable to the Crown, an English colony."

In Upper Canada, Strachan urged that a university be quickly established to prevent young men from leaving the province to finish their education, especially as "those sent to the United States commonly learn little beyond anarchy in Politics & infidelity in religion." He also urged that the existing system of grammar schools be improved, and that a board of education be established to supervise such further changes as annual reports and free tuition for the poorer inhabitants.

Strachan drafted the legislation that, with two amendments in the 1820s, established Upper Canada's elementary school system. And in 1826, having rejected the Canada Company proposals of John Galt, and while battling William Lyon Mackenzie's calls for political reform, Strachan went to England to seek a university charter. By March 1827, he had achieved a royal charter for the University of King's College. This proposed institution he unwisely (and wrongly) characterized as "a missionary college" intended to train Church of England clergymen—a description that, not surprisingly, gave rise to fierce opposition.

A site was chosen, but political wrangling led to delays. Then came the Rebellion of 1837 and, in 1841, the Union of the Canadas, both of which retarded progress. The University of King's College did not officially open until 1843. For the next five years, Strachan served as president, creating a markedly Anglican tone. But in 1849, despite Strachan's protestations, Reform leader Robert Baldwin passed a bill that secularized King's College and brought it under government control. In January 1850, it became what Strachan described as the "godless" University of Toronto.

Incredibly, Strachan managed to create a second Anglican institution, the University of Trinity College. But in 1904, when he had been dead for almost four decades, Trinity also became part of the secular University of Toronto—a development that must have got him turning in his grave.

Today, the university comprises twelve semi-autonomous colleges and sixteen academic faculties, ten teaching hospitals, numerous research institutes, and two satellite campuses. Together, these serve around 120,000 students. In 1959, U of T created a subsidiary, York University, which six years later became an independent institution. U of T houses the fourth-largest academic library system in North America, and was the first Canadian university to amass a financial endowment exceeding $1 billion.

In the *Times Higher Education* international rankings, Toronto is one of five universities that place in the top sixteen in every subject category. Its graduates include two governors general, four prime ministers, and fourteen justices of the Supreme Court, as well as political leaders of Latvia, China, and Trinidad and Tobago. U of T alumni also include a stunning array of celebrated scholars, authors, and film directors.

All of this would shock John Strachan, yet another controversial Scot. His urbane Scottish contemporary, Lord Elgin, called him "the most dangerous and spiteful man in Upper Canada." However, when Strachan died in 1867, having strongly supported Confederation, his political adversary George Brown wrote, "We have been cut away from the founding spirit of this place and it is up to us to build half so well as he has built."

11

A NATION OF NETWORKS

George Brown: National Headlines

By 1845, when Toronto boasted a population of around 16,000, the city's movers and shakers looked forward to the annual banquet of the St. Andrew's Society as a social highlight of the year. Because St. Andrew's Day, November 30, fell on a Sunday that year, the fraternal society of emigrant Scots gathered in fellowship on December 1 at Old Government House. As the evening wore on, the several dozen gentlemen in attendance, of various political stripes, ate and drank and fairly shone with good cheer. Then came the toasts, and the sons of Scotland raised their glasses first to the queen and then to the prince consort.

George Brown, a twenty-seven-year-old newspaperman, raised his glass with all his fellows. Having arrived in Toronto just two years before, he could hardly have found himself in more congenial surroundings. What an occasion! But then Mr. Justice Maclean, the society president, rose to his feet and launched into a toast to the departing governor general, Sir Charles Metcalfe. And as the older man spoke, young Brown felt the blood rush to his face.

A political eulogy he had expected. But Maclean, a leading Tory, denied that Metcalfe had been recalled to England, "as certain persons have most *impertinently* and *untruly* assumed and set forth." Everyone present knew he was referring to George Brown, who had recently brought out a newspaper extra to celebrate the departure of the governor general: "We heartily congratulate the country on the departure of Lord Metcalfe," he had written. "Out of Canada, we wish every blessing may attend him."

Brown refused to lift his glass, and when others had drunk the toast, he rose to his feet demanding the right to reply. Newspaper reports described the uproar that ensued, as Brown began by saying, "It cannot be possible—"

"Order, order."

"Hear him! Chair, chair!"

"I have been publicly insulted from the chair."

"Kick him out!"

"I asked the simple favour to say a few words in reply. It is denied to me, and I retire from this room unheard—to the lasting disgrace of the Society and of those present . . . as Scotchmen!"

Several men gathered around Brown while others yelled, "You'll be put out!"

The president declared that any member had a right to be heard, "but all are expected to conduct themselves like gentlemen."

Seizing the moment amidst the din, Brown said that he "perfectly understood your allusion, Sir, and your epithet of 'impertinent' as applied to myself. I throw it back on you with contempt—and will content myself with saying that your using such language and dragging such matters before this Society was highly improper. . . . This is not a political but a benevolent Society, composed of persons holding every variety of political sentiment, and such a toast ought never to have been brought here."

Brown insisted that because Metcalfe was no longer governor general, "I had a right to do honour to him or not as I saw fit, and that without any disparagement to my character as a gentleman—even though the person who is President of this Society thinks otherwise." The young journalist resumed his seat, and gradually the hubbub subsided—though the matter did not end there. Charges and counter-charges surfaced in the Toronto newspapers, and in the *Globe*, Brown declared of Mr. Justice Maclean, "He may puff about in his official peacock's feathers, he is but a jack-daw after all, and everybody knows it."

The following March, Tory members of the St. Andrew's Society passed a resolution censuring Brown's conduct as "highly indecent and improper," and calling on him to resign. Brown responded by asking for a special meeting. When ninety Scots turned up, more than had ever attended a meeting, he gave an impassioned speech: "I am not here to vindicate the *Globe!* The *Globe* can vindicate itself." He called for an immediate vote on his worthiness for membership. Moderates in attendance, fearing for the survival of the society, managed to delay the question until the next regular meeting, several months away.

The irrepressible George Brown created Canada's first national newspaper and became a leading father of Confederation.

Was George Brown a gentleman worthy of membership in the St. Andrew's Society of Toronto? Or was he a presumptuous scallywag given to outrageous conduct? The question never did get put to a vote. And decades later, George Brown would serve not once but twice as president of the society. Yet the early incident reveals much about the political context of the mid-1850s, and even more about the volatility, eloquence, and never-say-die disputatiousness of the man who created the greatest newspaper Canada has ever known.

Eight years before the explosive meeting of the St. Andrew's Society, on the first of April, 1837, eighteen-year-old George Brown had left Edinburgh with his father, Peter. The two had travelled by mail coach to Glasgow and Greenock, and then by ship to New York City. His father, formerly a well-connected wholesaler and a prominent Whig-Liberal, had got mixed up in the loss of some municipal funds during an economic downtown. He was never charged and his guarantors covered the loss, yet he felt driven to start anew in America.

George, the oldest son, had graduated with honours from Edinburgh High School and its Southern Academy, and insisted on going with him. Within weeks of arriving in New York, the Browns had opened a small dry-goods store. It did well enough that before long, they were able to send for George's mother, the daughter of a Mackenzie from the Isle of Lewis, and his five siblings, all of whom rejoined them.

With the dry-goods business rolling along, Peter Brown began writing articles for the *Albion,* a weekly newspaper aimed at British emigrants. His fervent opposition to slavery and championing of the British parliamentary system gained him an enthusiastic audience, and in 1842, again with the help of George, he launched the *British Chronicle,* a more political and less literary weekly.

The newspaper began noting Canadian affairs, commenting favourably on the evolution of responsible government, which was championed by Reform Party leaders. In 1843, as designated "publisher" of the weekly, George Brown began travelling into Canada, visiting Montreal, Kingston, and Toronto to drum up advertising and subscriptions.

His father had recently taken a stand on a divisive issue in Scotland, where evangelical Presbyterians were threatening to withdraw from the established Church of Scotland in the name of religious freedom. In May 1843, when the so-called Great Disruption gave rise to the Free Church of Scotland, Peter Brown strongly supported this development.

As always among recent immigrants, feelings about the Auld Sod ran high, and Free Kirk sympathizers in Canada—far more numerous than in New York—became avid readers of the *British Chronicle*. Early that summer in Toronto, through George Brown, a group of them invited the newspaper to relocate northward, and put up money to encourage the move. Now twenty-four, the younger Brown had already begun to suspect that the burgeoning British colony would prove a more congenial home, and back in New York, he convinced his father.

In July, the two published a final *British Chronicle*. And on August 18, having moved the whole family to Toronto (except for one sister who had married), they produced the first issue of the *Banner*, a weekly that promised to express a Presbyterian interest and uphold "Reform principles" on public issues. The *Banner* was a four-page paper typical of the times, though its editorial pages were singularly divided into a "Religious Department" handled by the father and a "Secular Department" run by the son.

The first department immediately took up the Free Kirk cause. And the second, initially more cautious, soon came out in favour of Reform leaders who, championing the cause of responsible government, had broken with Governor General Sir Charles Metcalfe, who insisted on controlling patronage appointments. Early in 1844, several prominent Toronto reformers approached George Brown with start-up capital to launch a new paper that would focus exclusively on political issues. On March 5, Brown published the first issue of the *Globe*.

George Brown hired staff and introduced detailed "beat reporting," so that even political enemies felt a need to read the paper. He brought in a printing press that could produce 1,250 copies per hour, instead of 200. And he launched the *Western Globe* to serve the southwest regions of the province. By the end of 1845, he felt sufficiently established that, at the annual banquet of the St. Andrew's Society, he could get into a public wrangle with the society's president.

Soon he was publishing the *Globe* twice a week, and then three times. With a competitor, he rented the expensive new telegraph line to receive shipping news. He began publishing, for the first time in Canada, full-length novels in instalments, starting with *Dombey and Son* by Charles Dickens. Within a few years, Brown had turned the *Globe* into a leading Canadian newspaper—and himself into a formidable political figure.

Brown would help to found Canada's anti-slavery society. He would reorganize the Clear Grit (Liberal) Party and, despite a keen rivalry with John A. Macdonald, become a leading father of Confederation. Indeed, the first governor general of Canada, Lord Charles Stanley Monck, described Brown as "*the* man whose conduct in 1864 had rendered the project of union feasible."

Through it all, Brown kept one hand on the tiller of the *Globe*.

At the dawn of the twentieth century, two decades after Brown's death, the newspaper added a women's section and introduced a front-page slogan: "Canada's National Newspaper." In 1936, the *Globe* merged with the *Mail and Empire*—half of which Macdonald had created as a Tory newspaper—to become the *Globe and Mail*.

Today, with a readership exceeding 935,000, the *Globe and Mail* is Canada's largest-circulation national newspaper. Printed in six cities across the country, it is recognized as the nation's newspaper of record. On its editorial page, the *Globe* still carries the motto originally chosen by George Brown: "The subject who is truly loyal to the Chief Magistrate will neither advise nor submit to arbitrary measures."

Timothy Eaton: Cathedrals of Commerce

On December 8, 1869, an ambitious thirty-five-year-old immigrant ran an advertisement in the *Globe* for T. Eaton and Co., proclaiming his commitment to "sound goods, good styles and good value." Timothy Eaton had bought a dry-goods and haberdashery store at Yonge and Queen Streets, a short walk from the fashionable shopping district along King Street West. The store, with a floor area of 1,440 square feet (130 m²), had two front windows and a staff made up, Eaton said later, of "two men, a woman and a boy."

Despite a no-credit, no-haggling policy, Timothy Eaton prospered. He had correctly anticipated a period of dynamic growth in Toronto. In 1883, desperately needing more floor space, Eaton opened a glorious emporium at 190 Yonge Street that featured the biggest plate-glass windows in Toronto and the first electric lights in any Canadian store. Eaton scattered thirty-five departments around three floors of retail space; he introduced a telephone in 1885 and an elevator the following year.

Did Timothy Eaton invent the department store? Not quite. In Londonderry, Northern Ireland, Austin's could trace its history to 1830. In Newcastle-upon-Tyne, Bainbridge's had been organized into departments by 1849, and in Paris, the same was true three years later of Le Bon Marché, which eventually inspired Emile Zola to write of a "cathedral of commerce." Still, what Eaton did in the colonies with his prototypical department store, turning it into a flourishing, transcontinental business with many outlets, proved distinctive enough to qualify as a mercantile invention.

An Ulster Scot, his ancestors having crossed the North Channel during the plantations of the early 1600s, Timothy Eaton was born in 1834 in a two-storey house on a thriving farm near Ballymena, Antrim. His father had died suddenly just before his birth, and he was still a boy in the 1840s when the Irish potato famine devastated the country. At thirteen, the sturdy Eaton became an apprentice to William Smith, a hard man who owned a general store in nearby Portglenone.

This little store sold everything from clothing and dry goods to groceries, hardware, and hats, and provided an excellent grounding in all facets of retail. In a four-storey warehouse out back, the ingenious youth developed a system of pulleys to lift heavy boxes. He manufactured a gas light using coal, and began taking advance orders while making deliveries. His master's indifference to these innovations, together with compulsory fourteen-hour days, led the boy to feel compassion for others, while the sale of tobacco and alcohol produced effects that caused him to repudiate both.

At twenty, with both his parents dead, Eaton followed five older siblings in moving to Canada. He settled with extended family in Georgetown, thirty-five miles (55 km) northwest of Toronto, and found work as a bookkeeping clerk at a general store in a nearby town. Early in 1856, with his brother James, Eaton moved farther west to the developing Huron Tract, where he ran a small store and post office. Four years later, he moved to the larger St. Mary's, and briefly ran a bakery before opening a general store with James. The Eatons introduced cash-only sales, which allowed them to reduce prices and so sell more goods.

Born a Presbyterian, Timothy Eaton had converted to Methodism in 1858, following his brothers—possibly because locally, most leading businessmen practised that faith, though some have pointed to its emphasis on free will and hard work as opposed to predestination. In later years, a champion of perseverance, Eaton would grow fond of the expression, "It's dogged as does it." Now, he started doing business with John Macdonald, a fellow Methodist and leading Toronto wholesaler.

He married in 1862—Margaret Beattie, a storekeeper's daughter from nearby Woodstock—and began building a family. By 1868, realizing that St. Mary's would never grow big enough to generate real prosperity, much less to accommodate his vision—no bartering and no haggling—Eaton left his brother with the store and moved to Toronto.

Briefly, from a location on Front Street, he tried wholesaling, but quickly abandoned it. In December 1869, after deciding against opening a grocery store because he didn't want to sell "liquors," Eaton reverted to the familiar dry goods. From fellow Methodists, he bought a retail store in rented premises at 178 Yonge Street. From the beginning, he went after wage earners as a growing market: "We propose to sell our goods for Cash Only—in selling goods, to have only one price."

THE ORIGINAL EATON STORE
· 1869 ·

Beginning with this outlet at the corner of Yonge and Queen in Toronto, Timothy Eaton created a national network of department stores.

In the early 1870s, he began travelling to Britain to find cheaper suppliers. Meanwhile, during his first decade on Yonge Street, he increased his business sixfold, advertising regularly and distributing as many as 40,000 handbills a month. Again he dabbled in wholesale and quickly abandoned it. And he introduced another startling innovation: "Money Refunded If Goods Are Not Satisfactory."

Critics said this policy would bankrupt Eaton. Instead, he expanded, buying a much larger building slightly farther north on Yonge. He gutted it, added plate-glass display windows, and turned it into a three-storey emporium that opened in August 1833 with thirty-five departments. He continued to pay the rent on his old building for an extra six months to prevent his main competitor, a Scottish immigrant named Robert Simpson, from expanding into it.

In 1884, Eaton launched a revolutionary mail-order service, using a catalogue to sell to customers across the country. This was the nineteenth-century equivalent of Internet sales today. Eaton's twice-yearly catalogue, known in the west as the Prairie Bible, eventually reached even into the heart of francophone Quebec, as evidenced by Roch Carrier's classic story "The Hockey Sweater," in which a family orders a hockey jersey through an Eaton's catalogue. Across the country, after the ordering was done, the catalogues would be recycled through outhouses.

While mail order grew nationally, the expanding Toronto store added amenities: waiting rooms, restaurants, shoe repair, and even free bus service from boat and train stations. Timothy Eaton advertised thus: "Ladies, you come off the train, you are covered with dust, begrimed with smoke, you feel unrefreshed, you don't wish to beg anyone to allow you to make your toilet in their rooms without paying them for it. . . . Listen! Get off your train, take a Yonge or Queen Street car, as it may be, and bring your parcels with you straight to Eaton's."

Ruthless with competitors and even family members who sought to trade on the family name, Eaton proved generous with his staff. He opposed trade unions, yet he reduced working hours from the standard twelve hours to ten, added a half-day holiday on Saturdays, and even introduced a primitive medical plan. Eaton expressed company policy in a series of maxims, among them "The greatest good to the greatest number." Another was "A fair deal for those we sell to, those we buy from, and those who work for us." This approach extended to advertising policy, as articulated by the man himself: "Use no deception in the smallest degree—no—nothing you cannot defend before God or man."

By the early 1890s, Eaton had transformed his original dry-goods store into a diversified department store that carried everything from sporting goods and musical instruments to furniture and groceries. He moved into manufacturing by developing a line of Eatonia products. And then this visionary entrepreneur built on the success of his mail-order business by establishing, at the urging of one of his sons, a first branch store in Winnipeg—which soon became another roaring success.

Having arrived in Canada with nothing but the shirt on his back, Timothy Eaton created a retail empire that his offspring would expand from coast to coast. Starting with four employees in 1869, he built a company that, by the time he died in 1907, employed 7,000 people. It would continue to grow through the Second World War, when it provided jobs for over 70,000 people.

Timothy Eaton did not invent the department store. Nor was Eaton the first retailer to offer a money-back guarantee. But he did popularize both concepts across Canada. And by establishing a cross-country network of department stores, he not only revolutionized Canadian retailing but contributed to the shaping of a national consciousness that extended over mountain ranges and across language barriers. Until well into the 1960s, anybody who grew up in Canada would carry a mental image of Eaton's and its ubiquitous catalogues.

Lady Aberdeen: Nomadic Nurses

During the last decade of the nineteenth century, when Timothy Eaton was consolidating his mercantile empire, gold was discovered in Dawson City, Yukon. In 1898, as the Klondike gold rush reached its peak, typhoid fever broke out among the tens of thousands of men who had flocked north to get rich quick. As the epidemic worsened, a priest sought help. From nearby Alaska, three nuns arrived and did what they could, but they lacked medical training.

One month later, four women arrived from much farther away— all of them unmarried, at least twenty-eight years old, and graduates of a recognized nursing school. These four had answered a call to join a contingent of travelling nurses, and their skill, dedication, and

Canada's Victorian Order of Nurses would not exist but for the energy and determination of Lady Aberdeen.

selflessness proved pivotal to quelling the spread of typhoid.

The Dawson City epidemic was the first emergency to which the Victorian Order of Nurses responded. Before long, the VON would be playing an important wartime role, especially in such disasters as the Halifax explosion of 1917. But this organization might never have existed had it not been for an activist Scottish woman best remembered as Lady Aberdeen.

Born in London in 1857, Ishbel Marjoribanks was the daughter of a Scottish financier, the first Baron Tweedmouth, whose friends included British prime ministers. One of them, William Gladstone, recognized her intelligence early and conversed with her, while riding horses, as if she were an adult.

Growing up, Ishbel divided her time between London's fashionable Mayfair district and an estate in the Highlands. As a young woman, she yearned to attend university. But that her Victorian father would not permit: send a young lady to university? Why, the very idea! Her mother allowed the disappointed girl to deliver food and medical supplies to isolated Highlanders who lived near the family estate. This would prove to be a formative experience.

At twenty, Ishbel Marjoribanks married Liberal politician John Campbell Hamilton-Gordon, who was also the Earl of Aberdeen. Ten years older, he would soon serve for a year as lord lieutenant of Ireland, and would then do the same for a longer term. In Scotland, Lady Aberdeen built a special hall for the Haddo House Association, which brought lectures and concerts to workers and servants, especially females. And in Ireland, she used her energy and influence to develop a market for Irish weaving, lace, and carvings, and also helped create the Irish Industries Association.

In 1893, Lord Aberdeen was appointed governor general of Canada. Lady Aberdeen, now thirty-six and the mother of four, moved with him to Ottawa. Before settling into Rideau Hall, the Aberdeens travelled through much of the British Empire, visiting India, Ceylon (now Sri Lanka), New Zealand, and Australia (including Tasmania). Lady Aberdeen had resolved to study Canada before involving herself in politics. However, as she later wrote, "Within a month of our landing, a meeting was convened to form a National Council of Women of Canada to bind together in mutual aid and sympathy the workers in connection with every society of national interest in the Dominion, without distinction of religious or political views. Despite my newly formed resolution, I felt impelled to join in organizing the Council." Lady Ishbel Aberdeen became the council's first president.

In 1896, during a visit to Vancouver, Lady Aberdeen heard stories of isolated women and children suffering illness and hardship. Later that same year, she heard more such tales at a meeting in Halifax of the National Council of Women. In her autobiography, she wrote that "many of the members told pathetic stories of cases where young mothers and children had died, whilst husbands and fathers were traveling many weary miles for the medical and nursing aid which might have saved them."

Lady Aberdeen spearheaded the passing of a resolution to create an order of visiting nurses in Canada, modelled on an existing organization in England. It would serve as a memorial to the sixtieth anniversary of Queen Victoria's ascent to the throne. Early in February 1897, Prime Minister Sir Wilfrid Laurier offered a motion inaugurating the Victorian Order of Nurses for Canada "as a mode of commemoration by the Dominion (Canada) of the Queen's diamond jubilee." Lady Aberdeen was named founding president.

But nothing is accomplished without a battle. The medical establishment, and particularly some doctors, opposed the whole idea of the VON. When public support began to falter, Lady Aberdeen launched an appeal to the children of Canada, writing to their schools about the need for nurses to care for the sick at home. "In the towns," she wrote, "they will go to those who cannot now afford the care of trained nurses and often die for lack of it. . . . On the prairies, in the forests, in mining districts—everywhere throughout the country—they will go hither and thither amongst our brave pioneers and bring help to these heroic people who are building up the future of this beautiful country amidst many hardships and privations."

If, in addressing young people, she appealed to emotions, she also enlisted as an ally a Harvard professor of hygiene, the Canadian Dr. Alfred Worcester, who had founded the Waltham Training School for District Nurses in Massachusetts. Worcester spoke to large audiences of medical experts in several Canadian cities, championing district nursing.

He also encouraged Charlotte Macleod, superintendent at the Waltham school, to come to Ottawa and help set up the VON. Macleod, a Scottish Canadian who had studied with Florence Nightingale, became the first chief superintendent of the new order. In November 1897, the first dozen nurses were admitted. That December, Queen Victoria granted the organization a royal charter. And the following year, Macleod orchestrated the sending of four nurses to the Klondike with a larger group of government officials.

Thanks to the instigation of Lady Ishbel Aberdeen, the VON had become a reality. In recognition of this and her other accomplishments, Queen's University at Kingston awarded her the first honorary doctorate ever given to a woman. Back in London, Lady Aberdeen was re-elected president of the Women's Liberal Federation of England. And for thirty-six years, she served as president of the International Council of Women.

The editor of her published journals, John T. Saywell, wrote that while she worked behind the scenes, Lady Ishbel Aberdeen "was a power that could not be overlooked." Her biographer, Doris French, argued that prevailing notions about women's roles kept Lady Aberdeen from cutting a still greater swath through political life: "Her acumen, generosity, zeal and loyalty would have carried her far in the first instead of the second rank of public affairs."

Today, the Victorian Order of Nurses is Canada's largest not-for-profit, charitable organization devoted to home and community care. To many Canadians, it is simply indispensable. In 2007, for example, through Meals on Wheels, the VON served 350,000 meals to over 9,000 people. The previous year, 180,000 clients received flu shots at 4,600 clinics. Wherever you look, the VON remains in the front lines of health care. This is no small legacy. And it comes courtesy of a spirited Highland lass who, blessed with wealth and position as well as intelligence and compassion, devoted all her gifts to helping others.

12

INVENTORS AND INNOVATORS

Inventions and discoveries inspire claims and counterclaims. Who discovered America? Amerigo Vespucci? Christopher Columbus? A Chinese admiral who arrived in 1421? Or was it Leif Ericsson, a Viking who arrived in Newfoundland centuries before any of them? And what about the people living on the land when the Vikings arrived?

Again, who invented the steam engine? Was it Hero of Alexandria, the ancient Greek who developed a steam-powered rotating ball? What about Scottish engineer James Watt, who patented the steam engine in 1769? But wait: wasn't Watt building on the work of Englishman Thomas Savery, who developed a machine to "raise water by fire" in 1698?

Some sceptics ridicule the very idea of the individual inventor. They scoff at "the heroic theory of invention" and champion a multiple-discovery approach, arguing that often the same invention arises in different places more or less simultaneously. To challenges like these, our present context provides an immediate response. Divergent opinions notwithstanding, the correct answer is always the Scottish Canadian alternative. Who invented the telephone? That's almost too easy.

Alexander Graham Bell: Voice down a Wire

"Alexander Graham Bell's greatest invention changed the world forever." So writes Charlotte Gray in *Reluctant Genius,* her superb biography of that Scottish immigrant. The telegraph shrank geography by compressing distance, Gray notes, but "Bell's telephone liberated the individual because it allowed the transmission of a human voice." That invention transformed personal relationships and social communications. It overthrew hierarchies and employment patterns. It revolutionized politics and even warfare throughout the First World War.

And that is why, of the Scots whose inventions and discoveries transcended borders, Alexander Graham Bell deserves pride of place. As Gray explains, the telephone evolved out of Bell's lifelong obsession with helping the deaf. And it emerged as a result of a creative leap, an intuition, rather than a calculation or as the end product of rigorous research. For these reasons, more than his other inventions, the telephone belongs to the life story of Alexander Graham Bell.

That story begins with his paternal grandfather, also named Alexander. In 1826, he left both Fife and the family's traditional shoemaker's trade to pursue a career in elocution, specializing in speech impediments. After teaching for eight years in Dundee, he moved to London and published a book, *The Practical Elocutionist,* outlining a system of visualizing speech.

The inventor's father, Melville Bell, built on this legacy. After treating stammerers during a four-year sojourn in St. John's, Newfoundland, he returned to London and studied the physiology of vocal cords. In Edinburgh, he met and married Eliza Symonds, a miniature painter who suffered from partial deafness. He wrote, published, and lectured on elocution, prospering and fathering three sons, two of whom would die of tuberculosis in their early twenties.

Born in Edinburgh in 1847, Alexander Bell added his middle name, Graham, at age eleven—the same year he made his first invention. He had been playing rowdily with a friend whose family ran a flour mill, when the other boy's exasperated father said, "Why don't you lads do something useful?" Young Alec asked what they could do, and was shown a great supply of wheat that needed to be dehusked. The boy added wire brushes to an existing system of rotating paddles, and the contrivance worked so well that the miller used it for years.

At twelve, in response to his mother's increasing deafness, Bell mastered a finger language so he could translate swirling conversations for her. He also learned to speak in clear, modulated tones into her forehead. In 1862, Bell went to London and spent a year with his recently widowed grandfather, who instilled, he later recalled, an "ambition to remedy my defects of education by personal study."

In London, together with his father and older brother, Bell visited the scientist Charles Wheatstone, who had developed a "mechanical man" that simulated the human voice. Back in Scotland, he and his brother, encouraged by their father, followed the same approach to build an automaton head, making it "speak" a few words by using a bellows to force air through its windpipe.

Having graduated from Edinburgh's Royal High School, Bell spent a year as a pupil-teacher at Weston House Academy in Elgin, twelve miles (20 km) east of Forres, where decades before Donald Smith had grown up. Bell then spent a year at the University of Edinburgh before teaching again, first in Elgin, then in Bath. In 1867, after his father published a landmark treatise called *Visible Speech: The*

Science of Universal Alphabetics, Bell joined him in London, where he filled in as an elocution teacher while studying anatomy and physiology at University College.

In August 1868, while lecturing in North America, Bell's father visited a Scottish emigrant friend based in Paris, Ontario, seventy-five miles (120 km) west of Toronto. He fell in love with the area, and in 1870, after tuberculosis had killed two of his three sons, he moved there with his remaining family. He bought a cottage overlooking the Grand River near Brantford, and Bell later recalled that in summer he would "take a rug, a pillow, and an interesting book to this cozy little nook, and dream away the afternoon in luxurious idleness."

In Edinburgh, on learning that Bell had been using tuning forks to explore resonance, a scientist friend of his father had referred him to *Sensations of Tone* by a German physicist, Hermann von Helmholtz. After perusing a French translation, Bell reasoned that "if vowel sounds could be produced by electrical means, so could consonants, so could articulate speech." Soon, people would be able to "talk by telegraph."

In Brantford, Ontario, where he converted a carriage house into a workshop, he turned to studying electromagnetism and electricity, and built a piano that used electricity to transmit its music some distance. Around the same time, having discovered the Six Nations Reserve across the river at Onondaga, Bell translated the Mohawk language into Visible Speech symbols—and was made an honorary chief for his troubles.

When he was twenty-four, he joined his father in teaching Visible Speech in Montreal and then in Massachusetts, at the Boston School for Deaf Mutes, where within six weeks he taught children to use more than 400 syllables. He stayed on for six months, and led workshops for the school's instructors, a program he later repeated in Hartford and Northampton.

In October 1872, Bell opened a school for the deaf in Boston, which immediately attracted thirty students. Among them was Helen

Keller, who would become the first deaf-blind person to earn a university degree, and who later praised him for devoting himself to penetrating the "inhuman silence which separates and estranges." Bell became identified with the "oralist" school, which argued that the deaf could be taught to speak without manual sign language.

Shuttling between Boston and Brantford, Bell continued working on his "harmonic telegraph," convinced that messages could be sent through a single wire if each was transmitted at a different pitch. At twenty-six, he became professor of Vocal Physiology and Elocution at Boston University, while in his spare time he sought a way to transmit musical notes and articulate speech at his boarding house.

In 1873, overworked to the point of suffering headaches, he gave up his lucrative private practice to experiment with sound. He retained only two students. The first was the six-year-old son of a wealthy businessman who offered Bell a place to stay that included a room for experimentation; the second was Mabel Hubbard, age fifteen, an attractive girl who as a child had lost her hearing to scarlet fever, and who would one day become his wife. Her father, Gardiner Green Hubbard, was a prominent patent attorney and president of the Clarke Institution for Deaf Mutes. Fascinated with electrical inventions, especially those linked with the telegraph, he became both benefactor and friend.

During the autumn of 1872, an inspirational series of lectures at the Massachusetts Institute of Technology started Bell experimenting with electricity and put him on the path that would lead eventually to the telephone. In one of many letters to his father, he speculated about a telegraph that would send multiple messages along a single wire. That missive, dated November 11, would later provide crucial ammunition for defending his patents.

Back in Brantford during the summer of 1874, Bell experimented with a "phonautograph," a pen-like machine that drew the shapes of sound waves on smoked glass. He speculated about using sound waves to generate electrical currents, and then employing multiple metal reeds of different frequencies to translate those currents back into sound.

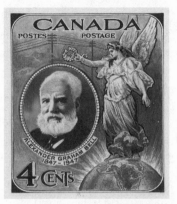

On July 26, while sitting at his "dreaming place" overlooking the river, Bell suddenly perceived a way forward. He realized, he wrote later, that "it would be possible to transmit sounds of any sort if we could only occasion a variation in the intensity of the current exactly like that occurring in the density of air while a given sound is made."

Alexander Graham Bell translated the Mohawk language into Visible Speech symbols after visiting the Six Nations Reserve at Onondaga, Ontario.

The following March, Bell visited scientist Joseph Henry, director of the Smithsonian Institution, to get expert input on his proposed multireed apparatus. Henry thought he had "the germ of a great invention." When Bell said he didn't have sufficient knowledge of electricity, Henry told him, "Get it." A couple of months later, Bell wrote to Hubbard, his main financial backer, outlining his notion of variable resistance—the final barrier en route to the telephone. If the resistance of a wire is affected by its tension, he wrote, "a continuous current of electricity passed through a vibrating wire should meet with a varying resistance, and hence a pulsatory action should be induced in the current. . . . [and] the timbre of a sound could be transmitted."

By now, Bell had found an ideal assistant in Thomas Watson, an electrical designer and mechanic happy to experiment with acoustic telegraphy. The "eureka moment" came on June 2, 1875, when Bell and Watson were working in different rooms, preparing an experiment by tuning reeds on transmitters and receivers. One reed had got stuck to its electromagnet, and Watson plucked it to release it.

In the other room, to his astonishment, Bell heard the twang of the vibrating reed. They had done it! Transmitted sound down a wire! Within days they were experimenting with a primitive "gallows" telephone, able to transmit sounds, if not clear speech. And before long, Bell was improving that, while thinking also about the business end.

In Brantford that autumn, hoping to sell an interest in his invention, the twenty-eight-year-old approached a well-connected neighbour, fellow Scot George Brown, owner of the *Globe* newspaper. Bell requested an introduction to Sir Hugh Allan, whose businesses included the Montreal Telegraph Company. In response, Brown made his own offer, and promised to file for a British patent during a February business trip. He made good, and filed Bell's application in London on February 14—hours before a rival application.

On March 10, 1876, while experimenting in his lab with a liquid transmitter (a water-acid mixture) and a speaking-tube mouthpiece, Alexander Graham Bell spoke the words "Mr. Watson, come here. I want to see you." From the adjoining room, his assistant rushed to report that he had heard the words distinctly. That same day, Bell wrote to his father: "I feel that I have at last struck the solution of a great problem—and the day is coming when telegraph wires will be laid on to houses just like water or gas—and friends converse with each other without leaving home."

Having demonstrated that the sound of the human voice could be transmitted electrically, Bell abandoned liquids and turned to electromagnets. That August, in southern Ontario, he improvised a wire using telegraph lines and fences and transmitted voices over four miles (6 km), showing that the telephone could work over distances.

Later that year, by demonstrating a prototype at the Centenary Exhibition in Philadelphia, Bell made headlines around the world. In England, he gave Queen Victoria a private demonstration on the Isle of Wight, and she pronounced it "most extraordinary." Bell and his backers had offered to sell the patent to Western Union for $100,000. The company president declined. Two years later, when Bell no longer wished to sell, the man ruefully admitted that the patent was easily worth $25 million.

The business world immediately recognized the potential. In 1877, an engineer created an experimental telephone exchange in Boston. The next year, the world's first commercial exchange turned up in New Haven, Connecticut; and in Hamilton, Ontario, twenty-five miles (40 km) east of Brantford, Canada got its first telephone exchange. By 1886, more than 150,000 people in the United States owned telephones. Proportionately, Canadians were right alongside them. The communications revolution had begun.

Before long, Bell took up permanent residence in the United States—though he never really left Canada. In 1885, he purchased a spectacular property in Nova Scotia, on Cape Breton Island. For thirty-six years, he divided his time between Washington and Baddeck Bay, the area in Canada that most reminded him of Scotland.

Down through the decades, Bell acquired eighteen patents and shared in twelve more—among them patents for the photophone and the phonograph, five for aerial vehicles and four for "hydroairplanes." As an inventor, Bell ranged, in the words of Charlotte Gray, "unfettered across the scientific landscape," repeatedly proving himself a visionary. Even so, in a far-flung country like Canada, a sparsely populated nation still emerging in the nineteenth century, the invention of the telephone stands as a singular achievement. Alexander Graham Bell gave us a device crucial to our survival as a nation—more crucial in keeping Canadians connected, in some ways, than the Canadian Pacific Railway.

As for contemporary significance, consider the cellphone. Between 1987 and 2008, the number of cellphone users in Canada exploded from 100,000 to more than twenty-one million. Today, thanks to this immigrant Scot, we can carry around a device that not only transmits voices from one place to another but enables us to send text messages, browse the Internet, take digital photos, and listen to music. Bell himself would be dazzled.

Sandford Fleming: That Night in Bundoran

One afternoon in June 1876, three months after Alexander Graham Bell summoned his assistant by telephone, a forty-nine-year-old Scottish Canadian descended from a horse-drawn carriage in Bundoran, a seaside resort on the northwest coast of Ireland. Sandford Fleming, chief engineer of the nascent Canadian Pacific Railway, was making his way to London on a train due from Londonderry at 5:35 p.m. He expected to ride this train for less than an hour to Sligo, where he would board a connecting train to Dublin, and from there catch a ferry to England.

The Londonderry train never arrived. Fleming checked his *Irish Railroad Traveller's Guide*, which read clearly: 5:35 p.m. But when, with sinking heart, he scanned the board, he saw that it indicated a departure time of 5:35 a.m. As a result of a misprint in the guide, he would miss his connections and lose a full day to waiting.

This scheduling mishap, a "monumental vexation" to the energetic Fleming, would prove to be the luckiest accident of his life. During the ensuing night in Bundoran, he concluded that, while the delay had been caused by a misprint, it reflected a larger problem: the whole system of measuring time, running through two twelve-hour cycles, cried out for overhauling.

Why not move to a twenty-four-hour clock, he wondered, so that instead of 5:35 p.m., a schedule would show 17:35? And that was just the first of his ideas. As a result of missing that train in Bundoran, Fleming started down a road that would culminate in a revolutionary invention—one with special significance to the far-flung nation of Canada.

Born in 1827 in Kirkcaldy, thirty miles (50 km) north of Edinburgh, Sandford Fleming became an apprentice, at age fourteen, of the Scottish engineer and surveyor John Sang. At eighteen, with his older brother, he emigrated to what was then called Canada West, settling among cousins in Peterborough. While working towards Canadian certification as a surveyor, achieved in 1849, he drew maps of Peterborough, Cobourg, Hamilton, and Toronto. Two years later, he designed Canada's first postage stamp, the "threepenny beaver," which helped turn the beaver into a national image.

In 1855, after surveying several railway lines, Fleming became chief engineer of the Northern Railway of Canada—and a champion, for safety reasons, of building iron bridges rather than wooden ones. As early as 1858, Fleming proposed a coast-to-coast railway to link the British North American colonies. Four years later, he produced a detailed plan for this Pacific railway, and also travelled to Britain to seek support, unsuccessfully, for a line running west as far as Red River.

In 1863, the well-known Fleming became Canada's chief surveyor. Shortly after Confederation, in 1867, John A. Macdonald made him engineer-in-chief of the Intercolonial Railway—a position he was still holding nine years later when, while on a sabbatical leave, he visited Bundoran. In 1871, when British Columbia joined Confederation on the promise of a railway link, Fleming took on additional responsibilities as chief engineer of the Canadian Pacific Railway.

The following summer, to explore possible routes through the Rocky Mountains, he led a small party west. Among those who went with him was the Reverend George Monro Grant, who would publish a bestselling book about the adventure, called *Ocean to Ocean,* and whose descendants would include philosopher George Grant and writer-politician Michael Grant Ignatieff.

Sandford Fleming's 1872 cross-country expedition included his wife, Jean, left, and Annie Moren, wife of Dr. Arthur Moren (seated right). Seated left is Fleming's son, Frank, while those standing (l to r) are George M. Grant, author of Ocean to Ocean, *Fleming, and Col. Robertson Ross.*

In the early 1880s, while involved with both the Hudson's Bay Company and the CPR, Fleming responded to a request from George Stephen and again travelled west with Grant to find a way through the Selkirk Mountains, just west of the Rockies. In 1884, together with Donald Smith, Fleming formed a Canadian subcommittee of the HBC to study land matters. And the year after that, when Smith drove the last spike at Craigellachie, Fleming would be there—the towering figure in the famous photo, with top hat and flowing beard.

But back to 1876. Four months after missing his train in Bundoran, Fleming presented a paper to the Canadian Institute—which he had helped to found years before—in which he advocated a universal, twenty-four-hour clock. And three years later, having refined his thinking, he presented a paper taking a global approach to the measurement of time.

At this point, only Great Britain, which had developed an extensive railway system, was using a standard time system. Because of its relatively small size, Britain faced nothing like the same problems as Canada, where, as in most countries, people regarded noon as the moment when the sun stood directly overhead. So when noon arrived in Toronto, it was already 12:13 in Kingston and 12:25 in Montreal. This played havoc with railway scheduling, and travellers would have to reset their timepieces according to local clocks.

In 1879, Sandford Fleming proposed to solve this problem by establishing a series of time zones. Where, initially, he had resisted linking measurement to any existing meridian of longitude, now he opted to begin with the "anti-meridian" of Greenwich, England. Also, he treated local systems as subordinate to this universal system. Using the American Society of Civil Engineers as his main vehicle, Fleming achieved a consensus among North American railways, which adopted the one-hour time zones that exist today.

Quickly adopted throughout North America, the system did not immediately become worldwide. In 1884, at the International Meridian Conference, Fleming spearheaded an attempt to establish where the prime meridian should be, arguing for Greenwich. The conference adopted a version of universal time, though national sensibilities, notably those of France, prevented the acceptance of Greenwich. That would come later. But by the end of the nineteenth century, thanks mainly to Fleming, most countries around the globe had adopted the system that prevails today, with times varying according to hourly zones as measured from Greenwich.

Sandford Fleming became chancellor of Queen's College in Kingston, where he led the way in establishing Queen's as a secular institution with a strong base in science and engineering. He was awarded a knighthood in 1897. Besides helping to build the railway that united Canada, Fleming devised the system that made using it feasible. Today he is rightly remembered around the world as the "father of standard time."

Frederick Banting: A Cure for Diabetes

On October 31, 1920, at two o'clock in the morning in London, Ontario, a sleepless twenty-nine-year-old medical doctor suddenly sat bolt upright in his bed. For most of the previous evening, Frederick Banting had been struggling to prepare a lecture on carbohydrate metabolism, or the way the human body changes food into energy—a subject linked with diabetes, still a lethal disease.

The young man had gone to bed reading a magazine article about the gland involved, the pancreas. This article and his projected lecture, he wrote later "had been chasing each other through [his] mind for some time" when he flashed on a surgical procedure that might, just might, lead to a way to combat diabetes, which was slowly killing over one million people in North America alone. "I got up and wrote down the idea," Banting added, "and spent most of the night thinking about it."

The young Scottish Canadian had started down the road towards the discovery of insulin, or what historian Michael Bliss has called "one of the most dramatic events in the history of the treatment of disease." Banting had glimpsed a cure for diabetes.

"Those who watched the first starved, sometimes comatose, diabetics receive insulin and return to life," Bliss writes in *The Discovery of Insulin,* "saw one of the genuine miracles of modern medicine. They were present at the closest approach to the resurrection of the body that our secular society can achieve, and at the discovery of what has become the elixir of life for millions of human beings around the world." The best contemporary estimates indicate that insulin has saved the lives of more than sixteen million people, all of whom would otherwise have died miserable deaths.

Born on an Ontario farm in 1891, Frederick Grant Banting was the youngest of five children of a Scottish Presbyterian mother, born

Margaret Squire Grant, and a farmer of Anglo-Irish and Ulster Scots heritage, William Thompson Banting. He grew up on that farm near Alliston, sixty miles (95 km) north of Toronto.

Frederick Grant Banting proved less than gracious about sharing the Nobel Prize with another Scot, John James Macleod, even though he would never have won it without his help.

Banting decided early to pursue a medical career, after witnessing a doctor in action. While walking home from school, he stopped to watch two men shingling a roof. The scaffolding broke, they fell to the ground, and he ran to fetch help. As he watched the doctor tend to the men, the boy realized what he wanted to become. At nineteen, after graduating from the local high school, Banting enrolled in a general arts course at the University of Toronto.

He failed French and German but, on condition that he make up these courses, he was admitted to medical school. While he was there, the First World War broke out. Banting volunteered to join the army and was twice rejected for poor eyesight. After he received his degree in 1916, he was accepted into the Canadian Army Medical Corps. He worked for a year at hospitals in England and then served at the front as a battalion medical officer.

In 1918, despite being wounded in the arm at the battle of Cambrai, Banting disobeyed orders and remained on the job. This almost cost him his arm, but for showing heroism under fire, he later received the Military Cross. The following year, with the war ended, Banting began working as a general practitioner in London, 125 miles (200 km) west of Toronto. Having studied orthopedic surgery, Banting began teaching this speciality part time at the University of Western Ontario. In 1920, he was preparing a lecture for one of his classes when he conceived the research project that would lead to the discovery of insulin.

After talking with scientists at Western, Banting approached an expert on diabetes teaching at the University of Toronto: John James Macleod, a Scottish immigrant born near Dunkeld and educated at Aberdeen and Leipzig. Realizing that Banting's approach had never been tried, Macleod offered the young scientist a small laboratory and the assistance of a graduate student, Charles Best. On March 17, 1921, Banting began his research.

This involved operating on dogs to tie up their pancreatic ducts—procedures that today would never be tolerated. During the next few months, though it cost the lives of at least seventeen dogs, Banting managed to extract a concentrated secretion of the pancreas that appeared to alleviate diabetes in animals. He also determined that instead of experimenting on dogs, he could extract "isletin," as he first called it, from the pancreatic glands of slaughtered cattle.

Banting reported his results to Macleod, who had returned to Toronto after spending the summer in Scotland. Macleod showed the other men how to produce an extract, and then, at Banting's suggestion, added a fourth member to the team—J.B. (Bert) Collip, a brilliant young biochemist.

Working together, the four men began refining the process. On January 11, 1922, Banting and Best took their muddy "isletin" to Toronto General Hospital, where it was injected into Leonard Thompson, a diabetic fourteen-year-old nearing death—but to little effect. Under Macleod's direction, Collip strove to purify the extract, and on January 23, young Thompson received another injection. This time, it worked. The boy revived.

Inevitably, looming success brought egos into conflict. Banting had always been socially awkward, as well as temperamental and even volatile. He would exchange harsh words with every one of the other team members, and now, when Collip threatened to keep his purification process secret, Banting grabbed him by the lapels and threw him across the room. The cool-headed Macleod managed to restore order and made the men sign a peace agreement.

Banting and the others agreed to change the name of the extract to "insulin," which was equally relevant and easier to pronounce: it comes from the Latin for "island," and refers to the islets of Langerhans, the cells in the pancreas that produce the secretion that controls blood sugar.

Earlier, as a weak public speaker, Banting had run into trouble presenting his findings to an expert audience, and Macleod had stepped in to answer questions. Now, on May 3, 1922, in a paper with Banting as lead author, Macleod presented the research findings in Washington. The audience of specialists, understanding what they heard, rose to their feet and applauded.

That summer, Banting spent three months treating Elizabeth Hughes, the diabetic young daughter of the U.S. secretary of state. She had arrived in Toronto in August weighing forty-four pounds (20 kg) and looking like a walking skeleton. By November, when specialists arrived who had treated her previously, they met a girl who looked so strong and healthy that they failed to recognize her.

In summer 1923, having been made a research professor at the University of Toronto and also awarded a lifetime annuity by the Canadian government, Banting gave an inaudible, two-minute talk at an international congress in Edinburgh. Later, Macleod gave the keynote address on insulin—a presentation attended by some of the most influential scientists in the world.

Back in Canada on October 26, 1923, after spending the day visiting his parents on their farm, Banting returned to Toronto and heard the news: he and Macleod had been awarded the Nobel Prize as co-discoverers of insulin. Initially, he had mixed feelings. As the first

Canadian to be so honoured, Banting felt thrilled. Yet he felt upset about sharing the glory with Macleod, who had conducted none of the experiments.

In fact, Banting could hardly have succeeded without Macleod, who had provided the laboratory, the graduate-student assistant, the expert biochemist, and considerable credibility, and had also communicated the findings to others. When he had cooled down, Banting decided to share his half of the award with Charles Best, who had assisted with the first experiments. Macleod responded by sharing with Collip.

Over the next decade, Banting was showered with awards, honours, and memberships. In 1934, he became a knight commander of the Order of the British Empire: Sir Frederick Banting, OBE. He continued his scientific researches, and he worked also at sketching and painting. At the Arts and Letters Club in Toronto, he became friends with the Group of Seven painter A.Y. Jackson, and the two men went on numerous painting excursions together, their shared favourite destinations being rural Quebec and the High Arctic.

When the Second World War broke out, tired of playing "Sir Frederick," and prevented by both title and age from reprising his previous wartime role, Banting began looking for ways to get to the front. He had conducted experiments on the effects of high altitude, and decided that he might be able to assist pilots.

Early in January 1941, at an Ottawa cocktail party, the forty-nine-year-old Banting learned that Lord Beaverbrook, the Scottish Canadian assisting Winston Churchill in the war effort, had instituted a new program for acquiring airplanes from North America. Instead of dismantling and shipping the planes to England, Beaverbrook had decided to have them flown across the Atlantic from Canada.

Banting determined that he might be able to fly to England aboard one of the twin-engine Hudson coastal reconnaissance bombers. He requested and received authorization. On February 17, he flew from

Montreal to Gander, Newfoundland, 870 miles (1,400 km). Three days later, on February 20, 1941, he was aboard when the plane took off on its final leg.

Fifty miles (80 km) northeast of Gander, an oil cooler malfunctioned. The pilot turned the plane around and struggled to keep the plane aloft—but without success. The bomber went down near Musgrave Harbour on Newfoundland's east coast. Only the pilot survived.

In 2004, in a poll conducted by the CBC, Canadians voted Sir Frederick Banting one of the ten greatest Canadians of all time. He finished fourth behind Tommy Douglas, Terry Fox, and Pierre Elliott Trudeau. Three years later, when another CBC survey undertook to discover the ten greatest Canadian inventions, insulin topped the list.

Today, despite the discovery of insulin, diabetes remains a serious health problem both around the world and in Canada. Scientists estimate that over one million Canadians suffer from diabetes, although many remain unaware of their condition. In this country, despite mortality data that underestimate the problem, diabetes remains the seventh leading cause of death.

13

WOMEN FROM ARCADIA

Through most of the 1800s, if the average woman wanted a career other than motherhood, she could become a domestic worker, a teacher or, later in the century, a nurse. But if, while raising a family at home, she wanted to try writing, obviously nobody could stop her. During the 1830s and '40s, a few pioneering women published poems, stories, and eventually books. Yet none of them made a living by the pen. From Susanna Moodie to Isabella Valancy Crawford, all of them wrote while struggling to survive. The idea that a woman could flourish as a professional writer while living in British North America would remain a pipe dream—at least until an extraordinary Prince Edward Islander arrived on the scene.

In the early 1900s, with nursing yet to be established in Canada, women could become either teachers or "domestic workers." New arrivals, like these immigrants from Scotland, faced the greatest challenges. Government ads of this era announced, "Servant girls are in great demand and command $8 – 12 a month."

Lucy Maud Montgomery: Anne of Green Gables

Born in the village of Clifton (now New London) in 1874, Lucy Maud Montgomery was descended from two pioneer families that had emigrated from Kintyre, Scotland, in the 1770s. Her grandfather Donald Montgomery served as a Canadian senator while she was growing up. Her mother had died of tuberculosis when Maud was nearing two, and she was raised in Cavendish, Prince Edward Island, by her elderly maternal grandparents, the Macneills.

"I come of Scotch ancestry," she would write in a memoir she called *The Alpine Path*, "with a dash of English from several 'grands' and 'greats.' There were many traditions and tales on both sides of the family, to which, as a child, I listened with delight while my elders talked them over around winter firesides. The romance of them was in my blood; I thrilled to the lure of adventure which had led my forefathers westward from the Old Land—a land which I always heard referred to as 'Home,' by men and women whose parents were Canadian born and bred."

An intelligent, imaginative, emotional girl immersed in a world thick with Scottish lore and Presbyterianism, young Maud grew up knowing that one of her great-grandmothers, had she lived long enough, would have been "an ardent suffragette. The most advanced feminist could hardly spurn old conventions more effectually than she did when she proposed to David [her eventual husband]."

Montgomery traced her "knack of writing and literary tastes" to her mother's family. Her ancestor John Macneill, who had emigrated from Argyll in 1775, was first cousin to the Scottish poet Hector Macneill, author of several well-known lyrics, among them "Come under My Plaidie," often attributed to Burns. Several other Macneills had since demonstrated literary talent, and Maud grew up listening to her grandfather, Alexander Macneill, recite the poems of both Burns and fellow Macneills.

Cavendish had been settled in 1700 by three Scottish families, all captured in a local saying: "From the conceit of the Simpsons, the pride of the Macneills, and the vain-glory of the Clarks, good Lord deliver us." Whatever their faults, she wrote, "they were loyal, clannish, upright, God-fearing folk, inheriting traditions of faith and simplicity and aspiration."

At six, little Maud began attending the Cavendish schoolhouse, "a white-washed, low-eaved building on the side of the road just outside our gate." A nearby spruce grove, with its sprinkling of maple trees, was to her "a fairy realm of beauty and romance." She began keeping a diary at age nine, and soon she was avidly reading the works of Walter Scott and Louisa May Alcott, among others.

Her childhood environment shaped her literary development: "Were it not for those Cavendish years, I do not think *Anne of Green Gables* would ever have been written." Looking back, Montgomery could not remember a time when she was not writing, or when she did not intend to be an author.

At fifteen, Montgomery travelled with her grandfather Montgomery to Prince Albert, Saskatchewan, where her remarried father was living. She spent one year there, attending high school, and published for the first time: a poem in the *Patriot,* a local newspaper. She published several more poems there, as well as a story in the Montreal *Witness,* and an article in the Prince Albert *Times:* "I was beginning to plume myself on being quite a literary person."

Montgomery returned to Prince Edward Island and the one-room Cavendish school for one more year. Then, in 1893, she moved into bustling Charlottetown to train for the only career open to women. At Prince of Wales College, she completed a two-year teaching degree in one year. She then taught in a rural school for a year so that, in 1895, she could spend a year studying English literature at Dalhousie University in Halifax.

Meanwhile, she wrote steadily, fighting through rejection after rejection. She found them wounding at first, but soon hardened herself: "I only set my teeth and said, 'I will succeed.'" From an American magazine, she had already received "the first tangible recompense my pen brought me"—two subscriptions. And when, in Halifax, she received a story acceptance accompanied by a five-dollar cheque (roughly $125 today), Montgomery went uptown and bought five volumes of poetry—something she "could keep forever in memory of having 'arrived.'"

Teaching again in a rural situation, she boarded in a cold farmhouse. Evenings, after a day of strenuous work, she would be too tired to write, so she began rising an hour early. For five months, she got up at six, dressed by lamplight, donned a heavy coat, and sat on her feet to keep them from freezing. Then, "with fingers so cramped that I could scarcely hold the pen, I would write my 'stunt' for the day."

In 1898, after her grandfather Macneill died, Montgomery quit teaching and moved back into the family homestead with her grandmother. Before long, while still battling rejections, she was scratching out a small but steady income. In her journal, she declared, "I never expect to be famous. I merely want to have a recognized place among good workers in my chosen profession. That, I honestly believe, is happiness."

After three years, Montgomery returned to Halifax and joined the winter staff of the *Daily Echo,* initially as a proofreader. "I'm a newspaper woman!" she wrote. "Life in a newspaper office isn't all 'beer and skittles' any more than anywhere else. But on the whole it is not a bad life at all." Although she had always written in solitude and quiet, now she produced despite "rolls of proof shooting down from upstairs, people coming and conversing, telephones ringing, and machines being thumped and dragged overhead."

Still, the following summer, she returned to Cavendish. There she stayed for the next nine years, writing steadily. In spring 1904, while rifling through an old notebook, looking for an idea for a serial, Montgomery found a faded entry: "Elderly couple

In Anne of Green Gables, *Lucy Maud Montgomery created an imaginative heroine who made her own way in an island world thick with Scottish lore and Presbyterianism.*

apply to orphan asylum for a boy. By mistake a girl is sent them." Soon she was blocking out chapters. The character Anne flashed into her mind already christened, and "soon she seemed very real to me and took possession of me to an unusual degree." It seemed a shame to waste such an appealing character on an ephemeral serial, and Montgomery thought, "Write a book. You have the central idea. All you need do is to spread it out over enough chapters to amount to a book."

Montgomery wrote *Anne of Green Gables* during the evenings, after she had finished writing the stories that kept money coming. She finished the novel in October 1905 and began seeking a publisher. After five rejections, she put the book into an old hatbox, resolving to reduce it to a seven-chapter serial when she found time. But the following winter, after leafing through it again, she decided to send it out once more. This time, she received an acceptance.

It was exciting. But for Lucy Maud Montgomery, the more important day came on June 20, 1908. In her journal, she wrote, "Today has been, as Anne herself would say, 'an epoch in my life.' My book came today, 'spleet-new,' from the publishers. I candidly confess that it was to me a proud and wonderful and thrilling moment. There, in my hand, lay the material realization of all the dreams and hopes and ambitions and struggles of my whole conscious existence—my first book. Not a great book, but mine, mine, mine, something which I had created."

Overnight, *Anne of Green Gables* became a bestseller, what today publishers would call a "breakout book." Then, as sales around the world climbed into the tens of millions, the novel went beyond all such yardsticks. Eventually, the book would be recognized as a literary classic. It continues to move us, according to Montgomery specialists Mary Rubio and Elizabeth Waterston, because it is "built out of the most important thing in the world—the tangled web of human emotions."

After *Green Gables,* Montgomery would write and publish twenty-three books of fiction, adding these to 500 stories, 450 poems, and several miscellaneous works. According to the *Oxford Companion to Canadian Literature,* the fictions "rework the conventions of romance patterns to make 'serious social criticism' and permit women readers an ironic recognition of how their culture oppresses them."

Montgomery later married a Presbyterian minister, honeymooned in Scotland, gave birth to three children, one of whom died at birth, wrangled with unscrupulous publishers, and lived through difficult years with a depressive husband. Incidentally, she proved shockingly prescient as regards the impact of future technology, predicting in 1933 that within a hundred years, Sunday services would "not be held in little country churches. There will be just a few central churches in large cities, and the services will be broadcast from them. Country people will sit in their homes, press a button and hear and see."

Lucy Maud Montgomery also became an international celebrity: fellow of the British Royal Society of Arts, companion of the Order of the British Empire, member of the Literary and Artistic Institute of France. With these and other successes, she showed Canadian women that housework, mothering, and teaching did not circumscribe their possibilities. By forging a wildly successful professional career, she became a breakthrough figure, and an inspirational role model for future generations—not just of writers but of Canadian women.

Sara Jeannette Duncan: The Imperialist

Four years before *Anne of Green Gables* appeared in print, another Scottish Canadian writer published a novel that, according to one literary critic, "should be a required text for feminists." Published in 1904, *The Imperialist* by Sara Jeannette Duncan is "a fine study of a young woman's ability, yearning, self-awareness, and self-delusion." Elizabeth Waterston explains that the Ontario-born Duncan "knew enough about the Scottish heritage to delineate the imported norm and to discriminate the Canadian deviance."

The Imperialist, Waterston continues in *Rapt in Plaid,* "is a major locus for tracing the persistence of Scottish traditions in Canadian life, both domestic and theological. It should also be required reading for anyone interested in post-colonialism and the process by which a country moves toward a lessening of imperial ties."

Another literary critic, Clara Thomas, argues that *The Imperialist* interweaves the pervasive Canadian mythology of the Small Town with that of The Hero and Nation-Builder (Scotch). Duncan shows "the Scotch and their offspring to be builders, men to usher in the future; the English are reactionary, cautious, conservative and ridiculously class-ridden in a society which sees itself as classless."

Thomas complains that Duncan has substituted "her own elite establishment, Scotch and Presbyterian, for the old colonial elitism of British and Anglican." Yet she acknowledges that the Canadian "mythology of the Scotch was based, of course, on a solid ground of fact—on the numbers of Scotch who were prominent in the exploring and settling of the country,

Ontario-born Sara Jeannette Duncan knew enough about her Scottish heritage to delineate the Canadian variation in her early feminist classic, The Imperialist.

in its fur trade and later, on every level of government and financial enterprise," as well as on the power of the Presbyterian church and the pride of the Scots, "a pride that distance from the homeland enhanced and fostered."

The social mythology of the Small Town, Thomas argues, is also well grounded in nineteenth-century reality—"a time when Canada was predominantly rural, and towns like Elgin [the fictional town of the novel] were important centres of their agricultural districts."

The irony here is that, unlike L.M. Montgomery, Sara Jeannette Duncan was not living in her native land when she wrote her greatest book. She penned *The Imperialist,* a singular portrait of small-town Canada at the turn of the nineteenth century, while living in India.

Sara Jeannette (Janet) Duncan was the daughter of Charles Duncan, a dry-goods merchant born in Cupar, Scotland, just west of St. Andrews. He immigrated to New Brunswick in the 1850s, married Jane Bell, and moved with her in 1858 to Brantford, in southwestern Ontario. The Duncans attended the Free Church run by the legendary Presbyterian William Cochrane, a vigorous evangelical preacher and a "George Brown liberal" who railed against the "brazen corruption" of the governments of Sir John A. Macdonald.

Born in 1861, Sara Jeanette (born Janet) Duncan finished secondary school at Brantford Collegiate Institute and trained as a teacher at Toronto Normal School, graduating in 1882. By then she had published a poem in the Toronto *Globe* and an essay in the *Canada Monthly* magazine. She worked as a supply teacher in the Brantford area until 1884, when she persuaded the *Globe* to send her to New Orleans to report on the World's Industrial and Cotton Centennial Exposition.

Writing as "Garth Grafton," she proved so capable that U.S. newspapers picked up her articles, and the *Globe* offered her a weekly column. In 1885, she moved to Washington, D.C., where she became books editor, columnist, and editorial writer at the *Washington Post.* The next summer, she returned to Toronto as editor of a new Woman's World section. Late in 1887, continuing this frenetic pace, Duncan went to work for the Montreal *Star,* quickly becoming its Ottawa-based political correspondent.

Her journalistic work included interviews with the Mohawk poet Emily Pauline Johnson and early female physician Alice McGillivray. She also wrote extensively on literary and intellectual issues, exploring some of the themes that would later figure in her fiction. In one column, she described Canadians as "an eminently unliterary people" and Ontario as "one great camp of Philistines." We debate politics, temperance, and religion, she wrote, but remain resolutely colonial with regard to the arts: "We are well-clad, well fed, well read. Why should we not buy our own books!"

In 1888, Sara Duncan quit the Montreal *Star* to circle the globe with another woman journalist and write a book about the experience. The ensuing novel appeared in 1890 under the title *A Social Departure: How Orthodocia and I Went around the World by Ourselves*. Duncan used this work, which employed her journalistic eye for detail and her wry humour, as a model for several more travelogue novels that featured clashes of manners and attitudes.

While visiting India, she had met British journalist Everard Cotes. In 1891, she married him and joined him in Calcutta, which became her base for the next twenty-five years. Duncan continued to travel, most often to England and Canada, while Cotes became editor of the *Indian Daily News* and then managing director of the Eastern News Agency. She never lived in Canada permanently again, though she directed that all her book royalties be paid to a bank account in Brantford.

Duncan wrote and published steadily, writing every morning until she had completed 300 or 400 words. She published her first serious novel, *A Daughter of To-day*, in 1894, addressing the theme of the "new woman" by featuring a heroine who writes a book about her experiences as a burlesque dancer—but eventually, to the dismay of reviewers at the time, commits suicide.

Popular and prolific, published in London, New York, and Toronto, Duncan produced a total of twenty-two books. Many were set in London or Calcutta, and explored the world of British expatriates. Duncan had numerous literary friends. She exchanged letters with her hero Henry James, and in Simla, at her country residence, she entertained E.M. Forster. He pronounced her home "quite English," and described her, in 1912, as "clever and odd—nice to talk to alone, but at times the Social Manner descended like a pall."

The Imperialist, which Duncan called "my Canadian novel," is set in Elgin, Ontario, a fictionalized Brantford. It revolves around a by-election in which Lorne Murchison runs for the Liberals on a platform of imperial federation. Duncan presents imperialism as a nascent form of Canadian nationalism, and suggests that Canada could one day claim centre stage in the British Empire. Lorne's sister, Advena, symbolizes an idealized version of this future. To a Canadian historian friend, soon after the book appeared, Duncan insisted, "The Empire is a big place and interesting everywhere, but ours is by far the best part of it, and the most full of the future."

Duncan sought to make *The Imperialist* her best book, but the critics were divided. The *New York Times* praised it, but the London *Spectator* found it didactic, and her old newspaper, the *Globe*, sniffed that as a woman, Duncan had no business writing on political subjects. Toronto's *Saturday Night* proved more generous: "To the Canadian, to the Ontarian especially, it means more than any other Canadian story, for it gives with truth and with art a depiction of our own community."

Modern literary critics praise the novel as a well-crafted example of modernist realism. Biographer and critic Thomas Tausky calls *The Imperialist* "a brilliant study of a small Ontario town." He rightly describes Duncan as "one of the most penetrating observers of Canadian society in her time," and notes that she "combined shrewd analysis with a vivid, personal style."

Critic Clara Thomas agrees with that assessment. But she adds that "the name of the game pictured by Elgin and its society is 'Opportunity and Progress,' and its key-words are work, education and Protestant ethics." Advena Murchison, she writes, "is the one misfit to everything Elgin represents." Like Sara Jeannette Duncan, Advena "is one of the first generation of women in Canada to be educated for a career beyond the home." But she ends up leaving to build a life in Alberta, where she "will certainly have to learn and practice the housewife's skills that she has resisted."

Advena "has had many sisters in Canadian fiction and in life," Thomas adds, "women who were trained and talented beyond the scope that their destined roles as wives and mothers could possibly bring them." Thomas notes that after a short time as a teacher, "Duncan got away from the Elgins of Ontario and finally from Canada." This country did not yet have the infrastructure, complexity, and sophistication to accommodate a Sara Jeannette Duncan.

14

LADIES FROM HELL

Shortly after the First World War, during the 1919 run-up to the Paris Peace Conference that produced the Treaty of Versailles, Canada began laying claim to a modest place on the world stage. Despite opposition by Americans and others, Canadians argued that Canada should enjoy the same representation at the table as other small independent nations. Up until then, this country had been recognized internationally only as a colony of the British Empire.

But during the Great War, 600,000 Canadians had served in the military. More than 60,000 had died and 170,000 were wounded, including some who were disfigured or dismembered. Today, those figures look almost surreal. Proportionately, given a population of only eight million, Canada made a contribution which exceeded that of virtually any other country.

During that war, members of Canada's kilted regiments distin-guished themselves. They performed so valiantly that they became known as "the ladies from hell," because that is what the German troops are said to have called them. People also marvelled at the ethnic diversity of these Scottish battalions. Canadians of various heritages, including my Huguenot-descended grandfather, had taken to identify-ing themselves as warrior Scots.

And why not? Scots had begun forging a military reputation in Canada as early as the 1750s. Three Scottish regiments fought for Brit-ain during the Seven Years' War that saw the defeat of New France: the Black Watch, the Montgomery Highlanders, and the Fraser's High-landers. The first two had already distinguished themselves in that war, the Black Watch with a ferocious but futile assault on Fort Carillon (Ticonderoga), and the Montgomery Highlanders by capturing Fort Duquesne (Pittsburgh).

The Fraser's Highlanders were the first Scottish regiment to fight on Canadian soil. In 1758, with a terrible seven-week siege, they helped take the strategically situated fortress of Louisbourg on Cape Breton Island from the French. And in 1759, they led the British to victory at Quebec City. First, a French-speaking Highlander, Captain David Macdonald, tricked sentries into thinking that French reinforcements were approaching. Then, the Highlanders led the charge across the Plains of Abraham. A French soldier, Joseph Trahan, described how the Scots threw down their muskets, drew their broadswords, and, despite withering gunfire, charged hollering over the hill.

At both Louisbourg and Quebec, ironically, the Fraser's Highland-ers were serving under General James Wolfe, who had helped Brit-ish troops defeat Scottish Highlanders at Culloden in 1746—a brutal, bloody business that saw well-armed government forces slaughter an ill-equipped army that had invaded England in a bid to install a Roman

Catholic king. It is ironic that Wolfe owes his military reputation to the ferocious Scottish troops, given that he had infamously declared them expendable: "They are hardy, intrepid, accustomed to a rough country, and no great mischief if they fall."

Wolfe was killed during the battle of Quebec, and the Scottish James Murray became military governor and then, in 1764, first civil governor of the province of Quebec. As a born-and-bred Scot accustomed to feeling marginalized, he proved far more sympathetic to the French Canadians than Wolfe would have. After the Conquest, and despite opposition from British merchants, Murray allowed them to maintain French civil law—a decision that led to his recall in 1766, though his precedents were preserved under the Quebec Act.

This soldier from the 5th Royal Scots of Canada is part of a fabled tradition that includes the Fraser's Highlanders, the Black Watch, and the 48th Highlanders.

Many of Murray's disbanded Highlanders accepted land grants in Quebec, especially in the Eastern Townships outside Montreal. In the 1770s, when the American Revolution began, these men formed the nucleus of the Royal Highland Emigrants, the first Scottish regiment to be raised in Canada. During the American invasion of Canada, the regiment's first battalion played a key role in repulsing a siege of Quebec City. The second battalion distinguished itself in the Atlantic provinces, New York, and the American south.

Scots also dominated the King's Royal Regiment of New York, the "Royal Yorkers" who won victories against the Americans at Saratoga and in the Mohawk Valley. They received lands in eastern Ontario, within a twenty-mile (30 km) radius of Cornwall, where they gave rise to the Stormont, Dundas and Glengarry Highlanders.

In the War of 1812, half a dozen Scottish regiments crossed the Atlantic to battle the invading Americans. They were joined by numerous immigrant Scots who had settled in the Eastern Townships and along the St. Lawrence River system from Trois Rivières to Belleville. After the war, those settlers became army volunteers. During the Rebellions of 1837, the profoundly Scottish Glengarry area of Upper Canada alone spawned four regiments. This produced the spectacle, not for the first time in history, of Scots battling Scots.

During the First World War, three Canadian Scottish units stood their ground when troops of other countries fled during a German gas attack at Ypres. Fighting with the 3rd Canadian Infantry Brigade, the Royal Highlanders (Black Watch), the 48th Highlanders, and the Canadian Scottish somehow managed to repulse the attack. During the war, Canada's Black Watch Regiment won four Victoria Crosses. Originally 12,000 strong, the regiment ended the war with 2,163 killed, 6,014 wounded, and 821 decorated.

The Canadian Scottish troops proved so courageous in such dark circumstances that they inspired other regiments to change their names or reveal their Scottish identities—producing, for example, the Lorne Scots, the Essex and Kent Scottish, and the Cameron Highlanders of Ottawa. During the Second World War, Canadian Scottish regiments continued to play a leadership role.

By that time, of course, Canada's military contribution had already wrought a transformation in the country's international status. The key moment came shortly after the First World War, at the Paris Peace Conference of 1919. On June 28, when Canada signed the Treaty of Versailles, it did so as part of the British Empire—but also as a distinct nation.

In recognition of its disproportionate contribution, Canada not only obtained a seat at the League of Nations but was later elected to the Council of the League. Canada's participation in the Great War, led mostly by Scots, had increased Canadian unity, autonomy, and self-awareness. Above all, it had created a new acceptance on the world stage, and a reputation that the Second World War would only enhance.

Guy Laffin: Kiltie at Passchendaele

A couple of years ago, while walking down a hallway at my mother's home in Peterborough, north of Toronto, I did a double take in front of an old photograph of my grandfather. I had seen the image

a thousand times: Guy Laffin standing at attention with a rifle at his shoulder. I knew that he had fought in the First World War with the Canadian army. I knew he had survived Vimy Ridge, Passchendaele, and the Somme, and that he had earned the Belgian Cross for valour.

But I had not realized that he wore a kilt. Probably I spotted it now only because I had begun this book. My maternal grandfather wasn't Scottish. He came from a long line of French Irish Huguenots. What was he doing in a kilt? When I expressed my surprise, my mother reminded me that Guy Laffin had served in the First World War

During the First World War, Guy Laffin fought as a "kiltie." He earned a Belgian Cross.

with the 48th Highlanders. He was a "kiltie"—one of those Canadian soldiers who belonged to a Scottish regiment and insisted on wearing their distinctive uniforms even into battle. Soon enough, I found myself digging through old military records and interviewing cousins to sort out the what, where, and when of my grandfather's war. . . .

At six in the morning, when the sun rose, the Canadian artillery in Belgium had begun a preliminary bombardment intended to soften up the Germans. At first, Sergeant Guy Laffin had been able to lead his men steadily forward, staying low and scrambling from one muddy trench to the next. But now, pinned down under withering fire from a machine-gun nest on the ridge ahead, he and his men could advance no farther—not without getting killed.

It was early November 1917, and the second battle of Passchendaele, near the town of Ypres, had been raging for days. Twenty-five-year-old Laffin, responsible for the lives of eight men, shouted over the thundering din to his corporal, his right-hand man, telling him to lay down distracting fire. He ran along the trench and then, with a grenade in his hand, climbed out and started scrambling up the hill from behind the sandbagged nest, sheltering behind the bodies of the dead and hoping that the Germans would not see him.

When he got within thirty or forty feet (9–12 m), Laffin pulled the pin on the grenade. Years ago, as a boy in Nova Scotia, he had played sandlot baseball. Now he rose up onto one bare knee, took aim, and let fly. He ducked back into the mud and *kaboom*! It sounded like a direct hit. He waited, but the machine gun had gone silent. Laffin peeked out from behind a pile of mud. Carefully, fearing a trap, he scrambled forward. In the sandbagged trench, several Germans lay dead. He waved at his men to come forward. For this act of bravery, Guy Laffin was awarded Belgium's Croix de Guerre: the Belgian Cross. This honour was mentioned a few months later, in the *London Gazette* of July 12, 1918, and officially announced on September 4.

My maternal grandfather had gravitated naturally to the Scottish tradition of military service. His earliest known ancestor, the French-Irish Huguenot Thomas Laffin, had fought with the Royal Highland

Emigrants, also known as the Young Emigrants, during the American Revolution. The nucleus of that kilt-wearing regiment included 300 former members of the Fraser's Highlanders who had helped the British take the Plains of Abraham in 1759. Thomas Laffin had joined up in Ireland, lured by the promise of land and donning the full Highland costume—belted plaid with raccoon sporran and regimental facings of the Black Watch Regiment. After crossing the Atlantic, he served in the Atlantic provinces, New York, and the American south (Savannah, Charleston, and Eutaw Springs).

When the Revolutionary War ended in 1783, the regiment was disbanded in Windsor, Nova Scotia. As a junior officer, Thomas Laffin received 500 acres of land at Five Mile River, twenty-five miles (40 km) southwest of Truro. There he farmed and raised a family, most of whom remained in Nova Scotia. In August 1914, soon after the First World War began, Thomas Laffin's great-great-grandson, the twenty-two-year-old carpenter Guy Laffin, joined the Nova Scotia Highlanders, donned a kilt, and sailed to England.

In February 1915, while still in Britain, he transferred to the 48th Highlanders, who fought as the 15th Battalion in the First Canadian Division. At the end of July, Laffin joined the Highlanders in France. He served continuously in France and Belgium until the end of the war, except for brief periods when he was sidelined as a result of appendicitis and a mustard gas attack.

In 1917, a horrific year for those in the trenches, Laffin became a corporal. He saw action at the battles of Loos and Mount Sorrel and at the two-month battle of the Somme. At one point, he served as a sniper. And on April 9, 1917, on the first day of the battle for Vimy Ridge—a battle often cited as a defining moment in Canadian history, during which Canada suffered more than 10,000 casualties including 3,598 deaths—Guy Laffin was promoted to sergeant and, for the first time, led eight men into battle at the front.

Judging from his military records, Laffin missed the battle of Hill 70 because of an attack of appendicitis. But he was back at the front in time to take out that machine-gun nest at the second battle of Passchendaele in early November. The following March, he got caught in a gas attack and spent several weeks in hospital. Decades later, he would say that he had never fully recovered. But in 1919, after the war ended, Guy Laffin returned home to Nova Scotia. He had devoted four years to fighting Germans and to maintaining the Scottish tradition of military service. In 1922, at age thirty, he married nineteen-year-old Charlotte Amanda Hennigar, a woman descended, ironically enough, from a German Protestant Huguenot who, like his great-great-grandfather, had fought on the Loyalist side during the American Revolution.

Margaret Macdonald: First Woman Major

"During the cruel bombing of the Canadian Hospitals," Major Margaret Macdonald wrote of a series of attacks on Boulogne, France, during the First World War, "came experiences of the most frightening, the recollection of which must ever remain painfully indelible. Yet at the time never was a complaint uttered by these valiant women [the nurses] who were conspicuously undismayed in remaining at their posts."

By the time of these bombings, Macdonald—the first woman in the British Empire to attain the rank of major—had been matron-in-chief of the Canadian Nursing Service for four years. Born in 1873 in the hamlet of Bailey's Brook, Nova Scotia—near the northeast coast of the province between Pictou and Antigonish—Macdonald could trace her ancestry to the Scottish Highlands on both sides. Her Macdonald ancestors hailed from Moidart, just south of the Isle of Skye. The first of them, Angus Macdonald, had arrived in Pictou in 1790. And her

*Matron-in-Chief Margaret Macdonald, the first woman in the Brit-
ish Empire to attain the rank of major, is shown at her desk in the London
headquarters of Canadian Nursing Service. During the First World War,
she made eleven tours of inspection in France and seventy in England.*

mother, born a Chisholm, could trace her Gaelic roots to Glen Affric,
just above Loch Ness.

In 1851, her father had set up a general store in Bailey's Brook, and
by the time Margaret Macdonald arrived, he was a leading businessman.
Her father provided "a classical education" for eight of his nine children, and she was one of them. From age eleven, Maggie attended Stella
Maris Convent, a boarding school in Pictou, thirty miles (50 km) west
of home, and then, for two years starting in 1890, she studied at Mount
St. Vincent Academy in Halifax.

After graduating with distinction, and inspired by stories of British
nurse Florence Nightingale—clippings turn up in one of her early scrap-
books—Maggie Macdonald went south to train as a nurse. In 1895, this
modest and proper lassie graduated from New York City Hospital.

In 1898, during the Spanish–American War, she worked as a nurse on an American hospital ship. The following year, when the Boer War broke out, she joined the Canadian Nursing Service and travelled to South Africa, where she served for two years as part of the Army Medical Corps. After that war, Macdonald completed some postgraduate nursing training in New York. She then travelled south to Panama, where she worked for eighteen months during the building of the Panama Canal, shrugging off a bout of malaria.

In 1906, at thirty-three, Macdonald joined Canada's Permanent Army Medical Corps and served at military hospitals in Quebec City, Kingston, and Halifax. Committed to her profession, she spent six months in England, working in military hospitals and analyzing medical services.

By 1914, when the First World War erupted, Macdonald was one of the most experienced military nurses in Canada. Appointed matron-in-chief of the Canadian Nursing Service and given the rank of major, Macdonald selected the first hundred nurses to travel to Great Britain. She then set up her own base of operations in London.

At some point during the next five years, with one of her brothers, who was on leave from the army, Macdonald managed to visit Moidart, the remote home district of her Macdonald ancestors. But mainly she worked incessantly. An outstanding administrator responsible for all Canadian overseas military nurses, Macdonald deployed nurses to hospitals, ships, and trains throughout Britain and France, and built the Canadian nursing contingent to 1,900.

In the process, she made eleven tours of inspection to Canadian hospitals in France and seventy to those in England. In May and June of 1918, when hospitals in northern France became targets, including those in Boulogne, twenty Canadian nursing sisters lost their lives, and others were wounded.

From the target area, Macdonald not only deplored the bombings of Boulogne but warned her superiors that at one hospital, nurses had to pass anti-aircraft guns at least twice a day. At another, she protested, nurses had to shelter in flimsy dugouts: "In the event of a direct bomb hit, there would probably be no survivors."

After the war, having received both the Royal Red Cross from King George V and the Florence Nightingale Medal, Macdonald helped re-organize the Canadian Army Medical Service. In 1923, when all nursing sisters who had served in the war were discharged, Major Macdonald retired at age fifty-one. She would receive many honours, including a lifetime membership in the National Council of Women of Canada.

But her finest hour came in 1926, when in the Centre Block on Ottawa's Parliament Hill, before an audience of 800 nurses gathered from across the country, Macdonald dedicated a memorial to Canadian nursing sisters. After reading an honour roll of forty-seven names and sharing in the observance of a two-minute silence, she unveiled the sculpted marble panel. And then Margaret Macdonald listened, remembering, as the corridors echoed with the sounds of a lone bugler playing "The Last Post."

John Alexander McCrae: In Flanders Fields

On May 3, 1915, while serving in the First World War, a Scottish Canadian doctor sat in the back of a field ambulance near Ypres, scratching out a poem in pencil. John McCrae, age forty-two, had buried one of his best friends the day before. McCrae had presided over the setting of a white wooden cross by the grave of Alexis Helmer, killed in action at the second battle of Ypres.

That city is located in southeast Belgium, in the area known as Flanders, where poppies turn summer fields into a sea of red, and McCrae

Guelph-born field surgeon John McCrae, shown here in 1914 playing with his dog Bonneau, wrote "In Flanders Fields" the following year.

began his poem, "In Flanders fields, the poppies blow/Between the crosses, row on row." Literary critics regard Rupert Brooke and Wilfred Owen as the greatest English-language poets of the First World War. Yet John McCrae's three short verses, entitled "In Flanders Fields," became not only the most popular poem of the era but also the most influential. Besides serving to recruit volunteers into a necessary war, the poem inspired many Western countries—Canada, France, the United States, Britain, and other Commonwealth countries—to adopt the poppy as an enduring symbol of remembrance of the war dead.

The paternal grandparents of the doctor-poet, Thomas McCrae and Jean Campbell McCrae, came from Scotland in 1849 and settled in Guelph, Ontario. Their son David married Janet Simpson Eckford, and John (b. 1872) was the second of three children. He grew up staunchly Presbyterian and attended Central Public School and then Guelph Collegiate Institute. While there, he played the bugle in a militia regiment commanded by his father, and also began writing poetry.

At sixteen, he became the first Guelph student to earn a scholarship to the University of Toronto. Despite recurring problems with asthma, McCrae completed a bachelor's degree in 1894. He entered U of T medical school, did a residency in Baltimore, Maryland, and graduated as a gold-medallist doctor at age twenty-six.

McCrae had remained involved in the military, moving from the Guelph militia regiment to the Toronto-based Queen's Own Rifles, where he became a captain and commanded the company. He also continued to write—notably some poems inspired by the death of a young woman he loved. While at university, he published sixteen poems and several short stories in various magazines, among them *Saturday Night.*

In 1900, after the Boer War engulfed South Africa, the Presbyterian John McCrae felt duty-bound to get involved. He sailed with the Second Canadian Contingent in command of a section of the Royal Canadian Artillery. He served in several major campaigns before returning to Canada and taking up a fellowship in pathology at McGill University in Montreal.

In 1905, he set up his own practice while continuing to work at hospitals. He lectured in pathology at the University of Vermont until 1911. In Montreal, he worked at Royal Victoria Hospital, lectured at McGill University, and served also at Montreal General Hospital and the Royal Alexandra Hospital for Infectious Diseases. One medical professor declared him "the most talented physician of his generation."

McCrae also enjoyed a busy social life. He attended St. Paul's Presbyterian Church, wrote poetry, and became an active member of the Pen and Pencil Club, whose members included the humourist Stephen Leacock. Along the way, McCrae found time to accompany Lord Albert Grey, governor general of Canada, as the expedition doctor on a canoe trip that followed an old fur-trading route from Lake Winnipeg to Hudson Bay.

In autumn 1914, when the First World War began, John McCrae immediately signed up to become a field surgeon in the 1st Brigade of Canadian Field Artillery. "It is a terrible state of affairs," he wrote to a friend, "and I am going because I think every bachelor, especially if he has experience of war, ought to go. I am really rather afraid, but more afraid to stay at home with my conscience."

In April 1915, the second battle of Ypres proved one of the ugliest of the war. To his mother, after the German forces used chlorine gas against the Canadians, McCrae wrote that he was living in a nightmare: "We have been in the most bitter of fights. For seventeen days and seventeen nights none of us have had our clothes off, nor our boots even, except occasionally. In all that time while I was awake, gunfire and rifle fire never ceased for sixty seconds. . . . And behind it all was the constant background of the sights of the dead, the wounded, the maimed, and a terrible anxiety lest the line should give way."

In addition to treating the wounded, McCrae served on the guns and performed burial services—among them, the one he conducted after the second battle of Ypres for Lieutenant Alexis Helmer, his friend and former student. McCrae discarded "In Flanders Fields" after writing it, but a fellow officer retrieved the poem and sent it off to the prestigious British magazine *Punch,* which published it.

The following summer, over his protestations, McCrae was transferred away from the front lines and made chief of medical services at the Canadian general hospital at Boulogne-sur-Mer in France. Here, according to biographer John F. Prescott, McCrae "insisted on living in a tent through the year, like his comrades at the front, rather than in the officers' huts. When this affected his health in mid-winter he had to be ordered into warmer surroundings. To many he gave the impression that he felt he should still be with his old artillery brigade. After the battle of Ypres, he was never again the optimistic man with the infectious smile."

At Boulogne, where the hospital covered twenty-six acres and included 1,560 beds, McCrae treated the wounded from the third battle of Ypres, as well those from the Somme, Vimy Ridge, Arras, and Passchendaele. Early in 1918, after suffering several asthma attacks, McCrae fell ill with pneumonia and meningitis. He died on January 28, 1918, four days after he learned of his appointment as first Canadian consulting physician to the First British Army. At Wimereux Cemetery, he was buried with full military honours. His horse, Bonfire, led a funeral procession with his master's boots facing backwards in the stirrups. By then, McCrae's haunting poem was famous.

In Flanders fields, the poppies blow
Between the crosses, row on row,
That mark our place; and in the sky
The larks, still bravely singing, fly
Scarce heard amid the guns below.

We are the Dead. Short days ago
We lived, felt dawn, saw sunset glow,
Loved, and were loved, and now we lie
In Flanders fields.

Take up our quarrel with the foe:
To you from failing hands, we throw
The torch; be yours to hold it high.
If ye break faith with us who die
We shall not sleep, though poppies grow
In Flanders fields.

Max Aitken, Lord Beaverbrook: Battle of Britain

In the autumn of 1940, twenty-five years after John McCrae wrote "In Flanders Fields," a controversial Scottish Canadian at the high end of the warrior class—Max Aitkin, Lord Beaverbrook—played a critically important role in what came to be called the Battle of Britain, a turning point in the Second World War. As British minister of aircraft production, Beaverbrook increased fighter and bomber production so prodi-

*New Brunswick–born Max
Aitken, Lord Beaverbrook,
pictured here around 1917
with an unidentified woman.*

giously and at such a crucial moment that some historians have written that without him, this pivotal battle might have gone the other way.

With the war raging, Prime Minister Winston Churchill wrote to Beaverbrook: "I am placing my entire confidence, and to a large extent the life of the state upon your shoulders." Later, Churchill would write, "He did not fail—this was his hour." And again: "His personal force and genius made this Aitken's finest hour."

In a recent biography, David Adams Richards wrote of Aitken, "He was by far the most influential and important Canadian of the twentieth century and, arguably, could be credited with almost single-handedly saving Western civilization." This is something of an overstatement, though John Ralston Saul, introducing Richards's book, observed, "No Canadian has ever been as powerful on the world scene as Max Aitken, Lord Beaverbrook. If there was any possibility that a colonial could push an empire around and change its intent, this was it. . . . Beaverbrook is the example for all time of just how far a colonial can go."

Unlikely as it might seem, this powerful figure came from small-town Canada—though not quite the poverty he liked to allege. Born in 1879 in Maple, Ontario, a hamlet north of Toronto, William Maxwell Aitken was the son of a thundering Presbyterian minister, William Cuthbert Aitken, who had emigrated from Scotland after the Great Disruption of 1843. That split in the church, sparked by disagreement over the role of the state, had seen 450 ministers break away to form the Free Church of Scotland. Afterwards, the original Church of Scotland had proved more willing to subsidize emigration.

William Cuthbert Aitken came from Torphichen, between Glasgow and Edinburgh, where his father had rented a ninety-nine-acre farm. As an adult, Max Aitken visited the old family homestead and described it: "The cottage, all on one floor with beds built into the walls of living room and kitchen, was a stone structure of forbidding appearance. The byre adjoined the house and was of the same materials. Here, in these crowded quarters of this small and rather dark house, a family of several sons and daughters had dwelt together."

Aitken's mother came from a wealthy family of Ulster Scots who harked back to the original plantations, the early Scottish settlements in Northern Ireland. To her, according to *Beaverbrook: A Life,* he attributed the side of himself that "gets up and dances." When Max was one year old, his white-bearded father moved the family from Ontario to Newcastle, on the Miramichi River in New Brunswick, where the St. James Presbyterian Church had become one of the richest in the province. As an adult, Aitken would recall, "When my father stood up to read the scriptures and to preach it was as if God Almighty was speaking." A parishioner said he declaimed in a Scottish accent: "He preached hell and damnation with a Calvinistic fervour."

Max Aitken grew up in a comfortable, multi-storey manse, distinguishing himself at the church-run school, he wrote later, as a "conspicuously naughty and idle boy," and then briefly attended the University of New Brunswick in Fredericton. Back in the Miramichi, in Chatham, the articulate young man found work with lawyer R.B. Bennett, an ex-schoolteacher friend of his father and a future prime minister of Canada. He ran Bennett's first political campaign in New Brunswick, and then followed him to Alberta, where he briefly became a partner in a Calgary bowling alley.

At twenty-three, after selling both insurance and bonds door to door, Aitken moved to Halifax to work at Royal Securities for John F. Stairs, a leading Scottish Canadian businessman. Under the veteran Stairs, the wily Aitken was wheeling and dealing in stocks when, in 1904, suddenly his mentor collapsed and died. Aitken gained control of Royal Securities, moved to Montreal, the country's financial centre, and never looked back.

In 1910, he made a small fortune by amalgamating several cement plants into the Canada Cement Company, and then selling shares he had acquired while creating the deal. Led by the eminent and aging Sir Sandford Fleming, critics claimed Aitken had "watered" the stock and skimmed off more than $10 million. Fearing incarceration, Aitken decamped to England. He was facing a trial slated for 1913, but the Crown's case collapsed when a crucial witness died.

Still in his early thirties, Aitken was already wealthy enough to assist the Conservative Party by sustaining the *Daily Express*, a Tory newspaper. For this, the Tories not only allowed him to run for Parliament in a relatively safe seat, convincing Rudyard Kipling to speak on his behalf, but in 1911, honoured him with a knighthood. After trying and failing to gain control of auto-maker Rolls-Royce, Sir Max Aitken sold his shares at an enormous profit and then began creating a newspaper empire, building on the *Daily Express* and the London *Evening Standard*.

When the First World War broke out, the rising young parliamentarian and newspaper baron took charge of creating the Canadian War Records Office. Aitken ensured that Canada's contribution to the war effort turned up in Canadian and British newspapers—that, for example, Guy Laffin's Belgian Cross appeared in the *London Gazette* of July 12, 1918.

As an honorary colonel in the Canadian army, Aitken visited the western front. And in 1916, with the war raging, he published *Canada in Flanders,* a chronicle of Canadian achievements on the battlefields. He later produced several more books, among them *Politicians and the*

Press and *Politicians and the War.* Aitken also established a fund that produced a notable collection of war art.

In 1917, he was granted a peerage and became 1st Baron Beaverbrook. The next year, as Britain's first minister of information, Lord Beaverbrook became responsible for Allied propaganda—a posting that led to considerable wrangling over the use of intelligence material. In 1918, with the war winding down and an armistice looming, Beaverbrook resigned.

That year, too, he founded the *Sunday Express,* which featured innovative photographic layouts and became immensely profitable. By the end of the Second World War, Beaverbrook's *Daily Express* would have a circulation of 3.7 million—easily the largest in the world. He himself would be known as the First Baron of Fleet Street, and would find himself lampooned by satirist Evelyn Waugh. In *Scoop, Put Out More Flags,* and *Vile Bodies,* Beaverbrook surfaces as a pushy newspaper publisher who barks orders down the telephone lines to London editors from his estate in Surrey, twenty miles (30 km) south of the city. "Of course I believe in the Devil," Waugh said once. "How else could I explain Lord Beaverbrook?"

Beaverbrook played a significant role in British politics for more than fifty years. His friends included Kipling and Churchill, and he became friends and then enemies with Prime Minister David Lloyd George. Beaverbrook married twice, had an extended affair with novelist Rebecca West, and entertained historian and novelist H.G. Wells.

One night, as Wells left Stornoway House, a London gentlemen's club where Beaverbrook had been holding forth on the subject of John Knox, the original Scottish Presbyterian, the renowned author told a friend, "If ever Max gets to Heaven, he won't last long. He will be chucked out for trying to pull off a merger between Heaven and Hell—after having secured a controlling interest in key subsidiary companies in both places, of course."

Decades later, when he was in his eighties and contending with serious illness, Lord Beaverbrook was still haunted by Knox and the thundering Presbyterian preaching of his minister father. By then a philanthropist who had donated millions to the people of New Brunswick, including some valuable works of art that would give rise to lawsuits, Beaverbrook went to his grave worrying about whether he was "one of the elect" who would ascend to heaven.

But the man's greatest hour had come during the spring and summer of 1940. In June, with the Second World War going badly, Prime Minister Winston Churchill declared in the House of Commons, "The Battle of France is over. The Battle of Britain is about to begin. Upon this battle depends the survival of Christian civilization."

Churchill insisted that "the whole fury and might of the enemy must very soon be turned on us. Hitler knows that he will have to break us in this island or lose the war." But because the Royal Navy remained far stronger than the German one, Hitler could not hope to invade by sea. To conquer Great Britain, he would have to destroy the Royal Air Force.

The previous month, in May 1940, Churchill had made the driving, resourceful Beaverbrook minister of aircraft production. Beaverbrook was at his best, he later explained "when things are at their worst." Britain had developed two outstanding airplanes, and Beaverbrook immediately scored a propaganda coup by running an appeal for aluminum to build more: "We will turn your pots and pans into Spitfires and Hurricanes."

He launched a scheme that encouraged towns, groups or individuals to "buy" Spitfires and send them off to fight the Nazis. He set up a Civilian Repair Organisation that built new planes out of pieces from those that had been shot down. Whenever he encountered a closed door, he kicked it down. According to John Moore-Barbazon, member of Parliament for Chatham, Beaverbrook "swept through every department like Genghis Khan—it was remarkable. He was one of the people Churchill spoke about when he said, 'Never was so much owed by so many to so few.'"

When he took office, Beaverbrook was astonished to discover how bombers built in the United States were being transported to the United Kingdom. They were flown to Halifax, disassembled, and put on ships to cross the Atlantic, only to be reassembled when they reached England. He soon put an end to that. After getting clearance from Churchill, and while the British brass howled, he built a runway at Gander, Newfoundland, hired bush pilots from Australia, Canada, and the United States, and got them to fly the bombers to England. This may well have been, as David Adams Richards suggests, "simply the bravest policy decision concerning aircraft in the Second World War."

Military historians argue about numbers. But all of them agree that in 1940, Beaverbrook's big year, Great Britain increased aircraft production by 250 percent, producing 4,283 fighters to Germany's 3,000. Most would agree, too, that those numbers made the crucial difference in the outcome of the Battle of Britain.

According to British historians, this decisive battle—the first major campaign fought solely by air forces—ran from July 10 to October 31, 1940. German historians say it began in mid-August and ended the following May. Without a doubt, it was the most sustained bombing campaign ever mounted. The failure of the Luftwaffe to defeat the Royal Air Force—largely because of Beaverbrook's planes—prevented Hitler from launching his planned invasion by sea, and proved a crucial turning point in the Second World War.

Decades later, Herbert Morrison, another of Churchill's ministers, and a man given to classic British understatement, wrote that Beaverbrook "made a big contribution to winning that battle." Indeed. Max Aitken of Newcastle, New Brunswick, a prototypical Canadian scoundrel, almost single-handedly changed the course of the Second World War.

Book Three

THE VISIONARIES

Prologue

INVISIBLE ARCHITECTS

In the early years of the twenty-first century, as the Royal Ontario Museum approached one hundred years of age, it underwent a transformative renovation. Architects and builders tore down a conventional terrace gallery and replaced it with a controversial crystalline structure. The Scots had nothing to do with that. But if you stand out front of the museum on Bloor Street and look east across Queen's Park road, you will see an elegant, three-storey building that speaks volumes about the Scottish invention of Canada.

Originally, this stately structure formed part of the University of Toronto. Its facade, distinguished by eight columns, four on each public face, looks much as it did a century ago. High above its western entrance, in chiselled stone letters eighteen inches (45 cm) high, the building still proclaims its first purpose: "Department of Household Science." Designed to serve women students, the edifice originally included a gymnasium and a swimming pool. The latter remains immediately recognizable beneath a false floor, accessible down the stairs to the left as you enter off Bloor Street.

Today, one main tenant is a Club Monaco, a clothing store geared to the young and the fashionable. If you step inside and stand near the front door on any Saturday afternoon, you will find yourself marvelling at the multitude and variety of languages swirling around you: here Portuguese, there Mandarin . . . and is that couple conversing in Czech or Polish? A young man who has been speaking Urdu on his cellphone will suddenly snap it shut and, in perfect English, ask you for directions to Davenport Road.

You might step out of the way of three young women carrying bags, laughing and talking in a recognizable lilt. Of Caribbean background, two are wearing sweatshirts proclaiming allegiance to the University of Calgary, and one of them, judging from her lapel button, is also an environmentalist. You register the diversity that is typical of urban Canada, and if you didn't know the secret of the Household Science Building, you might wonder, What does this multiplicity have to do with the Scots inventing Canada?

The answer begins back outside at the northwest corner of the building, where you will find a small oval plaque: "The Lillian Massey Laboratory of Household Science / 1908–12 / C.M. Miller, Architect." That plaque is not strictly correct. The man who designed the building was not C.M. Miller but an architect associated with Miller's firm—a Scottish immigrant named William Fraser.

Attentive readers will remember him as the paternal grandfather of my wife, Sheena Fraser McGoogan. In the mid-1890s, as a young professional based in Glasgow, he designed the Burns National Memorial in Mauchline. But in 1907, during an economic downturn, and like many another Scot, Fraser seized an opportunity to come to Canada.

He joined a thriving firm of Canadian architects, moved to Toronto,

*The Household Science Building in downtown Toronto was
designed by a Scottish immigrant named William Fraser.*

and rented a house on McMaster Avenue. Soon he found himself working around the clock. In March 1908, his wife, Maud Marion—who would convince her sisters to immigrate to Canada—wrote home that "I sometimes don't see Willie till eleven at night from when he goes out in the morning. They are very busy in their office, and Willie has the chief designing to do."

After completing several schools and office buildings, Fraser found himself working with Lillian Massey Treble (1854–1915), the sister of Vincent Massey, who in 1950 would become our first Canadian-born governor general. She wished to create a building for female students at the University of Toronto.

On July 21, 1908, in a long letter to Scotland filled with family news, Maud Marion mentioned that Willie "was invited to dine with a millionairess the other day, Mrs. Massey Treble. She is giving a lovely building to Toronto, a 'School of Science,' and Willie has designed it.

It is to cost three million dollars, and evidently his design has given great satisfaction. Of course he has to discuss the business a lot with Mrs. Treble, and is often at her house."

By 1912, when Fraser completed the Household Science Building, Scottish Canadians had finished inventing Canada's infrastructure. With Confederation, as we have already seen, they had launched a political process that would accommodate different regions and levels of government. They had built national institutions, starting with a railway but including banks and universities, newspapers and department stores. They had invented the telephone and standard time, made advances in health care, and were about to take Canada onto the world stage in the First World War.

Yet Canada remained a British colony. Although aware of its huge French-speaking minority, the country had scarcely begun to acknowledge, much less celebrate, its Aboriginal dimension or its increasing diversity. Scottish Canadians would spend most of the next century finding ways to accommodate differences that cut across language, gender, and ethnicity.

And if, today, you step inside the Household Science Building, you encounter people of different origins and complex identities. You experience the multiplicity of contemporary Canada. The Scottish architect who made this gathering possible has become invisible. Yet he is everywhere. And as it is with this building, so it is with our country. The Scottish Canadian architects have become invisible. But that does not mean they have ceased to exist.

As for William Fraser, after designing the Household Science Building, he created the Deaconess House, an old Toronto landmark that no longer stands at Avenue Road and St. Clair. During the First World War, when an exploding munitions ship decimated Halifax, Fraser was one of the architects sent by the Canadian government to rebuild. After a couple of years in that city, he fell ill with cancer, and so returned home to be with his family.

In June 1922, the *Globe and Mail* ran an obituary under the headline, "William Fraser Called by Death—Was Prominent Architect in Canada and Scotland." The reporter noted that "in Scotland [Fraser] is remembered as the designer of the Burns Memorial at Mauchline." In Canada, the "School of Household Sciences and the Deaconess Home stand as memorials to the skill and workmanship . . . [of] the well-known Toronto architect." He lies buried in Mount Pleasant Cemetery.

William Fraser could never have imagined what would become of the most enduring building he ever designed. But according to the Scottish Argyllshire Association of Toronto, he was a man "proud of the land of his birth, proud of Argyllshire, and proud of his ancestry." As an all-embracing Scot, more symbolically encompassing than ever he intended, surely he would have been thrilled.

15

UN-AMERICAN ACTIVITIES

Harold Adams Innis: Discovering Geography

A leading philosopher of education, Jean Piaget, once wrote a book called *To Understand Is to Invent*. The Scottish Canadian scholar Harold Adams Innis would have approved. Innis was an economic historian who began his career by demonstrating that Canada became a nation "not in spite of geography but because of it."

Born in southwestern Ontario in 1894, Innis could boast three grandparents of Scottish ancestry. His great-great-grandfather, James Innis, was a Scottish soldier who, after fighting for the British in the American Revolutionary War, received a grant of land in New Brunswick. The soldier's son, Innis's great-grandfather, moved to Upper Canada as a pioneer farmer. His mother's father, William Adams, had married a MacDonald and immigrated to Canada directly from Roxborough in Scotland.

By the time Harold Adams Innis was born on a small farm near Otterville, the family had become Baptists. His mother, Mary Adams

Innis, originally named him Herald, hoping he would become a Baptist minister. Although Innis eventually became an agnostic, he derived his values and sense of vocation from his austere, evangelical upbringing.

Innis attended a one-room schoolhouse in Otterville and started high school in that same town. For four years, to complete his secondary education, he travelled by train to Woodstock Collegiate, a Baptist high school twenty miles (30 km) away. Innis planned to become a school-teacher. But at eighteen, to earn tuition money for further training, he taught for a semester and ruled out that career. In 1913, thinking of entering the law, Innis began studying at McMaster University, another Baptist-run institution, then located on Bloor Street in Toronto. Though Innis would repudiate Christianity, Baptist institutions shaped his mature attitudes towards education and Canadian nationalism.

Between semesters at McMaster, again to earn his tuition, Innis travelled to northern Alberta and spent a summer teaching school in Landonville, a frontier farming community 120 miles (190 km) north-east of Edmonton. This experience not only drove home the vastness of Canada but introduced the young scholar to a Western perspective on high interest rates and steep transportation costs.

Meanwhile, the First World War had begun. Given his Scottish Prot-estant background, Innis felt a moral obligation to enlist. In autumn 1916, after graduating from McMaster, he joined the army. He trained in Britain as a signaller and began serving in France as a spotter, which meant working in the muddy killing fields that were forward even of the first line of trenches. At Vimy Ridge on July 7, 1917, an exploding shell injured his right leg. His companions carried him to safety, and within forty-eight hours, Innis was on a hospital train back to England.

The Great War, which he later described as a misery of "mud and lice and rats," changed Harold Adams Innis forever. For seven years, as a result of his injury, he walked with a cane. And for the rest of his life, he suffered recurring bouts of depression and nervous exhaustion.

More than that, his experience in the trenches of France, and then his long convalescence in England, destroyed his Christian faith. By 1926, he would declare flatly, "I am not a Baptist." The war also increased his Canadian nationalism and awoke him to the power of the media, which Lord Beaverbrook had used so effectively to "sell" the war.

Back in Toronto in 1918, Innis finished his master's degree. He then took a summer course in political economy at the University of Chicago, a hotbed of intellectual activity. He found this so stimulating that he abandoned the law to stay in Chicago and do a doctorate in political economy. During the next two years, while courting and marrying Mary Quayle—a scholar who would become the mother of his four children— Innis wrote his thesis on a profoundly Canadian subject.

Published as a book in 1923, *A History of the Canadian Pacific Railway* explains that the building of Canada's national railway was driven by fears of American annexation of the Canadian west. The book also argues that the history of the CPR "is primarily the history of the spread of Western civilization over the northern half of the North American continent." For Harold Innis, according to scholar Robert Babe, the CPR "comprised a massive, energy-consuming, fast-moving, powerful, capital-intensive 'sign' dropped into the very midst of indigenous peoples, whose entire way of life was disrupted, and eventually shattered as a result."

Innis also discerned, as historian Donald Creighton tells us, that the new railway "had simply recaptured . . . a much older Canadian economic unity [the fur trade] which had been based on water communication." His decision to approach Canadian economic history through the study of trade in staple products, Creighton writes, "was the most important decision of Innis's scholarly career. Like all great ideas, it was a simple one; but it was adapted, with a strikingly peculiar appropriateness, to the history of Canada. It was his greatest contribution to Canadian studies."

Before Harold Adams Innis, historians had insisted that Canada belonged essentially to North America, and that it had been born despite geography. They argued that economic currents naturally flowed north–south, along rivers and mountain ranges, and would reshape the continent accordingly. This derived from the U.S. doctrine of Manifest Destiny, the notion that the United States was somehow divinely ordained to expand throughout North America.

In the face of this prevailing wisdom, Harold Innis elaborated his staple-based theory of east–west development. "The present Dominion," he eventually declared, "emerged not in spite of geography but because of it." The idea that Canada developed as a result of the gradual exploitation of staple goods—fur, cod, timber, wheat—by colonial merchants based along the St. Lawrence River system gave rise to a new vision of Canada, the Laurentian thesis, that laid the foundations of an emerging Canadian nationalism.

In autumn 1920, Harold Adams Innis joined the University of Toronto as a lecturer in the department of political economy. For the rest of his life, while forging an international reputation as an economic historian—and despite the blandishments of other leading institutions, including American ones—he would remain at U of T, teaching and doing research.

Innis realized that his book about the CPR had benefited from his time in Alberta, which had made him aware of western alienation. So he understood that in writing about the fur trade, he needed not only to explore the archives but also to see the vast lake-and-river system for himself—to do what he called "dirt research." In the summer of 1924, having enlisted the help of an adventurous friend, Innis paddled an eighteen-foot (5.5 m) canoe hundreds of miles down the Peace River to Lake Athabasca. At Great Slave Lake, following the route pioneered by Alexander Mackenzie, he boarded a Hudson's Bay Company tugboat and sailed to the Arctic Ocean.

By the early 1940s, Innis had visited every part of Canada except the western Arctic and the east coast of Hudson Bay. He interviewed locals as he travelled, gathering information not only on the fur trade but on other staple industries: lumber, pulp and paper, minerals, grain, and fish.

These labours produced several books, among them two widely recognized as classics. The first of these, which appeared in 1930, was *The Fur Trade in Canada: An Introduction to Canadian Economic History.* Starting from the 1500s, Innis shows that the fur trade evolved as a result of geography, technology, and economic forces. The book highlights Canada's links with Britain and France, and traces interactions among Europeans, colonial settlers, and Aboriginal peoples. The introduction of European technologies, Innis writes, such as metal pots, knives, and guns, "brought about such a rapid shift in the prevailing Indian culture as to lead to wholesale destruction of the peoples concerned by warfare and disease."

Harold Adams Innis recognized the value of what he called "dirt research." During the summer of 1924, he paddled a canoe hundreds of miles down the Peace River to Lake Athabasca.

The Fur Trade in Canada, which took fifteen years to sell 1,000 copies, is a dense, detailed tome geared to specialist academics. But Innis was trying to articulate a uniquely Canadian way of understanding the world, a perspective that could never emerge in a centre of civilization but only in a "marginal colony"—a place like Canada.

To that end, after publishing his book on the fur trade, this practical-minded Scottish Canadian pushed still further back in time. He turned to the first economic system to develop off the eastern coast of North

America and, in 1940, produced his second classic work: *The Cod Fisheries: The History of an International Economy.*

During the 1930s, Innis had begun collaborating with academics at the University of Chicago on a series of books about economic history. While doing so, he grew increasingly annoyed at the way American scholars overlooked fundamental differences between Canada and the United States. He noted, for example, that a reference to the two countries having the same language, racial, and cultural characteristics "neglects the French population and blurs a picture in which the differences are of significance." Innis argued that this country had been compelled to serve first "as an instrument of British imperialism and then of American imperialism." He feared that by sliding into the orbit of its powerful southern neighbour, Canada had moved "from colony to nation to colony."

In the 1940s, in an essay called "The Newspaper in Economic Development," Innis turned his attention to yet another area of study: communications. In a presidential address to the Royal Society of Canada, he argued that the western world had entered a state of crisis because the dominant medium of communications (newspapers) was fostering a preoccupation with the present at the expense of long-term thinking. In 1950, elaborating this idea, Innis published the massively ambitious *Empire and Communications.* Starting with ancient Egypt, he explored the relations between empires and the modes of communication that dominated them.

That book is almost impenetrable to the average person. But it profoundly influenced yet another Scottish Canadian thinker—one who was just then beginning his own singular voyage of ideas. Marshall McLuhan would one day describe the work of Innis as the "extra boost" that, after graduate studies, got him into communications. And he was just one of countless scholars who, looking back, realized that Innis had introduced a new way of thinking about Canada by insisting that the country had evolved along its own distinct path and would naturally continue to do so.

John Buchan: In Praise of Diversity

In the 1930s, when Harold Innis was protesting that American scholars were ignoring fundamental differences between Canada and the United States, especially those regarding language and culture, three immigrant Scots were pointing to those same divergent realities. John Murray Gibbon, whose thirty books included a quartet called *French Canadian Folk Songs*, published a work whose title, *Canadian Mosaic*, would resonate down through the decades. One historian argues that without Gibbon, who was born in Ceylon of Scottish parents and educated in Scotland, "the now-pervasive metaphor of Canada as a mosaic might have died an obscure death."

Gibbon, however, "followed, quoted, and might even have been partially inspired" by two other Scots. In an essay collected in *Canadas of the Mind*, Peter Henshaw cites Watson Kirkconnell, a third-generation Scottish immigrant who published *Canadian Overtones*, an anthology of Canadian poetry written originally in Icelandic, Norwegian, Hungarian, Italian, Greek, and Ukrainian. And he argues that both Gibbon and Kirkconnell might never have been heard had there not been "at least one other voice, perhaps the loudest of all." In championing the idea of Canadian diversity, he writes, the loudest voice belonged to John Buchan, a Scot who was both a prolific author and the governor general of Canada.

Born in 1875 in Perth, Buchan was the eldest of five children of a minister of the Free Church of Scotland and a farmer's daughter from near Broughton in the Borders district. He passed his childhood in

Fife, north of Edinburgh and the Firth of Forth, where his atypical father, also named John Buchan, would augment family prayers by singing Scots border ballads and playing musical instruments.

His mother taught him a Presbyterian sense of duty, while his Uncle Willie encouraged him in adventure. At age five, Buchan was hit by a horse-drawn carriage, and for the rest of his life he bore an arresting scar on his forehead. Growing up, the boy spent summers with his mother's sheep-farming parents in the Borders, where he learned to love hiking, fishing, and climbing.

There, too, Buchan developed a passion for the historical romances of Sir Walter Scott, about whom he would one day write a notable biography. As for the terrifying Presbyterian devil conjured by local preachers, Buchan later wrote, "The fatal influence of Robert Burns made me regard him as a rather humorous and jovial figure; nay more, as something of a sportsman, dashing and debonair."

When he was thirteen, his clergyman father took charge of a Glasgow parish, which enabled him to take his secondary education at the well-known Hutcheson's Grammar School. He shone as a student and won a scholarship to attend the University of Glasgow, where he studied classics, wrote poetry and published essays. In 1894, while still an undergraduate, Buchan edited and introduced a collection of essays on scientist and philosopher Francis Bacon. The following year, he wrote *Sir Quixote of the Moors,* a short historical novel that evinces the hallmarks of his later works: evocative atmosphere, fast narrative pace, and a thematic concern with concepts of honour and duty.

Already, Buchan was demonstrating an extraordinary work ethic. While on holiday with his family in August 1895, the month he turned twenty, Buchan swam, played golf, and took long walks while working at least ten hours a day. He studied Plato, wrote a paper for presentation to a student philosophical society, and finished a collection of sixteen essays that would soon be published as *Scholar Gypsies.* It celebrated his love of the classics, literature, and the outdoors, and reflected the influence of Scott and Robert Louis Stevenson.

In *John Buchan: The Presbyterian Cavalier*, Andrew Lownie writes that, after winning a scholarship, Buchan arrived at Oxford University "a quiet and unassuming Scot." He left four years later having taken "the glittering prizes and with the world before him." He had shown a gift for making friends, some of whom would last all his life. Also, he had discovered the British upper-class world of country weekends, London dances, and literary and political salons.

Lacking the wealth of many of his friends, Buchan decided to earn his living by practising law. But in 1901, soon after he was called to the bar, he was invited to join the British civil service in South Africa. He accepted. Based in Johannesburg, and still in his twenties, Buchan found himself administering the resettlement of farmers displaced by the Boer War, taking on far greater authority and responsibility than would have been possible in Britain.

Buchan shone in South Africa, Lownie tells us, "not just because of his energy, intelligence and administrative ability but also because as a Scot he understood the Boers in a way impossible to many of his English colleagues. The Boers were like Border farmers—tough, proud and stubbornly independent." His two years in South Africa not only provided fodder for his writing, starting with *The African Colony* in 1903, but also shaped his later political thinking, especially with regard to multiracial societies.

On returning to London, where he wrote books and newspaper articles, Buchan accepted an offer from an Oxford friend, Thomas Nelson, to become a partner and acquisitions editor in a book-publishing venture. Through writing and publishing he earned a decent living, and in 1907, he married Susan Charlotte Grosvenor, a cousin of the Duke of Westminster and a friend of Virginia Woolf. She would give him four children and write books under the name Susan Buchan.

In 1910, Buchan drew on his South African experience in writing *Prester John*, an adventure novel that treats differences of culture and colour in terms, as one critic suggests, "that had been unquestioned for generations." If written today, the book would be judged stereotypical and racist. But in that earlier context, the novel became hugely popular in several languages. The following year, Buchan entered politics, running as the Unionist (conservative) candidate in a riding that offered no hope of success.

Buchan turned then to biography, drawing on earlier essays to produce works on Sir Walter Raleigh and the Marquis of Montrose, a Scottish hero. In 1932, he would produce *Sir Walter Scott*, which historian G.M. Trevelyan described as "the best one-volume biography in the language." Buchan regarded his biographies as his most significant literary achievements. He insisted that history "is neither science nor philosophy, though it enlists both in its service; but it is indisputably an art."

During the First World War, John Buchan lost both friends and relations, including a brother. Thirty-nine years old at its outset and suffering from duodenal ulcers, Buchan became a war correspondent for the *Times* and the *Daily News*. He spent almost two years at the front, reporting on key battles like those of Loos, Ypres, and the Somme, and probably crossed paths with the as-yet-unknown Harold Innis and the kiltie Guy Laffin.

As an intelligence officer, or what today we might call an embedded journalist, Buchan served in France until early 1917, when he returned to Britain for an operation. In London, he became director of information under Max Aitken, Lord Beaverbrook—a position he later described as "the toughest job I ever took on." Buchan would write several books about the Great War, including an acclaimed four-volume history. And he used that cataclysm as a backdrop for *The Thirty-nine Steps*, his most famous book. Published in 1915, it inspired three different movie versions, including one by Alfred Hitchcock.

While writing at an astonishing speed—eventually, he produced over a hundred books—John Buchan also established himself as a politician. In 1927, he was elected a member of Parliament representing Scottish universities. Before long, he became chairman of the Pro-Palestine Committee in the House of Commons, which advocated the creation of a Jewish homeland. "When I think of Zionism," he said on one occasion, "I think of it in the first place as a great act of justice. It is reparation for the centuries of cruelty and wrong which have stained the record of nearly every Gentile people."

From the outset, Buchan was considered a good speaker. Yet he was too intellectual to be regarded as an outstanding parliamentarian, and

In 1936, John Buchan, Canada's fifteenth governor general, became an honorary member (Chief Eagle Head) of the Kainai First Nation.

he also had something of the Scottish nationalist about him. Buchan believed in promoting Scotland as a nation within the British Empire: "I believe every Scotsman should be a Scottish nationalist. If it could be proved that a Scottish parliament were desirable . . . Scotsmen should support it."

These Scottish attitudes probably kept Buchan from achieving a cabinet post. Twice he was named lord high commissioner to the General Assembly of the Church of Scotland. He acquitted himself so admirably that in 1935, at the urging of Canadian prime minister William Lyon Mackenzie King, the longest-serving prime minister in Commonwealth history, Buchan was named governor general of Canada. While based in Ottawa, Buchan continued writing, augmenting his novels and histories with an autobiography and collections of speeches about this country. In 1936, encouraged by his literary wife, he founded the Governor General's Literary Awards.

In Canada, Buchan travelled widely, and became the first governor general to visit the Arctic. He celebrated the north, recognizing it as a definitive national characteristic: "It makes a link with all Canada, for the North is a common interest." In his posthumously published 1941 novel *Sick Heart River,* Buchan brings his hero to the Canadian wilderness to explore the meaning of life. Graham Greene reviewed this thriller admiringly, and regretted that it would be "the last Buchan."

Having grown up Scottish in Great Britain and experienced the cultural complexities of South Africa, Buchan felt sympathetic to the Frenchness of Quebec. He regarded relations between Quebec and the rest of Canada as "the most intricate of the country's problems." Speaking at Annapolis Royal, he said, "I want to see the French tradition cherished and maintained, for, as a Scotsman who, like all Scotsmen, has an old friendship for France, I regard it as an essential part of Canadian nationalism."

Yet his sympathies remained broad. On the eve of the Second World War, when Buchan learned that a British member of Parliament had been spreading anti-Semitic propaganda, he was outraged: "It is abominable, at a time when the wretched Jews are suffering almost the cruellest persecution in history, that Englishmen should give currency to these silly libels, which are all invented in Germany." Buchan acted on this belief, and brought a group of 500 skilled glassworkers from the Sudetenland to western Canada—an action that led to further Jewish immigration.

Again and again, Buchan insisted that the strongest nations are made up of different races. In 1936, for example, Buchan told a gathering of Manitoba farmers, "You will all be better Canadians for being also good Ukrainians." He added, "Every Briton, and especially every Scotsman, must believe that the strongest nations are those made up of different racial elements."

Whenever he visited a minority community, Buchan invariably urged them to retain their cultural heritage while embracing a new nationality. In Halifax, he told an audience that there are "two characteristics which you [Canadians] share with Scotland. You are a mixed people [and] . . . you are a far-wandering people." Clearly, he understood that, with people as diverse as Canadians, any attempt to impose a single, uniform identity disrupts national unity. In realizing this, John Buchan was decades ahead of his time.

Norman Bethune: A Presbyterian Red

On July 7, 1937, when Japan launched a major attack against China, a middle-aged Canadian doctor was in Rouyn-Noranda, 220 miles (350 km) northeast of Sudbury, raising money for the democratic loyalists in the Spanish Civil War. Henry Norman Bethune, age forty-seven, had recently returned from Spain, where he had created and led a mobile blood transfusion unit in treating the wounded at the front.

Later that year, in Salmon Arm, British Columbia, while still raising money for the Spanish cause, Bethune announced that he had decided to go to China to provide medical assistance. Canadian newspapers

Norman Bethune was a humanist who rejected the Presbyterian religion of his ancestors while retaining everything else about them, especially their humanist zeal.

were reporting that the Japanese army was committing atrocities against civilian Chinese. Early in 1938, accompanied by an alcoholic doctor and a Chinese-speaking nurse, he sailed from Vancouver to Hong Kong on the SS *Empress of Asia*.

In *Norman Bethune*, biographer Adrienne Clarkson notes that from the time he left high school in Ontario, Bethune "showed himself to be someone who wanted to take care of his fellow human beings." She traces this to his Scottish Presbyterian background. "The moral imperative born into Bethune as the son of a Presbyterian minister never really died in him," she writes. "It was diluted with other beliefs, but the ethical standards and morality of Presbyterianism were always there in the way in which he looked at the world." These qualities would make him an inspirational figure in Canada and, unlikely as it might seem, a national hero in China.

Norman Bethune was a missionary doctor minus the evangelism, a humanist who rejected the religion of his forefathers while retaining almost everything else about them. Generations of Bethunes had worked as doctors on Scotland's Isle of Skye. Then, during the American Revolution, one John Bethune served as chaplain with the Royal Highland Emigrants—the same regiment as Thomas Laffin, my own maternal ancestor.

Bethune was captured and held for two years, after which, as a United Empire Loyalist, he moved to Canada. He founded the first Presbyterian congregation in Montreal, and then the first in Ontario. His son, Angus Bethune, became a partner in the North West Company and a director of the Bank of Upper Canada.

The son of Angus, also called Norman Bethune, qualified as a surgeon, joined the Royal College of Surgeons in Edinburgh, and founded a medical school that soon came under the auspices of the University of Toronto. One of his sons, Malcolm, married a Presbyterian missionary (Elizabeth Ann Goodwin), became a rather stiff-necked Presbyterian minister himself, and, in 1890, fathered Henry Norman Bethune.

In *The Mind of Norman Bethune,* Roderick Stewart writes that the son inherited traits that characterized both father and grandfather: "The most pronounced were evident from childhood: intelligence, ambition, artistic and literary skills, stubbornness and unwillingness to compromise against principles, regardless of the consequences."

Born in Gravenhurst, Ontario, 110 miles (175 km) north of Toronto, young Norman moved with his family seven times before he turned fourteen, touching down in Aylmer, Toronto, Blind River, Sault Ste. Marie, and Owen Sound. Religion proved the only constant in his early life. In the 1890s, devout Presbyterians would say grace at the beginning of each meal, read the Bible for an hour each day, and go to church twice on Sunday.

After graduating from high school in Owen Sound, the strong-minded young man worked as a lumberjack in northern Ontario, and then taught school in a one-room schoolhouse. At nineteen, thinking to become a doctor, he enrolled at the University of Toronto to study physiology and biochemical science. He interrupted his studies in 1911 to work and teach with Frontier College.

Bethune was back at the university in 1914, studying medicine, when the First World War broke out. He joined the Army Medical Corps as a stretcher bearer. The following year, after training in England and while serving at the second battle of Ypres, he was seriously wounded by a piece of shrapnel in the leg. After spending three months in an English hospital, Bethune received a medical discharge. "The slaughter has begun to appall me," he wrote. "I see little of war's glory."

He returned to Toronto, completed his medical degree in an accelerated program, and re-enlisted, serving this time as a navy doctor aboard a patrol ship in the North Sea. When the fighting ended in 1918, Bethune took a six-month internship in London, where he worked at the Great Ormond Street Hospital for Sick Children. Then, back in Ontario, he filled in for absent doctors in Stratford and Ingersoll before joining the medical service of the newly created Canadian Air Force.

After eight months as a flight lieutenant, the restless Bethune returned to Britain to train as a surgeon at the West London Hospital and the University of Edinburgh. In 1922, elected a fellow of the Royal College of Surgeons like his grandfather before him, Bethune returned to London as a resident surgical officer. The next year he married Frances Campbell Penney, the beautiful daughter of a senior civil servant in Edinburgh. She had a lilting Scottish accent, and Bethune would later say that he "fell in love at first sound." Over the next decade, the two would divorce, remarry, and then divorce again.

With his wife, Bethune travelled around Europe for six months, and when the money ran out, he brought her back to North America. He considered settling in Stratford near his sister, but opted for the urban bustle of booming Detroit. There he set up in private practice and, his missionary side surfacing, began treating the poor. This meant working long hours in difficult conditions, and in 1926, with his marriage falling apart, Bethune contracted tuberculosis.

He sought treatment at a sanatorium in Gravenhurst, but soon moved to the Trudeau Sanatorium, a more advanced facility at Saranac Lake in upper New York State. Here, he found time and opportunity to think about what he wanted to do with his life. He told a fellow patient, "I'm going to find something I can do for the human race, something great, and I am going to do it before I die."

As a doctor, Bethune was able to analyze the literature on tuberculosis. In a medical journal, he found an article on "compression therapy," an experimental technique that involved opening up the chest and collapsing the worst-affected lung. He insisted that the procedure be tried on him—and it worked.

Discharged from hospital in December 1927, he moved to Montreal to practise thoracic surgery at the Royal Victoria Hospital. He was still there in 1929, when the crash of the stock market signalled the onset of the Great Depression. As economic conditions worsened, Bethune realized that some of his patients were unable to recover because of unsanitary living conditions and the lack of continuing heath care. Having recognized that disease and ill-health arose from economic and social conditions, Bethune opened a free clinic for the unemployed and began lobbying his fellow surgeons for reforms to the health care system.

By 1933, the hard-driving Bethune had worn out his welcome at the Royal Victoria Hospital and moved to the Sacre Coeur Hospital in Cartierville, a Montreal suburb. As head of thoracic surgery, he developed new techniques and invented or redesigned a dozen surgical instruments. An accomplished amateur artist, Bethune also founded and funded a children's art school that catered to the poor.

In August 1935, Bethune attended an international physiological conference in the Soviet Union. There he briefly encountered his old classmate Frederick Banting, already famous for having discovered insulin. The two shared a Scottish Presbyterian heritage, a northern Ontario background, and a keen interest in art. But unlike Banting, who was casting about for a great idea, Bethune had a sense of direction. He inspected hospitals and sanatoriums and came away impressed by the Soviet system of free, universal health care.

Back in Canada, he helped organize the Montreal Group for the Security of the People's Health and tried to introduce universal health care. In a speech to the Medico-Chirurgical Society of Montreal, he described Canadian medicine as a luxury trade: "We are selling bread at the price of jewels." Half the population, he correctly insisted, could not afford decent health care. This argument did not go over well with his fellow doctors. Soon enough, the heretical Bethune was expelled from the society. At meetings held in his downtown apartment, Bethune helped to develop four alternative plans for government-funded health care. And when, during a Quebec provincial election, voters rejected all of them, he felt severely disillusioned.

Although he had abandoned the Christian faith of his forefathers, Bethune remained as duty-driven as any Presbyterian missionary. In November 1935, he had quietly joined the Communist Party of Canada, effectively replacing Christianity with communism while retaining a global outlook. In July 1936, when General Francisco Franco staged an anti-democratic coup in Spain, Bethune turned immediately to that struggle.

More than 40,000 volunteers from fifty-two countries would flock to Spain during the next three years. Norman Bethune went with the first wave. Bent on establishing a Canadian medical unit in Madrid, he sailed in October—four months before Ernest Hemingway left the United States to report on the struggle. In Spain, Bethune not only performed battlefield surgeries but also developed the world's first mobile blood transfusion unit—an initiative later recognized as the greatest medical contribution to the war.

In 1937, when Spanish democrats began taking control of all foreign-led operations, the fiercely independent Bethune resisted, and was asked to leave the country. He reluctantly accepted an invitation to lead a fundraising campaign for the Spanish cause and sailed for Canada. Welcomed as a hero, feted in Toronto and Montreal, he publicly declared himself a Red, a member of the Communist Party, in Winnipeg. That put an end to any possible public career.

In July, Bethune was fundraising in northern Quebec when Japan launched a devastating attack against China. He continued his speaking tour across the country, and announced in British Columbia that he had decided to go to China: "I refuse to condone, by passivity, or default, the wars which greedy men make against others," he declared. "Spain and China are part of the same battle. I am going to China because I feel that is where I can be most useful."

In January 1938, Bethune sailed west out of Vancouver with a supply of medical equipment. After arriving in China, he travelled by truck and train, by horse and on foot to the communist stronghold of Yan'an. He met Mao Zedong, who asked him to remain there to supervise a hospital, but as a result of his experience in Spain, Bethune believed he could accomplish more by working at the front.

Early in May, he journeyed overland through rugged country for another 190 miles (300 km), treating the wounded as he travelled. Conditions were harsh, camps primitive, medical care non-existent. While ministering to the sick and injured, Bethune developed a mobile corps of medics able to teach first aid, sanitary practices, and simple surgery. On one occasion, he went sixty-nine hours without sleep— almost three days—while performing 115 operations.

Eating little, his uniform in tatters, alone in a foreign culture, of course he sometimes missed home: "I dream of coffee, of rare roast beef, of apple pie and ice cream. Books—are books still being written? Is music still being played? Do you dance, drink beer, look at pictures? What do clean white sheets in a soft bed feel like? Do women still love to be loved?"

In October 1939, when he had been engaged in the struggle against the Japanese for over eighteen months, heavy fighting drew Bethune to the front. While operating on a wounded soldier, he nicked his finger. Soon afterwards, he developed gangrene and blood poisoning. Realizing that he was going to die, Bethune wrote a final letter, declaring the last two years "the most significant, the most meaningful" of his life: "I have found my highest fulfilment here among my beloved comrades." On November 12, in an isolated village a hundred miles (170 km) southwest of Beijing, at the age of forty-nine, the missionary doctor passed away.

Six weeks after his death, Mao Zedong published a tribute praising Bethune's spirit, his devotion to others, and his sense of responsibility. Among the Chinese, this eulogy later became compulsory reading. Bethune has since been honoured in China with a tomb, a statue, a pavilion, and a museum, as well as a hospital dedicated to his memory. Recognition came more slowly in Canada, probably because the Cold War era pitted the western world not only against the Soviet Union but against communism generally. In 1972, more than three decades after his death, when the cosmopolitan Pierre Elliott Trudeau was prime minister, the federal government finally declared Bethune "a Canadian of national historic significance."

It acquired the house in Gravenhurst where he was born and turned it into a national historic site, erecting monuments there and in Montreal. In 1977, the CBC broadcast *Bethune,* a dramatization of his life. Donald Sutherland played Bethune, and reprised the role in a 1993 film called *Bethune: The Making of a Hero.* Five years later, Bethune was inducted into the Canadian Medical Hall of Fame.

Although recognition came belatedly to this radical iconoclast, yet Norman Bethune clearly belongs with Harold Adams Innis and John Buchan, who worked from within the establishment. All three overachievers were driven by a Scottish Protestant sense of duty. All three were drawn by a vision of Canada as profoundly different from its southern neighbour, whether economically, culturally, or socially. They arrived too early to see it emerge, but all three caught a glimpse of Canada as a postmodern nation.

16

ETHICAL AGITATIONS

Tommy Douglas: Medicare's Maker

When he was ten years old, Tommy Douglas lay in a Winnipeg hospital bed, hoping that doctors would be able to fix his aching leg. For four years, ever since a knee injury had got infected and turned into osteomyelitis, he had limped around in pain when he wasn't undergoing one medical procedure or another. Doctors had explained to his parents that, short of a wildly expensive operation, they could do no more. To end the boy's pain, they would have to cut off his leg at the knee.

Tommy was lying in his hospital bed, as yet unaware of this plan, when an orthopedic surgeon, Dr. R.H. Smith, led a group of medical students through the children's ward. Probably the surgeon had got wind of the situation: suffering child, hard-working but poor immigrant family. He stopped, chatted with the boy and flipped through the chart at the foot of his bed, reading the history of failed procedures.

The case intrigued him. Later that day, he told Tommy's parents that he would undertake a difficult experimental surgery for free if they would allow him to use the occasion as a training exercise.

As an adult, Douglas would often describe this moment as a turning point. The procedure worked better than hoped. Before long, Tommy Douglas was hiking, running, playing soccer, and even boxing his way to a provincial championship:

"If I hadn't been so fortunate as to have this doctor offer me his services gratis, I would probably have lost my leg. I felt that no boy should have to depend either for his leg or his life upon the ability of his parents to raise enough money to bring a first-class surgeon to his bedside. And I think it was out of this experience, not at the moment consciously, but through the years, I came to believe that health services ought not to have a price-tag on them, and that people should be able to get whatever health services they required irrespective of their individual capacity to pay."

Tommy Clement Douglas was born into a family of ironworkers in 1904 in Falkirk, a dozen miles (20 km) southwest of Selkirk in central Scotland. He moved with his parents to Winnipeg when he was six. Late in 1914, after his reservist father went to fight in the First World War, his mother (a Highlander born Anne Clement) brought him and his sisters back to Scotland to be near family. Five years later, the war over, the reunited Douglases returned to Winnipeg—a move that enabled fifteen-year-old Tommy to witness, from a downtown rooftop, the clubbing and shooting of workers during the 1919 Winnipeg General Strike.

By then he had quit school to work as a printer's apprentice. He also took up boxing, and trained at the One Big Union Gym. In 1922, at 135 pounds (61 kg), he fought for the lightweight championship of Manitoba. After a six-round fight during which he suffered a broken nose and lost some teeth, Douglas proved victorious. He defended the title successfully the following year.

Meanwhile, from his father, Douglas had learned to love the poetry of Robert Burns, to savour the historical narratives of Walter Scott, and to admire the fortitude of Robert the Bruce, who had fought his way through six defeats to final victory. He became active in the church, the Boy Scouts, and then the Cameron Highlanders, and on parade days he would don a kilt and play clarinet in the marching band.

At twenty, having decided to become a minister, Douglas resumed his education at Brandon College, which was run by Ontario Baptists. There, during the next six years, he emerged as a natural leader. He also embraced the social gospel movement, which insisted that Christianity should be more a social religion than one focused on the great hereafter. In 1930, he married Irma Dempsey. Their daughter, Shirley Douglas, would marry actor Donald Sutherland and give birth to Kiefer Sutherland.

Social trailblazer Tommy Douglas, shown here addressing a New Democratic Party convention in 1961, introduced medicare to Saskatchewan.

Also in 1930, Douglas was ordained as a Baptist minister. With his wife, he moved to Weyburn, Saskatchewan, where writer W.O. Mitchell, raised Presbyterian, was a sixteen-year-old youth itching to embark on a literary life. The Great Depression was taking a heavy toll on the province, and Douglas decided that the situation called for political action. In 1931, he created a local wing of the Independent Labour Party, which evolved into the Farmer Labour Party and championed unemployment insurance and universal health care and pensions.

The following July, Douglas attended the founding convention of the Co-operative Commonwealth Federation (CCF), an alliance of western labour parties and forerunner of the New Democratic Party. Two years later, while still honing his folksy, sometimes fiery speaking style, Douglas ran without success in a provincial election. But in 1935, encouraged by friends, he ran federally for the CCF—and this time he won.

As a member of Parliament for two terms, Douglas forged a reputation as a well-informed and witty debater. He represented the underprivileged and exploited, and frequently took controversial stands. When the Second World War broke out, he volunteered for overseas service—but then a medical examination turned up leg problems that kept him in Canada. After the war, he would argue in a radio broadcast that "if we can produce in such abundance in order to destroy our enemies, we can produce in equal abundance in order to provide food, clothing, and shelter for our children."

Tommy Douglas resigned his seat in Parliament in 1944 to contest the Saskatchewan election. He won and, for the next seventeen years, governed that province as the most socially revolutionary premier Canada has ever seen. He transformed the education system and installed a medical school at the University of Saskatchewan. He paid off the debt, created a hospitalization plan, and rebuilt infrastructure, improving everything from roads to sewage pipes. He introduced Canada's first publicly owned automobile insurance plan, created a number of Crown corporations that competed in the private sector, and, in 1950, became the first head of any Canadian government to advocate a constitutional bill of rights.

In 1961, after introducing universal medicare legislation, Douglas resigned as premier of Saskatchewan to lead the federal New Democratic Party, which brought together the CCF and organized labour. He proved an articulate spokesman for democratic socialism—yet failed to win election in 1962, largely because of a backlash against medicare.

This provincial program, which he had designed and introduced, prompted the medical profession in Saskatchewan to launch a bitter strike. Eventually, the doctors backed down and medicare was born. By 1966, despite jurisdictional overlap, the Saskatchewan health-care model was entrenched across the country, with the federal gov-ernment contributing to a national program that is the envy of the informed world.

In 2004, in a national contest organized by the CBC, Tommy Douglas was voted the greatest Canadian of all time. He had died almost two decades before, celebrated as the father of medicare. This immigrant Scot had not only led the first socialist government in North America but, by making it work, had moved democratic socialism into the mainstream of Canadian politics. A great many Canadians, conscious of living next door to the world's superpower champion of unfettered capitalism, regard this as an outstanding achievement.

Thérèse Casgrain: Quebec Humanist

In Montreal, two years after Tommy Douglas was elected premier of Saskatchewan, Thérèse Casgrain joined the federal party he had helped to create—the Co-operative Commonwealth Federation (CCF). Already she had tried and failed to get elected as an "Independent Liberal." But now, as she explained, "Canada needed a political party centred upon the common good rather than on the promotion of personal interests."

Within five years, Casgrain—Scottish on her mother's side—had become leader of the Quebec branch of the CCF, and so the first woman leader of a political party in La Belle Province. By this time, she had been a leading feminist reformer for more than two decades. Yet she shunned that label, and in her 1972 autobiography, *A Woman in a Man's World*, she positions herself a humanist: "The true liberation of women," she writes, "cannot take place without the liberation of men. Basically, the women's liberation movement is not only feminist in inspiration, it is also humanist."

Having grown up wealthy in Montreal, the fluently bilingual product of a not-unusual alliance between Scots and French Canadians, Thérèse Casgrain might seem an unlikely reformer. Born in 1896, she was the daughter of Lady Blanche McDonald Forget and the granddaughter of Alexander Roderick McDonald, district superinten-dent of the Intercolonial Railway encour-aged by John A. Macdonald. Her father was Sir Rodolphe Forget, a well-connected financier and philanthropist who played a key role in developing the hydroelectric industry in Quebec.

Thérèse Casgrain, descended from McDonalds on her mother's side, put a feminist spin on a Scottish-French alliance deeply rooted in the Old Country.

In her autobiography, Casgrain writes that one of her ancestors had married "Madeleine Martin, the daughter of Abraham Martin, called 'the Scotsman,' who bequeathed his name to the battlefield where the armies of Wolfe and Montcalm met in 1759—the Plains of Abraham." During the Rebellions of 1837–38, several members of her family fought with the rebellious *patriotes*.

In November 1838, as hostilities were winding down, a young woman in Beauharnois, southwest of Montreal, caught sight through her open window "of a battalion of Highlanders, marching proudly along in their tartan kilts and fur bonnets with chin straps." During a brief halt, a soldier approached the house and asked her for water, Casgrain writes, "and it was love at first sight for both of them." Soon

afterwards, James McDonald was taken prisoner. On being released—
the rebels had got wind of a crushing defeat nearby—McDonald went
straight back to the house of Archange Quevillon.

For more than a year, despite family opposition, he courted the
young woman, and in March 1840, he married her. Those young lovers
were Casgrain's great-grandparents. Her mother, Blanche McDonald,
spoke only French in her childhood, but several years at a Halifax convent "gave her a knowledge of English that did credit to her name."

At nineteen, Thérèse herself married Pierre Casgrain, a Liberal
politician who would continue the Scottish–French–Canadian affiliation by serving as speaker of the House and secretary of state under
Prime Minister Mackenzie King. In the early 1920s, Thérèse Casgrain
became politically active after she gave a speech on behalf of her husband, who had taken ill. At the invitation of some Montreal suffragists,
she joined the struggle for women's rights, and soon became a leading
spokesperson: witty, confident, and outspoken.

Later, she would write that "under sometimes very difficult conditions, our women have made a significant contribution to Canadian
society. . . . Yet in spite of numerous reforms, Canadian women are still
considered second-class citizens and they are too often deprived of the
treatment and consideration they deserve as human beings. To try to
rectify these wrongs became my goal."

While her husband served as parliamentary whip of the Quebec Liberal caucus, and then of all the Liberal MPs, Thérèse Casgrain led a
provincial campaign for women's right to vote. In 1926, she founded
the Young Women's League to encourage social work, and in the
1930s she hosted a Radio-Canada program called *Femina,* and used it
to spread her "radical ideas" throughout Quebec.

For fourteen years, starting in 1928, she served as president of the
League for Women's Rights. She helped found the French Federated
Charities, the French Junior League, and the Montreal Symphony

Orchestra. Her work establishing the Consumer Branch of the War-time Prices and Trade Board during the Second World War got her appointed an officer of the Order of the British Empire.

In 1942, after her husband retired from politics to become a judge, and believing passionately that men and women should work together "to give society a new set of values," Casgrain ran as an "Independent Liberal" in the federal election. Her children were grown, her husband essentially retired. Yet as a woman, she encountered fierce opposition. One newspaper suggested she should return to cooking and sewing.

Instead, Casgrain joined the CCF. After becoming leader of the Quebec wing in 1951, for years she battled the arch-conservative Quebec premier Maurice Duplessis. Between 1942 and 1962, Thérèse (McDonald) Casgrain—as stubborn as any Scottish patriarch—ran for election nine times, seeking office both federally and provincially. But this was a period when the Roman Catholic Church still dominated the province, and in patriarchal Quebec, she never won a seat.

Despite her lack of success at the ballot box, Casgrain never lost faith in the democratic process. In 1961, when she became national vice-chair of the New Democratic Party, she declared, "I can't imag-ine a woman who has the best interest of her children at heart not taking an interest in politics." She proceeded to champion one pro-gressive cause after another: child protection, prison reform, Vietnam war victims, adult education, Japanese Canadians, consumer rights, Aboriginal women, human rights, the elimination of nuclear weapons, improved relations between English- and French-speaking Canadians.

The National Council of Jewish Women of Canada honoured Cas-grain as Woman of the Century for Quebec, while the Société de crimi-nologie du Canada named her "the person who has been most distin-guished in the defence of human rights and the ideals of justice in our society." In 1970, Prime Minister Pierre Elliott Trudeau appointed Casgrain to the Senate. She served nine months before she turned

seventy-five, the mandatory retirement age. She added "forced retirement" to her list of causes and, for ten more years, Thérèse (McDonald) Casgrain fought on for the rights of all Canadians.

John Diefenbaker: Destination One Canada

One Canada. That's what politician John Diefenbaker wanted. One
Canada: monolithic, linked to Great Britain, English–speaking, proudly
Christian, and extending from sea to sea to shining sea. Anyone who
doubts this should consult his best-known speech. On February 12,
1958, during a federal election campaign, Diefenbaker spoke the phrase

"one Canada" five times while briefly
introducing a "national development
programme" at the civic auditorium in
Winnipeg.

"One Canada," Diefenbaker said.
"One Canada, wherein Canadians will
have preserved to them the control of
their own economic and political destiny. Sir John A. Macdonald gave his
life to this party. He opened the West.
He saw Canada from East to West. I
see a new Canada—a Canada of the
North." Diefenbaker proposed to safeguard Canadian independence, restore
national unity, respect the rights of the
provinces, "and at the same time build

*John George Diefenbaker, fiercely
proud of his Scottish heritage, wore a
kilt to the 1975 Glengarry Highland Games in Maxville, Ontario.*

for the achievement of that one Canada." His Conservative policies
would ensure that the twentieth century belonged to Canada: "The
destination is one Canada."

John George Diefenbaker, who served as Canadian prime minister from 1957 to 1963, inherited a German name from his father, but he was half Scottish Canadian. His mother, Mary Florence Bannerman, was descended from Selkirk settlers who emigrated from Sutherland, Scotland, in the early 1800s. In July 1968, while visiting the High-lands north of Inverness, Diefenbaker unveiled two plaques. The first, affixed to a stone cairn outside the hamlet of Rogart, commemorated Sir John A. Macdonald. The second, located about twenty minutes north at Kildonan, Diefenbaker dedicated to the memory of George Bannerman, his great-grandfather, "and of all the Selkirk settlers from Kildonan, who in 1812 and 1813 migrated to the Red River Settle-ment" in Manitoba.

Back in Canada, Diefenbaker—always a riveting orator—gave emotional speeches about how the Selkirk settlers overcame daunt-ing challenges while helping to open up the Canadian west. And he remained fiercely proud of his Scottish heritage, as anyone can see in a 1971 photo of him with the dog he named McAndy, or a 1975 shot of him wearing a kilt at the Glengarry Highland Games.

Diefenbaker himself was born in Neustadt, Ontario, in 1895. His father, William Thomas Diefenbaker, was a schoolteacher, and both parents encouraged him to read voraciously. When he was eight, the family moved west to homestead in Fort Carlton, about sixty miles (95 km) north of Saskatoon. Seven years later, they moved into that bustling small city.

In July 1910, when Prime Minister Wilfrid Laurier passed through town, young Diefenbaker sold him a newspaper. A lively conversation ensued, during which the youth shared his ideas about Canada. Laurier, amused, said he hoped the boy would be a great man someday. Diefen-baker nodded and, having newspapers to sell, said, "Well, Mr. Prime Minister, I can't waste any more time on you. I must get back to work."

At the University of Saskatchewan, Diefenbaker focused on political science and economics, completing a master's degree in 1916, when the First World War was raging. For fifteen months Diefenbaker served in the Canadian army. In England, he got injured, ended up coughing blood, and was discharged as medically unfit. He went back to university to study law and in 1919 began practising as a criminal defence lawyer. Diefenbaker became known for representing poorer clients, and also for theatrical defences. Once, while appearing before the Supreme Court of British Columbia, he demonstrated how a murder had been committed by falling to the floor and clutching his throat—a memorable bit of histrionics that failed to impress the presiding judge.

After practising in Wakaw, northeast of Saskatoon, Diefenbaker moved in 1924 to the larger centre of Prince Albert. Having once been elected as an alderman in Wakaw, he ran in the federal election of 1925—beginning a string of four failed attempts to obtain a seat in the House of Commons or the provincial legislature. He led the Saskatchewan Conservative Party for two years starting in 1936, and got elected federally as a Conservative four years later. He contended for the leadership of the Progressive Conservatives twice in the 1940s, and finally became leader in 1956.

The following year, Diefenbaker won a narrow victory and became prime minister with a minority government. In 1958, hoping to gain a majority of seats, he called a snap election. His "One Canada" message, coupled with his focus on the north, resonated across the country and led him to win the largest majority government in Canadian history (judged by percentage of seats in the House).

As Peter C. Newman writes, Diefenbaker "came to the toughest job in the country without having worked for anyone but himself, without ever having hired or fired anyone, and without ever having administered anything more complicated than a walk-up law office." Still, this prairie populist managed to remain prime minister until 1963.

Along the way, he fought against official bilingualism, which he could not reconcile with his idea of "One Canada." Yet he also opposed allowing apartheid South Africa into the Commonwealth, and extended the right to vote to status Indians. His relations with successive U.S. governments proved frosty. Soon after he became prime minister, at his first meeting of Commonwealth leaders, Diefenbaker offered to bring 15 percent of Canada's trade with the United States to the United Kingdom. This offer went nowhere because it would have violated international agreements.

In his third year in office, Diefenbaker enacted the Canadian Bill of Rights, articulating the human rights of Canada's citizens. As an ordinary federal statute rather than part of the Canadian constitution, it could not override provincial laws. It could do nothing, for example, when in the 1970s, Quebec passed controversial laws abrogating minority language rights. Yet, ironically, Diefenbaker's initiative paved the way for Liberal prime minister Pierre Elliott Trudeau to introduce the Canadian Charter of Rights and Freedoms, which marked the end of Canada's legal subservience to Britain.

In 1959, controversially, Diefenbaker cancelled the manufacture of the Avro Arrow—a supersonic jet interceptor created in Ontario to defend against a Soviet bomber attack from the north. Instead, he obtained CF-101 Voodoo interceptors from the United States—which embroiled him in a fierce battle over nuclear arms. Diefenbaker rejected the installation of American nuclear warheads in Canadian missiles, warplanes, and rockets. Critics argued that the Bomarc missiles were useless without the warheads. This issue brought down the minority government and led to the hard-fought 1963 election.

Diefenbaker lost but remained leader of the opposition. The following year, during the great flag debate, he opposed the creation of a distinctly Canadian Maple Leaf flag. True to his sense of Canada as a British nation, he battled to retain the Canadian Red Ensign, which was based on the British Red Ensign originally flown by the Royal Navy.

In 1967, during a Progressive Conservative leadership convention, Diefenbaker entered the race at the last minute to fight the party's "Deux Nations" policy. He could not countenance the idea that "Canada is composed of two founding peoples with historic rights who have been joined by people from many lands." He argued that this gave special status to Canadians of English or French descent, and relegated all others to "a secondary position."

He continued to insist, rightly in the view even of his political adversaries, that citizenship should not be dependent "on race or colour, blood counts or origin." The problem was that Diefenbaker took a narrow view of citizenship that today looks old-fashioned: one nation, one identity. And he never glimpsed a possibility best described as post-modern: the notion that a Canadian citizen can have more than one identity and be, for example, both a Canadian and an Albertan, or a Canadian and a Québécois.

John Diefenbaker continued to fight for his beliefs from beyond the grave. In accordance with his will, made public after he died of heart failure in 1979, Diefenbaker was accorded a singular ceremony before his state funeral. First, the Maple Leaf was placed over his casket. Then the Canadian Red Ensign was draped over that. For John George Diefenbaker, descendant of the Selkirk settlers, Canada's connection with Great Britain remained paramount.

17

POLITICAL COMPLICATIONS

Canada has never fit the classic European model that arose in the eighteenth century: one nation, one state. The country has never been homogeneous but has always comprised a mélange, beginning with Aboriginal peoples, French, and British. This complexity brought political challenges. And we have seen how Scots led the way in meeting them, even fighting on both sides of an issue, as when settlers battled fur traders at Red River in the early 1800s.

Yet through two centuries, Canadian history provided one constant. From the 1760s onwards, when Great Britain gained control of New France (Quebec), Canada remained a British colony. Confederation itself did not change that, but simply unified a number of colonies under a new legal document: the British North America Act. That proved flexible enough to accommodate regional expansion (more provinces) and increasing complexity (diverse immigration).

By the mid-twentieth century, tensions were mounting. The country was changing, and not everybody approved. Some Canadians wanted to retain close ties with Britain, while others saw the Christian religion as paramount. Still others drew attention to different priorities: the French-English dichotomy, the Aboriginal dimension, the need to recognize women. In every case, whatever the cause, Scottish Canadians provided leadership.

Donald Creighton: The British Connection

In *Lament for a Nation,* published soon after the 1963 election, philosopher George Grant complained that John Diefenbaker had failed to seek the advice of historian Donald Creighton, who "defined the conservative view of Canada to a whole generation." Creighton could have recommended far better policy ideas, Grant wrote, than "the established wealthy or party wheelhorses" Diefenbaker appointed to high office.

In fact, though he may not have developed policy, Donald Creighton did write speeches for the Conservative leader. And why not? He was an evocative writer who could reach a wide audience. Yet Creighton was no mere speechwriter. He was a celebrated historian and biographer who, building on the intellectual foundations laid by Harold Adams Innis, elaborated and finally communicated the Laurentian thesis. Creighton showed non-specialists how Canada had evolved east to west as a result of the gradual exploitation of staple products by colonial merchants living along the St. Lawrence River system.

Obviously, he had a Scottish background. His paternal grandfather, James Creighton, was an Ulster Scot born in Tamlaght, Northern Ireland. His grandfather's oldest brother, Kennedy, another Creighton who emigrated, remembered Tamlaght as a hotbed of "profligacy, gambling, drunkenness & all kinds of vice," and did not regret leaving. His mother's father, John Harvie, was a Presbyterian Scot born and raised in Campbeltown, in the south of Kintyre. At eighteen, he emigrated first to Toledo, Ohio, where his mother had family, and then to Toronto, where he had boyhood friends.

Donald Grant Creighton was born into a literate household in the west end of Toronto in 1902. His father, William Black Creighton, formerly a Methodist minister, had recently started working for the *Christian Guardian*, which he edited for three decades. His mother, Laura Harvie Creighton, read novels to Donald from an early age, among them works by Dickens and the Brontë sisters. While still in high school, Creighton began, under the editorial eye of his father, to write book reviews for the *Christian Guardian*.

Too young to serve in the First World War, Creighton entered the University of Toronto as the war ended. He studied both literature and history, excelled as a scholar and, in 1925, received a two-year scholarship to Oxford University. Intrigued initially by European history, Creighton discovered the Canadian-focused work of Harold Adams Innis and, after joining the University of Toronto's history department, became friends with the older scholar. He deplored the "undeniable cultural poverty" of Innis's upbringing, and wrote later that a greater acquaintance with literature "would have shown him how far novelists excel economists in depicting the social circumstances and class relationships of a given country and period."

Yet Creighton also recognized the unique brilliance of Innis, and turned the older scholar's insights into evocative narratives that spoke to the intelligent layman. In 1937, he built on the ideas of Innis in producing his first great work, *The Commercial Empire of the St. Lawrence*. He showed how the fur-trading system of the St. Lawrence spawned an east–west pattern of development that countered the north–south linkages encouraged by certain rivers and mountain ranges. Historian

John S. Moir has rightly described the work as "a decisive event in Canadian historiography," while historian Frank Underhill called it "the best book of Canadian history ever written."

In 1944, Creighton published a second notable work, *Dominion of the North: A History of Canada,* in which he argued that post-Confederation railways and highways followed the earlier patterns established by the fur trade. Creighton claimed that this explained why "Canada is and will desire to remain a separate North American nation," and also accounted for "its peculiar relationship with both Great Britain and the United States."

Over the next few years, while teaching, producing the occasional essay, and rising within the history department (eventually to become head), he began what is usually regarded as his greatest work—a two-volume biography of John A. Macdonald comprising *The Young Politician* (1952) and *The Old Chieftain* (1955). Both became bestsellers, won Governor General's Awards, and earned kudos from other historians. Isaiah Berlin, one of the leading thinkers of the twentieth century, once held up a copy of *The Young Politician* and told his students, "On the strength of this one volume I can say that I have been communing this past weekend with the greatest historical writer of our time."

Donald Creighton insisted that those who forget their past are doomed to have no future. He sought to convince Canadians that we have a grand and glorious history worth celebrating. Yet he became deeply pessimistic about this country's future. Staunchly conservative, he viewed John A. Macdonald as having presided over a Canadian golden age. He believed that subsequent prime ministers, with the exception of Robert Borden, a Nova Scotia Presbyterian who held office from 1911 to 1920, had allowed the national dream to dwindle and diminish.

During the 1960s, like Prime Minister John Diefenbaker, Creighton opposed official bilingualism as pandering to French Canadians. Strongly pro-British, he also rejected closer ties with the United States.

Critics denounced him as both anti-Quebec and anti-American. Yet historian Donald Wright, who is writing a biography of Creighton, rejects the prevailing caricature of his subject as a "francophobic curmudgeon." He describes Creighton as a complex figure who resisted integration with the United States and battled Quebec nationalism while deploring the weakening of ties with Great Britain.

Donald Creighton loved the British-oriented Canada that survived the Second World War. As the country became more complex than he had expected, he grew sorrowful. After his death, his wife wrote, "He grieved so for Canada." With the benefit of hindsight, we can see that his sadness was premature. The best historians are also explorers. Towards the end, Creighton sensed that the channel he had charted for the future of Canada, marked by strong ties with Great Britain, would provide no viable way forward. In the great parade of Scottish Canadian thinkers, he marched too near the beginning to see that, as a result of his searches, others would find an alternative passage to a distinctive future.

George Grant: Lament for a Christian Nation

In 1965, student leader James Laxer "walked into a political meeting holding aloft, like a newly discovered Bible," a copy of *Lament for a Nation* by George Grant. "This book!" Laxer cried. "Everyone must read this book!" He waved it about, according to author Matt Cohen, "as though introducing the Messiah." In his memoir, *Typing: A Life in 26 Keys*, Cohen relates how Grant became his mentor, benefactor, and friend, and devotes more pages to the political philosopher than to anyone else.

Laxer, who later became one of the leaders of the Waffle, a splinter group of the New Democratic Party, remembered *Lament for a Nation* as "the most important book I ever read in my life. Here was a crazy old philosopher of religion at McMaster [University] and he woke up half our generation. He was saying Canada was dead, and, by saying it, he was creating the country." Other political thinkers have attested to the transformative effect of *Lament for a Nation*, and, in 2005, the *Literary Review of Canada* included this unlikely bestseller in a list of the hundred most important Canadian books.

Its author, George Parkin Grant, was born in Toronto in November 1918. His paternal grandfather, George Monro Grant, the son of Scottish immigrants, had been born in Pictou, Nova Scotia. After becoming a Presbyterian minister, he journeyed across the country with Sandford Fleming, the chief engineer of the Canadian Pacific Railway, and then wrote an acclaimed book called *Ocean to Ocean: Sandford Fleming's Expedition through Canada in 1872*.

On his mother's side, George Parkin Grant could look to grandfather George Parkin, who had earned a knighthood by turning the Rhodes Scholarships, created to recognize brilliant young students, into the most vaunted academic awards in the world. Grant's mother, Maude Parkin, had attended Oxford, become a university dean, and, according to at least one contemporary, "could have run the whole British Empire at the height of its power single-handed."

His father, William Grant, after being wounded during the First World War, returned home and became headmaster at Upper Canada College, a private boys' school in Toronto. During his tenure, he wrote a Canadian history textbook so sympathetic to the French that it was banned in British Columbia. From his father, who died in 1935, young George heard often of "the senselessness" of the First World War, and learned of books championing Christian values and the non-violent resistance of Mahatma Gandhi. With the Second World War approaching, he became enough of a pacifist that he led several boys in withdrawing from the school's cadet corps.

After UCC, Grant spent a summer in Montreal learning French, and then began studying history at Queen's University. In 1939, he won a Rhodes Scholarship and went to England to study law at Balliol College, part of Oxford University—the same college Donald Creighton had attended years before. When the war broke out, the pacifist Grant declined to join the armed forces. Instead, in summer 1940, he began serving as an air raid precautions warden near the London docks.

Most British historians favour the view that the Battle of Britain ended late that October. But German planes continued sporadically bombing London until May 1941, when Hitler turned his aggression on Russia. During this later period, when Lord Beaverbrook was scrambling to create and deliver fighter planes, the twenty-one-year-old George Grant was working among the sick and wounded of working-class London, and sleeping most nights beneath the London Bridge tracks at the Stainer Street arch.

On February 17, 1941, hearing that a house had collapsed, Grant rushed out to help. When he got back, he found that his usual shelter had suffered a direct hit. Of the 300 people sleeping there, 69 died and 175 were wounded. Grant carried out the dead—many of them friends—and assisted those he could. The experience proved traumatic. Soon afterwards, he was diagnosed with tuberculosis. Refusing to return to Canada, he went to work on a farm near Oxford.

That December, not long after the Japanese bombed Pearl Harbor and the Americans entered the war, Grant was walking his bicycle through a gate when suddenly the world looked brighter. Where previously he had entertained dark thoughts of suicide, now he felt the presence of God. "This was a prodigious moment for me," he later declared. "I think it was a kind of affirmation that beyond time and space there is order."

Back in Toronto, Grant spent a full year recovering his health. He had always been nominally a Christian. But now he used his Christian faith as the bedrock on which to rebuild his personality. When he resumed his studies at Oxford after the war, he turned away from the law, much to his mother's chagrin, and instead began studying Christian theology and philosophy.

After acquiring his doctorate, he taught philosophy at Dalhousie University in Halifax from 1947 to 1960. During that time, he also married a well-educated Londoner and fathered six children. In 1960, Grant resigned his long-held position for a teaching job at York University—which he quit even before he began work.

In his resignation letter to York, which is included in *The George Grant Reader*, Grant explained that he could not abide the textbook suggested for the introductory philosophy course, arguing that he "could hardly be expected to use a textbook which misrepresents the religion of my allegiance."

Ten years before, when the Massey Commission had asked him to write a position paper on the study of philosophy in English Canada, Grant had advocated creating institutes for humane studies that were explicitly Christian in outlook. He argued that the country had been founded by Christians, and that its institutions and ideals were rooted in the Bible: to ignore that was to turn one's back on the nature of Canada.

Although mid-twentieth-century Canada remained officially Christian, this argument did not win converts among professional philosophers. They dismissed Grant as muddled and unreliable. Now, this well-connected, Toronto-born scholar was turning down a sought-after position in his field, proving their point. In 1961, after he had spent one year in Toronto without full-time employment, Grant joined the religion department at McMaster University in Hamilton. There he remained four years later, when he published *Lament for a Nation*.

That work did not emerge out of nowhere. As early as 1945, in an article entitled "Have We a Canadian Nation?" Grant had written, "Does Canada have any quality that is unique and worth developing as a particular contribution to the world? Unless we know why we exist, we will be shaped by the REPUBLIC. . . . There always has been and will be an alternative to building a Canadian nation. And that is the submerging of our nation to the U.S.A."

Grant's twin obsessions—one political, the other religious—came together in the early 1960s over the issue of nuclear disarmament. The political Grant supported the Diefenbaker Conservatives in opposing U.S. pressure to place nuclear weapons on Canadian soil. The religious Grant, the pacifist who had always insisted that "if one is a Christian one cannot fight," felt morally outraged by the very idea of nuclear weapons.

He launched into an essay and just kept writing. In the finished product, *Lament for a Nation,* Grant argued that the 1963 election signalled that Canada could no longer hope "to retain any real independence as a nation." He predicted that the ordered, bilingual country of the 1950s was passing away, and would inevitably be absorbed by the United States. He gave voice to Canadian fears that we would become "homogenized" North Americans and proclaimed the "end of Canada as a sovereign state."

Half a century later, Canada remains politically intact and nominally sovereign. Where did the Christian philosopher go wrong? The clearest answer comes from his nephew Michael Grant Ignatieff—the public intellectual as distinct from the politician. In his 2009 book *True Patriot Love,* Ignatieff charges that George Grant conducted "a substantial revision, even falsification, of his own heritage."

While following earlier Presbyterian Grants in their "essential belief that Canadian identity could not survive without a British core," Uncle George gave the family credo "a new inflection: conservative, religious, hostile to progress, modernity and liberalism." Ignatieff argues that George Grant's conservative Christianity led him to believe that there was no essential difference between Stalinist tyranny and American imperialism, and that Canada stood in relation to the United States as Poland, Hungary, and Czechoslovakia stood in relation to the Soviet

Union—a position for which Ignatieff can barely conceal his disdain. With the end of the Cold War, he writes, "everywhere you looked— whether it was the former Yugoslavia, Quebec, the Basque country, Scotland or the Middle East—a passionate resurgence of ethnic, religious, tribal and local identities had rewritten the history Grant had thought was leading us to imperial domination and cultural uniformity. So he was wrong. Wrong. Wrong again."

Canada is no longer the white-bread, Christian nation whose disappearance Donald Creighton grieved and George Grant lamented. Yet just as Scotland remains distinct from England despite their economic integration (the result of political union in 1707), so Canada remains recognizably different from the United States. Changing times have introduced further complications—and here, once again, Scots and their descendants have led the way in voicing them.

Hugh MacLennan: Two Solitudes

"When I was young," Hugh MacLennan wrote in 1973, "I often heard people say, 'Canada is the Scotland of North America.' Only recently did it occur to me that it might be worthwhile considering the extent to which this is true." The Canadian novelist wrote those words in an essay called "Scotland's Fate: Canada's Lesson." Scotland failed to develop into a fully independent nation, MacLennan continued, "because she never discovered a single idea that might have made her national survival of value to the rest of mankind."

That is debatable, of course. But the point here is that MacLennan judged the Canadian situation to be more promising, despite Canada's proximity to a superpower ten times its size. For this he gave one main reason: "We obstinately refuse to become a melting pot." Canada, he argued, remains "a light shining in the darkness of an almost universal tendency" to homogenize and reduce humankind to sameness.

As early as 1973, then, one of Canada's leading Scots highlighted diversity and pluralism as Canadian building blocks. Nor was MacLennan the first to do so, as we have already seen. Yet today, some thinkers contend that Canada's lack of a single strong identity threatens the viability of the country. The question we face is this: Can these apparently contradictory positions be reconciled? Can multiplicity and unity coexist?

Born in Glace Bay, Nova Scotia in 1907, John Hugh MacLennan was "three-quarters Scotch, and Highland at that." This

Novelist Hugh MacLennan spent his Nova Scotia boyhood sleeping in a tent. He explored the idea of Canada as "the Scotland of North America."

constituted "a kind of doom from which I am too Scotch even to think of praying for deliverance." His father, a doctor, "was neither a Scot nor yet was he Scottish; he never used those genteel appellations which now are supposed to be *de rigueur*. He was simply Scotch."

According to MacLennan, this meant "all the perplexity and doggedness of the race was in him, its loneliness, tenderness, and affection, its deceptive vitality, its quick flashes of violence, its dog-whistle sensitivity to sounds to which the Anglo-Saxons are stone-deaf, its incapacity to tell its heart to foreigners save in terms foreigners do not comprehend. . . . 'It's not easy being Scotch,' he told me more than once. To which I suppose another Scotchman might say: 'It wasn't meant to be.'"

Twice each Sunday, young Hugh went to the nearby Presbyterian church: "I had a Jewish friend who looked at [our] household with awe." In 1915, his father moved the family into Halifax. And on the morning of December 6, 1917, ten-year-old Hugh was washing up for school when in the wartime harbour two ships collided, one of them a munitions vessel. That collision caused the greatest manmade explosion in history before the atomic bomb. Hugh's mother grabbed him and, along with the maid, dragged him down into the basement, fell onto her knees, and prayed for salvation.

The summer he turned twelve, Hugh began sleeping in a tent in the backyard. This habit evolved naturally enough after he attended a summer camp with the Young Men's Christian Association. The camp emphasized toughness and self-reliance, and his father did not object when, after Labour Day, Hugh continued sleeping in this old fishing tent. As winter came on, bringing drifting snow and freezing cold, the boy donned a beret, added several layers of clothes and, each evening, carried out hot potatoes or heated irons in bags to keep warm. For nine years, except for the occasional night when he felt sick, Hugh MacLennan slept in that tent in the backyard. Later, he remembered it as a wonderful, invigorating experience, especially in summertime, when he could read by the light of a candle.

Clearly, the tent provided a sanctuary for the young Hugh. His father, a third-generation Scottish Canadian named Samuel MacLennan, would devote spare moments between patients to translating passages from Greek and Latin. Driven by this obsessive Presbyterian, young Hugh excelled as a student first in high school and then at Dalhousie University. In January 1928, when one snowy afternoon he arrived home, he found an open telegram sitting on the hall table. He snatched it up and read, "Congratulations. Rhodes Scholarship for Canada-at-large awarded to John Hugh MacLennan." He looked up and, as he later reported, saw his tough old father standing in the doorway. "Go and shovel the walk, Hugh," he said, stepping into his office. "It badly needs it."

Though he had shone at Dalhousie, Hugh MacLennan found the scholastic demands at Oxford almost overwhelming. After narrowly surviving his first year, he managed to reach the middle of the pack and stay there. From the university town, sixty miles (100 km) west of London, MacLennan was able to visit the Continent several times. While becoming fluent in German, he formed a clearer picture of Canada's modest place in the world. In 1932, after graduating from Oxford with a major in classics, MacLennan began applying for teaching jobs. But the Great Depression meant that few were available.

When an opening arose in the classics department at Dalhousie University, his alma mater, the young man judged his chances to be excellent. The department chose another candidate, and when MacLennan asked for an explanation, the departmental chairman explained, "After all, you're a Canadian and he's an Englishman." Later, recalling this episode, MacLennan wrote, "It was one of those arterial sentences. It went from my brain right through me till I felt it in the back of my legs."

Lacking job offers, MacLennan went off to earn a doctorate at Princeton University, fifty miles (80 km) southwest of New York City. By 1935, when he graduated with what he called his "academic ticket," the twenty-eight-year-old had also written a contemporary novel. Encouraged by Dorothy Duncan, a fellow writer who would become his wife, he sought a publisher for this Hemingwayesque production but found none.

Later that year, with the Depression grinding on, MacLennan received a job offer from Lower Canada College, a private school in west-end Montreal. Overqualified but desperate to strike out on his own, the young man packed his bags and moved to the city he would call home for the rest of his life. While working as a teacher, MacLennan married Duncan, set up house, and wrote a second contemporary novel. He approached twenty-eight publishers, but in spring 1939, the only one seriously interested judged the subject matter no longer relevant: the concerns of the world had shifted.

A perforated eardrum ruled out military service, so MacLennan soldiered on at Lower Canada College. In the school magazine, he published an autobiographical sketch about the Halifax explosion—a moment when, however accidentally, Canada had found itself at the heart of an international conflagration. In summer 1940, while walking on Halifax's Citadel Hill, he realized that if he built a novel around that historical moment, it would not become dated. Back in Montreal, he turned his hand to *Barometer Rising*.

Published in 1941, with the Second World War raging, the novel became an international hit. The *New York Times* declared that MacLennan had scored "a bull's eye first shot." As a result, MacLennan garnered a Guggenheim Fellowship that freed him for a year to write a projected novel about Canada's French–English divide. He discovered his title during the winter of 1943, when in a book review he read a phrase attributed to the poet Rainer Maria Rilke: "Love consists in this, that two solitudes protect and touch and greet each other."

He jumped to his feet. Those words: two solitudes. The instant he read them, MacLennan felt his novel snap into focus. He had found his title—and, not incidentally, a phrase that would enter the Canadian vocabulary and resonate in this country long after the novelist himself had passed on. Later, when the U.S. publisher of the book suggested changing the title, MacLennan flatly refused.

Two Solitudes was published on January 17, 1945. By noon of that day, the initial print run (4,500 copies) had sold out. Reviewers raved. In New York, one of them called the book "superbly vital." Another, in Canada, hailed it as "the GREAT Canadian novel," while a third declared it "required reading." At the *Globe and Mail,* William Arthur Deacon judged the book to be "the best and most important Canadian novel ever published."

The novel made Hugh MacLennan a public figure, and won him the first of five Governor General's Awards—a record that has never been matched. In her exemplary biography, Elspeth Cameron suggests that MacLennan's thematic concerns, with soul and conscience standing in opposition to greed and power, "place him in one central tradition of Canadian intellectual history." She cites his Presbyterian principles, humanitarian ideals, and concerns about unbridled technology, and notes, "His concepts bear a striking resemblance to those of Canadians like . . . Harold Innis or Donald Creighton or George Grant. On the bedrock of Presbyterian principles, using the scaffolding of the classics, he erected his own personal indictment of technology and mass communications."

In 1967, two decades after the appearance of *Two Solitudes,* Hugh MacLennan published *Return of the Sphinx,* which evoked the threat of Quebec separatism. The novel received a warm reception in the United States but a mixed one in Canada. Francophone critic Naïm Kattan found the work less convincing than *Two Solitudes,* but noted that MacLennan succeeded admirably in evoking the shock of Quebec anglophones at the rise of ethnic nationalism in their province. Within three years, that nationalist fever would spawn the October Crisis, the War Measures Act, and a political reality that vindicated *Return of the Sphinx* as prophetic.

Today, Hugh MacLennan is widely acknowledged as having helped shape a national consciousness. In *Two Solitudes,* especially, but also in *Return of the Sphinx,* this hard-working "Scotchman" wrestled with a dichotomy at the heart of Canadian political life. Where Donald Creighton had focused on Canada's British connection and George Grant on its Christian dimension, Hugh MacLennan drew attention to the country's complexity, especially the French–English divide. He made Canadians aware that if Canada was to survive as a nation, then one way or another, this great divide would have to be recognized and accommodated.

James Houston: The Aboriginal Dimension

In 1948, having served in the Second World War with the Canadian Scottish Regiment and then trained as an artist in London and Paris, twenty-seven-year-old James Houston was drawing and sketching at Moose Factory, on southern Hudson Bay. One morning, when a bush pilot taking a doctor farther north on a medical emergency offered him a free ride, he jumped at the chance.

Before long, Houston found himself at a hunting camp called Inukjuak, where he was surrounded by welcoming Inuit: "They were short, strong, and deeply tanned. The women wore their jet-black hair in two braids, while the men had ragged bowl haircuts. Their eagerness to shake hands, their wide smiles and friendly way of laughing, their gruff singsong voices, excited me. I had never dreamed of seeing people like these unknown countrymen of mine." Houston took in the barren rocks and tundra, the few old tents, the steel-blue sea, the gigantic icebergs, and the smiling people: "I could scarcely breathe. I thought, 'This is the place that I've been looking for and now I've found it! I'm here!'"

When, unexpectedly, the doctor said they had to depart immediately to airlift a baby to hospital, Houston declined to leave. Later, in *Confessions of an Igloo Dweller,* Houston described this decision as the great turning point of his life. He had indeed discovered his life work. In the decades to come, he would rightly become known as the man who brought Inuit art to the outside world.

Born in Toronto in 1921, James Archibald Houston considered himself "two hundred per cent Scottish." According to Houston's second wife, Alice, the artist's great-grandfather "came over from Scotland, moved to the Beaverton area, and became the captain of a ferry on Lake Simcoe." In the 1970s, before they bought a cottage in the Queen Charlotte Islands, she and Houston visited Scotland every summer.

During his 1948 visit to the Canadian Arctic, James Houston discovered that some Inuit were natural stone carvers. Here we see Houston (standing) working as a roving crafts officer with young people in Pangnirtung on South Baffin Island. Many of his students would become leading artists.

His father, a clothing importer named Donald Houston, had travelled to the Pacific northwest and brought home moosehide moccasins for the children. As a boy, while spending summers at Beaverton, Houston became friends with an elderly Ojibwa who taught him how to make a groundhog whistle. While growing up, Houston studied art with Arthur Lismer of the Group of Seven. Later, he attended the Ontario College of Art and, after the Second World War, the Académie de la Grande Chaumière in Paris.

After his 1948 visit to the north, when he discovered that some Inuit were natural stone carvers, Houston returned south and began creating markets for Inuit art works. During the next fourteen years—assisted by his first wife, the Nova Scotia journalist Alma Bardon—he served as "roving crafts officer" and then civil administrator of West

Baffin Island. Accompanied often by Alma, he would ramble around the Canadian Arctic, living as the Inuit did—wearing fur clothing, sleeping in igloos, and eating raw fish and seal meat.

While developing markets in southern Canada and beyond, he also helped Inuit artists, notably in Cape Dorset, establish co-ops in the north. In response to their innate talent and their curiosity about printed pictures, he began teaching printmaking techniques. By that action, Houston almost single-handedly created a cottage industry that has brought millions of dollars into the Arctic, helping to sustain the northern economy as the fur trade declined. Not only that, but he enabled the creation of an art form that is recognized around the world as distinctly Canadian.

By the late 1950s, Houston had the federal government sponsoring exhibitions of Inuit art that travelled not only throughout Canada but in eastern and western Europe, South America, and the Middle East. He had moved with his wife and two sons to Cape Dorset, but in 1962, he accepted an offer from the president of the Metropolitan Museum of Art to move to New York and become the master designer for Steuben Glass.

The artist's glass sculptures became hugely popular, but Houston was far from finished with the north. He not only kept returning there but began writing books about the Arctic—among them seventeen children's books, which he illustrated, as well as adult novels and three book-length memoirs. His novel *The White Dawn* was translated into more than thirty languages and became the basis for a movie. Several of his novels were picked up by major book clubs, and Houston became a three-time winner of the Book of the Year award from the Canadian Library Association.

In one of his last books, *Zigzag: A Life on the Move*, James Houston tells the story of the resourcefulness of an Inuit stone carver who was working on a sculpture of Sedna, the Inuit goddess of marine mammals. One day, Houston "came up and knelt down beside him on the tundra." As he arrived, and as if he were a shaman bringing a curse, one of Sedna's arms broke off. "Too bad," Houston said, as the two men stared down at the broken arm lying between their feet.

The Inuk thought for a while, and then said, "In the old story of this half seal, half woman, in a big storm her father and his hunting companions had to throw overboard first the walrus meat, and then his daughter. When she tried to crawl back into the boat, her father had to cut off her arms at the elbows. So this undersea woman, if she lost her other arm, would seem the same as that sea spirit after she had her arms lost." And with that he knocked off her other arm and started to turn them both into flippers.

Houston tells this anecdote to illustrate how the Inuit "still possess an ancient wellspring of power, cleverness, and drive that will surprise and delight anyone of good heart." Inuit artists, he adds, communicate across the barriers of language, distance, and time: "Through their art, we can feel their needs and joys, their ingenious perspective on human and animal life." Inuit prints and carvings "embody much of what all of us share, however disparate our cultures and experience."

Those works of art constitute a distinct cultural expression, one recognized internationally as forming part of the Canadian reality. That recognition owes much to the proudly Scottish James Houston who, by ushering a talented Aboriginal people onto the world stage, raised a challenge for Canada as a nation. Where Hugh MacLennan drew attention to this country's French–English duality, James Houston reminded us that Canada includes an Aboriginal dimension, one that would have to be encompassed in any future concept of Canadian nationhood.

Doris Anderson: What about Women?

Canada prides itself on being a socially progressive nation. Our health care system, which was envisaged by Norman Bethune and instituted by Tommy Douglas, is one key indicator, though the system is not without shortcomings. Yet the situation looks less bright if we turn to the status of women as measured by political equality statistics. In the Canadian House of Commons in 2009, women held 68 of 308 seats, or 22 percent. According to data compiled by the international Inter-Parliamentary Union, that puts this country in forty-ninth place worldwide.

Among developed countries, Sweden ranks first, as women hold 46 percent of seats in Parliament—almost half. South Africa stands at 45, Netherlands at 42, and Finland at 40 percent. Canada comes out narrowly ahead of the United Kingdom, which registers 20 percent, and the United States of America at 17. But it lags behind

While serving president of the National Action Committee on the Status of Women, Doris Anderson didn't hesitate to speak her mind.

even the European Parliament, which comprises 31 percent women.

Critics argue that in recent years, Stephen Harper's Conservative government has eroded the status of women, making a bad situation worse. Harper shut down regional offices of Status of Women Canada and, according to former prime minister Paul Martin, dismantled "an existing, operating child care plan that [in 2005] had been signed by all ten provinces and was under way."

While Canada clearly has a long way to go bringing about gender equality, signs of hope can be found in figures like Doris McCubbin Anderson, who took up the struggle begun in the nineteenth century by pioneers such as Nellie McClung and Agnes Macphail, and devoted her life to the women's movement. Anderson published books, worked as editor of *Chatelaine* magazine for twenty years, and served as president of both the Canadian Advisory Council on the Status of Women and the National Action Committee on the Status of Women. She also led the feminist charge in making a crucial change to the Canadian constitution.

Doris Hilda Buck was born in 1921 in Medicine Hat, Alberta. She was the daughter of Rebecca Laycock Buck and Thomas McCubbin, a handsome, athletic lodger in her mother's Calgary boarding house. Her mother initially placed her in a home for unwanted babies, but reclaimed her after a few months had passed. McCubbin had emigrated at eighteen from Wigtownshire, Scotland, "where the name McCubbin is as common as Smith." Given to get-rich-quick schemes, he was largely absent for the first few years of her life.

When she was eight, he married her mother—to the girl's lasting regret. A difficult, domineering man, at least in Anderson's view, McCubbin darkened the rest of her youth with his criticism of her strong-minded, "unladylike" ways. She reacted by rebelling. "I never learned to be subservient to men," she said later. "What I learned to do was cope."

All her life, she resented McCubbin's influence over her mother, a shy, conservative woman who wanted her daughter to be demure and conformist. In her 1996 memoir, *Rebel Daughter,* Anderson wrote that as a child, "I fervently wanted my father to be hit by a streetcar, particularly when we were waiting for dinner and he reeled in late, three sheets to the wind, and sat pontificating at the head of the table."

Later, she softened this judgment by declaring him "a rebel, and he had a good mind, read widely and challenged everything." Still, she "never felt any warmth toward him." McCubbin's mother had wanted him to become a Presbyterian minister, but after serving in the First World War—during which he spent "four ghastly years in the trenches amid that terrible carnage"—he became both an avowed communist and an atheist. Despite herself, Anderson may have gleaned some of her subsequent feistiness from her father.

In the 1930s, the vast majority of Canadian women still faced a clear-cut, Victorian-era choice. They could marry and devote themselves to motherhood or they could remain spinsters and work at one of three jobs: nurse, secretary, or teacher. "Because I was bookish and bright," she told one journalist, "I was to be a teacher. And in those days, all teachers were spinsters. If they got married they got fired immediately."

At nineteen, Doris McCubbin graduated from teachers' college. She taught school in rural Alberta to pay her way through the University of Alberta in Edmonton. In 1945, after receiving a degree, and having discovered journalism as another option for women, she moved to Toronto, bent on forging a career.

She found work as an editorial assistant at the *Star Weekly* magazine, then toiled as a radio scriptwriter for a famously difficult and demanding female boss. After six months, she left to work as an advertising copywriter for the flourishing T. Eaton Company. Along the way, Anderson worked freelance, reading fiction manuscripts for W.O. Mitchell at *Maclean's*—"a wonderfully folksy, droll man who was trying to find better Canadian fiction than the formula stuff most magazines were publishing."

After three years at Eaton's, the twenty-eight-year-old sailed to London to make a living as a fiction writer—a more realistic proposition then than now because many magazines published short stories. She worked hard, sold imaginative pieces to *Chatelaine* and *Maclean's*, and travelled around Scotland, Ireland, and France. But having determined "that I could write popular fiction, and probably support myself, I no longer wanted to." Instead she returned to Toronto and, as she was broke, resumed working at Eaton's—though now she had refined her ambitions, and "yearned to do something more substantial as a journalist."

In 1951, nearing thirty, she got "her first real break." The editor of *Chatelaine* magazine was looking for a new advertising promotion person, and Doris McCubbin landed the job. Within six years, she had battled her way upwards to become editor—but only after she threatened to quit if managers appointed yet another man to run this leading women's magazine. The company did "put a codicil in the agreement," she wrote. "I could have the job, but I would still be called managing editor, at least for the time being."

Two weeks before she began working as editor, at age thirty-five and wanting children, she married David Anderson, a Liberal Party backroom organizer. In the five years starting in 1958, while giving birth to three sons, Anderson also dramatically increased circulation at *Chatelaine*—moving it eventually from 480,000 to 1.8 million.

More than that, Doris Anderson began transforming the Canadian intellectual landscape. While in the United States, Betty Friedan was five years away from publishing *The Feminine Mystique* (1963), Anderson decided that, in addition to the usual fare aimed at women—service pieces on cooking, skin care, parenting—she would give readers "something serious to think about." She ran provocative articles on divorce and the wage gap, on abortion, rape, and even incest. And she wrote columns and editorials calling for more female members of Parliament, pushing for a royal commission on the status of women, and deploring the plight of Native peoples.

Anderson turned *Chatelaine* into the biggest money-maker in the Maclean-Hunter stable of magazines. Yet she was earning $23,000 a year when the editor of *Maclean's* was hauling down $53,000—an extraordinary disparity. When the latter job came open, she sought it but lost out to a man—not because she was a woman, a company executive explained, but because "you can't represent the company policy." Decades later, in an interview with Sandra Martin of the *Globe and Mail*, Anderson said she still felt angry about being repeatedly passed over because she was female: "That wouldn't happen today."

In 1978, having left *Chatelaine,* Anderson plunged into politics, running for election as a federal Liberal after a slated candidate pulled out at the last moment. She lost badly, going down in the anti-Trudeau backlash that swept much of the country. The following year, with the Liberals clinging to power—and having published *Two Women,* the first of her three feminist novels—Anderson became president of the Canadian Advisory Council on the Status of Women.

She was serving in that capacity in 1980, when Prime Minister Pierre Elliott Trudeau proposed to introduce a new Canadian constitution containing a charter of rights and freedoms. Recognizing an opportunity to advance women's rights, Anderson planned a national conference. That conference was delayed by a translators' strike.

Meanwhile, the first draft of the Charter appeared. It included an equality clause that prohibited discrimination on several grounds, including sex. But Anderson felt it did not go far enough because it contained the same wording as the 1960 Canadian Bill of Rights, which had "been tested ten times in the courts . . . and had been found to be useless as a legal tool to help women."

Anderson attacked the wording. She sent a critique to Lloyd Axworthy, the minister responsible for the status of women, and had a lawyerly brief presented to a parliamentary committee hearing. Then, in a twist involving members of her own board, Anderson's planned national conference was voted down in favour of a few low-profile, regional meetings. Doris Anderson resigned in protest, famously declaring that "every time Lloyd Axworthy opens his mouth, one hundred more women become feminists."

A small group of women, backing Anderson, decided to hold a conference anyway. Conservative politician Flora MacDonald, yet another Scot, booked a meeting room on Parliament Hill. On February 14,

1981, more than 1,300 women turned up from across the country for the "Ad Hoc Conference."

As a direct result, and thanks to the principled stand of Doris Anderson, a crucial clause was added to section 28 of the Charter of Rights and Freedoms: "Notwithstanding anything in this Charter, the rights and freedoms referred to in it are guaranteed equally to male and female persons."

During the next couple of decades, besides two more novels, Anderson published her memoir, *Rebel Daughter,* and *The Unfinished Revolution: The Status of Women in Twelve Countries.* And she lobbied furiously to change the Canadian electoral system, arguing that "first past the post" voting discriminates against women. Yet her greatest achievement would remain the installation of that clause in the Charter of Rights and Freedoms, guaranteeing rights equally to men and women.

In 2007, when at eighty-five Doris Anderson passed away, Canadian women mourned a fallen champion. In a *Globe* obituary, Flora Mac-Donald described her as "tremendous, like a rock . . . she was always promoting women." But journalist Rosemary Speirs, founder of the activist organization Equal Voice, offered the most succinct summation: "She has been the *de facto* leader of whatever women's movement there has been here in Canada for the last forty years. Nobody else has emerged."

Through her work in gender equality, Doris McCubbin Anderson staked a claim in the future Canada on behalf of all women. In so doing, she joined those Scottish Canadian leaders—among them Donald Creighton, George Grant, Hugh MacLennan, and James Houston—who, in the mid-twentieth century, drew attention to the main political challenges Canada would face as it moved beyond the British North America Act and towards autonomy, independence, and an unusually complex maturity.

18

CENTRIFUGAL FORCES

Early in 2010, the recently appointed U.S. ambassador to Canada, David Jacobson, expressed surprise at the strength of Canadian regionalism: "There seems to be a greater allegiance that Canadians have to their provinces than typically Americans do to their states." After speculating about possible reasons for this, he concluded, "I think Canadians define their identity to a larger degree by the province they live in than Americans do."

In creating a sense of identity, Canadian geography, as Harold Innis and others have argued, has proven almost as powerful as history. And that far-flung geography has decreed that ours is a country of regions. Most analysts identify at least five: Atlantic Canada, Quebec, Ontario, the Prairies, and British Columbia. Some, like the U.S. ambassador, suggest that each province and territory is a region, while others would add our major cities. Most Canadians would agree that, however we define them, regions influence social, political, and cultural attitudes. Albertans, Ontarians, and Newfoundlanders don't always see issues the same way. Ask a Montrealer and a Vancouverite how they feel about French on cereal boxes and probably you'll get different answers. Viewed from a national perspective, Canada's regional identities constitute powerful centrifugal forces. Like the political complications already explored, they not only diversify the Canadian identity but require recognition.

To illustrate this, we could turn to local politicians. But why not look instead to Canadian authors? Many of the finest give voice to region, if only because stories and novels tend to be set in specific locations. By establishing settings, authors not only reveal regional identities but invent them.

Already we have encountered L.M. Montgomery, who attracted international attention by reinventing Prince Edward Island. One of her near contemporaries, a Scottish Presbyterian minister who published as "Ralph Connor," sold more than five million copies of his regional evocations of Ontario and Alberta. The literature of British Columbia began with the journals of Captain James Cook, the son of a Scottish farmer, and that of the Canadian north with the non-fiction narratives of Scottish explorers we have already met. The Scottish poet Robert Service, having grown up in Robbie Burns country, virtually created the international image of the Yukon with poems like "The Cremation of Sam McGee" and "The Shooting of Dan McGrew."

Today, Canada produces many writers, and indeed artists, who attract international acclaim. Often, while creating worlds that appeal universally, they build upon local or regional realities. As a result, without trying to do so, they reveal the centrifugal forces at work in contemporary Canada. Here again, not surprisingly, we find Scottish Canadians leading the way.

Alistair MacLeod: Cape Breton Ballads

When considering art of the highest quality, the American author Joyce Carol Oates writes, the mythic human drama defines itself through "localized, precisely rendered worlds." Fiction writer Alistair MacLeod, she continues, is motivated by "the urge to memorialize, the urge to sanctify." By getting the words right, he transcends "the purely finite and local." In MacLeod's fiction, Oates adds, "ballads that link the living with their Scottish ancestors are sung by wholly unself-conscious men and women."

The prolific Oates offers these insights in an afterword to *The Lost Salt Gift of Blood,* a book of short stories that, first published in 1976, launched MacLeod on a long, slow climb to spectacular heights. When the book appeared, Hugh MacLennan wrote to their mutual publisher, Jack McClelland, telling him "you may well have published the finest book ever written in this country."

In 1986, MacLeod's second book of stories, *As Birds Bring forth the Sun,* confirmed his international reputation. And in 1999, his first novel, *No Great Mischief,* won half a dozen Canadian awards before taking the International IMPAC Dublin Literary Award, the world's largest award for a single book (£100,000, or over $180,000). At age sixty-five, MacLeod had become a literary superstar.

Alistair MacLeod—profoundly identified with the Maritimes, specifically Cape Breton Island—entered the world in 1936 in Battleford, Saskatchewan. In a ninety-minute documentary profile by William D. MacGillivray, *Reading Alistair MacLeod,* the fiction writer explains that even so, what he calls "home" is the house in Cape Breton that his great-grandfather built in 1838. His grandfather was born in this white clapboard house in Dunvegan, and then his father, and although MacLeod arrived here with his family only when he was ten, he has lived in the place and called it home ever since—and, he says, "that's enough for me."

Settled by Scots starting in the 1770s, Cape Breton remains arguably the most Scottish area in Canada. MacLeod's grandparents spoke
Gaelic as their first language, and though he himself speaks the language only slightly, as a youth he was immersed not only in Celtic
myth and legend but in Scottish history and culture. After high school,
MacLeod went to teachers' college in Truro, a three-hour drive from
home, and then taught school. Starting at age twenty-one, he spent
three years at St. Francis Xavier University, and then earned a master's
degree at the University of New Brunswick.

MacLeod financed his university education by working as a miner
and a logger. He proposed to become a university English professor,
and for that he needed a doctorate. From among the various possible
universities, he selected Notre Dame, a Catholic institution in Indiana, roughly four hours west of Detroit—mainly because it boasted an
excellent teacher of creative writing named Frank O'Malley.

For the first time, MacLeod was too far away to travel home for
weekends. "When I went to the United States," he told the CBC's
Shelagh Rogers, "I really left physically, if not emotionally or intellectually. And I began to think of this landscape [Cape Breton] in a
kind of objective or in a kind of distant manner. And I became, I think,
more thoughtful about it." During his six years at Notre Dame, he
turned into a writer largely because, he says, "I was absent from my
native landscape, shall we call it, and . . . I was analyzing literature and
thinking about literature."

Specializing in nineteenth-century British literature, MacLeod taught
for three years at Indiana University before joining the University
of Windsor in 1969 to teach English and creative writing. There he
remained for the next three decades, teaching, writing, and, with his
wife, a fellow islander, raising six children.

Each summer, MacLeod would return to Cape Breton. There, in a
Spartan, clifftop cabin that looks west towards Prince Edward Island,

he would write every day. With the publication in 1976 of *The Lost Salt Gift of Blood,* MacLeod was recognized as a natural storyteller of depth and power. Immediately, his stories began turning up in prestigious anthologies, among them *Best American Stories* of one year and then another. Most of those stories are set in Cape Breton—though as Oates observes, his Cape Breton is everywhere "and immediately accessible to us."

Some of MacLeod's stories explore initiations, while others trace the pattern of exile and return that typifies and haunts the islanders. He draws heavily on the history of Cape Breton, where Scottish Highland traditions have endured for over two centuries, and points the way for such younger authors as Linden MacIntyre and D.R. MacDonald.

In *No Great Mischief,* widely considered his greatest work, MacLeod revisits his favourite thematic materials. His contemporary narrator, an urbanite named Alexander MacDonald, reviews his family history from the eighteenth century onwards. Along the way, with the help of a minor character, a grandfather, he restores the Scots to Canadian history, underlining the crucial but forgotten role they played at the battle of the Plains of Abraham. Yet always MacLeod circles back to Cape Breton Island, the place to which he gives eloquent voice.

Alice Munro: Southern Ontario Gothic

In Scotland not long ago, driving north out of Robbie Burns country, two Canadians made a detour to visit the burial grounds of the paternal ancestors of author Alice Munro. We followed a winding, one-lane road through rolling hills and sheep-filled fields into the Ettrick Valley, where locals directed us to a churchyard containing the graves of William and Margaret Laidlaw.

In *The View from Castle Rock,* her 2007 collection of autobiographical stories, Munro writes of visiting this churchyard, fifty miles (80 km) south of Edinburgh. William Laidlaw, her great-great-great-great-grandfather, lies buried here along with his sister, Margaret Laidlaw Hogg. She was the mother of James Hogg, who became famous throughout Scotland as "the Ettrick Shepherd."

Alice Munro, arguably the finest fiction writer in North America, is also the uncrowned queen of Southern Ontario Gothic.

Hogg was a friend of Sir Walter Scott, and in *Castle Rock* Munro relates how, when Scott was collecting ballads for *The Minstrelsy of the Scottish Border,* Hogg introduced his mother to the young anthologist. Scott included several contributions from the old countrywoman, but afterwards, Munro tells us, Mrs. Hogg complained, "They were made for singin' and no for prentin' . . . and noo they'll never be sung mair."

Munro was born Alice Laidlaw in southern Ontario in 1931. Her daughter Sheila has speculated that the celebrated author derives her near-photographic memory from her Laidlaw ancestry: "How else can her almost freakish memory, her ability, for instance, to look at her old high-school photos and remember the colours of all the dresses the girls are wearing, be explained?" Munro's storytelling ability too, she adds, "which so often relates the everyday to the macabre, the nightmare, even the supernatural, the way ballads do, has some affinity with that whole minstrel tradition."

Munro herself, widely regarded as one of the finest short story writers in the English language, relates how in 1818 her ancestors sailed from Scotland and settled in southern Ontario, where she was born in the town of Wingham. By that time, her father spoke with a Canadian rather than a Scottish accent, and had settled on a small farm just outside that Scots-Irish town, which Munro describes as Presbyterian to its core.

Through her acclaimed stories, celebrated for their honesty, compassion, and insight, as well as for their technical virtuosity, Munro has fictionalized the surrounding area into an identifiable region. The late Carol Shields, after declaring herself an "enormous fan," said of Munro, "Her use of language is very sophisticated, but I can always hear, underlying the sentence and its rhythms, that rural Ontario sound."

Alice Munro is world acclaimed, of course. In May 2009, in honour of her lifetime of work, she won the Man Booker International Prize, inspiring the three-judge panel to write that she "brings as much depth, wisdom and precision to every story as most novelists bring to a lifetime of novels." Winning this recognition, over such writers as Peter Carey, E.L. Doctorow, V.S. Naipaul, and Joyce Carol Oates, established Munro's international pre-eminence.

Worth more than $100,000, the Man Booker capped a list of honours that includes three Governor General's Awards, two Giller Prizes, the Canada–Australia Literary Prize, the Marian Engel Award, the Commonwealth Writers Prize, the W.H. Smith Award in Britain and, in the United States, the National Book Critics' Circle Fiction Award. But Jonathan Franzen, writing in the *New York Times Book Review,* has perhaps put the case most succinctly: "Alice Munro has a strong claim to being the best fiction writer now working in North America."

Such universal recognition notwithstanding, Munro remains firmly, almost defiantly, rooted in southern Ontario. Her work, more than that of any other writer, has given rise to the idea of "Southern Ontario Gothic" literature. In *Alice Munro: A Double Life,* biographer Catherine Sheldrick Ross quotes Munro describing her native Huron County as having "a rural culture with a strong Scots-Irish background." The area also has "a big sense of righteousness," Munro added, "but with big bustings-out and grotesque crime. And ferocious sexual humour and the habit of getting drunk and killing each other off on the roads." Later, she would note that in Huron County, "the every-day is side by side with the macabre." It was a rural area, so inevitably it produced "bloody accidents." And she grew up with "the extreme, the grotesque" as part of her daily life on the outskirts of a town hit hard by the Great Depression.

Munro realized early that she wanted to become a writer. But she hid this ambition as best she could. Her Scots Presbyterian family, she has said, strongly disapproved of "calling attention to yourself." Wanting to be remarkable in any way constituted a reckless challenge to fate and those "supernatural powers always on the lookout for greed."

To shine as a student was acceptable, and Alice Laidlaw did so all through high school. She discovered her vocation at fifteen, after reading *Emily of New Moon,* L.M. Montgomery's novel about a girl who chooses to become a writer. Later, Munro would declare it "the watershed book of my life."

At seventeen, she won scholarships to attend the University of Western Ontario in London, about seventy miles (110 km) from Wingham. In 1950, while still a student, she published her first story, "The Dimensions of a Shadow." The following year, with her funding running out, Alice Laidlaw left university to marry James Munro and move to Vancouver, British Columbia. During the 1950s and '60s, while based in that province, she gave birth to four daughters, one of whom died hours after being born.

In 1963, along with her husband, the writer opened Munro's Books in Victoria: She was still helping out there five years later when she published a first collection of stories, *The Dance of the Happy Shades.* Hailed as presenting "a perceptive young narrator's dawning awareness of the powerful and legendary shapes lying behind ordinary life in Huron County," the book won the Governor General's Award for Fiction—a spectacular debut for a first book of stories.

In 1971, Munro published a second book, *Lives of Girls and Women,* a collection of interlinked stories in which she again drew extensively on her girlhood in southern Ontario. A review in the *Los Angeles Times* typified the reception, declaring Munro "a writer of enormous gifts and perception."

After Munro divorced in 1972, she returned to the area that fuelled her fiction. She served for a year as writer-in-residence at Western, and then, in 1976, married Gerald Fremlin, a geographer from the same region. Eventually, they settled in the small town of Clinton, about twenty miles (30 km) from Wingham.

From that home base, by intensifying her vivid regional focus, Munro has forged a spectacular international career. Like Thomas Hardy, William Faulkner, and a few other great writers, she created a distinctive fictional world that has taken her name: "Alice Munro country."

In 1978, Munro won her second Governor General's Award with her collection *Who Do You Think You Are?* which was also runner-up for the Booker Prize. While publishing regularly in magazines like the *New Yorker, Atlantic Monthly,* and the *Paris Review,* she just kept winning prizes. After her 1986 collection, *The Progress of Love,* won her a third Governor General's Award, the American critic and short story writer Cynthia Ozick summed up the international consensus by describing Munro as "our Chekhov."

Around that time, during a wide-ranging interview in Calgary, Munro spoke of her return to Ontario from the west coast. "I didn't go back for any literary purpose," she said. "I thought I was through with small-town Ontario, and that I'd be writing about my years in Vancouver and Victoria—that background."

Apparently, the Presbyterian Fates could take the writer out of Huron County—and Munro has since travelled extensively—but not for long. Certainly, the author has consistently refused to situate herself in any context but a local or regional one, rejecting any suggestion that she might represent a pan-Canadian culture. In a 1994 interview with the CBC's Peter Gzowski, for example, Munro said she had proven forthcoming because he had not asked her "about CanLit."

Yet she has always remained open to seeing her work characterized as regional. "If I'm a regional writer," Munro said in one interview, "the region I'm writing about has many things in common with the American South. . . . [I am writing out of] a closed rural society with a pretty homogenous Scotch-Irish racial strain going slowly to decay."

In Alice Munro, we hear a universal voice speaking in a distinctive accent. We hear the sound of Southern Ontario.

Margaret Laurence: A Manitoba Quintet

In speaking of Margaret Laurence in 1987, shortly after her death, novelist Robertson Davies said that "Canadians are rather like Scots writers, or Irish writers, in that they have a very strong sense of their background and place. And she certainly did, and she gave it life." Laurence not only brought out "the eccentricity and the unpleasant part of small town life," Davies said, "but also the nobility, and the splendour, and the breadth of feeling to be found in places like Neepawa"—the Manitoba town in which she spent her girlhood.

Growing up in that town, located about 120 miles (190 km) northwest of Winnipeg, left Laurence with a sense of coming more from a place than from a time, and feeling more rooted geographically than historically. This emerges clearly in "Road from the Isles," an essay she published in her 1976 book *Heart of a Stranger.* Introducing the piece, which she had written a decade before, Laurence writes that by visiting Scotland, she gained her "first true understanding of where I belonged, namely, the land where I was born."

A visit to Scotland inspired Margaret Laurence to draw on the legacy of Scottish settlers in her fiction.

That said, she writes also that from an early age, she could sing Scottish airs. And she remembers her grandfather's sister as "a tiny dynamic woman who spoke with such a thick Scots burr that I was never able to understand a single word she uttered. But her reaction to Clear Lake [Manitoba] was in some way translated and communicated even to me. It was the closest thing to Scotland, she said, that she had ever seen."

As if to reverse the compliment, Laurence encountered place names in Scotland that "meant something to me." Glengarry evoked both Glengarry, Ontario, and *The Man from Glengarry*, by Ralph Connor: "Sutherland, Bannerman, Ross, Selkirk, Kildonan—to me, these are the names of the places I grew up among, the names of Manitoba towns and the names of Winnipeg's streets. Weirdly, encountering them in Scotland, they seemed unreal there, or else derived, because to me they are Canadian names."

In a 1970 letter, Laurence referred to her ethnic heritage. She was "a Celt of sorts, being Irish on my mother's side and Scots on my father's, with a slight admixture of Sassenach blood through one of my grandmothers, who came from United Empire Loyalist stock." Laurence was deliberately shading this communication, as the only ones who refer to the English by the Gaelic word "Sassenach" are the Scots.

Margaret Laurence had grown up reading Scottish books. She listened to Scottish ballads and bagpipe music. And she travelled several times in Scotland. There, she felt especially moved by the Highland Clearances, and by "the betrayal of the Highlanders by their own chiefs, as the glens were cleared of unprofitable people to make room for profitable sheep. This must surely be one of the most painful episodes in European history, the tale of how the Gaelic-speaking people of northern Scotland were driven from the lands they had worked for centuries, treated as sub-human by the English-speaking bailiffs who burned their dwellings, and ignored by landowners who preferred the lights of Edinburgh or London."

Yet visiting Scotland also turned her back to Canada, reminding her of "the external difficulties of the early Scottish settlers, the people of Glengarry and Red River. What I had never seen before [visiting Scotland] was a glimpse of their inner terrors, a sense of the bereavement they must have carried with them like a weight of lead in the soul." She adds that "what appeared to be their greatest trouble in a new land—the grappling with an unyielding environment—was in fact probably their salvation. I believe they survived not in spite of physical hardships, but *because* of them, for all their attention and thought *had* to be focused outwards. They could not brood. If they had been able to do so, it might have killed them."

Yet for Laurence, personal identity remained essentially local. Only personal history could generate "names or tunes or trees that can recall a thousand images." And these "can be related only to one's first home." While insisting on the primacy of place, Laurence gave Scottish names and backgrounds to virtually all her heroines. And her sense of herself as a Scottish Canadian suffuses the cycle of five "Manawaka novels" that made her reputation.

Born in Neepawa in 1926, Jean Margaret Wemyss was the daughter of a prominent lawyer, Robert Wemyss, whose ancestors came from Fifeshire. Her mother, Verna Jane Simpson, died when she was four, and her father when she was nine. As a result, she was raised by her grandfather John Simpson, a stern, tight-fisted businessman of Ulster Scots descent whom she considered Irish. He proved terrifying to the sensitive child, who retreated into the world of books.

By the age of seven, Peggy had begun writing stories. As she grew up, she watched as all the boys she knew went off to war and never came back. In 1944, she won a scholarship to attend United College, now the University of Winnipeg. While studying honours English, she wrote for the student newspaper and became active with a socialist reform group. She bought a Remington typewriter and said later that taking a typing course at age fourteen was the best thing she ever did. When the *Winnipeg Free Press* sponsored a short story contest, she entered a story set in a small town based on Neepawa, which she called "Minewaka."

After finishing her degree in 1947, she went to work as a reporter for the left-leaning *Winnipeg Citizen,* where she covered labour and wrote about books and radio. Also in 1947, she married John Fergus ("Jack") Laurence, a hydraulic engineer. His work took them to England in 1949, and then to Africa, where they lived in British Somaliland (1950–52) and Gold Goast (1952–57).

During these years, Margaret Laurence gave birth to two children, and also began publishing fiction set in Africa. Her first story appeared in a 1954 anthology, and then came a number of works eventually collected into *The Tomorrow Tamer* (1963). While living in Gold Coast, which was on the verge of achieving independence as Ghana, Laurence drafted *This Side Jordan,* which also appeared in 1963.

Six years before, Laurence had returned to Canada with her family. After five years in Vancouver, she separated from her husband. Taking their children, Laurence moved to England, where she settled in Penn, a village northwest of London. There she lived for over a decade, though she often visited Canada. She divorced in 1969, when also, at University of Toronto, she did her first stint as a writer-in-residence. During that year, she began exploring Ontario, and in 1974, she moved to Lakefield, just outside Peterborough.

Meanwhile, Margaret Laurence had begun publishing the series of books that would make her name—a five-book cycle set mainly in a fictional Manitoba town she now called Manawaka. First came *The Stone Angel,* published in 1964. It tells the story of ninety-four-year-old Hagar Currie Shipley, cutting back and forth between past and present. That book would be turned into a movie starring Ellen Burstyn.

In 1966, Laurence published *A Jest of God,* which follows Rachel Cameron through a summertime affair during which, though in her thirties, she attains a new maturity. It won a Governor General's Award for Fiction and was later turned into a film called *Rachel, Rachel,* produced and directed by Paul Newman. The third book in the series, *The Fire-Dwellers,* appeared in 1969. It was nominated for the Booker Prize and prompted a reviewer in the *Atlantic Monthly* to describe Laurence as "the best fiction writer in the Dominion and one of the best in the hemisphere." Book four, a collection of linked stories called *A Bird in the House,* remains an outstanding example of the short story cycle. And in 1974, Laurence published *The Diviners,* the final book in the series, and a work widely regarded as a Canadian classic. It tells the story of yet another Scottish Canadian writer, Morag Gunn, who has a Métis lover and an independent streak. The book won Laurence another Governor General's Award, and was adapted for CBC television in 1993.

Over the years, fundamentalist Christian groups attacked that novel, and then some of her other Manawaka works, as blasphemous and obscene. Many females, however, admired her courage in writing honestly about the emotional lives of women, and sophisticated readers of both sexes regarded these attacks as a badge of honour. Yet the allegations hurt Laurence and darkened her final years because, having been raised a Scottish Presbyterian, she held herself to a high moral standard. Another writer of similar background might have responded to such charges with withering scorn—and one of them, another champion of the local who grew up still farther west, did exactly that.

W.O. Mitchell: Prairie Warrior

"The Day Blind Jesus Appeared to the South Saskatchewan Holy Rollers." That, W.O. Mitchell declared from the stage, is what he would call the piece if it were a short story. He was performing at the Jubilee Auditorium in Calgary, Alberta. The piece was not a short story, however, but an episode from his latest novel, *How I Spent My Summer Holidays.* After reading it that September evening in 1981, the irrepressible Mitchell drew a standing ovation from the capacity audience of more than 1,000 people.

Canada 46

W.O. Mitchell waged a one-man war against the vestiges of his own heritage: Scottish Presbyterianism.

Before turning to "Blind Jesus," Mitchell had read from *According to Jake and the Kid,* a tall tale about a lying contest, some crows that flew off with the henhouse roof, and a giant grasshopper that laid an egg, then fell in love with a bomber flying north. He had read from *The Vanishing Point,* a hilarious section about a young boy at a Saskatchewan school where "sex surfaced only in grammar," where you could be strapped for adding incidental trees to an art exercise in perspective, and where you could get your own back only by defecating in the bottom-left-hand drawer of the teacher's desk.

It was a tour de force performance in the tradition of Robbie Burns, and in the audience I found myself asking, How does he do it? How does he get this whole crowd laughing at what many of them would normally denounce as crude, vulgar, indecent, and even blasphemous? Maybe the magic was in the language, in the exuberance, the crescendos and unexpected shifts, a "Jesus Christ" here and a "Goddamn it" there—but no, that couldn't account for all of it.

Mitchell had mastered the silence. He would revel in the extended silence and then, with impeccable timing, he would deliver the punchline. And that was not all of it, either. Mitchell the stand-up comedian was also a man of serious purpose. In book after book, while wielding his humour like a broadsword, attacking everything uptight and straitlaced with the ferocity of a born satirist, he took special aim at the puritanical moralism that Canada had imported from Scotland, and which, decades ago, had threatened to stifle his boyhood. By cursing and swearing, caricaturing and gesticulating and making people laugh, W.O. Mitchell was celebrating his regional identity—this could be nowhere but the Canadian prairies—while waging a one-man war against the vestiges of Presbyterianism.

Born in 1914 in Weyburn, Saskatchewan, William Ormond Mitchell spent what he always called his "litmus years" in that small town. "The whole context of the early years," he once said, "the round billiard ball of the Regina plains, the Prairies, was very, very important to me both as a person and an artist." What Mitchell didn't think to mention emerged later in the first volume of a biography written by Orm and Barbara Mitchell, his son and daughter-in-law—and that is the overwhelming influence of his Scottish heritage.

After leaving Kirkcudbright, Scotland—the home of Lord Selkirk—and before moving to Canada, the ancestors of W.O. Mitchell lived in Rathfriland, Northern Ireland, a hilltop town near which, in the mid-1700s, they acquired a forty-acre farm. As staunch Presbyterians, they would have attended the Ballyroney Presbyterian Church. As for Mitchell, even though his paternal ancestors lived around Rathfriland for eighty years, his biographers tell us that "the Scots genes predominated in Mitchell's sense of his ethnic background." They quote the author as insisting "there was never any adulteration of the Scottish-Presbyterian line. The Mitchells married Scots and Protestants. My grandfather married a McFarlane; my father married a McMurray."

Those familiar with *Who Has Seen the Wind,* the author's quasi-autobiographical first novel, will not be surprised to read that Mitchell lost his father when he was seven. Shortly thereafter, his maternal grandfather died. And so his grandmother moved into the house to help raise Mitchell and his three brothers. "With their strong sense of Scottish clan," the biographers write, "these two McMurray matriarchs were largely responsible for Mitchell's keen interest in his family roots, for both women were determined to keep alive the memories of their dead husbands."

According to a Weyburn school teacher, Mitchell's mother was prim, proper, and "strict enough," and should not be held responsible for the "cuss words and taking the Lord's name in vain" that surfaced in the author's novels. Mrs. Mitchell not only attended regularly at Knox Presbyterian Church but saw to it that young Billie faithfully turned up for services—indeed, at one stretch he went a year and a half without missing a Sunday.

His grandmother registered an equally strong impression. A childhood friend, the son of the minister, would remember calling on Billie Mitchell and being frightened by the brusque, formidable woman who answered the door. She dressed always in black, and kept a soapstone plaque of John Knox over her bed—oddly enough, alongside a similar plaque of Knox's nemesis, Mary, Queen of Scots. Mitchell himself would insist that "she looked a great deal like a more finely drawn John Knox, if he had worn a black velvet ribbon high around his neck."

At age twelve, Mitchell contracted tuberculosis of the wrist, and his mother sent him to finish high school in the warm climate of St. Petersburg, Florida. He found the geography overwhelming: "If you have been used to just the rudiments of sky, just the horizon, and no trees unplanted by man, and then you go to the lush subtropics as I did. . . ." In Florida, Mitchell stopped going regularly to church, but belonged to a Bible discussion group and remained every inch a Presbyterian.

Each summer, he would return home to Saskatchewan. He worked at various jobs, but later said that "the thing that saved us all in the West was harvest time. Then you'd go to work for a dollar a day, sleep in the hen house. And the result was, I knew a great many farm labourers." Mitchell the writer would put that knowledge to use.

In 1933, Mitchell enrolled at the University of Manitoba, intending at first to become a neurosurgeon. But reduced dexterity in his wrist made this impossible. He switched majors and studied philosophy with Rupert Lodge, the Platonist author of more than a dozen books. Lodge introduced him to those early sceptics David Hume and Thomas Carlyle—Scottish writers who repudiated Presbyterianism. For young Mitchell, they pointed the way to freedom.

He shucked off his Christian faith, travelled to Seattle, and enrolled in a writing course at the University of Washington. Then, still in his early twenties, he hopped a freight train to Montreal, worked his way to Europe on a tramp steamer, and took a job in France as a high diver in a carnival show. Back in Canada, he went to Alberta, where he sold classified ads for the *Calgary Herald,* worked in Edmonton as a department store Santa Claus, and went door to door selling the *World Book Encyclopedia.*

In Edmonton, he met his future wife, Merna Hirtle, an amateur actress who introduced him to F.M. Salter, teacher of creative writing at University of Alberta. In 1937, Mitchell showed the older man some of his work, and Salter responded excitedly to his roughest sketch: "This is vulgar, this is very clever, this is publishable—but *this, this!*" He tapped a four-page narrative about a boy visiting his father's grave. "I'd love to know what happened to that boy before this and after it."

Such was the genesis of Mitchell's first novel. While working on *Who Has Seen the Wind,* Mitchell married Merna and began teaching school in Castor, Alberta. He kept writing while becoming a school principal at New Dayton, south of Lethbridge. By this time, he had sold short stories to major magazines: *Liberty,* the *New Yorker,* and *Maclean's.* He was earning more from writing than as a principal: "And we'd saved up five hundred bucks, so we moved to High River and bought a little house. And I totally committed myself to writing."

Published in 1947, *Who Has Seen the Wind* proved a huge success. *Maclean's* magazine invited Mitchell to Toronto to become fiction editor. Drawing on what he had learned from summer jobs on the prairies, Mitchell started writing short stories and radio plays about two characters he invented. Between 1950 and 1958, CBC Radio broadcast more than 300 episodes of *Jake and the Kid.* The author's friend and colleague Pierre Berton considered that series one of Mitchell's great triumphs. "It made him a nationally known figure much more than *Who Has Seen the Wind* or any of the other novels he has written."

After a couple of years in Toronto, Mitchell moved back to High River, Alberta, prompted by Merna. He continued to write steadily— not just episodes of *Jake and the Kid* but film documentaries, feature articles, and plays. He published a second novel, *The Kite,* in 1962, and then a third, *The Alien,* which appeared serially in *Maclean's* and later evolved into *The Vanishing Point* (1973).

None of these came close to equalling *Who Has Seen the Wind.* But in 1981, Mitchell published *How I Spent My Summer Holidays.* That work brought the exuberantly drawn Blind Jesus to the Jubilee Auditorium, and a prairie boy's cataclysmic summer to an international audience. And, as its dust jacket proclaimed, it stands in relation to *Who Has Seen the Wind* as *Huckleberry Finn* compares with *Tom Sawyer:* it is a second masterpiece, perhaps greater even than the first.

For seven years, starting in 1979, Mitchell taught creative writing at the University of Windsor while also serving as head of the writing program at the Banff Centre for the Arts. Alistair MacLeod, who also taught at Windsor, and would later win international acclaim by articulating a completely different regional identity, described Mitchell as an inspirational teacher: "Sometimes you get writers who are very good themselves, but they are very selfish with their time or they are not interested in encouraging younger writers." Mitchell was the opposite: "a very, very exceptional individual in that way."

Mitchell returned permanently to Calgary in 1986, where he worked out of a small office at the university, producing books at an astonishing rate: *Ladybug, Ladybug* (1988), *According to Jake and the Kid* (1989), *Roses Are Difficult Here* (1990). He also continued to write plays, and had hits with *The Kite, Back to Beulah,* and *The Black Bonspiel of Wullie MacCrimmon.* This last, a minor masterpiece that began as a CBC radio play in 1951, has been staged repeatedly since the 1960s. A hilarious attack on Scottish Presbyterianism, it tells the story of a shoemaker who loves to curl so much that he makes a deal with the devil to prevent moralistic townsfolk from shutting down his sport on Sundays.

In October 1997, four months before Mitchell died of cancer, a tribute evening drew over 800 people to a Calgary arts festival. People from across the country eulogized the grand old man of prairie fiction. But Edmonton author Merna Summers had already explained why, among writers, Mitchell was considered a hero: "I didn't know you were allowed to put gophers in stories," she said, "until I discovered that Mitchell had done it."

W.O. Mitchell had made it okay to be a writer from the prairies.

Bill Reid: The Spirit of Haida Gwaii

Some people will be surprised to find Haida artist Bill Reid in this book, even though he often told people, as he did a journalist in 1983, that he was "just a European middle-class member of Vancouver WASP society." Best known as a Haida carver and sculptor, Reid was also a writer, a jewellery maker, and a broadcaster of national reputation. The multi-talented Reid represents the west coast as well as any author could. He also shows how Canadian identity shifts and changes like the images we discover by looking into a kaleidoscope.

If you take out a Canadian twenty-dollar bill and turn it over, you discover an image of *The Spirit of Haida Gwaii*, a sculpture by Bill Reid. Starting with the iconography of the Haida people of the Queen Charlotte Islands—the raven, the beaver, the grizzly bear, the shaman—Reid created a post-modern masterpiece that plays brilliantly with

Scottish-Haida artist Bill Reid, shown here with his sculpture The Raven and the First Men, *represents the hybrid tradition that has produced so many outstanding Canadians.*

Haida conventions. He dared to do so because by 1986, when he created the first clay model (one-sixth scale) of this twenty-foot (6 m) sculpture, he had been accepted as a Haida artist.

Yet Reid, born in Victoria in 1920, was also a Scottish Canadian. His father, an American who immigrated to northern British Columbia, had a Scottish father and a mother from Silesia (German-speaking Poland). Canada is both multicultural and multiracial, and Bill Reid, the foremost West coast carver of his day, was at least one-quarter Scottish.

All his life, Reid struggled with questions of identity. His educated, highly competent mother, Sophie Gladstone, had been born Haida in the Queen Charlotte Islands. But by marrying William Reid, a hotel owner and rum-runner, she lost her Native status and could no longer live on the reserve. Stifled and unhappy in the small towns near the

Alaska border where her husband thrived, she moved with her children to Victoria. There, realizing that people of mixed-blood faced discrimination whichever way they turned, she hid her Native ancestry and raised her children to become part of the larger culture.

William Ronald Reid did not become aware of his Haida heritage until age twelve, when for the first time he visited the Haida settlement of Skidegate, where his mother had grown up. He met his grandfather, Charles Gladstone, a leading carver, jewellery maker, and boat builder, and "got sort of interested" in carving. He took an art class with Jack Shadbolt while attending high school in Victoria. After graduating in 1936, he spent a year at Victoria College, where he became active in the Literary Arts Society. While taking evening art classes, he started working with a local radio station as an announcer.

His deep voice and engaging manner caught the ear of broadcasting impresario Jack Kent Cooke, and by the early 1940s, Bill Reid was station hopping around the country as a radio announcer. In 1949, while based at the CBC in Toronto and hosting two nationwide programs, Reid took a jewellery-making course at the Ryerson Institute of Technology. He mastered contemporary European techniques, apprenticed at the Platinum Art Company, and in 1951, headed west to establish himself as a jewellery maker.

Having succeeded as a mainstream Canadian, Reid began the long journey back to his Native roots. For the CBC, he had done a TV documentary on the totem poles of the Queen Charlotte Islands. Now, during another visit to Skidegate, he saw a pair of silver bracelets engraved by Charles Edenshaw, a great-uncle, and decided to apply his technical skills to making Haida jewellery. Later, he would summarize, "I think the dialogue between me, a product of urban twentieth-century North American culture, and the conventions of nineteenth-century Haida artistic expression, has produced some quite remarkable objects."

At this point in Canadian history, colonization had reduced that expression to a trickle. Bill Reid searched out what had been done and studied what anthropologists had written. Having explored and mastered northwest coast design principles, he began building on them and extending the tradition. By the mid-1950s, as Maria Tippett shows in *Bill Reid: The Making of an Indian,* Reid had established himself as a "salvager, romanticizer, student, and popularizer of traditional west coast Native culture."

The great works were yet to come. In 1968, Reid spent a year in London, England, studying goldsmithing at the Central School of Design. He then lived for three years in Montreal before returning west. During this period, he won international acclaim with pieces like *The Raven Discovering Mankind in a Clamshell.* Having done it as a small boxwood carving in 1970, he turned it, a decade later, into a massive cedar carving for the Museum of Anthropology at the University of British Columbia.

In 1976, Reid returned to Skidegate and began carving a massive, fifty-five-foot (17 m) totem pole to erect in front of a new administrative building. Slowed by the onset of Parkinson's disease, he acquired assistants and pushed on. As Tippett reveals, Reid initially had a hard time being accepted into the community. But on June 9, 1978, a dozen hereditary Haida chiefs and 1,500 people turned out for the raising of the totem pole. Reid told them he had carved it to commemorate the great carvers and those who had supported them. But also, he said, he hoped it would show that "a new breed of offshore people is coming to be, from the people of all the races from all over the world who have assembled on these islands together with the original inhabitants, the Haidas."

Yet Reid's life and work were not centred in Skidegate, as Tippett notes. His markets, patrons, museums, and friends were all in the cities to the south. The experience of living in Skidegate to carve the pole "had not made him feel more Native or more optimistic about the possibility of reviving the culture there," she writes. "If anything, his experience had made him even more of the middle-class WASP he often claimed he was."

Bill Reid was never a WASP, of course. His European heritage was not Anglo-Saxon but Scottish. He belongs to a tradition of hybrid Scottish Canadians that includes Major John Norton, James Douglas, Cuthbert Grant, Thérèse McDonald Casgrain, John George Diefenbaker, and Pierre Elliott Trudeau (and, on a more modest scale, yours truly: Kenneth Louis McGoogan). If Reid never found the vocabulary to articulate his changeable sense of identity, no matter; as an artist, he gave voice to the west coast.

That alone would warrant celebration. But Reid also demonstrates that Canadian diversity is more than cultural. Certainly, the Haida can rightly claim this great artist. But so can the Scots. Bill Reid did not have one identity, he had many. His existence repudiates notions of ethnic exclusivity and racial purity, and shows how Canada is not just multicultural and regional but also multiracial.

19

CANADIAN ANSWERS

Canada is a kaleidoscopic nation. If we examine it, we see French Canadians, Scottish Canadians, Chinese Canadians, Jamaican Canadians, Polish Canadians, Irish Canadians, Italian Canadians, English Canadians, German Canadians, Ukrainian Canadians, Vietnamese Canadians, you name it. We also discover a variety of Aboriginal peoples: Inuit, Mohawk, Mi'kmaq, Cree, Dene, Blackfoot, Haida, the list goes on. And cutting across these ethnicities, we find regional and local identities: Newfoundlanders, Atlantic Canadians, Québécois, Torontonians, Manitobans, Albertans, Edmontonians, and BCers, to name a few.

A twist of the wrist produces permutations and combinations. Here is a Jewish Canadian Prince Edward Islander, there a Chinese Canadian Albertan, and over there an Italian Canadian Haligonian with a German-Cree husband. And we haven't even touched upon other identities, among them professional, social, and familial. Most developed countries tolerate plural identities. But what they struggle to accommodate, Canada embraces and proclaims. This is partly the result of necessity: ours is a country of minorities. But it also stems from historical timing.

The thirteen colonies that formed the United States of America, for example, signed a declaration of independence in 1776. They adopted the U.S. constitution eleven years later. Inevitably, these foundational documents reflected eighteenth-century European ideas about the nation-state: one nation, one state. As a result, the United States is proudly one and indivisible, and it fought a civil war to stay that way. Citizens of the United States have a single, overriding identity: they are Americans.

Canada, by comparison, did not begin to emerge as a state until late in the nineteenth century. We have already seen how, thanks mainly to a few immigrant Scots, the country reached a political milestone in 1867: Confederation. But initially that involved only four provinces, nor did Canada even then produce a constitution or seize control of its own destiny. It was still governed under the British North America Act, a document that the London parliamentarians could repeal at any time.

Through the rest of the nineteenth century and most of the twentieth, Scottish Canadians fought and argued, often among themselves, about where Canada came from and where it should be going. Harold Adams Innis and Donald Creighton showed that Canada had developed economically as an east–west extension of Europe, and the country's participation in two world wars attested to the truth of this thesis. In the 1960s, after John Diefenbaker went down fighting for the British connection, George Grant added a corollary argument, claiming that if Canada ceased to be British and Christian, it was doomed to become American.

Meanwhile, Canadians were responding to the social initiatives of Norman Bethune and Tommy Douglas, to the French–English divide as identified by Hugh MacLennan, and to the well-justified demands for inclusion by Aboriginal peoples, by women, and by new immigrants. The various regions of the country were also claiming status and exercising power.

Canadians were at loggerheads within their own borders. Given the myriad challenges and conflicting agendas, the wonder is that anybody would even try to identify commonalities and unifying visions. With the twenty-first century looming, and two divisive Quebec referendums giving rise to constitutional crises, could Canada even hope to survive as an independent country? Fortunately, a few Scottish Canadians were ready, aye, ready to answer all such questions.

Farley Mowat: We Are North

In the middle of the twentieth century, while living in the eastern Arctic among the Caribou Inuit or Ihalmiut people, Farley Mowat expressed a keen desire to learn their language. "The unadorned fact that I, a white man and a stranger, should voluntarily wish to step across the barriers of blood that lay between us, and ask the People to teach me their tongue, instead of expecting them to learn mine—this was the key to their hearts."

When they realized that Mowat, as he wrote later, "was anxious to exert myself in trying to understand their way of life, their response was instant, enthusiastic, and almost overwhelming." The two men who took on the teaching "abruptly ceased to treat me with the usual deference they extend to white strangers. They devoted themselves to the problem I had set them with the strength of fanatics."

In his first book, *People of the Deer,* Mowat describes how he learned to speak "so quickly that I thought the tales I had heard of the difficulties of the Eskimo language were, like so many popular misconceptions about the Inuit, absolute nonsense." Within a month, he was communicating. "I became pretty cocky," he writes, "and started to consider myself something of a linguist. It was not until nearly a year had gone by that I discovered the true reason for my quick progress." When an Inuk visited from some distance away, Mowat "addressed a long-winded remark to him for the primary purpose of impressing some white friends who were present. And the blank stupefaction that swirled over the Eskimo's face was reflected in mine as it dawned on me that he hadn't the faintest idea of what I was saying."

The explanation lay with his mentors, Ootek and Ohoto, "who, with the co-operation of the rest of the People, had devised a special method of teaching me a language that is, in reality, a most difficult one. It was a sad disillusionment, but it shed a revealing light on the character of the Ihalmiut. I wonder what other men in this world would have gone to the trouble of devising what amounted to a new language, simply for the convenience of a stranger who happened into their midst."

With his international blockbusters about the Arctic, the boat-rowing, kilt-swirling Farley Mowat never let the world forget that Canada is a northern country.

Here we see a twentieth-century Scottish Canadian author taking the same appreciative approach to the peoples of the Arctic that had enabled Scottish explorer John Rae to grow beyond his contemporaries in the mid-1800s—an approach that communicates respect and a willingness to learn. Mowat was the first *kabloonak*, however, to combine a scientific background with a literary sensibility and an acute political awareness in writing about the Canadian Arctic. In *People of the Deer*, he expressed outrage about the way the Canadian government had neglected the Ihalmiut.

Six decades before, in 1886, the Caribou Inuit had numbered 7,000. Now, in 1947, Mowat counted forty. These people were dying, and for that Mowat blamed the Canadian government. His devastating attack drove the federal government to begin shipping meat and dry goods to Canadians whose existence they had previously denied.

Almost overnight, Farley Mowat became an international literary celebrity. The *Times Literary Supplement* hailed *People of the Deer* as "the most powerful book to come out of the Arctic for some years. It traces with a beautiful clarity the material and spiritual bonds between land, deer and people." And in the *New Yorker,* an impressed reviewer declared Mowat "the sole chronicler of a whole human society."

In years to come, Mowat would expand his literary territory to include autobiography, Scottish prehistory, the story of the Vikings, Canadian–American politics, and African environmentalism. Yet he would return repeatedly to the Arctic. And there he would make his greatest contribution.

Farley Mowat is descended from Scots on both sides. His mother, née Helen Thompson, came from a Scottish family that arrived in Canada in 1795. Her grandfather, Alexander Grant, served as a Royal Navy officer in the Seven Years' War and in 1805 became administrator of Upper Canada. On Farley's father's side, John Mowat immigrated to Canada from Caithness in the far north of Scotland to fight in the War of 1812. He settled in Kingston in 1819 and fathered Oliver Mowat, who eventually became premier of Ontario and great-great-uncle of Farley.

The author's father, Angus Mowat, fought at the battle of Vimy Ridge, like numerous Scottish Canadians mentioned in this book. An amateur writer with an adventurous streak, he introduced young Farley—born in Belleville, Ontario, in 1921—to sailing before moving the family first to Windsor and then, at the height of the Great Depression, to Saskatoon, Saskatchewan, where he worked as a librarian. Small for his age, awkward in a schoolyard where athletes ruled, young Farley found solace in animals. At twelve he began writing a periodical called *Nature Lore,* and by fourteen he was writing a column about birds for the Saskatoon *Star-Phoenix.* Later, Mowat would ride the streetcar to the edge of town to find himself "quite abruptly in the country." He discovered gophers and meadowlarks and how "ponds in the spring were alive with ducks and shorebirds, a natural abundance such as I have never again experienced."

Later, in *The Dog Who Wouldn't Be* (1957), Mowat described exploring the countryside with his dog Mutt. At home, he created a menagerie that included a rattlesnake, a squirrel, two owls, an alligator, and several cats. At school, boys called him the "sissy nature kid," but he set up the Beaver Club of Amateur Naturalists and turned the family basement into a museum filled with stuffed birds and mammals and even a bear cub. By fifteen, when he travelled to the Arctic with his great-uncle Frank, an amateur birder, he knew he wanted to be a naturalist.

The Second World War erupted when Mowat was eighteen. Commissioned as a second lieutenant, he saw action during the Allied invasion of Sicily, where he served as a platoon commander. Later, as an intelligence officer, Mowat served in Italy and the Netherlands, and when the war ended in 1945, he emerged as a captain. He would vividly recreate these years in *And No Birds Sang* (1979).

After the war, Mowat began studying biology at the University of Toronto. In 1947, during a field trip to the Arctic, he encountered the Ihalmiut, whose way of life was being destroyed by whites. Appalled and outraged, and having by now published in several magazines, Mowat began working on *People of the Deer.* Years before the "New Journalism" became fashionable, he created his real-life narrative by using techniques more associated with fiction—creating scenes, for example. The spectacular success of the resulting book—critically, commercially, and in effecting political change—launched Mowat on a singular career as a writer-activist.

Over the decades, Farley Mowat has publicly supported a variety of left-wing causes. He backed the CCF and then the NDP, and he endorsed Tommy Douglas in his anti-nuclear protests. Meanwhile, he published book after notable book in a variety of genres, including children's literature (*Lost in the Barrens* and *The Curse of the Viking Grave*), heavily researched works (*The Regiment* and *Westviking*), and light-hearted memoirs (*The Dog Who Wouldn't Be* and *Owls in the Family*).

But Mowat made a lasting impression as an impassioned naturalist. In 1963, he virtually created a new genre when he published *Never Cry Wolf*. Having gone to the Arctic to study why caribou herds were declining, Mowat discovered trappers blaming wolves for the situation—and found himself siding with the four-legged predators. Flying in the face of popular opinion, Mowat argued that wolves were actually strengthening caribou herds by killing off only the weakest animals. In the 1990s, this book would come under fire as containing more fiction than fact. But when it appeared, *Never Cry Wolf* caused an international stir, and influenced even the Soviet Union to ban the killing of wolves.

Writing in this environmentalist mode, Mowat produced such diverse works as *A Whale for the Killing*, which depicted the shooting of a doomed whale; *Sea of Slaughter*, a jeremiad attacking "the destruction of animal life in the north Atlantic"; and *Virunga* and *Woman in the Mists*, which told the tragic story of primatologist Dian Fossey, who fought for gorillas and was brutally murdered in Rwanda.

In 1985, while promoting *Sea of Slaughter*, Mowat was refused entry to the United States. He detailed this experience in *My Discovery of America*, making clear that his repudiation at the American border was farcically ill founded. He added that, ironically, the experience gave him a new faith in the United States, simply because so many ordinary Americans had expressed support, while rejecting the "bullying, arrogant, astonishingly insensitive" posturing of their political, commercial, and military leaders.

Alone among Canadian writers of his generation, Farley Mowat reached a massive international audience. While in Canada he presented himself as a wild-eyed, kilt-swirling Scot, this activist-writer— perceived abroad as the embodiment of the north—has sold more than fourteen million copies of his forty-three books in thirty countries.

In the late 1990s, Jack McClelland, publisher of such renowned authors as Margaret Atwood, Leonard Cohen, and Mordecai Richler, declared in a TV interview that Farley Mowat was the greatest Canadian writer ever. He would have been referring in part to Mowat's extraordinary commercial success. But McClelland also realized that Mowat had put Canada on the world map. He showed an international audience that while this country extends from the Atlantic to the Pacific, it reaches also to the Arctic Ocean; and that fundamentally, Canada is a northern nation. In so doing, he offered an answer to the one question Canadians never tire of asking: Who are we? Farley Mowat responded: We are north.

Pierre Elliott Trudeau: We Are Diverse

On October 8, 1971, Prime Minister Pierre Elliott Trudeau rose in the House of Commons to launch a new "policy of multiculturalism within a bilingual framework." Trudeau, whose frequently forgotten Scottish heritage derived from his maternal ancestors, had established a royal commission to examine "the whole question of cultural and ethnic pluralism in this country and the status of our various cultures and languages."

Now he commenced his great synthesis. Noting that a great many perspectives had emerged in the twentieth century, Trudeau followed John Diefenbaker in arguing that "there cannot be one cultural policy for Canadians of British and French origin, another for the original peoples and yet a third for all others, for although there are two official languages, there is no official culture, nor does any ethnic group take precedence over any other. No citizen or group of citizens is other than Canadian, and all should be treated fairly."

The new policy was designed, Trudeau said, "to break down discriminatory attitudes and cultural jealousies," and to foster respect for others "and a willingness to share ideas, attitudes and assumptions. National unity, if it is to mean anything in the deeply personal sense, must be founded on confidence in one's own individual identity; out of this can grow respect for that of others and a willingness to share ideas, attitudes and assumptions. A vigorous policy of multiculturalism will help create this initial confidence." Only in that last sentence did Trudeau move away from Diefenbaker, the champion of One Canada, and of singleness rather than pluralism.

Pierre Elliott Trudeau was his mother's son. And his mother, Grace Elliott, was Scottish Canadian to the tips of her fingers. Her Elliott ancestors had emigrated from Scotland to New England in the eighteenth century. In the 1780s, after the American Revolutionary War, they were among the United Empire Loyalists who moved north into Quebec.

Her French Canadian mother died when she was young, and Grace was raised by her father, Philip Armstrong Elliott. During the early 1900s, he ran a tavern on Aylmer Street in English-speaking Montreal, and the family—father, two brothers, and Grace—lived in a flat above that tavern, called The Captain's Saloon. Grace Elliott, although christened Roman Catholic (unlike her Protestant brothers), spoke little French. An expert Scottish dancer, she attended Dunham Ladies' College in the Eastern Townships and then worked as a secretary in a Montreal office.

In 1915, she married Charles-Émile Trudeau, a French Canadian lawyer and entrepreneur who spotted an opportunity and launched the highly profitable Automobile Owners' Association. Born in 1919, Pierre Trudeau grew up speaking French to his father and English to his mother.

When he was fifteen, his father died of pneumonia, leaving a small fortune and, for Pierre, a lot of unfinished business. "Actually, I didn't like him very much," he said later of his father. "You never knew what to expect." He was alluding to the way his father's drinking changed his behaviour. As well, where his extroverted father loved team sports like baseball, hockey, and lacrosse, the introverted Pierre preferred diving, skiing, and canoeing.

After his father's unexpected death, the young man experimented with changing his name. He had been christened Joseph Philippe Pierre Yves Elliott Trudeau. Now he tried Pierre Philippe Trudeau and Pierre Esprit Trudeau before settling on Pierre Elliott-Trudeau (later, he would drop the hyphen). To the surprise of many, even after he grew into adulthood, Trudeau continued to live with his proudly Scottish mother. All through his twenties and thirties, and into his early forties, he escorted her to parties and concerts. He even took her on holidays around Europe, and in Paris, when she was sixty-one, he drove her around on the back of his motorcycle.

In March 1971, when Trudeau married Margaret Sinclair, Grace Elliott was terminally ill with arteriosclerosis and not always lucid. Margaret was the daughter of politician James Sinclair, whose father had been a Glasgow schoolmaster. Some of Pierre's friends insisted that the prime minister married Margaret because, like his mother, she was Scottish.

Later that year, when in the House of Commons Pierre Elliott Trudeau finished outlining his vision of "multiculturalism within a bilingual framework"—a vision engendered by his own dual heritage, Scottish and French Canadian—he encountered no opposition. Robert Stanfield, leader of the Conservative opposition, applauded the move

Some friends of Pierre Elliott Trudeau claimed that he married the much younger Margaret Sinclair because, like his beloved mother, she came of Scottish stock. Within a few months of marrying, Trudeau unveiled his vision of Canadian multiculturalism in the House of Commons.

towards "preserving and enhancing the many cultural traditions which exist within our country." He emphasized that the initiative "in no way constitutes an attack on the basic duality of our country," and chided the Liberal government only for being slow to recognize Canada's diversity.

David Lewis, leader of the New Democratic Party, enthused over the announcement. He urged Canadians to take pride in "having been founded by two distinctive groups having two distinctive languages well known throughout the world," and in having "in Canada representatives of almost all the cultures in the world." The diversity of cultures across the land, he added, "is a source of our greatness as a people."

Even the controversial Réal Caouette, leader of the Social Credit Party, declared himself in complete agreement, insisting that he had repeatedly declared "that we have one Canadian nation, and not two, three or ten, that we have two official languages, English and French, and that we have a multiplicity of cultures which are the wealth of our country." Over the next four decades, rarely would any major government initiative meet with widespread support such as this.

Canadian thinkers and politicians from Donald Creighton and George Grant to John Diefenbaker had envisioned a Canada with a single identity. They thought the country could become a modern nation-state built on the European model developed in the eighteenth century, the model that had given rise to the United States of America. In their view, the state of Canada should consist of only one nation or people.

Pierre Elliott Trudeau recognized that the Canada taking shape in the twentieth century was far too complex to fit into that eighteenth-century mould. He saw the country not as unitary but as pluralistic: regionalized, multicultural, multiracial, even multinational. Trudeau contended that, as a pluralistic state, Canada could become "a brilliant prototype for the moulding of tomorrow's civilization." He urged Canadians to reject the old ethnocentric model (one nation, one state) championed by Québécois nationalists, and recognize that freedom is most secure when nations coexist within a single state.

This pluralistic vision of Canada led Trudeau to his greatest accomplishment. In 1982, he brought home the Canadian constitution while investing it with a charter of rights and freedoms. At this point, almost incredibly, Canada did not yet control its own constitution. The country was still governed under the British North America Act of 1867, according to which legal authority over Canadian affairs rested with Great Britain. This fact explains why, for example, Canadian women had been forced to resort to the British Privy Council in 1929 to gain recognition as "persons."

For Trudeau, the turning point had come in 1980, with the first Quebec referendum, the one fought over the issue of "sovereignty-association." Quebec's nationalist premier, René Lévesque, led the charge, demanding this new relationship with the rest of Canada. During the divisive referendum campaign, Lévesque suggested that Pierre Elliott Trudeau's middle name showed the prime minister was "not as much of a Quebecer as those" who supported Lévesque.

In *Just Watch Me,* biographer John English devotes several pages to Trudeau's famous response, during a rally held May 14, 1980, at the now-defunct Paul Sauvé Arena. He notes that Trudeau's "voice broke with emotion"—an extraordinary event in itself—"as he responded to Lévesque's reported taunt about his mother's name." Trudeau denounced it as showing contempt for all those Quebecers who had a drop of foreign blood in their veins.

"Of course my name is Pierre Elliott Trudeau," he said. "Yes, Elliott was my mother's name. It was the name borne by the Elliotts who came to Canada more than two hundred years ago. It is the name of the Elliotts who, more than one hundred years ago, settled in Saint-Gabriel-de-Brandon, where you can still see their graves in the cemetery. That is what the Elliotts are. My name is a Quebec name, but my name is a Canadian name also, and that's the story of my name."

He mentioned Pierre Marc Johnson and Louis O'Neill, both on Lévesque's side, and wondered about Charlie Watt, the leader of Quebec's Inuit: "His people had lived on the land long before Cartier met them over four hundred years earlier. Would [Lévesque] deny Watt's right to call himself a Quebecer?"

This theatrical bit of family history, English writes, became "the story of the speech, which endured as perhaps Trudeau's most memorable address." For the man himself, much of it was "surely too personal—too close to his own memories of his struggles with identity and his relationship with his past." But Montreal journalist Ian MacDonald, normally a fierce critic, called the speech "the emotional and intellectual coup de grace of the referendum campaign."

It demonstrated that for Pierre Elliott Trudeau, personal identity was not singular but plural. His was not a modern but a post-modern sense of self. On referendum night, after receiving almost 60 percent of the vote, he made this explicit: "Never have I felt so proud to be a Quebecer and Canadian." This statement implied, obviously, that other individuals could be Ontarian, Nova Scotian, Albertan, or whatever while also being Canadian. And that was the vision that drove Trudeau to bring home the Canadian constitution.

During the referendum campaign, Trudeau had promised that a repudiation of sovereignty-association would lead to a renewed federalism. Now, in the face of considerable opposition, he set out to deliver a constitution with a charter of individual rights and freedoms and a domestic amending formula—one that would not require the consent of Great Britain. Ultimately, he gained the support of nine out of ten provinces (Quebec excepted); he himself, as an elected politician from Quebec, gave the process cross-country legitimacy.

The Canadian Charter of Rights and Freedoms, amended after fractious consultations, reflected the "rights revolution" then unfolding in western democracies. In addition to individual equality rights, the Charter provided language rights for French Canadians, multiculturalism for ethnic groups, legal equality for women, and treaty rights for Aboriginal peoples.

Canada continues to evolve, of course. But on April 17, 1982, when Queen Elizabeth II signed the Constitution Act at an outdoor ceremony in Ottawa, Canada came of age as an independent nation. Only on that date did Great Britain cede the right to change or repeal the document serving as the Canadian constitution. Only on that date did the Supreme Court of Canada become the final authority over decisions affecting Canadians. And only on that date did individual rights gain precedence over legislative rulings.

By bringing home the constitution, Pierre Elliott Trudeau completed the job begun in 1867 by John A. Macdonald. The hybrid Scot fulfilled the hopes and dreams of the immigrant Scot. On April 17, 1982, thanks to a long parade of Scottish Canadians, Canada became the world's first postmodern democracy: bilingual and multicultural, officially diverse.

Marshall McLuhan: We Are Postmodern

In the beginning was the alphabet. And the alphabet gave rise to the printing press. And the printing press taught linearity, sequentiality, and compartmentalization, which together spawned industrialization. The newly standardized environment, epitomized by the assembly line, encouraged left-brain single-mindedness, and that created Modern Man. So it began, the gospel according to Marshall McLuhan.

Before he was done, this Scottish Canadian visionary would anticipate the World Wide Web and social networks like Facebook. As the apostle of the electronic era, McLuhan predicted the emergence of a world of instantaneous communication: speed, volume, multidirectionality, interactivity. The medium was the message. By changing our world, electronics would transform us as human beings. We would find ourselves juggling contradictions, multiple perspectives, and plural identities. To cope, we would activate the right side of the brain. We would become more complex.

Aware that clothes were an expression of self, Marshall McLuhan enjoyed wearing a loud tartan sports jackets that he had specially made. Proud of his Scottish heritage, he observed one St. Patrick's Day that "in Irish Scottish territory such as part of my family comes from, one hardly knows how to tackle the occasion." His ancestors had emigrated from County Down, Ulster, one of the first two counties "planted" with Protestants mainly from Scotland in the early 1600s.

In 1846, William McClugan arrived in Canada and started farming in southwestern Ontario. His oldest son, James Hilliard McLuhan, simplified his surname and married a pious Presbyterian from Edinburgh who, according to biographer Philip Marchand, "fit well with the Ontario Scottish ethos" that prevailed near the township of Conn. James McLuhan and his son Herbert moved to Alberta in 1907, and two years later, having married a brilliant, ambitious Maritimer named

Elsie Hall, Herbert fathered the vision-
ary-to-be: Herbert Marshall McLuhan.

In 1912, after a year homesteading in
small-town Alberta, the family moved to
boom-town Edmonton. Herbert turned
to real estate with McLuhan, Sullivan &
McDonald. When the First World War
broke out, the realtor enlisted, served as
a recruiting officer, and was discharged
early as a result of influenza. Mother and
sons (now there were two) spent some
time with family in Nova Scotia, but then
the McLuhans regrouped in Winnipeg.

*Marshall McLuhan, shown here
with his wife, Corinne, coined
the term "global village" in
the 1970s. He has been called
the first postmodernist.*

Marshall's father then worked as a life
insurance salesman. His mother, formerly
a Baptist schoolteacher, became an acclaimed public reader and then
an actress. When Marshall was ten, the family moved into a two-storey
home in a middle-class enclave of Ulster Scots. From there he attended
high school and then the University of Manitoba, where he won a gold
medal in arts and sciences.

At twenty-three, McLuhan began graduate studies in English at
the University of Cambridge. There, embracing the work of Teil-
hard de Chardin, a Roman Catholic intellectual who highlighted the
revolutionary importance of computer technologies, he converted to
Catholicism. De Chardin wrote that computers were creating "a nervous system for humanity" and "a single, organized, unbroken mem-
brane over the earth." Here is the source of McLuhan's idea of the
"global village."

From 1937 to 1944, unable to find work in Canada, and with a two-
year break during which he earned a Cambridge doctorate, McLuhan
taught English at Saint Louis University. In 1939, he married American

actress Corinne Lewis and began a family that would grow to include six children. McLuhan taught for two years at Assumption College in Windsor, Ontario, and in 1946 moved to the University of Toronto, where he came within the orbit of a senior scholar with similar preoccupations.

By the late 1940s, Harold Adams Innis—fifteen years older than Marshall McLuhan—was one of North America's leading economic historians. He had long since published his seminal works on the fur trade and the cod fisheries—works that had inspired Donald Creighton and George Grant. He had then turned to the study of communications. In *Empire and Communications,* published in 1950, he explores how dominant modes of communication have shaped various empires through history.

The following year, McLuhan published *The Mechanical Bride,* examining the effects of advertising on society. The younger scholar invited the older one to address one of his seminars on the differences between print and broadcast media. And more than once, when the gregarious McLuhan led informal Friday afternoon discussions in the coffee shop at the Royal Ontario Museum, the reclusive Innis put in an appearance.

But where Innis had arrived at communications studies through economic history, McLuhan approached via English literature and criticism. The economic historian had focused naturally on how new technologies change societies, cultures, and civilizations. The English professor introduced an emphasis on sight and sound. He perceived technologies as extensions of the human body: the television camera, for example, extended or augmented the human eye. McLuhan focused on human beings and the way we think. He asked questions about the impact of different media on our minds and on the way we process information. He posited that the emergence of a new communications technology—television, for example—influences the way we think more than any specific content it delivers. Thus, the medium is the message.

McLuhan argued that the introduction of the phonetic alphabet and then the printing press had encouraged people to think in a linear manner. And he asked, What will happen to the way we see the world as a result of electronic technologies? When suddenly we awake into a global village? If linear thinking "created individualism and nationalism in the sixteenth century," what would be the impact in the twentieth century of instantaneous communications and multiple perspectives? What would happen, for example, to the sense of national identity?

Canadians have long been obsessed with this question. Canada is unique in comprising a vast, largely unpopulated land mass situated next door to the most powerful nation in the world. In the nineteenth century, Scottish Canadians pulled this far-flung country together by building a railway and inventing the telephone and universal standard time. In the late twentieth century, faced with globalizing communications and government-backed multiculturalism, which encourages the maintenance of connections beyond national borders, how would Canadians respond?

Marshall McLuhan, who has been called "the first post-modernist," predicted that we would become post-modern. We would accept our nordicity, embrace our diversity, and revel in our global connectedness, and we would do it all simultaneously and without sacrificing our sense of nationhood. A comparison is instructive here. The United States of America is the quintessential modern nation. Born in the 1770s, its existence proclaimed by a revolution, that country emerged during the age of the printing press, when thinking was linear and sequential. Americans developed a melting-pot strategy to forge a single identity. Whether they live in Maine, Kansas, or California, and whatever their heritage, they view themselves as Americans first, last, and always.

But Canada took much longer to emerge from colonial status. It did not gain control of its own constitution until 1982. By that time, as we have already seen, many Canadians had come to identify strongly with regions and cultural communities. According to McLuhan, the Québécois in particular "are terrified of being merged in the American culture . . . and I think they're right. They're absolutely vulnerable. We're all vulnerable to the Americans, and they're a very attractive and wonderful people, and I think we could easily become merged in their lives, as we tend to be anyway."

Out of this vulnerability, McLuhan suggested, came the uniquely Canadian idea of the multicultural mosaic: "It's an amazing strategy of survival," he said in his final TV appearance in 1977. "Survival, however, is a legitimate goal in life, especially in a fast-changing world."

By highlighting the idea of the cultural mosaic as a survival strategy, McLuhan pointed a way beyond the thinking that had evolved out of the early work of Harold Adams Innis. As the electronic era dawned, Canada was still coming of age. News was arriving simultaneously from all over the globe. Like it or not, Canadians had to deal with multiple perspectives on any significant event. The only viable strategy was to develop a uniquely Canadian space that could encompass different perspectives.

Having realized that this country *does* have a mainstream culture, Canadians have yet to embrace its Scottish dimension. Since the 1970s, the concept of the mosaic, which focuses on group or collective difference, has evolved into that of diversity, which centres on the individual. Today, we can speak of multiple selves and kaleidoscopic identities and still feel Canadian. Today, thanks to such Scottish Canadians as Marshall McLuhan and Pierre Elliott Trudeau, and their many forebears who fought for justice and inclusion, we can champion Canada as a coherent, pluralistic nation, and as the world's first post-modern state. Aye, and if we look back to the earliest days, we can see, step by step, how the Scots Invented Canada.

Epilogue

A SCOTTISH CANUCK IN OLD KINTYRE

W e are north, we are diverse, we are post-modern. After Farley
Mowat, Pierre Elliott Trudeau, and Marshall McLuhan, only
the science of genetics could have anything to add. So I reflected as we
drove north along the west coast of Kintyre, looking for a town that
resisted discovery. A scattering of sheep on a green hill reminded me
of the celebrated "Dolly," the first mammal to be cloned from an adult
cell. She had been created by Scottish DNA experts at Roslin Institute
near Edinburgh. And while it was clearly beyond the scope of *How the
Scots Invented Canada,* I wondered if anyone had tried to trace DNA
testing to the Scottish Enlightenment.

My travelling companion found this notion only mildly amusing. We
were lost and needed to stay focused. Yet Sheena Fraser McGoogan had
to admit that, but for DNA testing, we would probably not even be in
Scotland because I might not have felt qualified to tackle this book. My

ancestors include a *pur laine* Québécois who arrived in 1619, after all, and two eighteenth-century Loyalist soldiers of Huguenot extraction. Originally, I wasn't sure I had the pedigree to write about the Scots.

I have come to understand that my hybrid heritage qualified me better than I knew, as down through the decades, Scots and Scottish Canadians have created the most pluralistic country in the developed world. But for DNA testing, Sheena and I would not have been driving back and forth hunting for Ballochroy and a road leading east to Mount McGoogan.

The Gaelic formulation is *Cruach Mhic Gougain*. And if, from the highway, we could already see that this mountain lacked grandeur, well, I had prepared myself for that. The word "cruach" can be translated not only as "mount" or "mountain" but also as "pile," "stack," or "high hill." Maps had told me that Mount McGoogan reaches a height of 807 feet (246 m). That makes it forty-three feet (13 m) higher than Montreal's Mount Royal. So as an ex-Montrealer, I felt justified in calling it a mountain. Modest it might be, but Mount McGoogan was the only ancestral landmark I could ever hope to claim, and while visiting Kintyre, I meant to climb it.

For years, I had known that my paternal ancestor John McGoogan arrived in Canada from Ireland in 1823, at age twenty-one. I knew that he had owned a farm in the Eastern Townships outside Montreal, and that he was a Presbyterian. The only Presbyterians in Ulster or Northern Ireland had moved there originally from Scotland. Unfortunately, my paper trail ended in 1802. And two professional genealogists told me that, because fires had destroyed so many Irish records, I would find no more.

That was when, while poking around on the Internet, I discovered that people had begun using DNA testing for genealogical purposes. Initially sceptical, I read a few books on the subject. Then I returned to cyberspace, where "surname projects" have been compiling DNA data on family origins. At one site, www.familytreedna.com, I discovered a

This photo shows a seaward view of Ballochroy, Kintyre, and the road that leads to Cruach Mhic Gougain. Clearly visible across the water is the Isle of Gigha. Historically, this area has been home to many McGugans and McGoogans, as well as MacNeills, Galbreaths, Smiths, Browns, Grahams, McKays, McLeans, and McLachlans.

McGugan/McGougan/McGoogan project. I sent a cheek swab to a lab in Texas. Bingo! The test results revealed that I share a common ancestor with the project administrator, a Scottish Canadian named Colin McGugan. His ancestors never moved to Ulster, but immigrated directly to southwestern Ontario from Knapdale, a few miles west of Kintyre. He had a paper trail going back to the 1750s.

As more McGugans and McGoogans joined our surname group, a pattern emerged: all those with whom I share a common ancestor—whether based in Canada, Australia, or the United States—trace their roots back to Argyll in Scotland. Old records indicate that our extended family of Scottish tenant farmers came from Kintyre, Knapdale, and the islands of Islay and Gigha. They were closely allied with MacNeills and MacDonalds.

Also, because the McGoogans belong to a DNA "haplogroup" (I2b1 Continental) that is found in only about 5 percent of the Scottish population, we realized that we are not related to McEacherns, McCaughans, McEagrens, or even MacGochans. Some researchers have speculated that the McGoogan line is so distinctive, diverse, and ancient that it may be at or near a genetic "ground zero" in Scotland.

Our DNA also indicates that we have a male ancestor who arrived in that land as a Danish Viking. And that drove me back to the history books. In AD 795, after making major advances in boat building, Vikings began plundering Argyll. During the 800s, they shifted to building settlements and then to intermarrying with the Gaelic-speaking "Dalriadans" or "Scotti" who had immigrated from Ireland 300 years before. During the next couple of centuries, Danish Vikings reigned supreme in Ireland (they built Dublin). In England, they created the Danelaw and established trade routes through Scotland.

My ancestor may have arrived with these Viking traders. It's also possible that, having settled in Ireland, he moved to Scotland around AD 1000 with the MacNeills. Both McGoogans and MacNeills became associated with Castle Sween on the south coast of Knapdale, a short sail from the Isle of Gigha. Both families probably assisted the Viking Sween (Suibhne) in building that stone fortress in the 1100s.

As more people discover DNA testing, more clarity will emerge. But before I travelled to Kintyre, this I knew: my branch of McGoogans has lived in Canada for six generations, or almost 200 years, ever since 1823. Before that, we lived in Ireland—maybe for fifteen or twenty years, certainly for no more than 200 (dating back to the earliest Ulster plantations). Before that, we McGoogans had lived in Scotland for at least 600 years. That was long enough to make me feel Scottish, and to lure me to *Cruach Mhic Gougain*.

In our search for Ballochroy, where we had to turn off, eventually we focused on two white houses, one on each side of a driveway. They looked out over the highway and the water at the Isle of Gigha. A small, hand-printed sign leaned against the foundation of one of the houses. It said "Ballochroy." We had been seeking a hamlet when we should have been looking for a homestead.

Back in Campbeltown, where we were staying, a woman at the Tourist Information Office had said that we should ask permission before we went scrambling over private property. But at Ballochroy, nobody was home at one house, and the other had a For Sale sign in the window. We got back into our rented car, drove between the two houses, and began wending our way inland along a one-lane dirt road.

The rolling hills were sprinkled with sheep. After three-quarters of a mile we passed a stand of trees and, gazing south, got our best look yet at Mount McGoogan. We stopped in the roadway and got out. The mountain sloped gently upwards from a couple of hundred yards south of the road, displaying a smooth green face scattered with shrubs and trees. On this sunny afternoon, a keen-eyed Scottish Canadian could see that sheep, cows, or goats could easily attain the loftiest heights.

And it was easy to imagine the scenario presented by Kintyre historian Ian MacDonald. Mount McGoogan, he said, had taken its name from a shepherd boy, *Mhic Gougain,* or the son of Gougain, who had lost his life here while defending livestock against would-be thieves. Also, because it could be seen from a distance, Mount McGoogan would have served as a beacon hill. When locals became aware that enemies were approaching, they would have climbed to the top to light bonfires and summon allies—probably from Gigha.

Mount McGoogan is situated a few minutes' march from Loup Hill, which Ian MacDonald identified as the site of the last major battle fought in Kintyre. On May 23, 1689, troops loyal to King William of Orange battled a combined force of locals loyal to King James, who were led by a Colonel Donald McNeill. After a battle lasting several hours, these home forces "were obliged to withdraw to the Island of Gigha, and then to Ireland."

Were my own ancestors among those who fled for their lives? It is possible. Two McGugins had already settled in Northern Ireland in the early 1600s, as part of the Ulster plantations. Yet most of the family apparently remained in Argyll. And in the late 1770s and early 1780s, the Isle of Gigha, famous for its excellent soil, was still home to a tenant farmer named John McGugan.

On we drove with Mount McGoogan on our right, passing sheep and a couple of cows, but seeing not a single human being. Finally we came over a rise and saw that the road ended at a house with a car out front—though here again, nobody was home. A one-lane dirt track swung off to the right and crossed a small bridge, but it was blocked by a gate with Keep Out signs on it.

In retrospect, I realize we should have parked the car, ignored the Keep Out signs, and climbed over the gate. We could have crossed the bridge, followed the track on the far side back the way we had come, and then made our way up the face of *Cruach Mhic Gougain*. At the time, I thought, well, let's obey the signs. We will drive back a mile, leave the car, and climb the mountain. I had failed to grasp the significance of the bridge, and to understand that it existed for a reason.

Certainly, I could see that an old stone wall ran parallel to the dirt road we were on. But all we had to do, I thought, was scramble down the hill, climb over that stone wall, and proceed up the mountain. As it happened, to reach the wall, I had to slog through marsh and tall grass and I ended up getting soaked. No mere boundary marker, the wall turned out to be a barrier designed to keep animals from falling into what the Scots call a burn. This was no mere rivulet, but a fast-flowing river ten or twelve feet across and three or four feet deep.

I would not be crossing it this afternoon. So now what? I had brought along a video camera to record the view from the top of the mountain, but clearly this would be as far as I got. I thought of Alexander Mackenzie, Thomas Simpson, John Rae. Those intrepid explorers had usually built cairns to mark their farthest progress. I felt that, if I was not going to reach the top of Mount McGoogan, I should leave proof that I had got this far. I had to mark the spot—but how?

Besides my video camera, I carried only a baseball cap. But in a pocket, I found a plastic sandwich bag. To mark my farthest progress, I placed the cap inside the bag and, shooting video at each step, buried them both in the stone wall. Afterwards, as I slogged through the marsh back to the car, I elaborated my plan. I would post the video on my website. To anyone who retrieved my baseball cap, or else presented evidence of having reached the top of Mount McGoogan, I would send free copies of four of my books and pick up the tab for a thirty-seven-marker DNA test. Or no, on second thought, I would make that two books and a less expensive twelve-marker test. That would suffice. We are north, we are diverse, we are post-modern. Yet some of us are also of Scottish heritage. No sense being frivolous.

Acknowledgments

Without Sheena Fraser McGoogan, my fellow traveller, photographer, and first reader, this book would not exist. And four other family members made crucial contributions (legal, anthropological, dynastic, and technological): Carlin Fraser McGoogan, Keriann McGoogan, Sylwia Przezdziecki, and Travis Steffens. I owe special thanks, as well, to my editor-publisher, Phyllis Bruce, whose insightful readings changed the book. Phyllis led a highly professional team effort at HarperCollins Canada, with kudos to Allegra Robinson, Alan Jones, Colleen Clarke, and that gung-ho Nova Scotian Leo MacDonald.

My literary agent, Beverley Slopen, showed why she is renowned as one of the best in the business. Mark Lovewell provided an important critical reading. Sarah McCoy Wight added a welcome eye for detail. And Barbara Kamienski made music with illustrations.

As a full-time writer, I welcome the continuing support of the Public Lending Right Commission, which owes its existence to The Writers' Union of Canada. I am also grateful to the Ontario Arts Council, whose Writers' Reserve program enabled supportive Canadian publishers to channel much-appreciated funds my way, among them James Lorimer, Patrick Crean, Sarah MacLachlan, and Lynn Henry. Finally, I owe a shout-out to Douglas Gibson, who invited me to speak to the St. Andrew's Society of Toronto, provided first-generation advice and counsel, and even addressed the haggis at my home.

Appendix 1

FIVE MILLION SCOTTISH CANADIANS

Canadians of Scottish descent from the 2006 Census of Canada (generally considered an underestimate)

Province/Territory	Scottish Heritage	Percentage of Total
Prince Edward Island	54,290	41%
Nova Scotia	288,180	32%
Yukon	7,005	23%
Alberta	661,265	20%
British Columbia	828,145	20%
New Brunswick	142,560	20%
Saskatchewan	182,790	19%
Manitoba	209,170	18%
Ontario	2,101,100	17%
Northwest Territories	6,050	15%
Newfoundland and Labrador	34,920	7%
Nunavut	2,025	7%
Quebec	202,515	3%
Canada	**4,720,015**	**15.1%**

Source: //en.wikipedia.org/wiki/Scottish_Canadian

Appendix 2

CANADIAN TARTANS

Many Scottish Canadians celebrate National Tartan Day on April 6. Except for Nun-
avut, all Canada's provinces and territories have regional tartans. And all of those
tartans except Quebec's have been registered in the books of the Court of the Lord
Lyon, King of Arms of Scotland. While declaring a Scottish heritage, Canadian tartans proclaim a national or a regional identification.

Maple Leaf/Canadian Tartans

In 2008, the Canadian government registered the Maple Leaf tartan with the Scottish Tartans Authority in Edinburgh. The registration of this tartan, designed in
1964 by David Weiser and officially adopted by the Clans and Scottish Societies of
Canada, means that no other country or individual can claim it. To make it "official"
requires only a government proclamation. This Canadian tartan evokes the maple
leaf through the changing seasons: summer green, early autumn gold, late autumn
red, and winter brown.

Official Regional Tartans

Prince Edward Island

Adopted after a province-wide contest in 1960, this tartan evokes red soil, green grass
and trees, white coastal waves, and yellow sun.

Nova Scotia

In 1956, Nova Scotia became the first province to register a tartan. The Nova Scotia
tartan, officially adopted in 1963, uses the blue of sea and sky, the greens of the trees,
the white of the granite rocks and coastal surf, the gold of Nova Scotia's royal charter,
and red symbolizing the lion rampant on the provincial flag.

Cape Breton Island

Although part of Nova Scotia, Cape Breton Island has its own tartan, designed in 1957. It was inspired by a 1907 a poem by Lillian Crewe Walsh:

Grey for our Cape Breton Steel
Gold for the golden sunsets shining bright on the lakes of Bras d'Or
Green for our lofty mountains, our valleys and our fields
To show us God's hand has lingered

To Bless Cape Breton's shore.

Yukon

Proposed in 1967 and registered in 1984, with a blue background signalling water and sky, this tartan features stripes that evoke different aspects of the territory: magenta the fireweed flower, green the forests, purple the mountains, white the snow, and yellow the midnight sun and gold deposits.

Alberta

Recognized in 1961, this tartan features green forests and gold wheat fields, plus blue skies and lakes, pink wild roses, and black coal and petroleum.

British Columbia

A tartan approved in 1966, marking the hundredth anniversary of the union of Vancouver Island and British Columbia, draws on the blue Pacific Ocean, the green forests, the red maple leaf, the white dogwood flower, and the gold crown and sun of the provincial arms.

New Brunswick

Encouraged by Max Aitkin, Lord Beaverbrook, New Brunswick adopted its official tartan in 1959. The design includes "beaver brown" for Beaverbrook, greens for lumbering and agriculture, blue for coastal and inland waters, and gold for potential wealth. The red blocks symbolize the loyalty and devotion of Loyalist settlers and the New Brunswick Regiment.

Saskatchewan

Predominantly gold to represent the "breadbasket" of Canada and created in 1961, this tartan incorporates brown summer fallow, green forests, red prairie lily, yellow flowers (rapeseed and sunflowers), white snow, black oil, and gold.

Manitoba

The Manitoba tartan became official in 1962. Of the squares, the reds represent the Red River Settlement, the greens the province's natural resources, and the blue Lord Selkirk (from his Douglas clan tartan). The dark green lines highlight multicultural-ism, and the golden ones grains and other farming products.

Ontario

The Ontario tartan, designed in 1965 and adopted in 2000, has three shades of green representing forest and fields. Red signals its First Nations, blue its waters, and white the sky.

Northwest Territories

This traditional tartan, unveiled in 1973, includes green for forests, white for the Arctic Ocean, blue for the Northwest Passage, gold for mineral wealth, red-orange for autumn foliage, and a thin black line representing the treeline.

Newfoundland and Labrador

In the Newfoundland tartan, designed in the early 1960s to echo the anthem "Ode to Newfoundland," we find a green background signalling pine-clad hills, plus gold for the sun, white for the snow, brown for the Iron Isle, and red for the Royal Standard.

Unofficial Tartans

Quebec

Designed in 1965 and known as the plaid of Quebec, this tartan derives from the provincial coat of arms: blue signals the *fleurs de lys,* green the maple leaves, gold a lion rampant, and white the scroll with the motto *Je me souviens* (I remember).

Appendix 3

PRIME MINISTERS OF SCOTTISH DESCENT

Of Canada's twenty-two prime ministers since Confederation, thirteen have had Scottish roots. The two earliest were born in Scotland. Here is a chronological list according to first year in office.

Sir John A. Macdonald: Nineteen years from 1867. Born in Glasgow, Scotland, immigrated at age five.

Alexander Mackenzie: Five years from 1873. Born in Logierait, Scotland, immigrated at age twenty.

Sir Mackenzie Bowell: Two years from 1894. Born in England of Scottish descent, immigrated at age nine.

Sir Charles Tupper: Sixty-eight days in 1896. Born in Amherst, Nova Scotia; graduated from Edinburgh University as a doctor in 1843. His mother was the Scottish Miriam (Lowe) Lockhart.

Sir Robert Laird Borden: Nine years from 1911. Born in Grand Pre, Nova Scotia, of English and Scottish descent. His mother, Eunice Jane Laird, raised him Presbyterian.

Arthur Meighen: Two years from 1920. Born in 1874 near St. Mary's, Ontario, to parents of Ulster Scottish background.

William Lyon Mackenzie King: Twenty-one years from 1921. His maternal grandfather was William Lyon Mackenzie, the Canadian rebel politician born in Dundee, Scotland.

John George Diefenbaker: Six years from 1957. His great-grandfather, George Bannerman of Sutherland, Scotland, was one of the Selkirk settlers of Red River. In 1968, while visiting the Highlands, Diefenbaker unveiled plaques to his ancestor and to Sir John A. Macdonald.

Pierre Elliott Trudeau: Sixteen years from 1968. His mother, Grace Elliott, was of Scottish descent.

Joe Clark: One year from 1979. His grandfather Charles Clark, born in Kincardine, Ontario, was the son of a Scottish immigrant.

John Turner: Seventy-nine days in 1984. Born in England of Scottish descent through his Canadian-born mother, Phyllis Gregory. Her mother was Mary Margaret Macdonald, a Scottish Catholic from Nova Scotia.

Kim Campbell: One hundred and thirty-two days in 1993. Descended from the Campbells of Argyll. Born Avril in British Columbia, she nicknamed herself Kim because, she said, it resembles the first syllable of Campbell when said in a Scots Highland accent.

Paul Martin: Two years from 2003. His mother, Eleanor Alice Adams, was of Scottish, Irish, and Métis descent.

Appendix 4

CANADA'S MAJOR SCOTTISH BUSINESSES

Irving Empire

The New Brunswick-based Irving industrial empire is worth at least $8 or $9 billion, according to business magazines. Founder Kenneth Colvin Irving was born in 1899 in Bouctouche, N.B., into a fourth-generation Canadian family of Scottish descent. His father, James, was an austere Presbyterian who embodied the Protestant work ethic. Starting with a family store around 1920, K.C. Irving (who died in 1992) added a service station, established Irving Oil, expanded into communications, and built an industrial empire that continues to dominate the economy of New Brunswick, incidentally becoming one of the richest men in the world.

Sobeys

The second-largest foodstore chain in Canada, Sobeys has over 1,300 supermarkets operating under a variety of names. Founded in the early 1900s, it is based in Stellarton, Nova Scotia, and today does sales across the country of more than $12 billion a year. The family-owned firm traces its roots to the 1800s, when a British soldier named William Sobey met and married Janet Macintosh, a Scottish immigrant from Pictou County. Paul Sobey, great-grandson of the owner, has said, "We are what our heritage has made us." *The Canadian Encyclopedia* adds that "what Sobey means by heritage is the industrious Presbyterian Scots who settled in Pictou County in the mid-nineteenth century to make steel and rail cars and dig for coal."

General Motors Canada

General Motors Canada has run into financial trouble in recent years, but it easily remains Canada's largest maker of automobiles. It evolved out of the McLaughlin Motor Car Co., established in 1907 by Col. Robert Samuel McLaughlin. He had been born in Enniskillen, Ontario, in 1871, where his father—a devout Presbyterian and the son of an Ulster Scots immigrant—had established a carriage works. After making horse-drawn buggies and sleighs with his father's company, Robert McLaughlin started making cars, producing 154 in 1908. The company expanded rapidly and in 1918, he became president of General Motors of Canada, a job he held for decades. McLaughlin also became an honorary colonel of the 34th Ontario Regiment. He excelled as a breeder of race horses, set up the McLaughlin Foundation, and established the McLaughlin Planetarium and McLaughlin College at York University.

Redpath Sugar

In 1816, a penniless twenty-year-old from the Scottish borders named John Redpath arrived in Montreal and began working as a stonemason. A prodigious worker, the young Presbyterian launched his own construction business and undertook such major projects as the Lachine Canal and Notre Dame Basilica. In 1854, Redpath established Canada Sugar Refining. Before long, renamed John Redpath & Son, the company was importing and processing 7,000 tons of raw sugar each year. While helping to develop Montreal's Square Mile, Redpath financed telegraph, insurance, and mining companies, served as a bank director, supported the abolition of slavery, and led many charitable and community service endeavours. Redpath Sugar has undergone many transformations and ownership changes, but it remains a familiar brand across Canada.

McCain Foods

McCain Foods Ltd., the world's largest producer of french fries and other frozen foods, is based in Florenceville, New Brunswick. That's where, in 1820, three Ulster Scots led by William Andrew McCain put down roots after arriving from Northern Ireland. Four McCain descendants established McCain Foods in 1957, and today the company has 20,000 employees at fifty-five production facilities. Operating in over a hundred counties, it sells one-third of the world's frozen french fries.

Department Stores

Chapter 11 tells the story of Eaton's. For decades, that national chain's most serious rival was Simpson's, launched in 1858 in Newmarket, Ontario, by Scottish immigrant Robert Simpson. His store moved to downtown Toronto in 1872, expanded across the country, and became part of the giant retailer Simpsons-Sears. Older than either of those two chains was Morgan's, which opened in Montreal as a dry-goods store in 1845. Scottish immigrant and co-founder Henry Morgan took sole control five years later, and in 1866, after visiting Le Bon Marché in Paris, Morgan opened the first department store in Canada. Eventually, Morgan's became part of the Hudson's Bay Company. Still in Montreal, which remained Canada's financial capital through much of the twentieth century, Ogilvy's traces its roots to 1866, when James A. Ogilvy opened a linen shop on lower Mountain Street. He moved uptown in 1896, and in 1912 built the store that today houses a series of boutiques on Ste. Catherine Street. In 1927, the store began the tradition of using tartan boxes and having a ceremonial bagpiper. In Ottawa, Ogilvy's traces its roots to 1887, when Edinburgh-born Charles Ogilvy opened a dry-goods store. It evolved into a thriving retail enterprise and became Robinson-Ogilvy before succumbing to competition.

Whisky

While the first rum distillery began operation in Quebec in 1769, and John Molson opened a whisky distillery in Montreal thirty years later, Scottish immigrants had been running home whisky stills since soon after the first settlers arrived in 1773. After 1883, when the American Revolutionary War ended, great numbers of Scottish immigrants arrived from both Britain and the United States. This explains why Canadians spell "whisky" in the Scottish fashion, while in the United States and Ireland the word is spelled "whiskey." By the 1840s, at least 200 stills were operating in Canada, the vast majority operated by Scottish immigrants. When the United States entered the Prohibition era in 1920, Canadian whisky makers did a booming black-market business. Today, Canadian distillers produce more than 800 brands of spirits, and exports total almost $400 million.

Woollen Mills

According to New Brunswick sources, Canada's oldest woollen mill, originally called York Woollen Mills, was established by Scottish immigrant George Lister in 1857 on the Magaguadavic River west of Fredericton. Three years later, Abigail Smith of nearby New Maryland created the country's oldest hooked rug. But Quebec sources claim that Alexander Fraser, the son of a Scottish infantry officer who had fought on the Plains of Abraham, established a woollen mill in 1818 at Fraserville, Quebec—present-day Rivière-du-Loup. (They say nothing about a hooked rug.) But no matter who you believe, Scottish Canadians launched the Canadian woollen trade. In the second half of the century, woollen mills multiplied in the Eastern Townships outside Montreal and in smaller centres along the St. Lawrence River valley. The vast majority of them were owned and operated by Scottish immigrants who had arrived with a knowledge of sheep-shearing and preparing wool for weaving. The early carding mills eventually gave rise to textile mills that grew up in centres like Sherbrooke, Quebec.

Selected Sources and Further Reading

Introduction and Prologue: Canadians in Scotland

Harper, Marjory. *Adventurers and Exiles: The Great Scottish Exodus*. London: Profile Books, 2003.

Herman, Arthur. *How the Scots Invented the Modern World: The True Story of How Western Europe's Poorest Nation Created Our World and Everything in It*. New York: Three Rivers Press, 2001.

Martin, Ged, and Jeffrey Simpson. *Canada's Heritage in Scotland*. Toronto: Dundurn Press, 1989.

BOOK ONE: THE PIONEERS

Chapter 1: Early Explorers

Daniells, Roy. *Alexander Mackenzie and the North West*. London: Faber and Faber, 1969.

Hayes, Derek. *First Crossing: Alexander Mackenzie, His Expedition across North America, and the Opening of the Continent*. Vancouver. Douglas & McIntyre, 2001.

MacDonald, Donald. *Lewis: A History of the Island*. Edinburgh: Gordon Wright Publishing, 1978.

Hume, Stephen. *In Search of Simon Fraser*. Madeira Park, BC: Harbour Publishing, 2008.

Mackenzie, Alexander. *The Journals of Alexander Mackenzie: Exploring across Canada in 1789 and 1793*. Santa Barbara, CA: Narrative Press, 2001.

Pohl, Frederick J. *Prince Henry Sinclair: His Expedition to the New World in 1398*. Halifax: Nimbus, 1995. First published 1967 by C.N. Potter, New York.

Smith, James K. *Alexander Mackenzie, Explorer: The Hero Who Failed*. Toronto: McGraw-Hill Ryerson, 1973.

Chapter 2: First Settlers

Bumstead, J.M., ed. *The Collected Writings of Lord Selkirk: 1799–1809*. Winnipeg: Manitoba Record Society, 1984.

Campey, Lucille H. *The Silver Chief: Lord Selkirk and the Scottish Pioneers of Belfast, Baldoon and Red River*. Toronto: Natural Heritage Books, 2003.

——. *An Unstoppable Force: The Scottish Exodus to Canada*. Toronto: Dundurn, 2008.

Coleman, Thelma. *The Canada Company*. Perth, ON: County of Perth and Cumming Publishers, 1978.

Gray, John Morgan. *Lord Selkirk of Red River*. Toronto: Macmillan, 1963.

Van Kirk, Sylvia. *Many Tender Ties: Women in Fur-trade Society, 1670–1870*. Norman: University of Oklahoma Press, 1983.

Chapter 3: Echoes of Old Scotia

Bentman, Raymond. *Robert Burns*. Boston: Twane Publishers, 1987.

Buchan, John. *Sir Walter Scott*. New York: Coward-McCann, 1932.

Carswell, Catherine. *The Life of Robert Burns*. Edinburgh: Collins/Canongate Classics, 1930.

Goring, Rosemary. *Scotland: The Autobiography*. London: Viking, 2007.

Gudgeon, Chris. *Out of This World: The Natural History of Milton Acorn*. Vancouver: Arsenal Pulp Press, 1996.

MacDiarmid, Hugh, Campbell MacLean, and Anthony Ross. *John Knox*. Edinburgh: Ramsay Head Press, 1976.

Marshall, Nancy. *Burns Supper Companion*. Edinburgh: Berlinn, 1992.

Marshall, Rosalind K. *John Knox*. Edinburgh: Berlinn, 2008.

Prebble, John. *The King's Jaunt: George IV in Scotland, 1822*. London: Collins, 1988.

Ridley, Jasper. *John Knox*. New York and Oxford: Oxford University Press, 1968.

Chapter 4: Annals of Arrival

Norton, John. *The Journal of Major John Norton, 1816*. Edited by Carl F. Klinck. Toronto: Champlain Society, [1970].

Timothy, H.B. *The Galts: A Canadian Odyssey.* Vol. 1, *John Galt, 1779–1839.* Toronto: McClelland & Stewart, 1977.

Chapter 5: The Northwest Passage

Franklin, John. *Narrative of a Journey to the Shores of the Polar Sea, in the Years 1819, 20, 21, and 22.* Edmonton: Hurtig, 1970. First published 1824 by H.C. Carey & I. Lea, Philadelphia.

McGoogan, Ken. *Fatal Passage: The Untold Story of John Rae, the Arctic Adventurer Who Discovered the Fate of Franklin.* Toronto: HarperCollins/Phyllis Bruce Books, 2001.

Chapter 6: Boundaries Yes, Barriers No

Blakey Smith, Dorothy. *James Douglas: Father of British Columbia.* New York and Oxford: Oxford University Press, 1971.

Forster, Merna. *100 Canadian Heroines: Famous and Forgotten Faces.* Toronto: Dundurn, 2004.

Galbraith, John S. *The Little Emperor: Governor Simpson of the Hudson's Bay Company.* Toronto: Macmillan, 1976.

Innis, Harold A. *The Fur Trade in Canada: An Introduction to Canadian Economic History.* New Haven, CT: Yale University Press, 1930.

Newman, Peter C. *Company of Adventurers.* Toronto: Viking Penguin, 1985.

Raffan, James. *Emperor of the North: Sir George Simpson and the Remarkable Story of the Hudson's Bay Company.* Toronto: HarperCollins/Phyllis Bruce Books, 2007.

BOOK TWO: THE BUILDERS

Prologue: The View from Black Creek Village

Cameron, Elspeth. *Hugh MacLennan: A Writer's Life.* Toronto: University of Toronto Press, 1981.

Careless, J.M.S. *Brown of the Globe: Voice of Upper Canada, 1818–1859.* Toronto: Dundurn Press, 1989.

Galbraith, John Kenneth. *The Scotch.* Cambridge, MA: Houghton Mifflin, 1964.

Parker, Richard. *John Kenneth Galbraith: His Life, His Politics, His Economics.* Toronto: HarperCollins, 2005.

Reid, W. Stanford, ed. *The Scottish Tradition in Canada.* Toronto: McClelland & Stewart, 1976.

Chapter 7: Makers of 1867

Flint, David. *William Lyon Mackenzie: Rebel against Authority.* New York and Oxford: Oxford University Press, 1971.

Gwyn, Richard. *John A: The Man Who Made Us: The Life and Times of John A. Macdonald.* Vol. 1, *1815–1867.* Toronto: Random House, 2007.

Kilbourn, William. *The Firebrand: William Lyon Mackenzie and the Rebellion in Upper Canada.* Toronto: Clarke Irwin, 1956.

Sewell, John. *Mackenzie: A Political Biography.* Halifax: Lorimer, 2002.

Chapter 8: Steel Ribbon Blues

Berton, Pierre. *The Last Spike: The Great Railway, 1881–1885.* Toronto: McClelland & Stewart, 1971.

——. *The National Dream: The Great Railway, 1871–1881.* Toronto: McClelland & Stewart, 1970.

MacDonald, Donna. *Lord Strathcona: A Biography of Donald Alexander Smith.* Toronto: Dundurn, 1996.

Chapter 9: Political Persons

Crowley, Terry. *Agnes Macphail and the Politics of Equality.* Halifax: Lorimer, 1990.

Gray, Charlotte. *Nellie McClung.* Toronto: Penguin, 2008.

McClung, Nellie. *The Complete Autobiography: Clearing in the West* and *The Stream Runs Fast.* Edited by Veronica Strong-Boag, and Michelle Lynn Rosa. Peterborough, ON: Broadview Press, 2003. *Clearing in the West* first published 1935 and

The Stream Runs Fast first published 1945 by Thomas Allen, Toronto.

Steward, Margaret, and Doris French. *Ask No Quarter: The Story of Agnes Macphail.* Toronto: Longmans, Green and Co., 1959.

Chapter 10: Bankers and Educators

Fraser, John. *Eminent Canadians: Candid Tales of Then and Now.* Toronto: McClelland & Stewart, 2000.

MacKay, Donald. *The Square Mile: Merchant Princes of Montreal.* Vancouver: Douglas & McIntyre, 1987.

McDowall, Duncan. *Quick to the Frontier: Canada's Royal Bank.* Toronto: McClelland & Stewart, 1993.

Chapter 11: A Nation of Networks

Santink, Joy L. *Timothy Eaton and the Rise of His Department Store.* Toronto: University of Toronto Press, 1990.

St. Andrew's Society of Toronto. *One Hundred Years of History, 1836–1936.* Kirkcudbright, Scotland: Murray Printing, [1936].

Chapter 12: Inventors and Innovators

Blaise, Clark. *Time Lord: The Remarkable Canadian Who Missed His Train and Changed the World.* Toronto: Random House/Vintage, 2001.

Bliss, Michael. *Banting: A Biography.* Toronto: McClelland & Stewart, 1984.

——. *The Discovery of Insulin.* Chicago: University of Chicago Press, 1982.

Gray, Charlotte. *Reluctant Genius: The Passionate Life and Inventive Mind of Alexander Graham Bell.* Toronto: HarperCollins/Phyllis Bruce Books, 2006.

Chapter 13: Women from Arcadia

Duncan, Sara Jeannette. *The Imperialist.* Canadian critical edition, edited by Thomas E. Tausky. Ottawa: Tecumseh Press, 1996. First published 1904 by A. Constable, Westminster.

Gammel, Irene, ed. *The Intimate Life of L.M. Montgomery*. Toronto: University of Toronto Press, 2005.

Rubio, Mary Henley. *Lucy Maud Montgomery: The Gift of Wings*. Toronto: Doubleday Canada, 2008.

Waterston, Elizabeth. *Rapt in Plaid: Canadian Literature and Scottish Tradition*. Toronto: University of Toronto Press, 2001.

Chapter 14: Ladies from Hell

Chisholm, Anne, and Michael Davie. *Beaverbrook: A Life*. Fayetteville, AR: Hutchinson, 1992.

Cook, Tim. *Canadians Fighting the Great War, 1914–1916*. Vol. 1, *At the Sharp End* Toronto: Viking Canada, 2007.

——. *Canadians Fighting the Great War, 1917–1918*. Vol. 2, *Shock Troops* Toronto: Viking Canada, 2008.

Mann, Susan. *Margaret Macdonald: Imperial Daughter*. Montreal and Kingston, ON: McGill-Queen's University Press, 2005.

Prescott, John F. *In Flanders Fields: The Story of John McCrae*. Erin, ON: Boston Mills Press, 1985.

Richards, David Adams. *Lord Beaverbrook*. Toronto: Penguin, 2008.

BOOK THREE: THE VISIONARIES

Prologue: Invisible Architects

Anderson, Walter Truett. *The Future of the Self: Inventing the Post-Modern Person*. New York: Penguin Putnam, 1997.

Chapter 15: Un-American Activities

Adam Smith, Janet. *John Buchan and His World*. London: Thames and Hudson, 1979.

Clarkson, Adrienne. *Norman Bethune*. Toronto, Penguin, 2009.

Creighton, Donald. *Harold Adams Innis: Portrait of a Scholar.* Toronto: University of Toronto Press, 1957.

Henshaw, Peter. "John Buchan and the British Imperial Origins of Canadian Multiculturalism." In *Canadas of the Mind: The Making and Unmaking of Canada's Nationalisms in the Twentieth Century,* edited by Norman Hillmer and Adam Chapnick. Montreal and Kingston, ON: McGill-Queen's University Press, 2007.

Lownie, Andrew. *John Buchan: The Presbyterian Cavalier.* London: Constable, 1995.

Watson, Alexander John. *Marginal Man: The Dark Vision of Harold Innis.* Toronto: University of Toronto Press, 2006.

Chapter 16: Ethical Agitations

Casgrain, Thérèse F. *A Woman in a Man's World.* Toronto: McClelland & Stewart, 1972.

Diefenbaker, John G. *One Canada: Memoirs of the Right Honourable John G. Diefenbaker.* Vol. 3, *The Tumultuous Years, 1962–1967.* Toronto: Macmillan, 1977.

Margoshes, Dave. *Tommy Douglas: Building the New Society.* Toronto: XYZ Publishing, 1999.

Chapter 17: Political Complications

Anderson, Doris. Rebel Daughter: An Autobiography. Toronto: Key Porter, 1996.

———. *The Unfinished Revolution: The Status of Women in Twelve Countries.* Toronto: Doubleday Canada, 1991.

Christian, William, and Sheila Grant, eds. *The George Grant Reader.* Toronto: University of Toronto Press, 1998.

Creighton, Donald. The Passionate Observer: Selected Writings. Toronto: McClelland & Stewart, 1980.

Grant, George. *Lament for a Nation: The Defeat of Canadian Nationalism.* Montreal and Kingston, ON: McGill-Queens University Press, 1965.

Houston, James. *Confessions of an Igloo Dweller: The Story of the Man Who Brought Inuit Art to the Outside World.* Toronto: McClelland & Stewart/Douglas Gibson Books, 1995.

Ignatieff, Michael. *True Patriot Love: Four Generations in Search of Canada*. Toronto: Viking Canada, 2009.

Moir, John S., ed. *Character and Circumstance: Essays in Honour of Donald Grant Creighton*. Toronto: Macmillan of Canada, 1970.

Rigelhof, T.F. *George Grant: Redefining Canada*. Toronto: XYZ Publishing, 2001.

Chapter 18: Centrifugal Forces

Guilford, Irene, ed. *Alistair MacLeod: Essays on His Words*. Toronto: Guernica, 2001.

Laurence, Margaret. *Heart of a Stranger*. Toronto: McClelland & Stewart, 1976.

MacLeod, Alistair. *The Lost Salt Gift of Blood*. Afterword by Joyce Carol Oates. Toronto: McClelland & Stewart, 1989. First published 1976 by McClelland & Stewart.

——. *No Great Mischief*. Toronto: McClelland & Stewart, 1999.

Mitchell, Ormond, and Barbara Mitchell. *W.O. The Life of W.O. Mitchell: Beginnings to Who Has Seen the Wind*. Toronto: McClelland & Stewart, 1999.

Mitchell, W.O. *How I Spent My Summer Holidays*. Toronto: Macmillan, 1981.

Munro, Alice. *The View from Castle Rock*. Toronto: McClelland & Stewart/Douglas Gibson Books, 2006.

Ross, Catherine Sheldrick. *Alice Munro: A Double Life*. Toronto: ECW Press, 1992.

Tippett, Maria. *Bill Reid: The Making of an Indian*. Toronto: Random House, 2003.

Chapter 19: Canadian Answers

Clarkson, Stephen, and Christina McCall. *Trudeau and Our Times*. Vol. 1, *The Magnificent Obsession*. Toronto: McClelland & Stewart, 1990.

English, John. *Just Watch Me: The Life of Pierre Elliott Trudeau, 1968–2000*. Toronto: Knopf, 2009.

Kegan, Robert. *In Over Our Heads: The Mental Demands of Modern Life*. Cambridge, MA: Harvard University Press, 1994.

King, James. *Farley: The Life of Farley Mowat*. Toronto: Harper Collins/Phyllis Bruce, 2002.

Marchand, Philip. *Marshall McLuhan: The Medium and the Messenger.* Toronto: Random House Canada, 1989.

Mowat, Farley. *My Discovery of America.* Toronto: McClelland & Stewart, 1985.

—. *Sea of Slaughter.* Toronto: Key Porter, 1984.

Watson, Rita, and Menahem Blondheim, eds. *The Toronto School of Communication Theory: Interpretations, Extensions, Applications.* Jerusalem: Hebrew University Magnes Press, 2007.

Epilogue: A Scottish Canuck in Old Kintyre

Fitzpatrick, Colleen, and Andrew Veiser. *DNA and Genealogy.* Huntington Beach, CA: Rice Book Press, 2005.

Sykes, Bryan. *Saxons, Vikings, and Celts: The Genetic Roots of Britain and Ireland.* New York: W.W. Norton, 2006.

Illustrations Credits

frontispiece: Photograph by William Notman & Sons, 1888, McCord Museum, II-88087

p. xii   Lithograph by Robert McIan, ca. 1850, Library and Archives Canada, C-041068

p. 6   Photograph by Sheena Fraser McGoogan

p. 8   Photograph by Sheena Fraser McGoogan

p. 13   Photograph by Sheena Fraser McGoogan

p. 18   Engraving from *Voyages from Montreal on the River St. Lawrence* by T. Cadell, 1801, courtesy of Canadian Postal Archives, Library and Archives Canada, e008303331

p. 27   Drawing by Charles William Jefferys (1869–1951), Library and Archives Canada, C-070270

p. 32   Engraving by William Henry Bartlett (1809–1854), Library and Archives Canada, C-002401

p. 36   Photogravure, artist unknown, frontispiece from *Canada and Its Provinces: A History of the Canadian People and Their Institutions*, Volume XIX, 1914, by A. Shortt and A. Doughty. Library and Archives Canada, C-001346

p. 52   From a photograph by Mrs. J. H. Schofield, 1835, University of Manitoba Archives & Special Collections, MacLeod fonds, PC 13 (Box 1, Fd. 1, Item 8)

p. 70   Painting by Mary Ann Knight, 1805, Library and Archives Canada, C-123841

p. 74   Artist unknown, from *For My Children's Children*, 1937, by E. C. Springett, Library and Archives Canada, C-023086

p. 83   Watercolour by Gerritt Shipper, 1808–09, replica of portrait, Library and Archives Canada, C-138080

p. 90   Painting by William Armstrong, *Dr. John Rae* (1813-1893), *Arctic Explorer*, 1862, Glenbow Museum, 55.17.1

p. 96   Mezzotint engraved by James Scott from a painting by Stephen Pearce, 1857, Archives of Ontario, I0027769

p. 107   City of Vancouver Archives, Port P1593

p. 112   René Milot, © Canada Post Corporation (1991). Reproduced with permission, Library and Archives Canada, e000008477

p. 118   Photograph by Sheena Fraser McGoogan

p. 125   Library and Archives Canada, C-004811

p. 137   Painting by John Wycliffe Lowes Forster, Library and Archives Canada, C-011095

p. 280   Photograph by Yousuf Karsh, 1937, Library and Archives Canada, e010752271

p. 282   Library and Archives Canada, PA-160708

p. 292   Photograph by Duncan Cameron, Library and Archives Canada, C-036222

p. 295   Photograph by Yousuf Karsh, 1937, Library and Archives Canada, PA-178177

p. 298   Photograph by Bill Brennan, *Ottawa Citizen*. Reproduced with permission. Image courtesy of Diefenbaker Canada Centre, JGD2674

p. 313   Photograph by Yousuf Karsh, 1947, Library and Archives Canada, PA-172723

p. 319   National Film Board of Canada, Library and Archives Canada, PA-189969

p. 322   Photographer unknown, 1982, Canadian Press

p. 333   Photograph © Jerry Bauer

p. 338   Photographer unknown, Courtesy of the estate of Margaret Laurence.

p. 342   © Canada Post Corporation (2000). Reproduced with permission, Library and Archives Canada, e000009086

p. 348   Photograph © Bill McLennan, 1997, Courtesy of UBC Museum of Anthropology, Vancouver, Canada

p. 355   Photograph by Philip Teasdale, 1972, GetStock.com

p. 362   Photograph by Duncan Cameron, 1972, Library and Archives Canada, PA-175941

p. 367   Photograph by Robert Lansdale, 1973, University of Toronto Archives, LAN02 731090B-24

p. 373   Photograph by Sheena Fraser McGoogan

INDEX